Huizhou

Huizhou

*Local Identity and Mercantile Lineage Culture
in Ming China*

Qitao Guo

UNIVERSITY OF CALIFORNIA PRESS

University of California Press
Oakland, California

Suggested citation: Guo, Q. *Huizhou: Local Identity and Mercantile Lineage Culture in Ming China*. Oakland: University of California Press, 2022.
DOI: https://doi.org/10.1525/luminos.119

Library of Congress Cataloging-in-Publication Data

Names: Guo, Qitao, author.
Title: Huizhou : local identity and mercantile lineage culture in
    Ming China / Qitao Guo.
Description: Oakland, California : University of California Press, [2022] |
    Includes bibliographical references and index.
Identifiers: LCCN 2021036622 (print) | LCCN 2021036623 (ebook) |
    ISBN 9780520385214 (paperback) | ISBN 9780520385221 (epub)
Subjects: LCSH: Mercantile system—China—She Xian (Anhui Sheng)—
    History. | Kinship—China—She Xian (Anhui Sheng)—History. |
    Merchants—China—She Xian (Anhui Sheng)—History. |
    She Xian (Anhui Sheng, China)—Social conditions—15th century. |
    She Xian (Anhui Sheng, China)—Social conditions—16th century. |
    China—History—Ming dynasty, 1368–1644.
Classification: LCC HF3840.H85 G86 2022 (print) | LCC HF3840.H85
    (ebook) | DDC 330.15/130951225—dc23

LC record available at https://lccn.loc.gov/2021036622
LC ebook record available at https://lccn.loc.gov/2021036623

30   29   28   27   26   25   24   23   22
10   9   8   7   6   5   4   3   2   1

For Andrea and Simon

CONTENTS

ACKNOWLEDGMENTS

I have incurred many debts of gratitude in the course of writing this book. It gives me pleasure to acknowledge the following people for their contributions: Emily Baum, Peter Bol, Cynthia Brokaw, Katherine Carlitz, Andrea S. Goldman, David Johnson, the late Harold Kahn, Marcus Kanda, Reed Malcolm, Joseph McDermott, Tobie Meyer-Fong, Steven Miles, Enrique Ochoa-Kaup, Archna Patel, Christopher Pitts, Kenneth Pomeranz, Brett Sheehan, Janet Theiss, Heidi Tinsman, the late Frederic Wakeman Jr., Jeffrey Wasserstrom, Zhang Guoyi, Zhang Ying, Zhao Guohua, Zhu Wanshu, Harriet Zurnderfor, and the outside reviewers.

The research for this project started with a grant from the National Endowment for the Humanities (2007–2008). I want to thank *Late Imperial China* for publishing an early article on Cheng Minzheng, portions of which are featured in chapters 1, 2, and 5 of this book and reproduced here with permission. An earlier version of my study on the late Ming cult of female chastity published in *Nan Nü: Men, Women and Gender in China* is the basis for chapter 4; I am grateful for permission to republish that work here. The University of California, Irvine, granted me several quarters of sabbatical leave during which I drafted and revised most of this book.

Finally, I want to thank Andrea and Simon for being there for me—and giving me the space when needed—while I completed this monograph; they have my deepest appreciation.

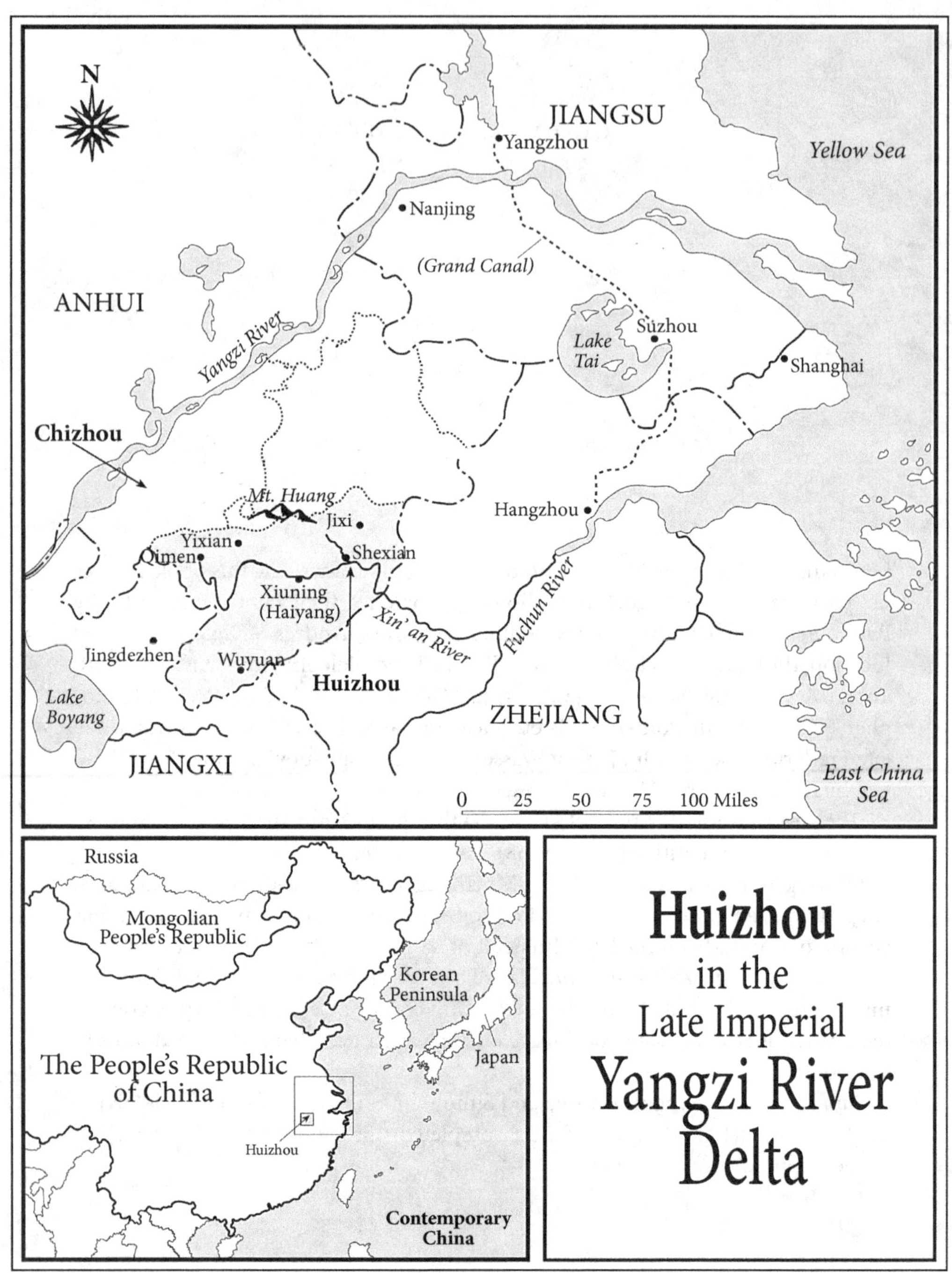

N
JIANGSU
Yellow Sea
Yangzhou
Nanjing
(Grand Canal)
ANHUI
Yangzi River
Lake Tai
Suzhou
Shanghai
Chizhou
Mt. Huang
Jixi
Hangzhou
Yixian
Qimen
Shexian
Xiuning
(Haiyang)
Xin'an River
Fuchun River
Jingdezhen
Wuyuan
Huizhou
ZHEJIANG
Lake Boyang
JIANGXI
East China Sea
0   25   50   75   100 Miles
Russia
Mongolian People's Republic
Korean Peninsula
The People's Republic of China
Japan
Huizhou
Contemporary China

Huizhou
in the
Late Imperial
Yangzi River
Delta

Introduction

This book studies the construction of local identity in Ming China (1368–1644). Its setting in time, roughly the second half of the Ming dynasty, was an era of vast changes in society, economy, gender practice, and intellectual and religious culture. Its setting in space, Huizhou, a single prefecture in the southeast, was a place of great significance in the late Ming empire that in many ways exemplified the concurrent changes. Huizhou became a stronghold of the lineage (kinship settlement based on the principle of patrilineal descent) and the homeland of arguably the empire's most powerful regional mercantile group, the Huizhou merchants (Huishang). It also produced a disproportionately large number of scholar-officials out of higher civil service exam degree holders. This social cohort, collectively termed the gentry in Anglophone scholarship, largely subscribed to a set of religio-philosophical precepts known as neo-Confucianism. Huizhou, claimed as the ancestral place of Confucian culture hero Zhu Xi (1130–1200), was hailed as a bastion of neo-Confucianism, and went on to become a center of the female chastity cult, while at the same time being marked by robust worship of popular local deities. How all of these developments came to be linked to one another and negotiated to form the Huizhou identity as a land of gentrified "prominent lineages" is the subject of this study.

The mid-Ming, which began about one hundred years after the establishment of the dynasty, was an embryonic moment for change. The economy accelerated, shifting from the founding emperor's ideal of self-governing village life to one interwoven with and animated by the forces of regional, and even empire-wide, markets. The rotational system of the *lijia* ("hundreds-and-tithings") that relied on the heads of local leading families to handle tax collection and delivery had been ineffective and in disarray for quite some time. The decay gradually ushered in the piecemeal fiscal rebuilding later known as the Single Whip reforms, which combined corvée and land taxes into one single cash payment, and in the end virtually waved the tax obligations of the gentry, as they enjoyed the privilege of being exempted from labor service. This long era of peace also nourished commercial landlordism, thereby promoting a monetized economy and the value of markets.

Toward the late fifteenth century, a top scholar-official, Qiu Jun (1420–1495), began to deliberate on a new state-market relationship in a chapter in his *Supplement to "Expositions on the Great Learning."* Believing that merchants did a better job of marketing goods than the state, he proposed an open market for traders, although as a devoted Confucian he still acknowledged the possible negative impacts of commercial activity on the moral fiber of the people. The *Supplement* was a significant set of policy deliberations that Qiu Jun presented to the newly ascended Hongzhi emperor in 1487, but it was also commercially published and widely circulated, anticipating the great wave of commercialization that was to sweep China in the sixteenth century.[1]

Huizhou, consisting of the six counties of Shexian, Xiuning, Wuyuan, Qimen, Yixian, and Jixi, emerged as a great beneficiary of sixteenth-century commercialization. This was partially because the lineages of this mountainous region fully supported their kinsmen's mercantile adventures. Indeed, in mid-Ming Huizhou a new social development, perhaps more notable than commercialization, was the strengthening of kinship associations. This took place through the compilation of lineage genealogies and by perfecting ancestral rites. Kinship solidarity and merchant success supported and enhanced each other.[2] The region became a stronghold of what I have elsewhere called "mercantile lineages," who built up massive kinship institutions that combined gentry leadership with merchant capital.[3] Paralleling all of these changes, as Timothy Brook has noted, was another mid-Ming trend—the retreat of the state from society and increased activism by local gentry.[4] It is against this spatial and temporal backdrop that my narrative begins.

This study of Ming Huizhou makes a signature contribution to the study of late imperial China by revisiting longstanding questions about Chinese lineage formation and practice as analyzed through new interpretive lenses and new sources. It advances the emerging body of work in English-language scholarship on the study of Huizhou (a well-developed subfield in Mainland Chinese scholarship); it historicizes the discursive development of lineage in one of the renowned strongholds of kinship settlements in late imperial China; and it sheds important new light on what has been termed the "localist turn" in the mid- to late Ming. Most importantly, perhaps, it weaves together intellectual, social, gender, and religious history, to offer a new and deep reading of the construction of Huizhou identity over the course of the Ming dynasty.

Scholarship on late imperial Huizhou can be largely grouped into two camps: an empirically robust but undertheorized Sinophone literature and a much smaller cluster of Anglophone studies. The richness of source materials combined with its distinctive social features has made the study of Huizhou central to post-Mao scholarship of Ming-Qing history in the People's Republic of China.

Indeed, Huizhou studies have developed into a historical subspecialty in China, called Huixue (Huizhou scholarship). Huixue may be defined as a special branch of regionally focused studies. It covers almost every aspect of Huizhou, but the greatest attention has been trained on Huizhou lineages and Huizhou merchants. As a whole, this scholarly literature tends to document and catalog without engaging the debates on late imperial society in Anglophone China scholarship.

Although a handful of English-language monographs have addressed the region of Huizhou, much of this work has been based on published collections or reprints of Ming-Qing documents, with the notable exception of Joseph McDermott's two-volume study of the development of Huizhou lineage in the sixteenth century, *The Making of a New Rural Order in South China*, which makes extensive use of the Huizhou *wenshu* (lineage imprints and manuscripts).[5] Most of these studies can be characterized as socioeconomic in focus, again culminating to date in McDermott's paired monographs, which chart the ascendance of the lineage and trace the ways in which lineage ancestral halls served as a kind of banking mechanism undergirding the financial ventures of Huizhou merchants.

My prior work shifted focus to popular cultural facets of Huizhou mercantile lineages.[6] What remains virtually unexamined is the discursive practices of local elites—whether in Huizhou or any other locality in Ming China—in developing their regional identity via the institution of the lineage. That is the work undertaken in this study.

As McDermott has noted, the lineage has over the past half-century "rightly come to occupy a central place in standard accounts of the social history of late imperial China."[7] Indeed, in the China history field, this trend can be traced back to Philip Kuhn's groundbreaking study *Rebellion and Its Enemies in Late Imperial China*, which was deeply influenced by approaches in structural anthropology and helped to mark the field's turn to regional history.[8] The role of lineage in state-society relations has been an enduring problem for the English-language field of late imperial China ever since.

More recently, the scholarship of Michael Szonyi has adopted a more dynamic approach to lineage as practice (rather than structure). His studies of kinship organization in northern Fujian have presented genealogical construction as a competitive practice in which interaction with the imperial state became a factor in evolving lineage form and function, and in which increasing social inclusiveness became a feature of kinship developed in an era that seemed to require ever greater efforts at social control. For Szonyi, lineage competition is manifest in the everyday politics of religious worship, as well as marriage strategies and tactics for avoiding military-service obligations.[9] Unlike the Fujian lineages that Szonyi studied, the Huizhou lineages that I analyze here were prominent and wealthy. Nevertheless, I share his approach of treating the representations of local kinship society as a key practice of lineage strategy. My study further mobilizes the toolkit of the new cultural history—with its attention to local rhetorical strategies, gender analysis, and religious symbolism—to themes first raised by the older anthropological and historical studies of lineage.

This study of mid- to late Ming Huizhou further engages with what Peter Bol has called the "localist turn," as shown in the case of Jinhua, Zhejiang (not far away from Huizhou), where literati elites started to conceptualize the locality through compiling local anthologies and gazetteers and making the home place a vital part of their identity.[10] Bol's work builds upon that of earlier economic and social historians such as Robert Hartwell and Robert Hymes, who have famously argued that the mid-Song turn away from national service to local strategies of engagement meant that the Southern Song elite was essentially the same group as the gentry of the Ming and Qing dynasties.[11] This continuity of local elites has contributed to viewing the Song-Yuan-Ming era as a discrete historical unit.[12] Peter Bol, in contrast, also argues for a localist turn for each major dynasty; for the Ming dynasty, the statist policies of the early Ming was followed by an era of government withdrawal from society and the rise of local elites. His emphasis is on the local initiatives, although for Bol, "a localist turn need not be anti-state per se" on the grounds that greater decentralization and elite autonomy could benefit everyone, "including the dynasty."[13]

This is where my inquiry into Huizhou cultural history fits in. We see an apparently similar localist turn in the region over the second half of the Ming dynasty—what I call the rise of Huizhou consciousness—as embodied most focally in a series of literati anthologies and gazetteers that glorified Huizhou history and cultural tradition. The glorification of the locality paved the way for the formation, around the mid-sixteenth century, of the Huizhou identity as a land of "prominent lineages." I show how vast changes in the intellectual, social, economic, religious, and gender realms during the second half of the Ming dynasty coalesced into the making of this Huizhou identity. Unlike Jinhua, Huizhou identity was not just local but also lineage bound. Hence, we see not only that localist manifestation varied in different regions, but also that the Huizhou story moves significantly beyond the localist-turn paradigm.

The projection of Huizhou identity constitutes the first half of this study; the second half addresses the development of the mercantile lineage culture upon which Huizhou identity was partially predicated. Over the course of the sixteenth century, local lineages became increasingly engaged in commerce, turning themselves into mercantile lineages. And yet, given the debasing of merchants in Confucian ideology and the deeply gentrified culture of Huizhou, mercantile activities were never considered fully honorable or culturally accepted in the collective discourse of Huizhou lineages. Partially, too, as a strategy to deflect outside criticism of the dominance of Huizhou merchants, mercantile interests were veiled behind the publicly projected image of Huizhou identity. This public erasure of merchant identity conveyed enormous meaning. It suggests that the merchants of Huizhou were dependent on home lineages as much in local discourse as they were in real life in terms of logistic and sociocultural support. As such, the projection of Huizhou self-identification was partly a move to consolidate local kinship society in an age of accelerating commercialization and the perceived loosening of established moral norms. This mercantile lineage culture, furthermore, was manifested in, and supported by, the local gender regime to make Huizhou the "Confucian heartland of women." It was further negotiated via religious symbolism with the popular God of Wealth being controlled by the patron deity of Huizhou lineages.

The book is structured in two parts. Part 1 covers the two chapters on the making of Huizhou consciousness and Huizhou identity. Part 2, in three chapters, addresses the reification of mercantile lineage culture, its engendered performance, and its symbolic representation in the local religious realm. Together, the two parts demonstrate the historical development of Huizhou from the mid- to the late Ming, while also revealing a discrepancy between name and substance. The success of Huizhou was predicated in large part upon this discrepancy.

Chapter 1 highlights the localist endeavors of Cheng Minzheng (1444–1499), a prominent official working at the imperial center who, in 1478, self-identified with his ancestral fatherland of Huizhou (also known as Xin'an), thereby devoting his life to raising the status of both the region and his Cheng lineage.[14] He compiled two important genealogies, one for his home branch in Xiuning County and the other covering all of the Huizhou Chengs in his *Composite Genealogy of the Xin'an Chengs* (Xin'an Chengshi tongzong shipu), a new genre at the time. He was also in charge of compiling the gazetteer of Xiuning. His most important Huizhou-focused work was the massive *Anthology of Xin'an Documents* (Xin'an wenxian zhi), consisting of one hundred *juan*, which highlights Huizhou's natural beauty, historical glory, and kinship solidarity. Fundamentally shaping the contours of Huizhou history, the *Anthology* is at least as important as any local gazetteer with regard to its role in shaping regional consciousness in the mid-Ming.[15]

Cheng Minzheng showed no conflict between commitment to locally focused endeavors and serving at the dynastic center. This dual outlook resonated with his philosophical predilections. He was an important thinker who helped transition from Zhu Xi's Learning of the Way to the populist moral-leveling thought of Wang Yangming (1472–1529), which tended on a metaphysical level to erase the distinctions between the imperial center and local society and between elites and commoners. Cheng Minzheng was not born in Huizhou, but he anchored himself there after his father moved back to the family's ancestral home in retirement.[16] As Minzheng often used his empire-wide connections to promote his localist endeavors, his identification with Huizhou had the potential to enhance his position in the central government. When he was dismissed from his central post, from 1488 to 1492, he stayed in his Huizhou home where he completed the compilation of some of his most important works, including *Anthology of Xin'an Documents* and two neo-Confucian philosophical collections. These works were partly motivated by his desire for political rehabilitation, in which he succeeded.[17] Indeed, Cheng

Minzheng's "localist turn" by no means suggests the separation of state and local society, but rather gave Huizhou a larger role in influencing the entire realm as a model Confucian society. Cheng Minzheng helped to enhance the Confucian characteristics of Huizhou by, among other activities, alleging kinship ties between the leading Song dynasty neo-Confucians—the two Cheng brothers—and his Huizhou Cheng descent line.

The foremost embodiment of regional consciousness in Huizhou was the lineage institution. Chapter 2 focuses on the 1551 edition of *Prominent Lineages in Xin'an* (Xin'an mingzu zhi), a massive genealogical gazetteer and a unique Ming genre that encompassed all of the acknowledged elite lineages in the prefecture. First, by contextualizing the composite genealogical gazetteer both textually and socially, this chapter demonstrates how Cheng Minzheng's influence played into its ultimate compilation and publication (of the Cheng-led sequence of prominent lineages). But the process also shows the evolution from one individual vision to a shared regional entity, as the genealogical gazetteer was collectively compiled by representatives of the local gentry and endorsed by all of the participating lineages.

More importantly, *Prominent Lineages in Xin'an* reflected the concurrent commercialization and development of kinship institutions. Drawing upon about eight hundred single-surnamed genealogies out of ninety Huizhou surnames (including many composite genealogies of the leading surnames inspired by Cheng Minzheng), *Prominent Lineages in Xin'an* marked the formation of a new Huizhou identity that was rooted in both regional and kinship ties, presenting the prefecture to the entire realm as a land of prominent—and Confucianized or gentrified—lineages (which was further confirmed in the 1626 *Prominent Lineages in Xiuning*, an expanded version of the 1551 genealogical gazetteer based on one county). Huizhou lineages claimed eminent ancestry, primarily defined as noted statesmen and scholar-officials (and even claiming descent from the royal families of ancient dynasties), making them socially privileged, morally worthy, and culturally admirable. And yet, *Prominent Lineages in Xin'an* actually covers both "famous" and "not-so-famous" lineages. This moral leveling resonated with the thinking of Cheng Minzheng and the popular Ming School of the Mind (also known as Wang Yangmingism), but also may be attributed to the editors' desire to make everyone happy by boasting about a region full of prominent lineages. Moreover, these Huizhou lineages now also embraced Confucian commoners, most notably "righteous" merchants and devoted kinswomen.

The new identity of Huizhou embodied in *Prominent Lineages* was multifaceted. Its public face was a land of prominent lineages, but its inner core was increasingly composed of what might now be called "mercantile lineages"—that is, it was gentry led and merchant based. This sublimating of merchant interests within the Huizhou identity was meaningful on several fronts: merchants were attached to their home lineages in terms of both kinship and finance; their business endeavors were often supported by the home lineages (in return, they gave back in order to enhance lineage institutions); and identification was kinship based rather than class based. In other words, Huizhou merchants, while dominant in markets and often viewed by outsiders in negative terms (as vividly narrated in popular tales), were morally elevated at home and yet never formed an independent class identity.

The three chapters of part 2 offer close readings of three manifestations of the now-matured mercantile lineage culture and Huizhou identity. Chapter 3 turns to the merchant biographies written by Wang Daokun (1523–1593), a prominent scholar-official from Huizhou. These biographies further reflect the subtle positioning of merchants within lineage discourse. Wang Daokun was both a product and producer of local mercantile lineage culture. He has received some scholarly attention, mostly in China and Japan, largely because of his literary reputation and his compilation of numerous merchant biographies. But a proper understanding of his contribution to Huizhou culture during the second half of the sixteenth century requires a balanced inquiry into all of his writings, especially his lineage documents, merchant biographies, and accounts of Confucian women. He elevated the status of merchants, helped Confucianize a mercantile ethical code, and further promoted the Huizhou social metamorphosis strategy widely practiced among local elite lineages of alternating learning and trade between generations or among brothers.

Wang never directly identified Huizhou tradesmen as "merchants," but instead used the term *chushi* (scholarly gentrymen without an exam degree), as many of them engaged in trade only after failing in the examination hall. And he actively promoted the virtues of merchants and women in the context of the lineage. He was first among late Ming scholar-officials to compile a new version of the *Biographies of Exemplary Women* (Lienü zhuan). Some of the leading entries on women and merchants were also printed in the genealogy he compiled for his own lineage, which he claimed was descended from the ancient Zhou royal house. At the same time, in keeping with the now wildly popular Wang Yangmingism, Wang Daokun held commoners in higher esteem than his famous Huizhou predecessor Cheng Minzheng. He equated family genealogies with official history and linked his home lineage to the symbolic center of dynastic power. In the end, if *Prominent Lineages in Xin'an* marked the emergence of a new Huizhou identity, Wang Daokun perfected Huizhou mercantile lineage culture, which ensured the prefecture's success both in commerce and in the placement of scholar-officials throughout the realm.

Gender also played an important role in Huizhou's mercantile lineage history. In the late Ming, the region became known for its virtuous women and devoted widows. Chapter 4 presents a new interpretation of the growing cult of female chastity in sixteenth-century Huizhou. Using the copious demographic data drawn from one massive genealogy of a leading Huizhou mercantile lineage, I show that the most important underlying factor in the formation of the female fidelity cult was the changing family-lineage structure, which was brought about by a high incidence of sojourning tradesmen in the region. Since the majority of young men in Huizhou left home for business and returned only "once in every three years," the age at which couples had their first child tended to be advanced. This demographic trend combined with a moderate average life span to make the nuclear family the norm. Situated in single-couple households, wives of sojourning husbands tended to be relatively free from the patriarchal monitoring of their sexuality. One effective way to ensure the fidelity of these abandoned women was to appeal to the larger lineage. This in part explains why Huizhou merchants were so eager to make contributions to consolidating home kinship institutions. In doing so, however, Huizhou merchants helped perpetuate the mercantile lineage regime that was subsumed within Huizhou self-identification, inhibiting development of an independent social identity.

This mercantile lineage culture was also embodied in the local religious order. Chapter 5 uses newly discovered archival materials, especially the late Ming ritual handbook, *Model Prayers to the Deities* (Qishen zouge), to examine the making of the Huizhou pantheon. *Model Prayers*, in six volumes, contains almost encyclopedic data about Huizhou's local cults, but its most notable feature lies in a regional pantheon that was headed by Wang Hua, a seventh-century Huizhou hero who had since accrued three facets of symbolic significance: he was the apical ancestor of the prominent and most populous descent line in the region; he was the patron deity of Huizhou; and, ultimately, he served as a link between local society and the dynastic center. This "ritual code" of Huizhou was a localized transformation of the Ming state religious system. Wang Hua emerged as the local proxy of the official City God, and his pantheon—as illustrated in some rare Ming dynasty Huizhou Wang genealogies—incorporated a large number of powerful deities from Buddhism and Daoism, as well as a number of locally worshipped spirits.

Interestingly, the ritual handbook was attributed to Cheng Minzheng, whose name was used to legitimate the hierarchical religious order of the Huizhou pantheon that fixed Minzheng's own sixth-century ancestor as an attendant of Wang Hua. Here we see local competition for symbolic capital, which nevertheless had the effect of achieving a power balance among local prominent lineages: the godly power of Wang Hua was balanced against the genealogical pedigree of the Chengs.

More importantly, as the Wang Hua pantheon was hierarchically structured, it served to control the power of many popular deities that were incorporated into its symbolic network, including the Wuchang pentad spirit, the locally worshipped God of Wealth, which channeled the power of money to good use while averting its potential harmful impacts. This lowly but popular patron deity of Huizhou merchants also played a key role in policing gender relations, helping to oversee kinswomen's sexuality and assure safe childbirth, both of which were critically important for sojourning merchants and their home lineages. Furthermore, as Wang Hua was also worshipped as the apical ancestor of all of the Huizhou Wangs, this tutelary deity of the region was turned into a generic patron deity of all Huizhou lineages. In this sense, the Wang Hua pantheon was virtually an extension of Confucian ancestral worship. Indeed, the local pantheon best exemplified the rise of Huizhou consciousness, but also became a religious representation of local mercantile lineage culture, reflecting and reinforcing the Huizhou identity.

Huizhou identity, I argue, was at once imagined and real, straightforward and multilayered. The historical roots of Huizhou prominent lineages were partly apocryphal, and yet by the sixteenth century had become real, as their mythic origins had been repeatedly asserted in the lineage genealogies and thus firmly established as local knowledge. These prominent lineages were further collectively enhanced by their outstanding achievements in official placements from Song-Yuan times onward and, later, over the course of the sixteenth century, in marketplaces. Huizhou identity was locally and lineage bound, but its core evolved historically. Huizhou had been self-claimed as a model Confucian society (as the so-called ancestral place of the three most important Song dynasty neo-Confucians—the Cheng brothers and Zhu Xi), and the lineage was supposed to be the best social embodiment of Song neo-Confucianism in local society. What came to be embodied in local kinship institutions and mercantile lineage culture, however, was mainly the moral leveling more associated with Cheng Minzheng (which to a certain degree also echoed the popular Ming School of the Mind). In practicing kinship, Huizhou kinspeople developed a variety of strategies that clearly broke the kinship guidelines set up by Song neo-Confucians in their construction of independent, large-scale ancestral halls worshipping apical ancestors; in co-opting merchant interests; in building and worshipping the local pantheon, which was syncretic and embraced both official and popular cults; and even in their public boasting of being a land of "prominent lineages." Most importantly, Huizhou lineages came to be increasingly composed of merchant interests, and yet such interests were elided in the representation of the regional self-identification. This development had much to do with the Huizhou social metamorphosis strategy of alternating between learning and trade, in which the merchants of Huizhou were overshadowed by the scholar-official gentry both socially and culturally. The gentry-led lineage also worked with sojourning merchants to tighten control over kinswomen, which had the effect of turning the region into a center of the female chastity cult. Indeed, devoted womanhood was key to the making and maintaining of mercantile lineages and Huizhou identity. All of this was also ritualized in the local religious order, as evidenced by the Huizhou pantheon that worked to protect and promote local mercantile lineages and their gender regime.

This study also adds a new dimension of internal competition to the mid-Ming rise of regional consciousness and shows that the consolidation of local elite lineages was not necessarily at odds with state interests. Not only were central alliances used to secure local preeminence, but local competition for cultural capital also strengthened the "harmonious" functioning of gentry kin communities. This enabled the region to successfully reproduce its power in the political and commercial realms of the state and provide key service to the center throughout late imperial times. As we learn from the Huizhou experience, the more locally rooted a society was, the more prepared it was to reach out to other regions and up to the center.

The distinction between Huizhou self-identification and its sublimated core of mercantile lineage culture ultimately suggests a manifest decoupling between the economy and sociocultural discourses: the more active the economy became, the more those central to the intensification of commerce—that is, merchants and mercantile lineages—embraced conservative social and cultural norms (a message that has implications for present-day China as well). While some western scholars of late imperial China have gravitated to the loosening, or "liberalization," of social mores in the late Ming, my study addresses the equally important conservative response to commercialization.[18] This focus recognizes that, perhaps ironically, home lineages embraced neo-Confucian orthodoxy even as they provided the financial, cultural, and logistical support to assure the success of Huizhou merchants. Huizhou, arguably the most commercialized region of the late Ming empire, did not prepare the social conditions that could have nurtured "capitalism" but built up gentrified mercantile lineage culture with Chinese—or Huizhou—characteristics.

This study focuses on elite discourses, but as I show there was interplay between discourse and social practice and between high and popular cultures. This emphasis is partly an intended shift away from my own previous work on popular culture.[19] But it is also an attempt to balance the use of various types of source materials. Here, I draw upon both the rich trove of newly uncovered Huizhou lineage imprints and manuscripts and so-called classical documents (*dianji wenxian*). Cheng Minzheng's philosophical treatises and Wang Daokun's genealogy nestle cheek by jowl with many *wenshu* documents. This includes the newly found ritual handbook *Model Prayers to the Deities*, handwritten labor and land contracts, as well as the many Huizhou genealogies stored in a variety of archives.[20] Over two dozen invaluable, pre-Qing Huizhou genealogies (along with seven from the Qing) are closely examined herein, many of which are massive in content and have never been studied. The result is a balanced exploration of all kinds of source materials that reveal the discrepancy between the projection of Huizhou identity and the actual workings of local mercantile lineage culture. Indeed, it is the richness of Huizhou sources that makes possible the reexamination of lineage matters through the lens of cultural history.

PART I

Local Identity

1

Cheng Minzheng and the Rise
of Huizhou Consciousness

In the winter of 1478, after thirteen years of service at the imperial court in Beijing, Cheng Minzheng finally visited his ancestral home, Huizhou. The Chenghua emperor approved Imperial Hanlin Academician Cheng's request to take a leave of absence, as his younger brother had just passed away in the village of Peiguo, in Xiuning County, leaving behind their aging parents. The key moment of this voyage, however, turned out to be Minzheng's visit to Huangdun (Yellow Mound), a rural canton in Huizhou's capital county, Shexian. There he went to see the main temple dedicated to his famous ancestor, Cheng Lingxi (514–568), and observed with great interest twelve sacred relics related to this deified Huizhou hero. Minzheng wrote a hymn for each of them and then distributed the verses to his kinsmen, many of whom responded with additional poems. These Huangdun verses were all compiled into a "huge collection" to be "shown to descendants," for which Minzheng wrote a foreword.

After conducting further research into the history of Yellow Mound, he observed that "Lord [Lingxi] originally lived in Xiuning's Huangdun, which was later ceded to Shexian."[1] To Minzheng, not only was Huangdun's county affiliation a matter deserving exegesis, so was its name. In an essay titled "Records from the Studio of Huangdun" (Huangdun shushe ji), he notes, "The Chengs, illustrious in the north, followed the Jin dynasty to move to the south by the time of Yuantan, who became prefect of Xin'an" (Xin'an was Huizhou's historical name). Given Cheng Yuantan's glorious achievements in governing Xin'an, Minzheng continues:

> Local people requested that he stay when his term ended, and he was awarded a mansion in the prefecture's Yellow Mound, where his offspring stayed and settled. His twelfth-generation descendant, General Yunhui, Lingxi, posthumously designated as Lord Zhongzhuang [loyal strength], rose up as a commoner, organizing the militia to resist the Hou Jing [rebellion, 548–552]. Appreciating his achievements in protecting the prefecture, the locals too honored him with a shrine at Yellow Mound.

> The Song house bestowed the title of Shizhong [permanent loyalty] on his temple, and his offspring thereafter increasingly prospered. Thus, the Chengs in Xin'an all honored the prefect [Yuantan] as the primary progenitor and Lord Zhongzhuang as the apical ancestor, calling themselves the Huangdun Chengs. My family also originated from Yellow Mound.

Having established the illustrious pedigree of his lineage, by highlighting Lord Zhongzhuang's contribution to Xin'an in particular, Minzheng turns to the crux of the naming matter:

> And yet, after examining various genealogies and prefecture gazetteers, I was still unable to figure out why the mound was so named. Lately, I have arrived at an interpretation: The *huang* of Yellow Mound was originally the character *huang* [bamboo]. It was so named because the place produced great quantities of bamboo. At the time of the Huang [Yellow] Chao rebellion [875–884], the rebels left no living humans in their path, except in the prefectures and districts with mountains and rivers that carried *huang* [yellow] in their names. The Chengs who hid [in Huangdun] therefore changed the word *bamboo* [huang] to *yellow* [huang] so as to avoid calamity. After a long time, this [name] became engrained in custom. Alas, how could the place where the good administrator [Cheng Yuantan] and loyal official [Cheng Lingxi], who had been awarded a mansion and offered sacrifices, have been blemished by the surname of a ruthless rebel! For more than seven hundred years, no one even has found this wrong! I therefore wrote out two huge characters, Huangdun [Bamboo Mound], and pasted them on my ancestral residence . . . so as to let our descendants know that I was the one who had restored the original name of this place.[2]

After consulting with his father (a top official who in 1472 retired to Huizhou) about restoring the rightful name of Bamboo Mound, Minzheng even decided to style himself "Huangdun." Upon his return to Beijing, he spread the bamboo story among his colleagues in the central bureaucracy, inviting them to write something to commemorate the event. Qiu Jun (1420–1495), the minister of the Board of Rites and Minzheng's mentor in statecraft, opened his celebratory poem directly: "This was the village in which Zhongzhuang once lived, where tens of thousands of shining stalks covered Bamboo Mound." An impressive cohort of other top officials from the Beijing court, including Peng Hua (1432–1496), Liu Zhen (1434–1501), Fu Han (1435–1502), Ni Yue (1444–1501), Xie Qian (1449–1531), Fei Yin (1436–1493), and Wu Kuan (1435–1504), joined Qiu Jun to help Minzheng legitimatize the "restoration" of "Bamboo Mound" by writing similar celebratory poems or essays. Minzheng again compiled these writings by "current gentrymen"—all prominent scholar-officials with metropolitan *jinshi* degrees—into a collection and wrote a "Preface for the Huangdun Records."[3]

In late imperial China, it was common practice for Confucian scholars to compose poems or conduct "evidential research," especially on things or places that were related to their native places or ancestral notables. Cheng Minzheng's case, however, turns out to be more than merely engaging in literati pastimes. There were hidden agendas—or intangible significations—in his renaming of Huangdun, but let us start with the tangible or semitangible. Imperial Academician Cheng, by publicizing the Huangdun story and thereby deepening his ancestral pedigree, would surely be able to enhance his standing among his colleagues in the central government. But he was also mobilizing his official contacts to influence local matters and strengthen the Cheng prestige back home in Huizhou, a region noted for its concentration of great families and prominent lineages with (claimed or real) deep roots in and sensitivity to ancestral pedigree. Central and local powers were intimately entangled. In this instance, Imperial Academician Cheng was concentrating on Huizhou local matters. When a Confucian scholar took a new style name, it tended to signal his new resolutions. Minzheng's new style signaled his newly found self-identification with Huizhou, which was not his or even his father's birthplace, but still his ancestral fatherland. It initiated a series of his remarkable locally engaged endeavors that significantly contributed to shaping the regional consciousness of Huizhou.

Cheng Minzheng was among the mid-Ming literati who first expressed the stirrings of the "localist turn." Seen from the standpoint of the neo-Confucian movement, it also marked the revival of literati "volunteerism" in various locally focused endeavors motivated by a commitment to "righteousness."[4] Underlying this revival was the inward turn of Ming neo-Confucians from an emphasis on textual studies to the cultivation of the moral self.[5] According to Ying-shih Yu, there was a political dimension to this intellectual shift. In the treacherous political environment of the early Ming, Confucian scholars avoided political involvement, instead turning inward to moral cultivation. This collective mentality intensified, creating an intellectual propensity to jettison "getting the monarch to spread the Way" (*dejun xingdao*) in favor of "awakening the people to practice the Way" (*juemin xingdao*).[6] Cheng Minzheng nevertheless aimed to spread the Way for both the monarch and the people. He was a "man who became aware and awakened first" (*xianzhi xianjue zhe*) in terms of both the philosophical positioning and the localist turn of the mid-Ming. However, his locally engaged endeavors were not purely motivated by a sense of "righteousness," but were also shaped by the special situation of Huizhou.[7] Cheng Minzheng focused on creating a new discourse by writing and rewriting the history of Huizhou and the Huizhou Chengs, anthologizing Xin'an historical documents, and compiling Cheng genealogies. This rewriting of history notably started with his renaming of Huangdun.

HUANGDUN, THE OLD XIN'AN PLACE

Huangdun was bursting with local and larger meaning for Huizhou. Several leading lineages claimed their original settlements in the place. One of the best documented was the claim by the Huang lineage. According to local folklore, their apical ancestor, Huang Ji, was appointed prefect of Xin'an by the first emperor of the Eastern Jin (r. 317–322). He was buried in a place called Yaojiadun ("mound of the Yao family"), where his son built a hut around his tomb. Their descendants settled in Yaojiadun, and then renamed it after their surname to become Huangdun (Yellow Mound).[8] Cheng Minzheng, in a preface he wrote for a Huang genealogy, acknowledged the settlement by the Huangs in Yaojiadun, though he skillfully avoided mentioning either Yellow Mound or Bamboo Mound.[9] It appears that Huang Ji arrived in Xin'an slightly before Cheng Yuantan, who, according to a 1298 tomb inscription, became prefect of Xin'an in 319 and died there in 322.[10] Huang Ji appeared to have served as the Xin'an prefect before Cheng Yuantan, even though *Prominent Lineages in Xin'an* (1551) mentions that Cheng Yuantan moved to the south during the Yongjia Disorder (304–311).[11] While we cannot be certain as to whether Huang Ji or Cheng Yuantan arrived in Xin'an or Huangdun first, the name Yellow Mound certainly testified to the Huangs' original claim. The actual timing of the sequence matters less than the importance such arcane territorial stakes held for latter-day lineage luminaries such as Cheng Minzheng and his Huizhou audience. For Cheng Minzheng, erasing the Huangs' monopoly of Huangdun worked to establish the Cheng precedence.

The real competitor for lineage preeminence in Cheng Minzheng's time, however, were the Wangs, whom Minzheng acknowledged in yet another preface he wrote for a Wang genealogy as "the most renowned" surname with "the largest number of kin branches," as expressed in a local saying: in Huizhou, "nine out of ten are surnamed Wang."[12] Cheng Minzheng's rewriting of the meaning of Huangdun may have worked to undermine—ever so slightly—the Wangs' standing, too. One Wang branch did not move to "Yellow Mound" until the early Tang, several hundred years after the Chengs and the Huangs, although the apical ancestor of the Huizhou Wangs was claimed to be Wang Wenhe, who crossed the Yangzi River in 197 and thereafter settled in Xin'an, definitely earlier than either Cheng Yuantan or Huang Ji.[13] By Cheng Minzheng's time, the Huizhou Wangs normally claimed direct descent from Wang Wenhe's Tang dynasty offspring, Wang Hua, a powerful regional warlord during the Sui-Tang transition period whose cult was dominant in later imperial Huizhou. Wang Hua was deified almost immediately upon his death in the early Tang, much earlier than the Song deification of Cheng Lingxi. It was Wang Hua's twenty-first descendent, Wang Wei of the Huangdun branch, who petitioned the Song court in 1222 to construct a temple to Cheng Lingxi in Huangdun. The emperor approved the petition the next year and honored the temple with the name Shizhong, thereby starting the state-sanctioned worship of Cheng Lingxi in Huizhou. Because of Wang Wei, as *Prominent Lineages in Xin'an* later noted, the Chengs "became increasingly more prominent."[14] Minzheng clearly cared most about the Cheng side of the story. His Huangdun tour focused on Cheng Lingxi's main temple and other mythologized relics, which, in his account, now appeared to dominate local religious life. For Minzheng, highlighting Huangdun shifted local audience attention to his deified ancestor, thereby making him a competitor with, if not a replacement of, Wang Hua in the local religious landscape.

Cheng Huangdun's strategy seems to have worked somewhat, at least in the eyes of a famous outsider. Not long after having enthusiastically responded to the "Bamboo Mound" episode, Qiu Jun was requested to write a preface for a newly revised genealogy for a Wang branch in Minzheng's Xiuning County. In this preface (1480), Qiu pays tribute to Cheng Lingxi as well as to Wang Hua. "In Xin'an," he writes, "only the two lineages of the Chengs and the Wangs are uniquely prominent. The ancestors of the two surnames [Cheng Lingxi and Wang Hua] were both notable heroes while alive and have since death enjoyed temple sacrifice in their home regions." The preface to the Wang genealogy was, of course, supposed to highlight the pedigree and accomplishments of the Wangs, so the author acknowledged some Song-Yuan notables in the Wang ancestry. He even confirmed Wang claims of direct descent from Duke Cheng of Lu (Lu Chenggong; r. 590–573 BCE)—a descendant of the Duke of Zhou.[15]

Herein lies a common strategy Huizhou lineages employed to build up local prestige: they claimed illustrious ancestry as far back into the ancient period as possible; the deeper the roots, the more prestigious the claim. Li Dongyang (1447–1516, *jinshi* 1464), Minzheng's colleague in the Board of Rites, in a 1488 preface he wrote for yet another Xiuning Wang genealogy, even repeated the Wangs' claim that they were descended from the mythical Yellow Emperor.[16] Some Cheng genealogies made such claims for the Chengs too.[17] As will be shown, Cheng Minzheng traced his lineage back to a prominent figure in the ancient Zhou dynasty, though not to the Yellow Emperor. He was an authoritative and innovative genealogist, and he understood the persuasive power of credibility in making claims about pedigree. His philological arguments about "Bamboo Mound" brought the seemingly incontrovertible force of erudition to bear on his ancestral pedigree, thus boosting a perception that the Chengs' roots in Huangdun, and the Huizhou region more generally, were the deepest—deeper even than those of the Huangs or the Wangs.

Longevity of local pedigree was not the only means by which Huizhou lineages shored up their claims to Huangdun, however. The place exuded additional luster because of its association with prominent figures in the neo-Confucian tradition. Most notable was the connection of Zhu Xi's (1130–1200) ancestors to Huangdun. This leading neo-Confucian synthesizer, though born in Fujian, was to become the most illustrious native son of Huizhou. In a preface he wrote for his kin in Huizhou's Wuyuan County, Zhu Xi noted what he had learned from his father, a true Wuyuan native: "our family ancestors had settled in Yellow Mound" before moving to Wuyuan.[18]

For the Chengs, however, the significance of Zhu Xi's bond with Huangdun lay in yet another connection: he was an avowed disciple of Cheng Hao (1032–1085) and, especially, Cheng Yi (1033–1107); and the state creed of neo-Confucianism in late imperial times was often simply called the Cheng-Zhu school. Zhu Xi's aura aside, some of the Huizhou Chengs even claimed that Cheng Hao and Cheng Yi, like themselves, were actually descended from Cheng Lingxi, or the Huangdun Chengs, despite the fact that they had been born and were active in the Luoyang area in the north.[19] Cheng Minzheng played a major role in publicizing and legitimating the claim, though he did not initiate it. This legitimating process would not be completed until the late Ming, by which time promoting the Cheng brothers' link to Huangdun was no longer simply a concern of the Cheng lineage, but rather a regional enterprise, since the claimed connection would confer prestige on the entire prefecture—or on any of its constituent counties.

During the Wanli reign (1573–1620), a cohort of thirteen Shexian gentrymen, led by Zhao Pang (fl. 1579–1615), compiled eight volumes under the title *Records of the Cheng-Zhu Native Place* (Cheng-Zhu queli zhi), with a foreword written in 1612 by the incumbent magistrate of Shexian, Liu Shen, to give the collection an official imprimatur.[20] The *Records of the Cheng-Zhu Native Place* champions the efficacious hills and rivers of Huangdun in nurturing such illustrious historical personages, while also enumerating the social and historical links of the Cheng brothers and Zhu Xi to Xin'an. The short introduction to volume one, "Record of an Efficacious Place" (Diling zhi), after noting the fostering of ancient sages in the special natural environment of their birthplaces, proudly points to the "twin links" of the ancestors of the "Cheng-Zhu three gentrymen," the "unprecedented genuine Confucians" (*kuangdai zhenru*) of Huangdun, now mostly written not as Yellow Mound but as Bamboo Mound. The volume also features an essay titled "Bamboo Mound," which is followed by the descriptions of six of the twelve relics linked to Cheng Lingxi on which Cheng Minzheng had written poems and of the two remarkable vestiges associated with Zhu Xi: "Zhu family street" in Huangdun and the "rainbow well" in Wuyuan.[21] But it was the Huangdun link that enabled Zhao Pang and his compatriots to call their home county (and by implication the larger prefecture) the "Native Place of the Cheng-Zhu."

Huangdun was quite simply the cultural and spiritual center of Huizhou in the collective memory of many prominent, pedigree-sensitive local lineages. Cheng Minzheng keenly grasped the significance of the strategic locale by adopting the modified place name as his style in 1478. This self-identification with Bamboo Mound signaled the resolution of Cheng "Huangdun" to rewrite Huizhou history—the history of local places, local figures, local descent lines, the status of the Chengs in Huizhou and that of Huizhou in the entire empire. Before we assess the accumulative impacts of this rewriting upon local consciousness, we need to first look at the writer himself.

HUANGDUN, THE NEW HUIZHOU MAN

The most visibly erudite scholar of Ming Huizhou, Cheng Minzheng was perfectly suited to the task of rewriting Huizhou history for his mid-Ming generation. Born in Beijing to a prominent family, Academician Huangdun (as he was later customarily called in Huizhou) was highly successful and widely connected. An enormously gifted and energetic man, Minzheng exuded absolute confidence. He mobilized his talents and fame with almost single-minded dedication to nurture a unique vision of Huizhou and the Chengs. To him, Huizhou, his ancestral Peiguo village, and the larger Cheng lineage were uniquely significant and beautiful. This vision framed his rewriting of the history, thereby helping fashion a new identity not just for his kinspeople but for all people of the region.

The only obstacle to Cheng Minzheng's claims for local supremacy seems to have been his outsider origins. He was neither born nor raised in Huizhou. But this outlier status gave him a firmer determination, more passion, and perhaps also a sharper perspective with which to complete his mission. Minzheng's immediate ancestors had moved north three generations earlier. During the Hongwu reign (1368–1398) Minzheng's great grandfather Ziling was relocated as part of a punitive military assignment, and eventually settled with his son Cheng (1390–1446) in Hejian Prefecture, in present-day Hebei Province.[22]

Minzheng's father, Xin (1417–1479), grew up and attended school in Hejian. Earning the metropolitan *jinshi* degree in 1442, Cheng Xin became an important official in various provincial and military administrative posts as well as at the imperial centers in Beijing and Nanjing.[23] While serving in Sichuan, Cheng Xin brought his eldest son, Minzheng, to the attention of the governor, Luo Qi (*jinshi* 1430). The mythologization of Minzheng as a genius started there when he was just ten years old, and soon Luo Qi recommended the prodigy to the Tianshun emperor. According to local lore, upon entering the palace, the boy was unable to step over the threshold, at which the emperor joked, "The young scholar's legs are short" (*shusheng jiaoduan*). To this first line of an antithetical poetic couplet, Minzheng is said to have instantly responded, "Your Majesty's threshold is tall" (*tianzi mengao*). The emperor was so pleased with this response that he sent the young pupil to study at the Imperial Academy, with all expenses covered. Grand Secretariats Li Xian (1408–1466) and Peng Shi (*jinshi* 1448), in particular, doted upon him, and Li Xian eventually became his father-in-law. Given such outstanding connections, the gifted Minzheng passed the metropolitan exam in 1466 at the age of twenty-two with a rank of second place among a class of 353 successful examinees.[24]

With bright career prospects clearly ahead of him, Minzheng was nevertheless not particularly suited to be a top bureaucrat, although he did rise from the post of imperial academician to lecturer to the crown prince, and eventually to vice minister in the Board of Rites. Minzheng gained a reputation for "often looking down upon his peers" and many colleagues "detested" him. He was impeached in 1488, whereupon he "returned home" to Peiguo for five years. Not long after he was called back to service, he became entangled in a deadly exam scandal in 1499. Minzheng, as one of the chief examiners of the metropolitan examination, was accused of leaking questions to two examinees, one of whom was none other than the future famous artist Tang Yin (1470–1524). Minzheng was imprisoned, although later absolved of wrongdoing, because an ugly power struggle lay at the heart of the case (two of his colleagues who had responded to his Huang-dun story, Fu Han and Xie Qian, were involved in a "plot" to take him down). Anger and humiliation soon led to his premature death, which earned him much needed sympathy and, eventually, a posthumous title as the minister of the Board of Rites.[25] Still, Minzheng's reputation appeared to have never recovered from this infamous scandal: no important figures wrote a *xingzhuang* (formal biography) or official epitaph for him; only his friend, an insignificant scholar named Qiu Tong, wrote one. Later Huizhou and Xiuning gazetteers contain some biographic sketches, as does the official *Ming History* in its section on "Literati."

If Minzheng cut a tragic figure as a high official, he achieved more success in his reputation as a first-rate scholar. Among the imperial academicians, according to a saying at the time, "Minzheng is noted for the wide erudition of his learning and Li Dongyang for the exquisite style of his essays."[26] The versatile Minzheng left behind a remarkable record of publications. Among them are collections of poems; two important annotated compilations of neo-Confucian philosophical works, *Oneness of the Way Collection* (Daoyi bian) and *The Classic of the Mind-and-Heart, Supplemented and Annotated* (Xinjing fuzhu); two massive compilations of historical documents, *Ming Essay Selections* (Ming wenheng) and *Anthology of Xin'an Documents* (Xin'an wenxianzhi); and a massive collection of essays in *Collected Essays of Bamboo Mound* (Huangdun wenji).[27] Many of the writings within *Collected Essays of Bamboo Mound* are concerned with Huangdun's beloved ancestral fatherland, though it also includes his lectures for the imperial princes concerning Confucian classics and policy recommendations to the throne. Indeed, along with *Xin'an Documents*, most of his written works are related to Huizhou, including the county gazetteer of Xiuning (*Xiuning zhi*; 1497) and two genealogies of the Chengs, namely *Composite Genealogy of the Xin'an Chengs* (Xin'an Chengshi tong-zong shipu; 1482)—along with its massive companion *Records of Bequeathed Glories of the Chengs* (Chengshi yifan ji)—and *Genealogy of My Peiguo Cheng Branch in Xiuning* (Xiuning Peiguo Chengshi benzong pu; 1497).[28]

After styling himself Bamboo Mound in 1478, this new Huizhou man fixated his mind on his newly adopted home region, especially when he was away from his Beijing office. Even his philosophic ponderings are mostly focused on the most famous native son of Xin'an, Zhu Xi. And yet, Minzheng also tried to reconcile the differences between Zhu Xi and his philosophical opponent, Lu Jiuyuan (1139–1194)—or rather, between the young Zhu Xi and the old Zhu Xi. Perhaps more importantly, however, Cheng Minzheng's new philosophic positioning also further facilitated his local engagement.

A ZHU XI DISCIPLE EMBRACING LU JIUYUAN

During his first banishment from the center of power, Cheng Minzheng completed some of his most important works, mostly while in Peiguo, from 1489 to 1492. In addition to compiling *Anthology of Xin'an Documents* (not published until 1497), he completed two philosophical books, *Oneness of the Way Collection* and *The Classic of the Mind-and-Heart, Supplemented and Annotated*. His foray into moral philosophy addressed a key issue at this critical juncture of neo-Confucian development in the Ming dynasty. That is, how to mediate between the two increasingly polarized streams within the neo-Confucian tradition: Zhu Xi's Learning of the Way (or School of the Principle) and Lu Jiuyuan's Learning of the Mind-and-Heart (or School of the Mind).

A disciple of the Cheng brothers, Zhu Xi created a single systematic program emphasizing "investigating things and extending knowledge" (*gewu zhizhi*), suggesting that one could reach the Way or moral principle only through intensive study of the classics. This greatest synthesizer of neo-Confucianism wrote and compiled a great body of philosophical, historical, and ritual works that eventually became a canonic collection. His younger contemporary Lu Jiuyuan had a different focus, advocating an intuitionalist, meditation-like shortcut to reaching the moral nature of the mind. In Lu's view, Zhu Xi had overtheorized sagehood, thereby undermining moral practice by diverting attention to textual studies. Lu accused Zhu of being "fragmented and disconnected" (*zhili*), whereas Zhu criticized Lu for being "empty and loose" (*kongshu*) in the famous 1175 Goose Lake debate.

Some later Confucians had attempted to mediate between the different modes of learning of Zhu and Lu. Wu Cheng (1249–1333), a leading neo-Confucian from Jiangxi, held that Zhu and Lu actually shared the same teaching, as they both tried to develop a single all-encompassing doctrine around the learning of the mind-and-heart. Zhao Fang (1319–1369), a Zhu Xi disciple from Cheng Minzheng's ancestral fatherland Xiuning, went a step further by specifically noting that Zhu and Lu at first differed but later in life reached a consensus.[29] Cheng Minzheng substantiated Zhao's claim by annotating the letters between Zhu Xi and Lu Jiuyuan (along with some comments by later Confucians) to show how these two Song dynasty neo-Confucian giants, who initially represented two opposite philosophical positions, eventually came together to reach an agreement on human nature and the approach to moral learning. His first philosophical foray carries a characteristic title, *Oneness of the Way*.[30]

Cheng Minzheng outlined his position on the unity of the Way and its historical transmission at the beginning of the *Oneness of the Way* as follows:

In the universe there is only one Way. The vastness of the Way originates from Heaven; in humans it inheres as human nature and is contained in the mind. How could there exist two kinds of mind? It is just that when it is obstructed by the selfishness of physical constitution, the [moral] nature becomes unnatural [immoral]. Therefore, the teachings of the Confucian school consist in the restoration of human nature. The fundamental way of restoring human nature lies in regaining the lost mind. As for Yan [Yuan]'s "Four Do Nots,"[31] Zengzi's "Three Reflections,"[32] and Zisi's "honor the moral nature [*zundexing*] and follow the path of inquiry and study [*daowenxue*]," as well as Mencius's "if one first erects that which is great, one will not be deficient in the small [human nature]," these sayings truly are as if uttered by a single mouth. Indeed, if the mind is not concentrated, how can one exhaustively explore moral principle, and how can one expect to thoroughly conform one's nature with the mandate? Beginning in the middle age, farther removed from the ancient sages, Buddhism and Daoism arose and meditation on the mysterious and enlightenment of emptiness was taken as lofty; etymological gloss prevailed and division of chapters and analysis of meanings was taken as worthy; florid words dominated and pleasing the public and winning acclaim was taken as an accomplishment. Therefore, the learning of the mind became obscured and failed to be practiced. Even the great Confucians like Dong [Zhongshu] and Han [Yu] were lacking in this, let alone others. Not until Master Zhou [Dunyi], born one thousand years later, elucidated the subtle meanings of the nature of the mind and promoted the ultimate power of moral practice was there a continuation of the proper transmission of Mencius. But actually, it was Master Cheng [Yi] who directly inherited it, so he said, "all the sayings and writings by the ancient sages and worthies are just meant to make people reign in the unrestrained mind, getting it again back into our bodies. [With the lost mind recovered], people will naturally seek to better themselves and discard lesser learning and thereby attain [the Way]." Therein lies the importance and the earnestness of his words, but what could be expected from subsequent scholars? In the end, no one was able to transmit the succession of the Way. Then, the two masters Zhu [Xi] and Lu [Jiuyuan] emerged after the corrosion of the Luo [Cheng Yi] Learning, and they lectured on their ideas along the east and west sides of the River, so that scholars under heaven all followed them. But the learning of the two masters could not help but differ in the early years and yet they reached agreement later in their lives. Scholars simply have failed to observe this evolving change, so as to assert that Master Zhu favored "inquiry and study," whereas Master Lu favored "honoring the moral nature," and that the two could not be reconciled throughout their lives. Alas, how could this have been good for moral practitioners? In fact, Master Zhu's "following the path of inquiry and study" is surely based on "honoring the moral nature"; how can it compare to the argumentation of later scholars who exerted all their energy on dividing chapters and analyzing the meanings of words? Master Lu's "honoring the moral nature" is surely complemented by "following the path of inquiry and study"; how can it compare with the quiet sitting of latter scholars whose minds were full of meditating on mysteriousness and awaking to emptiness? I genuinely fear that the learning of the nature of the mind will again be obstructed and submerged in the world, with scholars accustomed to thinking that the Way is not singular. It is on the basis of this examination that I have compiled the detailed [letters] in this collection.[33]

As expressed in this opening statement, Cheng Minzheng's view of the Way and of its successive transmission (and discontinuity) from the early Confucians down to the Cheng brothers is largely identical with that of Zhen Dexiu (1178–1235), a leading neo-Confucian scholar who upon Zhu Xi's death played a key role in winning official support for the Cheng-Zhu school and whom Cheng Minzheng greatly admired.[34] Quite strikingly, however, Cheng Minzheng included both Zhu Xi and Lu Jiuyuan as "two masters" (not just Zhu Xi alone) who inherited the Way, while at the same time documenting the different emphases of their learning in their early writings. The key sections of *Oneness of the Way* focus on how the two masters gradually reached an agreement starting in middle age, as shown in the letters from both admitting their own biased emphasis in earlier days. Notably, both the choice and order of the included letters appear to suggest that Zhu moved closer to Lu's position later in life. The fourth section, focusing on their views at later middle age, opens with Zhu's letter admitting that he had indeed overemphasized scholarly textual studies at the expense of "honoring the moral nature":

> Largely from Zisi onward, the method of teaching that has been highlighted and especially effective focuses on two things: "honoring the moral nature" and "following the path of inquiry and study." Now, what Zijing [Lu Jiuyuan] has spoken about is exclusively "honoring the moral nature," whereas what I have daily elaborated upon has a bit overemphasized the pursuit of "the path of inquiry and study" . . . I myself now realize that, although I've dared not to make irresponsible comments on moral principles, nevertheless I've often been ineffective at the key task of my own behavior and treating others. I should now work hard at self-examination to get rid of shortcomings and accumulate strengths so as to avoid falling again into this one-sidedness.

"From this letter," comments Cheng Minzheng, "we learn why Master Zhu became the greatest synthesizer of the [Song] Confucians. Those biased, opinionated people who are used to making arguments to belittle others should be startled and awakened. But Master Lu also had letters discussing the need to incorporate illuminating lectures and daily practice into learning, which are in complete agreement with Master Zhu, showing no conflict as they did in their middle age. Below is Lu's letter."[35]

Later in the same volume, after listing Zhu Xi's seven other letters (intertwined with several of Lu's letters and comments) where Zhu self-critiqued his former "fragmented and disconnected" approach, including a letter emphasizing "work on daily needs" (*riyong gongfu*), Cheng Minzheng commented, "Indeed, Master Zhu insightfully realized that he must rescue the scholars to overcome the 'fragmented and disconnected' flaw, and so in his letters he frequently referred to the issue, sending out warnings that were extremely alarming and sincere. This is what comes out of the talent of supermen and the learning of sages and worthies, who appreciated the justice of righteous principle, with no division between you and me. He is a paragon of virtue and learning who should be strictly followed for one hundred generations!"[36]

To later followers of the Zhu Xi School, Cheng Minzheng made too many concessions to Lu Jiuyuan; some believed he even completely betrayed the understanding of Zhu Xi. Notably, in the heyday of Wang Yangming's influence, Chen Jian (1497–1567) attacked Lu Jiuyuan and Wang Yangming as "ostensible Confucians and covert Buddhists" in his *Thorough Critique of Obscurations to Learning*. In the same treatise, Chen accused Cheng Minzheng of having paved the way for Wang Yangming to make his false assessment of Zhu Xi in his famous *Conclusions Reached by Master Zhu Late in Life*.[37] Wang Yangming, however, felt that his learning of the mind was "perfectly congruent with Zhu Xi's."[38] So did Cheng Minzheng, who must have exerted influence upon Wang Yangming. Cheng Minzheng was one of the cosupervisors (along with Li Dongyang) of the metropolitan exam in 1499 in which Wang Yangming earned the *jinshi* degree (criticism of irregularities during that exam was also the cause of Cheng's impeachment and eventual ruin).

Cheng Minzheng was a devoted Zhu Xi disciple, both intellectually and emotionally, and was widely known to be so. As Li Dongyang noted in his preface to *Collected Essays of Bamboo Mound*, his former colleague in the Board of Rites was "well versed in a multitude of various books and yet had closely examined the learning of Master Zhu in particular, feeling that [Zhu Xi was] his teacher."[39] Cheng Minzheng himself said it best in a private letter, "I'm stubborn and eccentric, but just love to read the books by Master Zhu; [I read them] while walking or sitting, so absorbed as to forget food and sleep." He went on in the same letter to explain how he had been misinterpreted: "What has been compiled in the *Oneness of the Way Collection* is all based on Master Zhu's mature sayings in his letters. Readers have not read them carefully, feeling that I was promoting Lu's learning."[40]

Cheng Minzheng was obviously responding to criticism of his *Oneness of the Way Collection*, but his philosophical leaning with regards to Zhu Xi was genuine. He clearly acted within the Zhu Xi position, trying to incorporate Lu's learning to enhance or restore what was in his mind the original, untainted learning of Master Zhu. Since Yuan times, and especially after Zhu Xi's learning had become state orthodoxy in the early Ming, scholars had been using Zhu Xi as a stepping stone to fame and power, ignoring the moral cultivation that was intrinsic to the Cheng-Zhu School.[41] From this perspective, Cheng Minzheng had shrewdly incorporated Lu to defend Zhu, all the while recognizing the degenerated and pragmatic use of Zhu Xi's ideas. Moreover, in identifying with Zhu Xi's ancestral place (where he now dwelled in banishment), the erudite Cheng Minzheng had succeeded in "following the path of inquiry and study." Indeed, he was uniquely positioned to argue for the primacy of inner self-cultivation over the external investigation of things—that is, to call attention to "honoring the moral nature" so as to unite Zhu-Lu learning. After all, belief in the unity of neo-Confucian doctrine still prevailed. As Peter Bol notes, "we should not read the great doctrinal split between Zhu Xi and Wang Yangming that emerged in the sixteenth century back into earlier periods . . . , and there was not such a sharp distinction between a Zhu Xi school and a Lu Jiuyuan school," both of which shared the common domain that was the learning of the mind or human nature.[42]

This, then, is the backdrop to Cheng Minzheng's annotation of a key anthology of classical and neo-Confucian passages on the mind, which he reissued in expanded, commentary edition. The original anthology is called *The Classic of the Mind-and-Heart* (abbreviated here as *Heart Classic*) compiled by Zhen Dexiu; and Cheng's compilation is *The Classic of the Mind-and-Heart, Supplemented and Annotated*. Although this work was largely ignored in China (whereas it was enormously popular in Tokugawa Japan and Choson Korea), de Bary elevates the *Heart Classic* as a key to understanding the larger neo-Confucian Learning of the Mind-and-Heart, "which preceded the divergence of neo-Confucianism into schools of principle and of mind and which represents the original matrix from which emerged the thought of Wang Yang-ming."[43] Indeed, the *Heart Classic* was a systematic compilation of the ideas of sages and Cheng-Zhu masters on the mind, or moral refinement; it begins with a famous yet obscure four-phrase classic aphorism on the mind and ends with Zhu Xi's inscription on "honoring the moral nature."[44] Cheng Minzheng's *Supplemented Heart Classic* was a further enhancement of his understanding of Zhu Xi's emphasis on the cultivation of the inner self (to supplement the investigation of external things).

The opening four-phrase aphorism of the *Heart Classic* is taken from the *Book of Documents*, attributed to the sage-ruler Yu: "The mind of man [*renxin*] is precarious, the mind of the Way [*daoxin*] is subtle. Have utmost refinement [*weijing*] and singleness of mind [*weiyi*]. Hold fast to the Mean." Zhu Xi's preface to the *Mean*, quoted as direct commentary on this line, emphasizes the undividedness, or oneness, of the mind while acknowledging two different sources of consciousness, "depending on whether it arises from the selfishness that is identified with the physical form or originates in the correctness of the innate moral imperative. . . . 'Refinement' means discriminating between the two and not letting them get mixed. 'Singlemindedness' [Oneness] means holding on to the correctness of the original mind and not becoming separated from it."[45] The method to accomplish this task, as some later sets of quotations show, is to maintain an attitude of reverent piety (*jing*), which was the focus of both the *Heart Classic* and Cheng Minzheng's *Supplemented Heart Classic*.[46] Serious reverence (as the basis for both self-cultivation and social action), as de Bary expounds, could mean an intense concentration on the matter at hand, but could also, in keeping with the teaching of the Cheng brothers and Zhu Xi, "invoke the ancient piety toward Heaven-and-earth as an undifferentiated reverence toward the whole creative power of the universe." Singlemindedness, or undifferentiated reverence, therefore, "is directed toward no specific object of worship but holds all things in proper respect . . . [and] one should deal with all persons as if they had a high dignity." At the same time, singlemindedness, as one quotation from Zhou Dunyi shows, "is having no desires." Put together, as de Bary argues, the *Heart Classic*, supplemented by Zhen Dexiu's other writings, "probably represents a more extreme view of human desires as evil, and a more austere, straitlaced ideal of human conduct than can be found in the Ch'eng brothers or Chu Hsi [Zhu Xi]," which later became "accepted as orthodox Chu Hsi teaching."[47]

Cheng Minzheng's further elaboration in his *Supplemented Heart Classic* added Cheng Yi's view on human desires to the opening set of quotations. When asked about "the mind of the Way" and "the human mind," Cheng Yi replied, "They are none other than heavenly principle [*tianli*] and human desires [*renyu*]. Certainly it [duality] is, but it does not suggest the existence of two things. It just means that the mind of one person, when in accordance with the Way and principle, is heavenly principle, and when following sensual wants, it is human desires. It must be apprehended at this division."[48] Before quoting Cheng Yi, however, Cheng Minzheng illustrated *weijing* and *weiyi* with the key precepts selected from the *Great Learning* and the *Doctrine of the Mean* in a way that resembled his elaboration in *Oneness of the Way*, balancing "following the path of inquiry and study" and "honoring moral nature." For Cheng Minzheng, the essence of the Cheng-Zhu Learning of the Mind-and-Heart, though hardly illustratable in words, can be best summed up by two terms: *jujing* (abiding in reverence) and *qiongli* (exhausting principle).[49] Sounding like Zhen Dexiu (again), Cheng Minzheng wrote a private letter to his student Wang Chengzhi discussing the meaning of his *Oneness of the Way*: "Indeed, 'honoring the moral nature' is a matter of 'abiding in reverence'; 'following the path of inquiry and study' is an effort of 'exhausting principle.' Nurturing each other, neither can be undone."[50] Little wonder, then, that toward the end of the *Supplemented Heart Classic*, Cheng Minzheng returned to the theme of *Oneness of the Way* by including dozens of Zhu Xi's letters, citing Zhu Xi as saying "'honor the moral nature' while also 'following the path of inquiry and study' . . . these two must be both worked on with no partiality."[51]

Cheng Minzheng's *Supplemented Heart Classic* was thus also a supplement to his *Oneness of the Way*. And these two neo-Confucian anthologies were united in the philosophic doctrine that was grounded in the Cheng-Zhu learning of the mind-and-heart, and balanced cultivation of the inner self with investigation of external things. Cheng Minzheng is not listed in Huang Zongxi's (1610–1695) *Case Studies on Ming Confucians*, an authoritative account of Ming Confucian thinkers, but he clearly played a role in bridging Zhu Xi's intellectualism and Wang Yangming's populist appeal. If Cheng Minzheng cannot be deemed an original thinker, at least he was a consistent one, which was a remarkable achievement, especially given the diverging trends within Confucian interpretation in the mid-Ming. He was consistent in insisting on the oneness of the Way. Whether heaven and man, inner and outer, or moral cultivation and social behavior, there was but "one thread uniting them" with no difference between them as regards the practice of the Way.[52]

This preoccupation with oneness—and with embodying the Way—pervades Cheng Minzheng's work. It was no coincidence that during his banishment, Cheng Minzheng anthologized not only philosophical sayings of sages and Confucian masters but also historical documents of Huizhou. Indeed, if the mind of the Way and the human mind were undifferentiated, there was no reason to separate one locality from the whole realm or to separate commoners from elites. This inclusivity shaped Cheng Minzheng's compilation of both his philosophic works and *Anthology of Xin'an Documents*; in turn, it informed the "localist turn" of this former classics lecturer at the imperial court in Beijing.

Anthology of Xin'an Documents

Anthology of Xin'an Documents (Xin'an wenxian zhi) was Cheng Minzheng's most important work. The anthology, comprised of one hundred *juan* in two collections, covers representative (often short) writings, or "sayings," by Huizhou notables and worthies (collection 1) and their biographical sketches, or "deeds" (collection 2), from the fifth to the late fifteenth centuries.[53] It was (and still is) the best embodiment of the Huizhou tradition of anthologizing. Here, too, Cheng Minzheng had a precedent for his endeavors. And here, too, he turned to none other than his beloved neo-Confucian exemplar, Zhen Dexiu, and the latter's anthology of the Han and pre-Han belles lettres according to neo-Confucian principles. One of the first guidelines of Cheng Minzheng's *Anthology* reads:

> Collection 1 completely follows the rules [regarding the selection criteria of historical essays] set by Zhen Xishan (Dexiu) in his *Wenzhang zhengzong* [Correct Tradition of Literature]. Of the writings [on institutions and rituals] by the former [Xin'an] worthies, those selected are only forthrightly pure and concerned with the established teachings; all others are not included, even if they have enjoyed great popularity.[54]

The *Correct Tradition of Literature*, according to the *Four Treasuries* editors, initiated a new trend of literati anthologizing that emphasized the transmission or embodiment of moral principles (as opposed to the earlier, other influential tradition of anthologizing started by *Selected Literature of Prince Zhaoming* of the Liang dynasty, whose criteria of selection focused on the literary values of exquisite writings).[55]

In collection 2, the biographies in various forms are all called *xingshi* (deed sketches), again following the precedent set by Zhen Dexiu in his *Correct Tradition of Literature: A Sequel* (Xu wenzhang zhengzong). If a selected biography was too long, Cheng Minzheng would shorten it by cutting out unnecessary details, "modeled on the rule Master Zhu set in his *Origins of the Yi-Luo Learning* [*Yi-Luo yuanyuan*]."[56] Indeed, the format of Cheng's *Anthology* is a combination of two sequential anthologies of "true and forthright essays." This format put his Zhen Dexiu-like philosophic position (or what he took as the genuine Zhu Xi position) into practice through compiling important, or representative, works by and on the former worthies of (and related to) his beloved ancestral place.

The *Anthology of Xin'an Documents*, as the editorial note of the eighteenth-century *Four Treasuries* put it, was a "gigantic project" produced out of the compiler's vast erudition in Huizhou history.[57] The modern edition consists of three thick volumes totaling 2,690 pages, and includes 1,087 essays and 1,034 poems (many of which marveled at the beauty of Huizhou's landscape). It was the first systematic anthology, and still is the largest and most comprehensive collection, of Xin'an historical documents of various genres. Shaping or, perhaps, reshaping the basic contour of Huizhou history over the past one thousand years or so, the *Anthology* contributed significantly to the forging of Huizhou consciousness in the mid-Ming epoch.[58] At the same time, Cheng Minzheng's regional focus was also balanced by his concerns for "all under heaven." As he eloquently wrote in the preface to *Anthology of Xin'an Documents*:

> Xin'an in our dynasty is in a key location [protecting the southern capital in South Zhili]. Situated at the foot of the Dazhang Mountain, it is marked by the steepness of its mountainous topography, overseeing other prefectures [in the lower Yangzi valley] from its uniquely lofty position. As noted by the former [Xin'an men] who measured it, Xin'an's altitude equals the peak of Tianmu Mountain [in Zhejiang]. Moreover, waters coming from Wuyuan enter westward into Po Lake; and waters coming from Xiuning enter eastward into Zhejiang. How marvelously steep and un-fathomably deep are its mountains and rivers!

After marveling at Huizhou's fabulous "mountains and rivers," Cheng Minzheng moves on to highlight its even more fabulous sociocultural legacy (after noting that the Daoist "immortals who filled the region since Qin and Han times" were hardly worth the value of its marvelous natural landscape):

> In founding our prefecture, Lord Zhongzhuang and Lord Wang of Yueguo [Wang Hua] rose up as commoners to organize righteous militias and protect their land and people from catastrophic disorders. In death they emerged as deities, display-ing incessant efficacy for more than a thousand years. Toward the middle era, the Xiuning Chengs moved north to Luo and generated two masters [Cheng Hao and Cheng Yi], while the Wuyuan Zhus moved south to Min and generated the Cultured Master [Zhu Xi]. Carrying on the orthodox tradition of Confucius and Mencius, they restored the vanished learning for eternity. How outstanding and great are its historical figures!
>
> Not long thereafter [in Xin'an] there emerged so many renowned masters and prominent Confucians, as well as a large cohort of [men and women noted for] their righteousness and filial devotion [*jiexiao*], military talents [*caiwu*], elderly wisdom [*yilao*], and maidenly chastity and ladylike elegance [*zhenyuan*]. Their names are enshrined in biographical sketches, and their deeds are widespread throughout the prefecture and local communities. But the texts recording them are scattered.

After a brief account of the anthologizing process that lasted for thirty years, Cheng Minzheng invoked the Duke of Zhou and Confucius, complimenting their having overcome difficulties to collect the records on archaic institutions and ritu-als. His anthology, he proclaimed in the end, would serve the public good for the entire prefecture and all under heaven:

> All like-minded men of my calling, seeing former worthies' good words and righ-teous deeds collected in this anthology, should think thoughts of lofty virtue and further put them into physical and mental practice every day. [The virtues] will

thereby spread from one family to the four seas, causing words to match deeds and glory to correspond with substance so that our literary works and virtuous deeds do not disappoint our ancestral notables. Moreover, by reading and following the Cheng-Zhu directives, we shall look up to Zou-Lu [the birthplaces of Mencius and Confucius] so that the mountains and rivers of Xin'an and the cultured notables nurtured therein will elevate not only one community, but also will enjoy fame throughout the realm. This glory will then not be transitory but will be transmitted to posterity. This anthology thus will not be mere scraps of useless paper.[59]

The preface makes multiple juxtapositions that powerfully highlight Huizhou's unique glories. Herein we see the pairing of the natural environs and the social landscape, words and deeds, like-minded living men and dead ancestors, north and south, one family/lineage and all under heaven. Moreover, Cheng Minzheng skillfully juxtaposes the two Cheng brothers with Zhu Xi (and the Xiuning Chengs with the Wuyuan Zhus), the ancestral place of Cheng-Zhu with Zou-Lu, the military commanders with civilian Confucians, Cheng Lingxi with Wang Hua, and the secular with the divine realms. Some of the juxtapositions seem to betray the author's implicit concerns, as will be analyzed in this and the following chapters. Here, we shall first deal with the explicit.

While focusing on Huizhou (or even just one family/lineage), Minzheng, who was temporarily banished from the central government, was never far away from "all under heaven." Metaphysically, there was no difference between locality and state as regards the cultivation and practice of Confucian virtues. After all, Minzheng was anthologizing Huizhou documents while reflecting on the oneness of the Way and the Cheng-Zhu interpretation of the mind-and-heart. His specific admission that he was following Zhen Dexiu's rule of essay selection—stressing the inherent message of Confucian ethics regardless of literary talent—seemingly reads like a cliché in the neo-Confucian tradition of literati anthologizing, but it was quite meaningful for his Huizhou-focused endeavor at this special juncture. *Anthology of Xin'an Documents* was in a sense a working out of Cheng Minzheng's new philosophical position of balancing *daowenxue* (follow the path of inquiry and study) with *zundexing* (honor the moral nature) in the realm of compiling historical documents. To be more accurate, his well-established *daowenxue* erudition allowed him to cover the essential documents of virtually all key aspects of the Huizhou past, whereas his new leaning toward *zundexing* allowed him to view the oneness between Huizhou local society and the entire empire, and between historical worthies and Confucian commoners. The unified pairing of center/locality with *zundexing/daowenxue*, with the latter supporting the former, is born out in the selected *Xin'an Documents*.

Collection 1 of the *Anthology of Xin'an Documents* covers various genres of writings, whereas collection 2 includes biographies on various exemplars of historical figures. One notable feature is the selection of a large number of writings by Zhu Xi, including thirty-eight essays, eighteen poems, and ten biographies. Among the selected writings by Zhu Xi are two studio poetic inscriptions titled *Zundexing* (Honoring the moral nature) and *Qiu fangxin* (Seek the original mind), in addition to a hand-copied version of Zhu Xi's *Zundexing* inscription by Zhu Tong (1336–1385), a high-ranking scholar-official from Xiuning in the early Ming.[60] Also included is a compliment from another Xiuning native, Zhao Fang, to Lu Jiuyuan that is also included in *Oneness of the Way Collection:* "The Confucians said that his learning looks like *chan* meditation, whereas the Buddhists said that our dharma contains no such thing. Surpassing in this way, he alone corresponds to the original mind [*chaoran duqi benxin*], waiting for the arrival of the sage generation after generation."[61] Herein we see Cheng Minzheng's leaning toward Lu Jiuyuan's learning as well as his reemphasis on Zhu Xi's concern with "honoring the moral nature."

But the *Anthology* as a whole is clearly also a product of his diligent pursuit of "the path of inquiry and study." For Zhu Xi, the purpose of "inquiry and study" was meant not just to conduct textual studies, but also to "embrace the worthies from the four directions, observe the things from the four directions, survey the terrains and circumstances of the mountains and rivers, examine the traces of prosperity or chaos, gains or losses of the past and present."[62] Cheng Minzheng was a good student of Zhu Xi. His interest in the mountains and rivers of Huizhou was not just for their great beauty, but probably also rooted in Zhu Xi's brand of "the path of inquiry and study." Moreover, as implied in his preface, Huizhou's marvelous topography partially accounted for its social glory. Zhu Xi is cited as noting that the Xin'an landscape of steep peaks and pure streams had helped nurture virtue among women and integrity among men.[63] In addition, *Xin'an Documents* contains two descriptions, or sightseeing records, of Mount Huang, along with other records and poems describing local scenes of hills and streams.[64]

Natural environs aside, *Xin'an Documents* focuses on Huizhou's political accomplishments and social marvels. Included in collection 1 are documents ranging from diplomatic protocols, memorials, personal letters, commemorative records of numerous local sites (including academies, bridges, ancestral halls, religious temples, studios, belvederes, lakes, and mountains, in addition to Mount Huang), prefaces or postscripts to important books and genealogies, statecraft essays, short treatises and miscellaneous writings on various meaningful subjects, lectures, stele inscriptions on key Huizhou heroes, ritual scripts, aphorisms, and a large number of poems. Collection 2 starts with the biographies of the two major heroes of Xin'an Prefecture, Cheng Lingxi and Wang Hua, followed by local worthies and notables in various fields, including accomplished civil and military officials and local administrators, eminent Confucians, noted literati, commoners (including merchants, often of local leading lineages) with particular virtues or talents (including medicine or divination), and a number of female chastity martyrs and devoted women.

Herein we already see the inclusiveness of his coverage, which is not confined exclusively to men of letters or scholar-officials. In terms of its coverage, *Anthology of Xin'an Documents* looks more like local gazetteers than other anthologies of writings, such as the aforementioned *Essential Writings of Xin'an*, which focuses mostly on literati essays and poems (with few biographies). Still, there was a fundamental difference between local gazetteers and literati anthologies of local writings. The former was usually called for by the central government and sponsored by local or regional officials. Compilation was usually undertaken by local literati or scholar-officials from the region, such as the aforementioned Zhu Tong, who in 1376 compiled the new version of the *Xin'an Gazetteer* (Xin'an zhi, no longer extant), or Cheng Minzheng, who compiled the *Gazetteer of Xiuning* (Xiuning zhi, initiated and sponsored by the county magistrate Ouyang Dan). In contrast, the document anthologies were normally initiated by the scholars themselves, even if they also solicited official support or connections. Due to this genre distinction, the literati anthology of local writings more readily represented the regional consciousness than local gazetteers, even though both tended to glorify the region.[65]

Genre distinction aside, the inclusiveness of Cheng Minzheng's anthologizing may also reflect his philosophic balancing of "the path of inquiry and study" with "honoring the moral nature," or his embracing the significance of internal cultivation, which in theory could work for everyone, not just learned scholars. While focusing on the famed and accomplished, the *Anthology* also covers biographies of "commoners," who were nevertheless unusual or who anticipated the future glories of their descendants, their immediate family lines, or their entire lineages. There is an account, for instance, of a Daoist immortal of the late Tang named Nie Shidao, a Shexian native whose descendants went on to earn five *jinshi* degrees during Song times.[66] But there was also an epitaph for an ordinary *chushi* (gentleman without an exam degree, a term later used to refer to an educated or righteous merchant) named Wu Bogang (1316–1400), who was noted for his virtue, including generosity and love for kinship, in his construction of an *yizhuang* (righteous estate) to assist kinspeople and cover ancestral rites.[67]

Another biographic sketch, for Bao Chun (1297–1376), was by an equally obscure Ming figure from Shexian (Zheng Yixiao). Bao's Song dynasty ancestors were noted for their indifference to government service, but their commercial wealth dominated the local community in Shexian. Bao Chun suffered the loss of both his sons but managed to adopt three grand-nephews to continue the family line. At the beginning of the Ming dynasty, upon the return of peace to the region, he took the lead in building communal waterworks and urging kinspeople to obey laws, and he was widely commended for his virtues.[68]

Another biographical epitaph on Bao Yuankang (1309–1352) of Tangyue in Shexian (written by Zheng Shishan [1298–1358], the famous Shexian neo-Confucian who followed Wu Cheng in the attempt to accommodate Zhu Xi with Lu Jiuyuan) concerns a more notable figure, especially with regards to his contributions to home lineage and local scholarly and ritual activities. Bao Yuankang stood out for having done three things: he skillfully managed the family fortune he inherited from his father and generously assisted kinsmen; he helped recover one hundred *mu* of ritual land for the Zhu Xi Shrine in Wuyuan; and he built the Shishan Academy where Zheng Shishan would lecture.[69]

Looking further into Zheng Shishan's writings, we find that he also authored an epitaph for Yuankang's father, Bao Jingzeng (1281–1335), a successful merchant, or commercialized landowner, whose fortune underpinned the prosperity of the Tangyue Bao lineage during the Yuan dynasty.[70] Notably, however, only the epitaph on Bao Yuankang is covered in *Anthology of Xin'an Documents*. Was this selection just a matter of preference? Or did it suggest Cheng Minzheng's penchant for scholarly involvement or kinship values over commercial success?

The answer becomes clear after reading two other selected essays regarding money or commerce and the preferred emphasis in some selected merchant biographies. One essay is a sardonic story by an obscure Yuan dynasty scholar from Xiuning named Wu Yingzi about a certain Kong Yuanfang, whose name literally means "a square hole at the center of something round" (surely a reference to a traditional Chinese copper coin). Mr. Kong used his riches to gain a high position and ended up being ruined; Minzheng appended a comment to the story: "he renounced virtue and righteousness" (*fangqi deyi*).[71] Moral tension over trade is more markedly expressed in the other piece on "Biographies of Traders" (Huozhi zhuan), by the prominent neo-Confucian Zhao Fang. Zhao Fang developed his own unique reading of this famous chapter of the Han dynasty *Records of the Grand Historian* as a hidden critique of the economic policy of Emperor Han Wudi. Zhao strongly reiterated the conventional concern over the immoral consequences of the obsessive pursuit of profits in commercial engagement.[72]

Two more examples further illustrate Cheng Minzheng's preference for selecting local worthies based on their contributions to local lineage institutions. The *Anthology of Xin'an Documents* includes an epitaph of Cheng Meng (1399–1465), selected from the biography section in the genealogical anthology of his home lineage, the Huaitang Chengs in Shexian. Cheng Meng authored the first slim-volumed Ming dynasty composite genealogy of the Xin'an Chengs.[73] Another epitaph included in the *Xin'an Documents* is for Cheng Jinghua (1379–1452), this time by the famed Qiu Jun, which emphasizes his leadership in local communities as well as in "building an ancestral hall to conduct ancestral rites" and "compiling the genealogy to clarify the descent line" of his home lineage, the Shanhe Chengs in Qimen.[74] It is quite clear that local worthies who had made notable contributions to lineage institutions were particularly dear to Cheng Minzheng.

The *Anthology of Xin'an Documents*, given its inclusive coverage, also includes biographic sketches of merchants. Even in these biographical sketches for merchants, however, we see Cheng Minzheng's preference for noncommercial matters.

One concerns a classically educated merchant, Cheng Decui, who followed his grandfather to migrate from Xiuning to Hubei and prospered in shipping and trade during the Song-Yuan transitional era. This self-claimed Song dynasty adherent (*yimin*) never cared about how much wealth he or his family had accumulated, but was genuinely interested in pursuing neo-Confucian learning. He traveled a long distance to join his Huizhou kinsman Cheng Ruoyong in order to study Cheng-Zhu learning under Rao Shuangfeng, who had been instructed directly by Zhu Xi's disciple, Huang Gan (1152–1221). Cheng Ruoyong, we learn from another biography included in the *Xin'an Documents*, was a Xiuning Chakou native who became the headmaster of the Anding Academy (Huzhou) and the Wuyi Academy (Fujian), attracting a large number of students, including Wu Cheng.[75] The merchant activities of Cheng Decui are overshadowed by his scholarly devotion and neo-Confucian links.

Another merchant biography, by the famous Shexian Confucian Cao Jing (1234–1315), concerns Cheng Kentang (1239–1310) of the Shuaikou Chengs in Xiuning, a prominent lineage known for its commercial success dating back before the founding of the Ming dynasty. Cheng Kentang gave up scholarly pursuits to engage in trade during the Mongol period. Due to his business acumen, he was able to pay off all of his family's debts. We are told that he was genuinely open-minded and never vied for material gain. He spent generously, purchasing land and building houses for ancestral rites, and he was willing to relocate his parents' grave for the sake of lineage interests, which was highly commended by his kinsmen.[76]

Most notably, the *Xin'an Documents* includes a merchant biography written by Zhu Xi. Zhu Que, Zhu Xi's maternal grandfather, controlled almost half the shops in the prefectural seat in Shexian, and at the same time was a kind family-man possessed of remarkable devotion and brotherly love as well as righteous generosity; even when his business declined dramatically in his old age, he never reduced his charitable contributions. In particular, he was keen on noticing scholarly talent, and married his beloved daughter to Zhu Xi's father when the latter was just a young student at the county school.[77] The coverage of such a good and wealthy shopkeeper carried enormous symbolic significance, given his relationship with Zhu Xi. Here again, however, Cheng Minzheng, and Zhu Xi, emphasized the non-merchant-related aspects of this businessman.

Unlike later sixteenth-century Huizhou notables, Cheng Minzheng hardly ever authored a biography or epitaph on Huizhou merchants, even though he must have appreciated the value of commerce from his own family background and his social dealings in Huizhou.[78] His father-in-law, Grand Secretariat Li Xian, authored an epitaph on Minzheng's grandfather, Cheng Cheng. Cheng Cheng initially managed the tilling of land at home in Hejian while his younger brother Yu chose to engage in the urban moneymaking trade. Before long, Cheng's farming became more profitable than Yu's business endeavors (the land the family owned turned out to be extremely fertile). Yu wanted to switch back to managing farm land,

and so Cheng happily let his brother take over while he switched to commercial pursuits. Cheng Cheng's new endeavor succeeded, and the family became wealthy enough that his son Cheng Xin (Minzheng's father) was able to concentrate on Confucian learning, eventually succeeding in the civil service exam.

Notably, Cheng Cheng's commercial career is mentioned only for the purpose of illustrating his brotherly love in the epitaph, which goes on to note that after the death of Yu, Cheng Cheng took care of Yu's children as if they were his own while ensuring that Cheng Xin diligently studied the Confucian classics.[79] The way in which Cheng Cheng's commercial endeavor is mentioned reveals a pattern in literati records of merchants that prevailed up until Cheng Minzheng's time: they were profiled not for their vocation but for their virtue (including their love for or interaction with scholarly activities and regional prominent lineages). This pattern clearly guided Cheng Minzheng's selection of merchant biographies for *Anthology of Xin'an Documents*.

Like Cheng Minzheng's coverage of Confucian women, which more or less imitated an established tradition, his coverage of merchants was highly limited, reflecting the reality of a still subdued commercialization (which, like the female chastity movement, would not take off until the turn of the sixteenth century).[80] The vast majority of selected documents are penned by or concerned with great military heroes, eminent scholar-officials, notable Confucians, and local kinship leaders. The coverage of merchants, however, was meaningful in mid-Ming Huizhou. Even placed within their social networks, these recorded merchants were still commoners, and their inclusion best represents the comprehensiveness of the *Anthology* coverage. It facilitated the spread of the Confucian identity of the entire Huizhou society (not just of the gentry class) to both the locals and an empire-wide audience. It also anticipated the enormous relevance of good merchants (as well as devoted women) to future Huizhou kinship society. Like his mentor and friend Qiu Jun, Cheng Minzheng sensed the need to cover commerce as it was gaining momentum toward its sixteenth-century boom, while at the same time conveniently signaling Confucian warnings regarding avarice.

Cheng Minzheng would come to see the value of money and merchants in publishing *Anthology of Xin'an Documents*.[81] The anthology was completed during his banishment in Xiuning, from 1489 to 1492, but was not printed until 1497. A lack of means was cited as one major reason for its delay. As Cheng Minzheng noted in his 1497 postface, following the endorsement of the governor of Southern Zhili Province and the support of local officials at the prefectural and county levels (from all six counties), descendants of local prominent lineages donated a large sum of cash in order to complete the publication of the gigantic project. Toward the end of the *Anthology* is a long list of 230 local benefactors from all six counties (Xiuning: seventy-seven; Shexian: forty-nine; Wuyuan: twenty-six; Qimen: forty-four; Yixian: twenty-six; Jixi: eight).[82] It is not that difficult to identify merchants or those who were closely affiliated with merchant families when checking this list against local genealogies. For the seven benefactors listed under Shuaikou village in Xiuning, for instance, at least four were merchants or affiliated with merchant families.[83] In fact, Cheng Minzheng was aware of the commercially active Shuaikou Chengs when he endorsed the 1486 expansion of the branch shrine to Cheng Lingxi in that village (first built in 1447 and then expanded to accommodate the enlarged lineage of six hundred kinsmen), noting the initiatives and contributions made by his wealthy kinsmen.[84] In his 1497 postscript to the *Genealogy of My Peiguo Cheng Branch in Xiuning*, Cheng Minzheng acknowledged the commensurability of farmers and merchants, although neither was equal to scholar-officials or gentry. As he put it: "learning can make you as great as a righteous official or prominent scholar, or at least a capable farmer or a good merchant [*lianggu*]."[85] In a preface to the lineage genealogy of another Xiuning Cheng branch in Wenchangfang, he wrote: "To be a good scholar when reading; to be a good farmer when farming; to be a good merchant when sojourning—all should work on the fundamental aspect of their respective vocations without negligence."[86]

Beyond valorizing the role of merchants, the *Anthology of Xin'an Documents* best illustrates the nature of the rise of regional consciousness in mid-Ming Huizhou. State officials, at every level, were involved in the compilation and publication of this "private" project, from beginning to end. Besides the status of the compiler (temporarily banished from the central government), officials at various levels not only endorsed the project but also directly contributed funds toward its publication. Among 230 benefactors were twenty provincial and (mostly) county-level officials. Surely, given Cheng Minzheng's potential influence upon return to the Beijing court, it was to their benefit to offer such support.[87] After all, this regionally focused anthology promoted the orthodox Confucian values that were universally applicable, good for all under heaven.

Even the perceived biases of the *Anthology* eventually worked to contribute to the promotion of not just Huizhou regional consciousness but also universal Confucian teachings. In promoting Huizhou to an empire-wide audience, *Anthology of Xin'an Documents* paid more attention to the Cheng heroes and worthies. Xu Chengyao, a Shexian native who passed the last-ever metropolitan exam, held in 1904, would later comment on the work, "Cheng Minzheng was strongly entrenched in the vision of his home village and lineage. His records of the Chengs are extremely detailed, which nevertheless are rich enough to make up for whatever is lacking in the *Gazetteer of Shexian*."[88] Collection 2 of the *Anthology* (covering the deeds of previous Huizhou worthies) starts with the entry on Cheng Lingxi, followed by one on Wang Hua, reversing the sequence of their placement in earlier anthologies such as the *Essential Writings of Xin'an*.[89] On the whole, Cheng Minzheng included far more documents on the Chengs than the Wangs—or any other author for that matter (except Zhu Xi, for self-evident reasons). Sixty-one Cheng authors and fifty-one Wang authors are cited in the *Anthology*.[90] Individual authors, moreover, could be cited multiple times in a more selective way so as to favor the Chengs. Nevertheless, Cheng Minzheng still tried wherever possible, or necessary, to maintain a power balance between the two most populous and prominent surnames and their deified ancestors: Chang Lingxi and Wang Hua, signaling their unique significance for Huizhou history and culture (as will be further illustrated in the following chapters).[91]

Most notably, Cheng Minzheng covered Cheng Hao and Cheng Yi in collection 2 of the *Anthology of Xin'an Documents*, treating the two Cheng brothers as legitimate Huizhou natives. There are two epitaphs on Cheng Hao followed by a detailed *nianpu* (life chronicle) of Cheng Yi by Zhu Xi, which is further enhanced with a lengthy supplement by Cheng Minzheng. These three constitute all of *juan* 62B, titled Daoyuan (Origins of the Way). This is preceded and followed by two *juan* sharing the same Daoyuan title: nine biographies on all the Cheng notables from Cheng Lingxi onward constitute *juan* 62A, and three biographies on Zhu Sen (?–?), Zhu Song (1097–1143), and their famous descendant Zhu Xi constitute *juan* 63. The first four *juan* of collection 2 cover virtually all the Cheng figures, while also extending beyond kin boundaries to include Wang Hua and Zhu Xi (as well as Zhu's father and grandfather).[92]

This favoritism for Cheng luminaries brings us back to the pairings Cheng Minzheng eloquently laid out in his preface to the *Xin'an Documents*: Cheng Lingxi and Wang Hua as the two most important deified regional heroes, and the two Cheng brothers and Zhu Xi as descendants of the two Xin'an or Huangdun lineages. The persuasive power of Cheng Minzheng's pairings lies in his use of what was already established to support the other complementary sets that were not yet widely accepted. In particular, to a local audience (especially those not surnamed Cheng), it would have been doubtful whether Cheng Lingxi was as powerful a local tutelary deity as Wang Hua or whether the Cheng brothers truly had blood ties with the Xin'an Chengs. These juxtapositions, then, when or if properly justified, could generate symbolic capital of enormous significance for the Huizhou Chengs.

I will deal with the issue of the Cheng Lingxi–Wang Hua juxtaposition in chapter 5. Here, it will suffice to look at the issue of pairing the Cheng brothers with Zhu Xi as native sons of Huizhou or, more accurately, of claiming Huizhou (or, more specifically, Huangdun) as their shared ancestral place. First, this localist look into the Huizhou ties of the Cheng brothers elevated both the Huizhou Chengs and Huizhou Prefecture as a whole, as it powerfully promoted, or helped legitimate, the image of Huizhou as the Cheng-Zhu ancestral place—that is, as a Confucian heartland for both local and empire-wide audiences. This was one key expressing of the rising Huizhou consciousness. Second, due to this logic, or strategy, on the part of Cheng Minzheng, in which the promotion of the Chengs at the same time also glorified the entire prefecture, his promotion of the Cheng surname succeeded in Huizhou. It eventually paved the way for the compilation, and publication in 1551, of another monumental record that further developed Huizhou identity as an epicenter of Confucian kinsmen and kinswomen, *Prominent Lineages in Xin'an* (to be explored in chapter 2). And third, Cheng Minzheng was not the first to claim that Xin'an was the ancestral place of the Cheng brothers. The *Anthology of Xin'an Documents* includes a document by his Yuan dynasty kinsman from Wuyuan, Cheng Wen. This postface, written for a collection of genealogical documents compiled by the descendants of the Cheng brothers in Henan, links the Cheng brothers directly to Cheng Lingxi, or the Huangdun Chengs.[93]

It was Cheng Minzheng, however, who played the most important role—in the most innovative way and at the most opportune moment of mid-Ming rising regional consciousness—in establishing the bloodline between the Cheng brothers and the Huizhou Chengs. Even before compiling the *Anthology of Xin'an Documents*, in a more visible and apparently more convincing way, he had successfully worked to build a commemorative shrine to the two Cheng brothers in Xiuning and compiled the most detailed, up-to-date composite genealogy of the Huizhou Chengs, which incorporated the branch of the Cheng brothers. Cheng Minzheng's involvement in the construction of home kinship institutions and of the Cheng Shrine was itself a key component of his localist engagement and of the development of Huizhou kinship society and regional identity as a whole, and thus calls for further analysis.

LINEAGE INSTITUTIONS

One area that demanded much of Cheng Minzheng's attention in his Huizhou-focused endeavor was to perfect home-lineage institutions, especially the compilation of the genealogies of the Huizhou Chengs. As he stated in 1482, "I have focused my attention on genealogical learning most" over the past "twenty years."[94] This focus can be attributed to two factors, one universal and the other specific to the development of Huizhou kinship society. The genealogy was central to the lineage institution, which had been an expansion of the extended family for the Song-Yuan neo-Confucian masters and thereafter became a local expression of the neo-Confucian movement. In the early Ming, Song Lian, Fang Xiaoru, and other top scholar-officials advocated for lineage formation and genealogy compilation, holding that lineage institutions, which in the Southern Song had been considered appropriate only for official and literati families, ought be spread to all families.[95]

For Huizhou, despite the later claim that the region had been a stronghold of prominent clans and great families since Tang and Song times, the building of lineage institutions came rather late. According to Joseph McDermott's study of Huizhou lineage history, it was still highly exceptional in Song-Yuan Huizhou to find a lineage with a genealogy, an ancestral hall of any sort, or a collective practice of maintaining graves. But around the mid-Ming, lineage order began to gain the upper hand against other rural institutions (such as the village worshipping association and Buddhist temples) and, eventually, by the late Ming, gained predominance in Huizhou villages.[96] Cheng Minzheng drew on previous works, but also made tremendous contributions to promoting this victorious advance of kinship organization in Ming Huizhou.

Above all, his contribution to the development of local lineage institutions lies in his masterful compilation of genealogies and lineage documents, which at the same time also provided him with the most workable channel to demonstrate, or claim, the Xin'an connection for the two Cheng brothers. In early 1482, upon completion of the three-year mourning period for his father, Cheng Minzheng contacted the kinsmen of various branches for his plan to compile a composite genealogy covering all of the Xin'an Chengs. They all supported it and their representatives lent him individual genealogies and lineage documents (which Cheng Minzheng had himself spent the "past twenty years" collecting). After six month of cooperation, with direct assistance in compiling and copying from fifty-six kinsmen (including Cheng Zuyuan of Shuaikou who, as noted earlier, later also contributed money to the cutting of the *Anthology of Xin'an Documents*), the *Composite Genealogy of the Xin'an Chengs*, in twenty *juan*, was cut and published in 1482, along with its massive companion *Records of Bequeathed Glories of the Chengs*, a thirty-*juan* anthology of historical documents relating to the Xin'an Chengs.[97] The composite genealogy covers more than ten thousand kinsmen of forty-four Cheng branches (some of which settled outside of Huizhou, such as in nearby Raozhou and Guangxin in northern Jiangxi). By definition, this massive composite genealogy was inclusive, covering all kinsmen, commoner or scholar, who could be proved to have descended from the same ancestry. While Cheng Minzheng was not the first genealogist in Huizhou to cover commoners, this inclusive coverage nevertheless corresponded with his philosophic position as a Cheng-Zhu disciple embracing the populist Lu Jiuyuan learning of the mind-and-heart.

Cheng Minzheng was truly an innovative genealogist in many ways, and his erudition gave his composite genealogy a solid evidential foundation. The *Composite Genealogy of the Xin'an Chengs* was the first fully developed extant genealogy in Huizhou that used the ancestral tree (*putu*) format of the lesser descent-line (*xiaozong*) rule to reach and cover the great descent line (*dazong*) of unlimited generations—backward to the first known apical ancestor and forward to every related concurrent kinsman. The "modern" Chinese genealogical protocol began in the Song, following the ruins of the great clans of the Tang aristocracy, spearheaded by Ouyang Xiu (1007–1072) and Su Xun (1009–1060), and emphasized the lesser descent-line rule of covering five generations.[98] In the fifteenth century, there was a revival in worshipping the apical ancestor, and Huizhou lineages were especially sensitive about their ancestral pedigree. Cheng Minzheng combined the lesser descent-line ancestral tree format and the great descent-line coverage to meet the needs of the prominent and populous Xin'an Chengs and the larger Huizhou kinship society. This genealogical format exerted a major influence upon the subsequent Huizhou genealogies marked by the *tuzhuan* (five-generation ancestral tree format, plus biographic sketch for each kinsman) pattern to cover all kinsmen (not just prominent figures in the ancestry) of unlimited generations in unlimited *tuzhuan* sheets.[99] As Cheng Minzheng determined that Ouyang's and Su's format of "one *tuzhuan*" did not reveal the composite feature of the descent line from the archaic ancestor, he borrowed the format of chronicle tables used in official histories (especially *History of the Han* and *History of the Tang*) and applied it to his *Composite Genealogy*.[100]

Cheng Minzheng's work also marked the first major composite genealogy not only for the Xin'an Chengs but also for the entire Huizhou kinship society. To be sure, it was built upon previous works, as best illustrated by the thirty-nine prefaces or postfaces to the previous Cheng genealogies covered in the composite genealogy, including three composite versions compiled in the Tang, Song, and Ming, respectively.[101] Of these three, only Cheng Meng's edition is extant; titled *The Various Genealogies of the Xin'an Chengs Threaded Together* (Xin'an Chengshi zupu huitong), it is about one hundred sheets in length.[102] Cheng Minzheng's genealogical work broke new ground, not just for its state-of-the-art format, but also for its sheer size and the quality of the publication, and especially for its contents.[103]

Key to the composite genealogy is a substantial essay in which Cheng Minzheng presents thirty-seven "genealogical clarifications" (*pubian*) in response to what he viewed as the "errors" of the previous Cheng genealogies, especially the three composite versions compiled in the Tang, Song, and Ming. The *pubian*, as well as the generational charts and documentation of the *Records of Bequeathed Glories of the Chengs*, authoritatively reconfirmed the ancient ancestry of the Chengs, tracing the earliest Cheng progenitors to the Zhou dynasty. Following Cheng Yi's identification, Cheng Minzheng demonstrated, with ample documentation, that the Chengs' first progenitor was Xiufu, the Zhou minister of war, who, after having assisted King Xuan of the Zhou (r. 827–781 BCE) achieve the revival of the dynasty, was enfeoffed as the Earl of Cheng (Chengbo), and whose descendants used the fief's title as their surname.[104] The next claimed and recognizable descendant of Xiufu was Cheng Ying (?–583 BCE), an unusual paragon of righteousness popular throughout Chinese historical and literary lore.[105] Cheng Ying's forty-first-generation descendant was Cheng Yuantan, whose twelfth-generation descendant was Cheng Lingxi.[106]

More notably, several key clarifications are intended to demonstrate the direct, albeit tenuous, blood ties not just of Cheng Hao and Cheng Yi to Cheng Lingxi but also of Cheng Minzheng's Peiguo Chengs to the two Cheng brothers. It was not novel for Cheng Minzheng to link the Cheng brothers directly to Cheng Lingxi. In addition to the aforementioned Cheng Wen, Hu Bingwen (1250–1333), a prominent neo-Confucian from Wuyuan, had also made the claim in his commemorative record to the Shrine to Local Worthies in the prefectural seat.[107] Cheng Minzheng not only added new twists to the link, but also used the genealogical tree and historical documentation to visually represent it and to set the stage for his new claim about the blood ties of the Xiuning Chengs to the Cheng brothers. One *pubian*

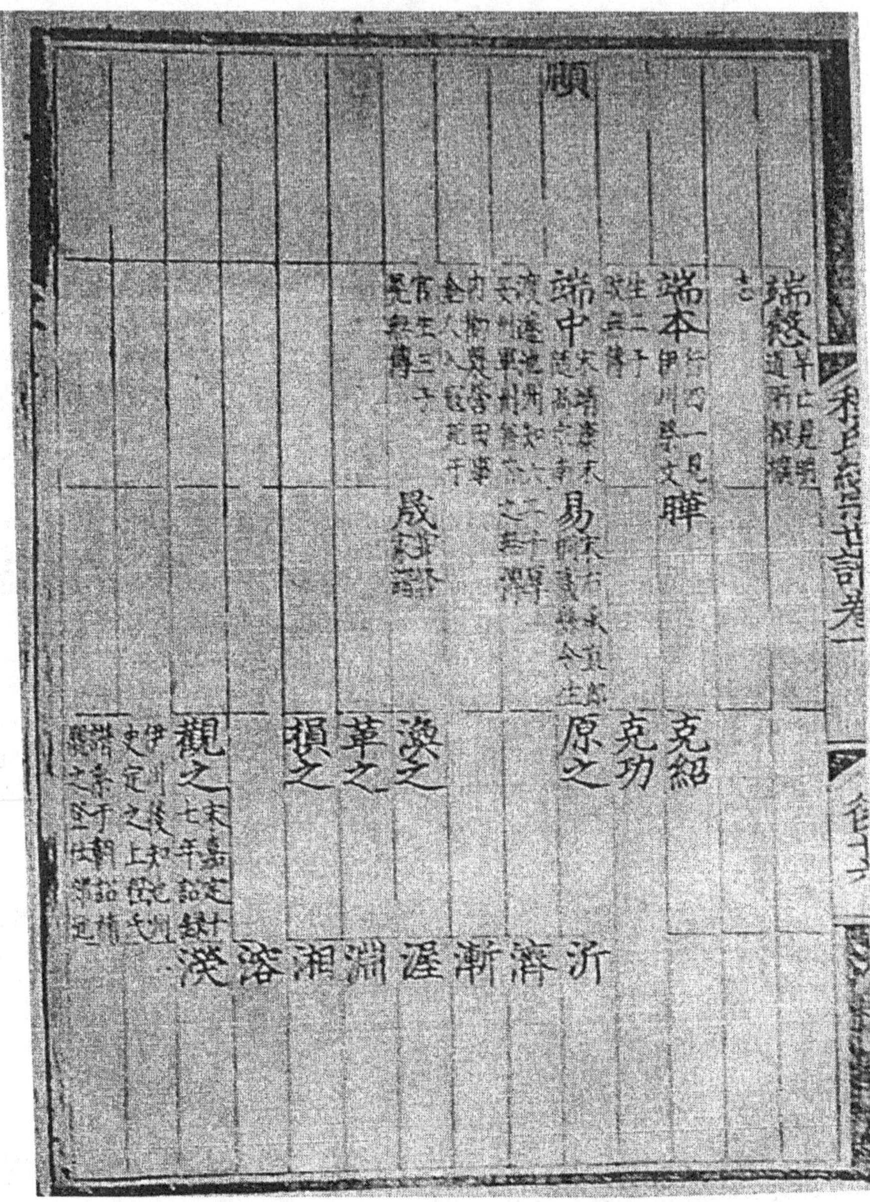

FIGURE 1. Cheng Yi and his descendants. The top register features Yi of the Cheng brothers; his son Duanzhong is indicated as having migrated to Huizhou's neighboring prefecture of Chizhou after the Song court was forced south. One of Yi's great grandsons, Guanzhi, became prefect of Chizhou. *XACST* 1.2.16b. Courtesy of Shanghai Library.

takes pains to show the movement of the descendants of the Cheng brothers south to Xiuning and nearby Chizhou and Jiankang in the early twelfth century, where they eventually converged again with their original kinsmen in Xiuning, including (through adoption) the Peiguo branch.[108] The kinship ties between the Chizhou Chengs and the descendants of the two Cheng brothers were further alleged in their ancestral tree.

How much pedigree did this composite genealogy, especially given its illustrious ancient ancestors and its identification of the Cheng brothers with Huizhou, add to Cheng Minzheng's descent line in Huizhou and add to Huizhou in the whole realm? And how did the added pedigree further enhance Cheng Minzheng's status among his colleagues in Beijing? The juxtaposition of these two questions speaks to the broader reach of Minzheng's Huizhou-focused endeavor, although we will not consider the second question until reaching the end of our story about Cheng Minzheng's localist turn. For now, let us address the first seemingly self-evident question by looking at his preface to the *Composite Genealogy* to see how it enhanced his descent line while also enhancing the entire prefecture of Huizhou in terms of its moral fabric and empire-wide fame.

The preface opens by noting the disappearance of noble families and their genealogies following medieval times. It then states that the Xin'an Chengs were surely such a noble descent line by listing the illustrious ancestors from Xiufu through Cheng Ying, Cheng Yuantan, and Cheng Lingxi down to the Cheng brothers who recovered, or "inherited," the tradition of the sages with their "learning of the Way." So illustrious was the Xin'an Cheng descent line that one kinswoman stood out, having mothered Zhu Xi's father. After briefly noting the process of compiling the *Composite Genealogy* and its enormous coverage, Cheng Minzheng continues:

> Should we just use the great prosperity of our noble lineage to distinguish [our-selves] from others in the four directions or glorify our offspring? Only because the progenitor made unusual contributions was he awarded the surname; [another an-cestor] performed absolute loyalty so that he was able to keep the surname; still [an-other ancestor] had an enormous achievement so as to benefit the homeland [of all Xin'an]—all of this has made our surname notably prominent down to the present. Therefore, in spite of my own unworthiness, and with the assistance from the worthy kinsmen of many branches, I have fulfilled my resolution to unify the entire descent line and completed the genealogy. Is it not a great fortune? All of the kinsmen [now covered in the genealogy] should henceforth never forget to think of the fountain of water and the root of tree, and should devote ourselves to the virtue of respecting the ancestors, honoring the descent line, and harmonizing the lineage [*zunzu jingzong muzu*]. We should maintain our inherited enterprise [and name], read our inherited books, protect all of the resting places of the ancestral bodies [graves] without losing [ritual land], and judiciously follow the rectification of the names without disorder-ing [the generational hierarchy]. Once the descent-line system has been established, social ethics should spread and moral teachings prevail. . . . If this should be the case, then [this compilation] indeed is not just the fortune of one descent line alone!

Cheng Minzheng ends the preface with a powerful forward-looking statement marked by his characteristically broad "all under heaven" vision (foretelling what he would state in his preface to the *Anthology of Xin'an Documents*): "How in the future can families all under heaven not learn from the Cheng descent line" about establishing lineage institutions and practicing Confucian ethics?[109]

Besides gaining pedigree, Cheng Minzheng also used the genealogical project to set an example for others to follow and largely succeeded. In addition to spreading the *tuzhuan* genealogical format, he popularized the motif of "respecting the ancestors, honoring the descent line, and harmonizing the lineage," which was to become the stock expression of subsequent Huizhou genealogies that set the descent-line rule or moral guidance for Huizhou kinship society.[110] In more general terms, with the Cheng brothers now genealogically affiliated with the Xin'an Cheng descent line, the entire region shined. Cheng Minzheng prevailed because he promoted the Xin'an Chengs along with the entire prefecture at the same time. Cheng Minzheng succeeded in capturing for Huizhou the fame of being the "ancestral place of Cheng-Zhu"—the heartland of Confucian kinship society—a key dimension of emerging Huizhou identity.

Indeed, Cheng Minzheng developed a strong sense of mission to build a "harmonious" kinship society in Huizhou out of his neo-Confucian conviction. He authored at least twenty-two prefaces or postscripts to other Huizhou genealogies as well as numerous records commemorating men and women who made notable contributions to or glorified through unusual virtue home lineages in Huizhou.[111] The *Records of Bequeathed Glories of the Chengs* covers many records on the construction or rebuilding of the branch shrines for Cheng Lingxi. Moreover, out of his immediate responsibility, Cheng Minzheng led projects perfecting the lineage institution for his home descent line at Peiguo.

After his father's death, Cheng Minzheng built an ancestral shrine for Cheng Xin in 1480 to the left side of the Chapel of Southern Hill (Nanshan An) near Peiguo. The Chengs and other benefactors had donated pieces of land to the chapel, noted Cheng Minzheng, which now totaled over eight *mu* and received annual rent from tenants and bondservants tilling the ritual land. First erected in 319, the chapel was rebuilt with financial support from local laymen during the Chunxi period of the Song dynasty (1174–1189) and again during the Jingtai period of the Ming dynasty (1450–1456). At this focal "praying place for the entire community," the Buddha was worshipped in the central shrine along with the two popular deified historical heroes, Guan Yu on the left wing and Zhang Xun on the right.[112] Indeed, according to Cheng Minzheng, the chapel was well selected to enshrine Cheng Xin's soul, not just because of the popular deities worshipped there but also because of the date of its first construction, 319, the same year in which Cheng Yuantan had become prefect of Xin'an. Clearly one of the oldest religious institutions in Xin'an, or, as Academician Huangdun put it, the "oldest" with the "most serene" setting, the chapel was another reminder to local people of the deep ancestry of the Peiguo or Huangdun Chengs of Xin'an.[113]

The ancestral shrine was not just to honor his father; it was also a central piece of the home-lineage building in which Minzheng was engaged. Cheng Xin's shrine, given the syncretic setting, was not purely Confucian, nevertheless it still functioned as a freestanding ancestral hall (away from dwellings) for the Peiguo Chengs as well as Cheng Minzheng.[114] In addition, Cheng Minzheng organized a Village Worship Society in 1482, initially consisting of thirty-six households of various surnames, to worship the deities at the Chapel of Southern Hill, now including Cheng Xin. He also helped set up additional ritual land and lineage corporate estates (*shetian*) for about two hundred Peiguo kinsmen to cover the spring and autumn sacrifices to the Earth God.[115]

Complementing all these lineage-related projects was *Genealogy of My Peiguo Cheng Branch in Xiuning*, printed in 1497, the same year in which *Anthology of Xin'an Documents* was finally cut. With the genealogy adding to a freestanding ancestral hall and corporate ritual land, all the key ingredients of the mature lineage repertoire were in place for the Peiguo Chengs.[116] The 1497 genealogy was significant for other reasons too. In addition to perfecting a genealogical format for the subsequent single-lineage genealogies to follow, Cheng Minzheng now felt justified in adding to his own branch genealogy two important seal inscriptions, first partially introduced in 1482 in the Huizhou-wide *Records of Bequeathed Glories of the Chengs*. The first, attributed to Cheng Yi, is titled *Chuanzong yinming* (Inherited Seal and Inscription). The seal consists of the four characters, *Chengbo zhihou* (descendant of Earl Cheng; that is, Xiufu or Qiaobo). The inscription reads:

> My apical ancestor Qiaobo [Earl of Qiao] was initially enfeoffed at Cheng; his descendants took the title of the fief-state as their surname. My departed father selected to settle near Cheng, restoring the title of Earl [posthumously bestowed]; the offspring called themselves "descendants of Earl Cheng." The third month of 1103, inscribed by [Cheng] Yi.[117]

The second seal, *Yichuan houren* (descendant of Cheng Yi), was the personal seal of the grandson of Cheng Yi, Cheng Cheng, whose descendants, according to Cheng Minzheng, had migrated back to Huizhou's surrounding areas and merged with their Xiuning (and especially Peiguo) kinsmen. As with *Records of Bequeathed Glories*, Cheng Minzheng placed the two seal inscriptions at the very beginning of *Genealogy of My Peiguo Cheng Branch in Xiuning*.[118] This served as further proof, for the genealogist, that the Cheng brothers were firmly established as descendants of the Xin'an Chengs, not just in genealogical terms, but more visibly with the newly constructed Cheng Shrine that was officially endorsed.

THE CHENG SHRINE IN XIUNING AND THE
CONFUCIAN TEMPLE

Cheng Minzheng was strategic in terms of his use of a multidimensional approach to drive his message home. He did not just rely on textual work, but also built a physical shrine named after the Cheng brothers in Xiuning in honor of local worthies to more visibly cement the link of the two Cheng brothers with Huizhou. As it turns out, the construction of the Cheng Shrine was not just a central piece of his Huizhou-focused enterprise, but in the end also paved the way for his most important policy proposal regarding the issue of canonizing the Confucian tradition as enshrined at the Confucian Temple in the capital. Moreover, one single thread running through the two projects, at both the local level and in Beijing, was Confucian moral teaching, which reflected his metaphysical positioning as embodied in two soon-to-be-compiled anthologies of philosophical sayings by ancient sages and neo-Confucian masters.

In the process of compiling *Composite Genealogy of the Xin'an Chengs* and *Records of Bequeathed Glories of the Chengs*, Cheng Minzheng came up with a plan to materialize the Xiuning ties of the Cheng brothers. Earlier, Henan Provincial Administration Commissioner Cheng Tai (*jinshi* 1453), Cheng Minzheng's elder kinsman from the village of Shanhe in Huizhou's Qimen County, had recommended to the imperial court that the Cheng brothers' shrine in their Henan home region be refurbished. The renovation started in 1478; after Cheng Minzheng paid a visit to the refurbished shrine, he wrote a commemoratory piece complimenting Cheng Tai's contribution to spreading neo-Confucian teachings.[119] Perhaps inspired by his tour to the new shrine in Henan, Minzheng began in 1481 to work on the construction in Xiuning of a Cheng Shrine in the style of honoring local worthies.[120]

In the twelfth month of 1481, he first wrote of his intention to Lou Qian (*jinshi* 1466), the imperial commissioner of Southern Zhili Province, emphasizing two points: first, as verified by the historical documents (including imperial conferral of honorary titles), the two Cheng brothers were descended from Cheng Lingxi. Cheng Yi's offspring moved back to Chizhou, and then Xiuning, in the Southern Song, eventually merging with the Peiguo Cheng descent line. Second, a new Cheng Shrine in Huizhou would be a project on which the rectification of local customs and promotion of Confucian teachings could truly rely (*chengyi fengjiao suoxi*); it would also encourage local students "to move their hearts toward the Way" (*xiangdao zhixin*). Lou Qian, Cheng Minzheng's *tongnian* or same-class graduate of the metropolitan exam, responded enthusiastically after apparently having been assured that the Cheng brothers did indeed have a relation to the Xin'an Chengs, reemphasizing that the two Cheng brothers had made the most important contributions to the Confucian tradition by resuming the learning of the Way from Mencius after the interruption of fourteen hundred years and by taking the promotion of "this culture of ours" (*siwen*) as their personal responsibility. Lou further instructed the new magistrate of Xiuning, Ouyang Dan (*jinshi* 1481), to supervise the project. Again, Cheng Minzheng wrote a commemorative essay, repeating what he had emphasized in his correspondence with Lou.[121] When the project was completed, dozens of prominent magistrates and local worthies of Xiuning, including Cheng Minzheng's father, Zhao Fang, and Chen Dingyu (1252–1334, a famed Confucian scholar mentioned in the following chapter), were worshipped along with Cheng Hao and Cheng Yi at the Cheng Shrine. Later, when Ouyang Dan asked Cheng Minzheng to preside over the compilation of the *Gazetteer of Xiuning*, Cheng Minzheng gained another officially sanctioned medium for promoting the ties of the two Cheng brothers to Cheng Lingxi and Huangdun.[122] He used three personal seals to sign his 1491 preface to the gazetteer; they were, in order, "Huangdun" (Bamboo Mound), "Keqin" (his alternative name), and "Yi-Luo yuanyuan" (Origins of the two Cheng brothers), the last of which was meant to echo, if not directly copy, the title of a key work by Zhu Xi.[123]

By 1488, Cheng Minzheng was reaching the zenith of his political career at the imperial court. The new Hongzhi emperor (r. 1488–1506) treated his former tutor with respect. Imperial mentor Cheng Minzheng was buoyed with optimism about his prospects for political advancement. His friend Qiu Jun had just been promoted to head the Board of Rites after submitting to the new emperor his famous *Supplement to "Expositions on the Great Learning."* In early 1488, another scholar-official, Zhang Jiugong (*jinshi* 1478), submitted a memorial revisiting the status of the Confucians enshrined in the Confucius Temple. Zhang recommended the removal of Xunzi from the temple along with some early interpreters of the classics whose writings were unacceptable to the followers of the Learning of the Way. The emperor sent it to his court for discussion, but the proposal was not accepted. Cheng Minzheng supported it, however, and so he submitted his own more substantial "Memorial on the Assessment and Correction of the Ritual Code" (Zou kaozheng cidian). This was Minzheng's most important memorial in which he articulated a guiding principle for the enshrinement criteria. The memorial begins:

> The ancient sage-king's rule of all under heaven heavily relied on coding the rites, which promoted virtues and rewarded merits [*chongde baogong*] so as to spread moral teachings and beautify the hearts of the people. . . . [Those qualified to be enshrined] must have had their writing in accordance with their behavior and their reputation in agreement with their life: they must make real contributions to those in alignment with the sage without any immoral trace in public records. This [criterion] is meant to uphold the meaning of promoting virtues and rewarding merits.

In other words, Cheng Minzheng placed personal moral quality and conduct above contributions to classic annotation or exegesis as the criteria for selecting the enshrined figures. Based on this new criterion, Cheng Minzheng expanded on Zhang's proposal for removals from and additions to enshrinement, all according to Cheng-Zhu judgments. Notably, Cheng Minzheng also recommended enshrining the fathers of Yan Yuan, Zengzi, Zisi, Mencius, the two Cheng brothers, and Zhu Xi, to be worshipped along with the father of Confucius, King Initiating the Sage (Qisheng Wang).[124]

Emphasis on spreading moral teachings was the single thread that united Cheng Minzheng's efforts at both the local and national levels: locally for constructing the Cheng Shrine in Xiuning and nationally for reforming the enshrinement criteria at the Confucian Temple. Both efforts showcased the commitment of Cheng Minzheng to the Learning of the Way, especially articulated by the Cheng brothers and Zhu Xi. Both efforts, of course, also revealed the practical concerns of Cheng Minzheng, one to elevate his descent line in Huizhou and Huizhou in the whole realm, and the other to fulfill at the center of power the responsibility of a loyal scholar-official and to further his political standing at this opportune moment with a newly ascended emperor.

And yet, while having succeeded at the local level, Cheng Minzheng failed miserably in Beijing. His memorial was almost instantly rejected (although eventually accepted and acted upon forty-two years later in 1530), partly because his proposal was too ambitious for such a fundamental issue regarding the canonization of the Confucian tradition and partly due to court factionalism. Moreover, barely two months later, this factionalism further led to his being dismissed (he was viewed as too ambitious on account of his sweeping reform proposal for the Confucian Temple). The stated accusation for the impeachment, ironically, pointed to dissolute or immoral faults in Cheng Minzheng's personal life, including sleeping with both the concubine of his uncle and a sing-song girl (possibly more than one) and "shamelessly" teaching them the *Book of Songs* and the *Book of Documents*.[125] We have no way to verify the credibility of the accusation. Cheng Minzheng did not even try to plead innocence, despite being urged to do so by some top officials, including Qiu Jun. His silent acceptance of the impeachment did not necessarily admit to the accusation, but more likely signaled his maturation in handling a political fall (as he may have known that self-defense could lead to a harsher punishment).

Upon return to Xiuning in banishment, he worked to clear his reputation by reestablishing himself as a leading scholar of his age with the compilation of some of his most important works. The *Oneness of the Way Collection* and *Classic of the Mind-and-Heart, Supplemented and Annotated*, with their balancing of "following the path of inquiry and study" with "honoring the moral nature," were partially meant to further prop up the guiding principle of his memorial on reforming the Confucian Temple. At the same time, they may have also served as a self-examination of his purported previous imprudence through revisiting the thoughts of former sages on human nature and moral cultivation. *Anthology of Xin'an Documents*, while presenting Huizhou as a model Confucian society, further supported and substantiated his philosophical position. Eventually, these works helped his return to political grace when in 1492 Beijing's power alignment shifted to his favor, with Qiu Jun being promoted to the grand secretariat.[126] Cheng Minzheng never stated that he intended to use his philosophic and locally focused works to pave the way for a possible return to the center of power in Beijing, but that ultimate outcome should be revealing enough for us to understand Cheng Minzheng's presumed unstated intention.

Indeed, Cheng Minzheng always had empire-wide matters at heart while acting on a local stage: from renaming the place of Huangdun to compiling *Anthology of Xin'an Documents* and the Xin'an Cheng genealogies. These compilations affected, or were affected by, his standing as an interpreter of Confucian thinking. We see the convergence of Cheng Minzheng's local and national interests most pointedly in the interpenetration between his contribution to the construction of the Cheng Shrine in Xiuning and his most important policy proposal presented in the "Memorial on the Assessment and Correction of the Ritual Code." In other words, state and society were seamlessly interconnected in Cheng Minzheng's localist endeavors.

CONCLUSION

Let us return to the opening story about Cheng Minzheng and his adoption of a new style name. The 1478 home visit of Sir Huangdun initiated a series of locally focused endeavors. Cheng Minzheng's self-style of "Bamboo Mound" was an individual choice, but it most vividly represented the rise of regional consciousness for Cheng Minzheng's generation. This becomes clear when compared to the style name of his father, Qingzhou (Sunny Islet).

In 1472, on the occasion of celebrating Cheng Xin's resettlement in his ancestral place, Cheng Minzheng had a volume of scenery and congratulatory poems by concurrent magnates collected and sent to his father, for which Cheng Xin wrote a foreword, "Record on a sunny islet" (Qingzhou ji). Cheng Xin first notes that when he was admitted to the official school in Hejian in 1433, he learned from the *Book of Songs* the meaning of *zhou*, a livable island. Realizing that the prefectural seat of Hejian looks exactly like an islet and inspired by an outing in this moment of great prosperity, Cheng Xin arrived at the idea of taking Qingzhou as a new style name. In 1450, he first visited the ancestral tombs in Xiuning on his way to an official appointment. While staying with some local elders at the foot of Zhi Hill, he crossed the nearby islet of Wenxi on a sunny day. Wenxi was so much like Hejian, except more beautiful. It was, he writes, truly worthy of the title Qingzhou, and the moment inspired him to resettle in his ancestral place after retirement. In 1472, his eldest son built a house for him in Peiguo. Cheng Xin, meanwhile, had purchased a piece of land in Xiuning with a pond islet, where he built a pavilion. Sitting in the pavilion, he imagined, would grant him a vision of the shared feature of both Hejian and Xiuning. On the occasion of prefacing the poetry volume his son collected for him, he happily reveals the origin of his style name.[127]

This self-styling of "Sunny Islet" seems to have foreshadowed—and perhaps inspired—the son's style name of "Bamboo Mound." However, there was a subtle yet fundamental difference between the two. Cheng Xin's style name, while celebrating the peaceful prosperity of the empire, signals his love of one particular natural feature that was shared by two locales: his birthplace and his ancestral fatherland. If it somehow symbolized a stirring of localist interest in the mind of a top official in the mid-Ming, it was also marked by the ambiguity of Cheng

Xin's regional identity. This ambiguity was also refracted in the actual planning of his retirement or local engagement. Even after his visit to Huizhou in 1450, he still set up a ritual land of five hundred *mu* back in Hejian, partly to maintain the tombs of his parents, partly to support his kinspeople and local tenants, and partly to prepare for his retirement there.[128] This estate in Hejian would later go unattended and fall barren, much to Cheng Minzheng's shame.[129] But how could it have been otherwise, especially after Cheng Xin purchased a piece of land in Xiuning, resettled there in retirement, and then died, leaving as his main trustee Cheng Minzheng, who was now completely focused on Huizhou?

Herein lies the main difference between the style names of the father and son. Cheng Minzheng's style was not derived from his love of natural scenery, but of his love of the Huizhou cultural landscape embodied in one place: Huangdun. It was not a simple invention of a new beautiful name, but an adaptation of, or reinscription over, one key locale. This was based on his profound understanding of Huizhou history and local kinship configuration, which, in combination with his insightful appreciation of the larger trends of the mid-Ming, signaled his new resolution. The two different styles marked the changing times between the two generations. Sunny Islet, while possibly signaling an initial rise of localist interest, still represented literati pastoralism, whereas Bamboo Mound was a straightforward (and simultaneously sophisticated, calculated, and erudite) expression of self-identification with Huizhou.

The year 1478 demarcated for Huizhou the localist turn of the mid-Ming, although the local engagement of its chief promoter must have started a bit earlier.[130] Cheng Minzheng's two most important Huizhou undertakings, the compilations of the Cheng composite genealogy and *Xin'an Documents*, had their forerunners in Cheng Meng's *Various Genealogies of the Xin'an Chengs Threaded Together* (1451) and Jin Dexuan's *Essential Writings of Xin'an* (1460). The evolution from these mid-century predecessors to Cheng Minzheng's works parallels that from Sunny Islet to Bamboo Mound in terms of their fundamental differences. The *Composite Genealogy of the Xin'an Chengs*, along with its massive companion *Records of Bequeathed Glories of the Chengs*, not only set the new standard for subsequent Huizhou genealogies but also firmly established the Huizhou ties of the two Cheng brothers and thus enhanced the already lofty pedigree of the Cheng descent line in the region. The *Anthology of Xin'an Documents* richly illustrated the established tradition of political and intellectual magnates with empire-wide influence (including the Cheng-Zhu masters), while also covering local figures whose contributions were limited mainly to their respective lineages. Cheng Minzheng's two magnum opuses contributed significantly to the reputation of Huizhou as the Cheng-Zhu ancestral place and paved the way for the formation of Huizhou identity as the Confucian heartland of kinship communities.

It is revealing that the man who best embodied and contributed to the rise of regional consciousness in mid-Ming Huizhou was not its native son, but a

Hanlin academician with empire-wide renown working at the imperial center, representing more state power than local society—or, we might say, he represented both. Cheng Minzheng identified himself with his ancestral place, but he broadcast his Huizhou stories to his colleagues in the central government, and they, in turn, endorsed his Huizhou endeavors by writing poems, prefaces to local genealogies, and epitaphs for local notables. These intriguing facets of Bamboo Mound's localist turn defined the rise of Huizhou consciousness from the very beginning—the presence of the state was intrinsic to the mid-Ming formation of regional consciousness.

The concrete undertakings of Cheng Minzheng's Huizhou engagement further illustrated the interpenetration between local and national interests. His engagement in the matters of the Cheng descent line was the expression not just of his interest in enhancing one family's pedigree and one lineage's solidarity but also of his "all-under-heaven" vision in setting a model for other families to follow with regard to establishing kinship institutions and purifying local customs. The mingling of personal, regional, and dynastic interests was most clearly embodied in his projects to identify with the Cheng brothers and his proposal to rectify the figures worshipped in the Confucian Temple. The rich documentation of Xin'an history and its strong kinship tradition was not just to glorify and promote Huizhou and its leading lineages, with the Chengs on the top, but was also intended to cause Confucian virtues to "spread from one family" and one region "to the four seas." After all, in Cheng Minzheng's metaphysical vision, as conveyed through his philosophical anthologies, there was no difference between the locale and the entire realm. Indeed, personal, familial, regional, and empire-wide practices were inherently united in the Confucian tradition from the very beginning. "Cultivate the self, regulate the family, administer the state, and establish peace under Heaven"— this was the gentlemanly ideal formulated in the *Great Learning*. Cheng Minzheng repeatedly lectured to the imperial prince on this key classic, and he found heroes in Zhen Dexiu and Qiu Jun, who further illuminated this classic in important writings for their own times, the *Extended Meaning of the Great Learning* and *Supplement to the Extended Meaning of the Great Learning*, respectively.[131]

While Cheng Minzheng contributed to shaping Huizhou consciousness, his Huizhou-focused projects were still transitional from the perspective of the subsequent formation of a new Huizhou identity as a land of "prominent lineages," with its core increasingly consisting of mercantile lineages. Notably, he built his father's shrine in a local Buddhist chapel (as opposed to the free-standing ancestral hall erected in the sixteenth century), and the coverage of merchants and women in his works was limited. As we will see in the following chapters, with the development of Ming society and economy and Huizhou mercantile lineage culture, the localist reach continued to deepen and widen. And so, too, did the interpenetration between the state and local society.

2

A Land of Prominent Lineages

In 1551, about half a century after Cheng Minzheng passed away, a monumental text came out that demarcated Huizhou from other places in Ming China. That text was *Prominent Lineages in Xin'an* (Xin'an mingzu zhi), a unique product of Ming dynasty genealogical literature that further enriched the regional consciousness of Huizhou. If Cheng Minzheng's *Anthology of Xin'an Documents* best represented the rise of Huizhou consciousness in terms of its historical roots, *Prominent Lineages* best defined the identity of Huizhou, while at the same time also capturing its emerging social characteristics over the half century following Cheng's death. The projection of Huizhou's self-identification looks straightforward, but it is also multilayered, reflecting the concerns local kinship communities developed amid accelerating commercialization.

Cheng Minzheng has never received any credit for the making of *Prominent Lineages in Xin'an*. Instead, it was another Xiuning native noted for upholding Zhu Xi's learning during the Mongol period, Chen Dingyu, who was believed to have compiled its forerunner, the similarly titled *Great Lineages in Xin'an* (Xin'an dazu zhi). Placing *Prominent Lineages* in the context of its textual history and the social and cultural changes of mid-Ming Huizhou, this chapter makes three interrelated observations.

First, Cheng Minzheng made significant contributions, albeit indirectly, to the production of the special genealogical genre of *Prominent Lineages*. Cheng Minzheng's *Composite Genealogy of the Xin'an Chengs*, the first of its kind, was over the course of the sixteenth century followed by other leading Huizhou lineages in the process of compiling, publishing, and distributing *Prominent Lineages in Xin'an*, suggesting the collective embrace of Cheng Minzheng's vision by gentry representatives of local elite lineages.

Second, *Prominent Lineages* publicly defined Huizhou as a land of prominent lineages composed of numerous great families with deep historical roots (real or claimed), but it also covered many not-so-famous kinship settlements, likely a sign of moral leveling in Cheng Minzheng's thinking, and now also resonating with popular Wang Yangmingism.

Third, and most importantly, many of these recorded lineages celebrated not just family pedigree (including both eminent ancestral origins and political-scholarly success) but also Confucian commoners, especially righteous merchants and devoted women, marking the emergence of Huizhou mercantile lineage culture. *Prominent Lineages*, more accurately, served as an accelerant to the emerging social trend of mercantile lineage culture rather than as its trigger.

To be sure, what I describe as mercantile lineage discourse is decidedly not how Huizhou elite lineages spoke of their own identity. They identified, as is evident in this massive text, as a land of prominent lineages. The substance of that stable outward projection was increasingly shaped, however, by mercantile interests. And this regional culture was at once locally concentrated and constituted of empire-wide outreach and appeal. Although partially a product of power-jostling among regional lineages over symbolic resources, *Prominent Lineages* celebrated an accepted ordering of the major local surnames, thereby facilitating their cooperation on various fronts (including elite intermarriage) that contributed to Huizhou's enormous success in both examination placement and commercial competition, which in turn further enhanced Huizhou mercantile lineage culture.

CHENG MINZHENG AND COMPOSITE GENEALOGICAL GAZETTEERS

In Ming China, Huizhou was the only region that produced prefecture- or district-wide composite genealogical gazetteers covering all of the recognized or participating lineages and their branches of various regional surnames, the most notable of which was *Prominent Lineages in Xin'an*. They were all privately compiled for a local gentry-led society, different from the pre-Song registers of empire-wide surnames that were officially assembled for an aristocratic polity and class marriage.[1] *Xin'an mingzu zhi* literally means "gazetteer of prominent lineages in Xin'an," but I will simply call it *Prominent Lineages*.[2] The text under scrutiny is based on the 1551 edition of *Xin'an mingzu zhi*; it also includes additional data that the modern editors have gleaned from other editions published during the Jiajing reign (1522–1566). It encompasses ninety surnames in total, covering all of their known kinship settlements in Huizhou's six counties; entries on kinship settlements were structured around the surname-county-village sequence.[3] For most of the covered kinship settlements or lineage-villages, there is a brief entry for each, covering the noteworthy figures in its ancestry and concurrent generation. The focus on local lineages (and their branches) and the brevity of each entry made it different from the genre of the local gazetteer (*fangzhi*, which was officially sponsored), and its composite coverage of all the recognized (or participating) elite lineages of different surnames made it different from the genre of the single-surname genealogy.[4]

The composite genealogical gazetteer was not just unique but also massive in scale; its modern edition totals 770 pages. Embodied in such a monumental work, quite naturally, is the distinctiveness of Huizhou society and culture. Still, a strong catalyst must have been needed to bring it about. In mid-Ming Huizhou, one apt catalyst for this venture may well have been Cheng Minzheng, a well-positioned and widely connected scholar-official whose love of his ancestral place was unprecedentedly strong and whose Huizhou- and Cheng-focused work was pathbreaking in terms of the making of regional consciousness and the promotion of the Cheng pedigree. As I will try to demonstrate, Cheng Minzheng played a significant role in the making of Huizhou's first prefecture-wide composite genealogical gazetteer. In the end, Cheng Minzheng may well have prepared the necessary condition for this unique Huizhou document, which was not printed until the mid-sixteenth century. In other words, to fully understand the backdrop of the *Prominent Lineages*, we need to contextualize the text both historically and socially.

When Cheng Minzheng first traveled to Huizhou, he encountered a region filled with great families, distinguished by ancient ancestries and remarkable achievements on the political, military, and intellectual fronts, as claimed in their individual genealogies. Most of these families, according to their genealogies, were descended from those who migrated to Xin'an from the north in the medieval period, especially during the Huang Chao rebellion of the late Tang (874–884 CE).[5] But as Joseph McDermott has shown, by Song times Huizhou was still a society composed mostly of recent migrants.[6] Many genealogical claims to ancient notables by Huizhou lineages were largely mythical, and not supported by neat ancestral trees. That said, myth could play a powerful role in discourse, especially when it was interspersed with seemingly truthful facts. By the mid-Ming, in particular, the mythical character of these claims did not matter much, as they had been repeated so many times in numerous editions of various single-surnamed genealogies that they were treated as historical fact.[7] Moreover, by mid-Ming times, many of these great families had truly grown into prosperous, populous lineages, with numerous branches spread throughout Huizhou's six counties.

A testament to the strength of the Cheng descent line, the number of branches from whom Cheng Minzheng solicited documents for his lineage-wide composite genealogy reached forty-four, representing in total more than ten thousand kinsmen. Most of the Cheng branches, like those of many other major surnames, were engaged in their own home lineage building in the mid-Ming. The Xiuning Shuaikou Cheng branch genealogy (1570), a revised "sequel" edition, for instance, incorporated numerous prefaces written for the earlier versions of the branch genealogy, as well as for the earlier Cheng composite genealogies (including Cheng Minzheng's preface to his *Composite Genealogy*).[8] Cheng Minzheng, while perfecting lineage institutions for his kinspeople in Peiguo, wrote a commemorative record for each of three Cheng settlements in Chakou, Shandou, and Shuaikou on the occasions of their expansion of Shizhong branch shrines honoring Cheng

Lingxi. In addition to the free-standing ancestral halls honoring their popular api-cal ancestor, noted Minzheng, the three Xiuning settlements had all set up corpo-rate land to cover sacrifice expenses for ritual gatherings of more than six hundred kinsmen in Shuaikou, four hundred in Shandou, and several hundred in Chakou.[9] More than half a century later, according to *Prominent Lineages*, the Shuaikou Chengs boasted about three thousand kinsmen.[10]

Still, in Huizhou the Chengs were not as populous as the Wangs. Already in Song times, in the words of a local aphorism quoted in the 1175 *Gazetteer of Xin'an*, "nine out of ten are surnamed Wang, all descended from Wang Hua."[11] By the late sixteenth century, one main descent line of the Shexian Wangs alone boasted six-teen branches of more than ten thousand kinsmen.[12] If this piece of evidence seems a bit late for our concern here, Zhu Xi, in a foreword he wrote in 1188 for a Xin'an Wang genealogy, commented that "No other lineage could possibly match the Xin'an Wangs for their prestige and prosperity."[13] Even Cheng Minzheng acknowl-edged their numerical superiority in a preface he wrote for a local Wang geneal-ogy.[14] Both before and during Minzheng's time, the Huizhou Wangs had compiled numerous independent branch genealogies. For instance, the 1487 version of a Xiuning Wang genealogy carries a foreword by Chen Dingyu, written in 1331 for its earlier, still "revised" edition, which follows Cheng Minzheng's 1487 foreword to the genealogy.[15] In the Yuan dynasty, local gentryman Wang Songtao compiled *Ancestral Records of the Wangs* (Wangshi yuanyuan lu), a ten-volume genealogy that traced the Xin'an Wangs back to the Yingchuan Wangs of Duke Cheng of Lu (directly descended from the Duke of Zhou and the Yellow Emperor).[16]

Wang Hua had long emerged as the leading patron deity of Huizhou, as acknowledged in Luo Yuan's *Gazetteer of Xin'an*. The prefecture's first official gazet-teer devotes an entire section, "Shrines and Temples" (Cimiao), in the first volume, to the God of Xin'an (Xin'an Zhi Shen).[17] A key element of the Wang lineage insti-tution, the cult of Wang Hua vastly overshadowed Cheng Lingxi in local popular worship in Cheng Minzheng's time (and throughout late imperial times). Cheng Minzheng, nevertheless, led the Huizhou kinship society in producing the first massive composite genealogy for a single Huizhou surname, a practice that was later followed by the Wangs and other surnamed prominent lineages.[18]

The concentration of many great surnames, and especially their rapid demo-graphic and social expansion (including the development of lineage institutions), nurtured the unique genre of composite genealogical gazetteer that encompassed all of the recognized and participating prominent lineages of the great surnames. It is curious that other regions with a similar concentration of prominent lin-eages did not produce a similar composite genealogical gazetteer in the Ming. Although I have no direct evidence of Cheng Minzheng's involvement with this unique Huizhou genre, the composite genealogical gazetteer is rife with the traces of his concerns: lineage rank and pedigree. Such a work would have been a natu-ral extension of his *Composite Genealogy of the Xin'an Chengs*. But according to

TABLE 1. Surname order in three composite genealogical gazetteers

A. *Great Lineages in Xin'an* (reprint 1667)
B. *Prominent Lineages in Xin'an* (1551)
C. *Prominent Lineages in Xiuning* (1626)

	A.	B.	C.
Cheng	1	1	1
Bao	2	2	—
Fang	3	3	2
Yu[a]	4	5	3
Yu	5	6	4
Huang	6	7	5
Wang	7	8	6
Xie	8	11	10
Zhan	9	12	13
Hu	10	13	14
Wu	11	14	18
Zhang	12	15	15
Chen	13	16	16
Li	14	17	17
Ye	15	18	19
Zhu	16	19	21
Zheng	17	20	22
Dai	18	21	23
Ren	19	9	8
Min	20	10	9

SOURCE: Table 1 is based on the three editions stored in Anhui Provincial Library, reprinted in Yu Chenghua et al., comp., *Huizhou Mingzu zhi*, 2 vols.

[a] The surname *Yu* ranked fourth and fifth in the first column refers to two different characters.

later evidence, an "ur-version" of sorts seems to have already existed in the Yuan dynasty. The renowned Yuan dynasty Confucian Chen Dingyu was believed to have compiled *Great Lineages in Xin'an*. This first Huizhou-wide genealogical gazetteer appears to have set a pattern for two subsequent versions: *Prominent Lineages in Xin'an* and *Prominent Lineages in Xiuning*. The two later genealogical gazetteers, although greatly enriched and with different focuses, largely followed *Great Lineages* in one key respect: the ordered placement of local prominent surnames headed by the Chengs (see table 1).

Why were the Chengs at the top of the surname sequence? How might the actual compilers have set the sequence and justified it to the local audience, especially given the social landscape of Huizhou in which the majority of elite surnames claimed in their single-surname genealogies to have celebrated ancestral pedigree and produced significant numbers of higher examination degree holders?

That the Chengs managed to secure the top position within the surname sequence in all of these prefecture- and district-wide composite genealogical gazetteers is highly suggestive of just the sort of maneuvering for prestige that so preoccupied Cheng Minzheng. It is possible that the mid- and late-Ming genealogical gazetteers simply followed the precedent established in the supposed original version, and yet since the claimed original edition is little more than a list of the recognized elite lineages and their local branches, it lacks sufficient explanatory matter to provide answers.[19] Looking to later sources for explanation, we see the third entry in the *fanli* (guidelines) of *Prominent Lineages in Xin'an*, finalized by Cheng Minzheng's kinsman from Shexian, Cheng Shangkuan, in 1551: "the ordered placement of various surnames listed here is based on the first arriving times of their ancestors in Xin'an."[20] As shown in chapter 1, however, the Chengs did not settle in Xin'an earlier than other prominent lineages, such as the Wangs and Huangs.[21] In fact, the "Surnames" section in the 1175 *Gazetteer of Xin'an* did not even mention the surname Cheng, listing instead Jian, Yu, Wang, Yang, Nie, Cha, Lü, Yu, Qian—nine in total, some of which were probably Xin'an aborigines.[22]

A more important gauge of social power—and potentially a key factor determining the surname sequence in the composite genealogies—could have been the number of metropolitan *jinshi* degree holders various lineages had produced. In this respect, the Chengs, though enormously successful, still came up short, as the Wangs were most dominant from the Song through the Ming-Qing periods: The Huizhou Wangs produced eighty degree holders in the Ming and seventy-eight in the Qing, whereas the Chengs produced fifty degree holders in the Ming and fifty-six in the Qing.[23]

Arguably, an even more decisive factor may have been the quality, rather than quantity, of the scholar-officials the local prominent lineages had produced. The two most prolific and influential scholar-officials from Ming Huizhou came from, not accidentally, the two most powerful regional lineages. These scholars were Cheng Minzheng and Wang Daokun (*jinshi* 1547). Here, the luck of seniority gave the upper hand to the former. By the time Wang Daokun came of age, the issue of genealogical order among local elite lineages had already been resolved and the precedent-setting mid-Ming genealogical gazetteer already printed. Yet, for all its traces of Cheng favoritism, it surely would have been indelicate for the mid-sixteenth-century compilers of *Prominent Lineages* (and, especially, Cheng Shangkuan) to have openly boasted about either the reputation of Cheng Minzheng or the prodigious Cheng *jinshi* production. This may explain, too, why these compilers needed to invoke the eminent Chen Dingyu to help justify their ordered placement of elite surnames. The first guideline entry reads: "*Prominent Lineages* is based on, and further expanded from, the old text [*jiuben*] by the Yuan scholar Chen Dingyu."[24]

Chen Dingyu was a leading figure in the neo-Confucian lineage of Huizhou, widely praised for having preserved and transmitted the authentic tradition of Zhu Xi's moral philosophy during the troubled Yuan era.[25] Like so many neo-Confucians, Chen Dingyu understood the social and moral functions of genealogy, having compiled one for his own kin and written numerous forewords or postfaces for the genealogies of other important Huizhou surnames.[26] In the process, conceivably, he must have collected information on many local prominent descent groups, thereby leading to the compilation of a composite genealogical gazetteer, similar to the *Great Lineages in Xin'an*. The problem, however, is that we simply do not have the original text of Chen Dingyu's *Great Lineages*, formerly assumed to be printed in the Yuan.[27] Indeed, had it been printed and circulated in the Yuan, Cheng Minzheng would surely have seized upon it to further boost the pedigree of Huizhou as well as of its Cheng descent line. His enormous erudition and passion for Huizhou's history and genealogies notwithstanding, Minzheng never mentioned *Great Lineages in Xin'an*, not even in the writings he wrote or compiled that paid high tribute to Chen Dingyu.[28]

Since no solid evidence exists to support the assertion that *Great Lineages in Xin'an* was printed in the Yuan, its authorship and the date of its first printing have become the subject of recent debate.[29] The most persuasive explanation to date now suggests that Chen Dingyu did compile something that eventually led to *Great Lineages in Xin'an*, but he did not have it cut.[30] Indeed, the primary sources support this assessment. The first guideline entry to another mid-sixteenth-century edition of *Prominent Lineages in Xin'an* clearly states that Chen's *Great Lineages in Xin'an* "was regrettably not cut and not printed. Occasionally, his manuscript [*chaoben*] can be seen; it is rather thin and offhand."[31]

The finalizer Cheng Shangkuan provides more details in his 1551 foreword to *Prominent Lineages*:

Xin'an is surely a prominent prefecture under heaven. *Gazetteer of Prominent Lineages* is to clarify the mixed [lines] and elucidate the hidden [meanings]; it stems from [natural] emotions and begins with righteousness. The Yuan dynasty Confucian, Chen [Dingyu], had once compiled *Great Lineages in Xin'an*, which, regrettably, was not widely spread [*wei shengxing zhe*]. Sir Zheng Shuangxi [*jinshi* 1530] and Sir Hong Jueshan [*jinshi* 1532], as his original compilation had been expanded, [endorsed] its printing. How substantially we can see the flourishing of Xin'an's cultural achievements; how summarily [this composite genealogical gazetteer] captures the key to success in this world! Amazing indeed! As for the data compilation [for the expanded version of *Gazetteer of Great Lineages*], the process started with Ye Benjing of Qimen, and continued with Dai Tingming of Xiuning, and so on, who had diligently worked on collecting [genealogical data] for over ten years. And yet, searching for the famed families, [we find that] many are still missing. . . . I have sincerely consulted prominent figures and compatriots of the six counties. I thereby further

> expanded this [genealogical gazetteer] based on the earlier editions, examining the surnames and successive migrations to fix it, proofreading to correct its errors, and monitoring the discrepancies [between various editions] to return to what is commonly accepted.

From the primary sources we can infer the following points. First, Chen Dingyu did compile a manuscript on prominent local lineages, which was nevertheless not cut in his lifetime. Second, it was Zheng Shuangxi and Hong Jueshan who, after seeing its expansion, had it first cut. It is not clear whether this first Huizhou composite genealogical gazetteer was titled *Great Lineages in Xin'an* or *Prominent Lineages in Xin'an*, but we can be sure that the first Huizhou composite genealogical gazetteer, presumably titled *Great Lineages in Xin'an*, cannot have been printed before the 1530s or 1540s. Third, the first edition of *Prominent Lineages in Xin'an*, or the expanded version of *Great Lineages in Xin'an*, took more than ten years of diligent data collection and compilation by Ye Benjing and, especially, Dai Tingming. And fourth, as the first edition was still considered incomplete, with many notable lineages or their branches "still missing," Cheng Shangkuan added additional data to it, and published the new edition in 1551, which is the earliest extant version of the genealogical gazetteer and the core text for the modern punctuated version of *Prominent Lineages*.

This understanding of the textual history can still hardly lead to an answer to the question as to why the list of elite surnames was ordered the way it was in *Prominent Lineages*, and especially why it was led by the Chengs. In fact, we still have no clue on exactly when Chen Dingyu's *Great Lineages in Xin'an* was first printed, which was the alleged origin of the ordered sequence of elite surnames that the later compilers of *Prominent Lineages* followed. Chen's "manuscript," "thin and offhand," may have been little more than a collection of hand-drafted notes of local lineages, not necessarily arranged in a sequential or hierarchical order. Even if they had been ordered, the unpublished manuscript was still a private document, and had yet to pass the test of acceptance from those local pedigree-sensitive lineages. All of this suggests that Chen's much vaunted "original" had never been printed, until, that is, it was needed for lineage development and local power politics in the mid-Ming. Rather than read Chen's *Great Lineages in Xin'an* as an ur-text that naturally explains the ordering of the surnames, then, it is likely that this list of prominent lineages was a product of the mid-Ming. It was opportunely brought into circulation (and then expanded with the ordered surnames) at the very time when Huizhou gentrymen were turning to the genealogical gazetteer to shore up prestige in the local arena and to promote their home prefecture to an empire-wide audience. This reading requires that we move from the manifest aspects of textual history to the hidden dimensions of social history to figure out the question as to when *Great Lineages in Xin'an* was first published or first readied for publication, with an eye to how that might have set the order of Huizhou elite surnames as now seen in *Prominent Lineages*.

When discussing the historical and social context of the unique Huizhou genre of genealogical gazetteers, we need to take Cheng Minzheng into account. Arguably the most influential and articulate scholar-official of mid-Ming Huizhou, he played a key role in building kinship institutions at the critical juncture of lineage development, including his innovative compilation of the composite and single-surnamed genealogies. He substantiated the blood links between Xin'an and the two Cheng brothers, which elevated the pedigree of both the Chengs in Huizhou and Huizhou in the entire realm. He also helped shape the regional consciousness that laid at the heart of *Prominent Lineages*. Intriguingly, there is textual evidence that, when properly contextualized, might reveal traces of Cheng Minzheng's possible involvement with the publication of *Great Lineages in Xin'an*.

Largely ignored is a preface that a certain Peng Ze (1459–1530) wrote, in late autumn of 1498, which endorsed the printing (not reprinting) of Chen Dingyu's *Great Lineages in Xin'an*. Peng Ze's preface is included in the expanded edition of the Huizhou composite genealogical gazetteer, published in 1667 by another Huizhou Cheng gentryman, Cheng Yitong.[32] Peng Ze was to become Huizhou prefect in 1500, and eventually minister of war, two official titles that were used to undersign his 1498 preface. This discrepancy between the dating of the preface and the official titles used is sometimes taken as evidence to question the authenticity of Peng's preface.[33] My assessment is exactly the opposite, because a forger would have had to have been particularly careful to avoid this kind of obvious dating mistake. In other words, the "mistake" should be read as an indication that the preface may have been truly written by Peng Ze in 1498, with his official titles added later at the time of printing or reprinting. After all, by 1667, Cheng Yitong no longer needed to manufacture any reasons to justify the reprinting of *Great Lineages in Xin'an*, since the previous editions of the composite genealogical gazetteers had already firmly established the Cheng-led placement of the local prominent surnames.

More importantly, this seeming detour to the preface by Peng Ze leads back to Cheng Minzheng. It also sheds new light on Huizhou lineage politics around 1498, the heyday of Cheng Minzheng's engagement in Huizhou matters. The printing of both *Genealogy of My Peiguo Cheng Branch in Xiuning* and *Anthology of Xin'an Documents* in 1497 marks the completion of Cheng Minzheng's tangible accomplishments in his Huizhou endeavor, and this energetic and widely connected Huizhou enthusiast surely was ready to embark on new ones to boost Cheng prestige as well as that of the entire Huizhou region. There is also reason to believe that Cheng Minzheng mobilized empire-wide official networks to achieve this goal. Although no tangible sources have been uncovered to suggest that Cheng Minzheng was behind Peng Ze's 1498 preface, a close examination of the preface itself and its intangible social embeddedness may provide clues about Cheng Minzheng's influence on, and even possible involvement in, its production.

Turning to the intangible social connections first, Peng Ze (*jinshi* 1490), a native of northwestern Lanzhou, was entwined in Minzheng's network of official friends and protégés. He earned the provincial *juren* degree in 1486, the same year in which Cheng Minzheng presided over the southern Yingtian exam, and in which Minzheng's close friend and colleague, Imperial Academician Li Dongyang, supervised the northern Shuntian exam where Peng Ze was registered.[34] Although a northerner, Peng Ze's ancestral place was Changsha, not far from Li Dongyang's native home. In 1512, at the request of Peng Ze, Li Dongyang wrote a foreword for a genealogy of Peng Ze's ancestral lineage in Hunan, in which he indicated that Peng Ze was "from my Changsha."[35] Going further back, the Changsha Pengs came from Ji'an in Jiangxi Province, and were related to the nearby powerful Anfu Pengs.[36] The first person Peng Ze contacted for support when planning the compilation of a Huizhou gazetteer was Peng Li (*jinshi* 1472), his kinsman from Anfu, who became the governor of Jiangnan Province (with jurisdiction over Huizhou) in 1498, roughly two years before Peng Ze's appointment as Huizhou prefect.[37] Peng Li's elder brother was none other than Peng Hua, who authored a commemorative record on the shrine to Cheng Minzheng's father as well as the essay "On Bamboo Mound."[38] What is more, the two Peng brothers' close cousin from Anfu was Peng Shi, the grand secretariat who, as already noted, had a high regard for the precocious Minzheng, the future son-in-law of his colleague Li Xian. It was Peng Shi, too, who authored the "epitaph" for Minzheng's parents while they were still alive.[39] Minzheng reciprocated by expending his own brush-and-ink capital for Peng Shi, writing two heart-felt verses and one memorial essay upon the latter's death.[40]

Likewise, Peng Ze would later pay his respects to his senior Minzheng through the occasional essay.[41] In a 1528 foreword he wrote for the aforementioned Shuaikou Cheng genealogy, Peng Ze piled the accolades on Minzheng, calling him "Minister of Rites Lord Bamboo Mound" (Da Zongbo Huangdun Gong), an "ultimate Confucian of the prosperous age" (*shengdai ruzong*), and best among all the top scholars the Huizhou Chengs had ever produced. For such a prolific scholar, quite revealingly, Peng Ze mentioned no specific works by Cheng Minzheng other than his *Composite Genealogy of the Xin'an Chengs*, while at the same time recognizing Minzheng's most cherished blood tie to Cheng Hao and Cheng Yi.[42] Given all of these ties, it seems plausible that Peng's 1498 preface endorsing the printing of *Great Lineages in Xin'an* might have been influenced by Minzheng. After all, Minzheng was a master in mobilizing his empire-wide official contacts to boost local Cheng prestige.

Peng Ze's 1498 preface further suggests Huizhou lineage politics at play in the *Great Lineages* project. The preface is short, conventional in content, and cautious in tone, especially when compared to the animated forewords he later wrote for the Shuaikou Cheng and his ancestral Changsha Peng genealogies. The preface opens with a general statement that a genealogy is intended to record the family pedigree and scholarly notables within a given ancestry. It goes on to identify two defining characteristics of "great lineages," both of which would have been readily acceptable to Huizhou kinship society and Cheng Minzheng. The first distinguishing characteristic is an objective one, concerning the ancient depth of ancestry, and it largely accords with the third guideline entry of *Prominent Lineages*. The second is relatively subjective, and it depends on the glory of ancestors, specifically those noted for having practiced or illuminated the Way, having fulfilled "loyalty and righteousness" or "filial devotion and friendship," or having made "remarkable accomplishments" in military campaigns, intellectual writings, or civil politics. "Short of these two" qualifications, declared Peng Ze, "there could be no great families." This was why, he explained, "the great Confucian, Sir Chen [Dingyu], traced the origins, and highlighted [the accomplishments], of those established families." As with many other genealogical prefaces, Peng Ze did not neglect the moral functions of a composite genealogy, briefly indicating that it would encourage kinspeople to revere ancestors and honor lineages and would purify local customs. All of this, concluded Peng Ze, distinguished great families from others, which was exactly what had been on the mind of Sir Chen when compiling *Great Lineages in Xin'an*.[43]

The cautious tone of the preface may further reflect the complicated web of social connections that lay behind it. Peng Ze, while enjoying various ties with Cheng Minzheng, was also a close friend of Wang Shunmin (*jinshi* 1478), a luminary of the Huizhou Wangs, although much less influential than Cheng Minzheng was. Peng Ze had been a colleague of Wang Shunmin in Yunnan prior to his Huizhou tenure. When planning his edition of the *Huizhou Gazetteer*, Peng Ze invited Wang Shunmin to preside over its compilation.[44] Peng had even taken a concubine from Wang Shunmin's lineage. This affinal relation, as a Wang document reasoned, partially explained why the new Prefect Peng so readily launched an investigation after a local Wang Hua temple suffered a terrible conflagration in 1501. After the inspection, Peng Ze immediately called upon all of the Huizhou Wangs to contribute to its reconstruction, in gratitude for which his portrait was to be placed in that temple, enjoying sacrifices along with Wang Hua.[45]

It seems, perhaps, not too far a stretch to read his ties with both the Wangs and Chengs into the terse balance Peng Ze tried to maintain between ancestral depth and ancestors' achievements when defining "great lineages" in his preface. The preface sensitively avoided the mention of any illustrious surnames (not even the glorious tie to the two Cheng brothers that he would later publicly acknowledge), let alone the ordered placement led by either of the two most populous and powerful surnames in mid-Ming Huizhou.

Peng Ze's cautious tone may also reflect a subtle difference between a manuscript and its printed version. Chen Dingyu's "old text" may have been little more than a hand-drafted list of local lineages, not necessarily arranged in a hierarchical order. Even if they had been ordered, the unpublished manuscript was still a private document, which had yet to pass the test of acceptance from those local pedigree-sensitive lineages. To get the genealogy cut, in other words, it would have to be ready for publication in accord with both textual and social norms. Textually, an ordered placement of all of the included elite surnames would have been a prerequisite for the cutting. Socially, an approval of such a placement from the majority of local kinship communities would have been necessary for it to be turned into a public text. Neither was an easy task to accomplish. It took decades, for example, for Dai Tingming and his associates to collect the information needed for the later *Prominent Lineages in Xin'an.* To reach consensus from local lineages on the list of ordered surnames could be an even more daunting challenge, for this would have required not just dedication or passion but also social skills and influence. In mid-Ming Huizhou, Cheng Minzheng, the most powerful advocate for both the Chengs and the entire prefecture and the most passionate about Huizhou lineage matters, would have been particularly suited to finesse the social engineering needed to complete this task.

All of this puts in perspective his efforts at forming direct links with the two Cheng brothers (to add the utmost intellectual luster to the Chengs). Here we see some echoes between Cheng Minzheng's maneuverings and Peng Ze's definition of "great lineages." This Cheng-Peng resonance notwithstanding, Peng Ze's endorsement did not lead to the instant printing of Huizhou's first composite genealogy. The deferral of the publication of *Great Lineages in Xin'an* actually lends additional support to my speculation that Cheng Minzheng was behind Peng's 1498 preface. Within months of the inking of the preface, in early 1499, Minzheng was implicated in the deadly exam scandal and died. Why should the cautious Peng Ze have pushed his endorsement further after Cheng Minzheng, quite possibly his powerful behind-the-scenes sponsor, had perished in disgrace? With Cheng Minzheng's sudden death, I suspect, gone too was the evidential paper trail linking him to Peng Ze's endorsement of *Great Lineages in Xin'an.* Had Cheng Minzheng not fallen victim to factional infighting in Beijing at the peak of his Huizhou achievements, perhaps he could have brought the composite genealogical gazetteer into being, or, at the least, left behind sufficient evidential traces to suggest that he was behind Peng Ze's endorsement of Chen Dingyu's *Great Lineages in Xin'an.*[46]

In the end, even though Cheng Minzheng's role in Peng Ze's 1498 preface cannot be confirmed, he had nevertheless laid the groundwork for the printing of Huizhou's first, Cheng-led composite genealogy. His remarkable erudition, activism, and stature (including his now established ties with the Cheng brothers) made it possible and acceptable to arrange the elite surnames in a Cheng-led sequence, which thereafter characterized all three district-wide composite genealogies. In fact, this (re)ordering of surnames was so successful that even other-surnamed publishers were loath to tamper with it. The third composite genealogy of Ming Huizhou, *Prominent Lineages in Xiuning,* focusing on one county, was compiled by the Xiuning gentrymen Cao Sixuan and cut by Wang Gaoyuan, and carried a preface from the cutter's famous Xiuning kinsman, Imperial Academician Wang Hui (*jinshi* 1590). Although in partial charge of publishing the 1626 composite genealogical gazetteer, the Wangs continued to honor the Cheng-led sequence first set down in *Great Lineages in Xin'an*. Cheng Minzheng's local activism made Cheng preeminence palatable to regional great families, most notably by dramatically publicizing his kin ties to the two Cheng brothers. This claimed blood distinction brought prestige to the entire prefecture, as amply evidenced in the late Ming *Gazetteer of Cheng-Zhu's Native Place*.[47] Cheng Minzheng's strategy of promoting the Chengs and Huizhou at once worked well both in his lifetime and long after his departure.

This regional prestige nevertheless also helped further strengthen the empire-wide appeal of the Confucian family-lineage values embodied in *Prominent Lineages*. The Yixian gentryman Cheng Guangxian, in his 1551 preface to the composite genealogical gazetteer, called Huizhou "the native place of Master Ziyang [Zhu Xi]," and wrote that the aim of the "extended edition of Chen Dingyu's compilation is to spread Ziyang [Zhu Xi] teachings," so that Confucian values would not "end in Xin'an," but would "robustly disperse through the four seas," thereby bringing about "peace all under heaven."[48] Cheng Guangxian's dialectic concern for localism and "all under heaven" was strikingly similar to Cheng Minzheng's vision. The rise of regional consciousness in Huizhou most notably started with Cheng Minzheng, and now culminated in the publication of *Prominent Lineages*, both of which had empire-wide appeal while at the same time being locally focused.

HUIZHOU IDENTITY AND MERCANTILE LINEAGE CULTURE

The textual history of *Prominent Lineages* was intertwined with the social underpinning of the publication, illustrating not just the deepening of regional consciousness of Huizhou as a land of "prominent lineages" but also the rise of mercantile lineage culture. If Cheng Minzheng provided the vertical context of the composite genealogical gazetteer, the socioeconomic development in the sixteenth century formed a horizontal milieu. If the highlighted tie between the Cheng brothers and Huizhou added luster to the entire region, the upsurge of the Cheng pedigree brought about by the same tie must have also added pressure to other prominent lineages in the region. They must have felt the same drive to distinguish themselves and their home region from other parts of the Ming empire, presumably more so during the vast socioeconomic change of the mid-sixteenth century. More specifically, the immediate backdrop of the *Prominent Lineages* compilation constituted two fronts: Huizhou lineages were flourishing in terms of both demographic-social growth and institutional construction, but at the same time they were also facing challenges in both sociocultural politics and gender relations that rapid commercialization had brought on.

The mid-Ming period (1450–1550) was stable and yet embryonic, laying down the social infrastructure for the rapid changes that accelerated in the late sixteenth century.[49] In Huizhou, the lineage had come to overshadow other socioreligious institutions (such as village worship associations and Buddhist temples) to become a dominant rural order, most notably by setting up lineage landed trusts and constructing ancestral halls, as well as compiling single-surnamed genealogies.[50] According to Zhu Wanshu, the editor of the 2004 edition of *Prominent Lineages*, the mid-sixteenth-century compilers collected data from about eight hundred genealogies of individual lineages.[51] The composite genealogical gazetteer culminated a concurrent boom in Huizhou in the compilation of individual lineage genealogies (each with a single surname) as their collective representation. For instance, the 1570 edition of *Genealogy of the Xiuning Gucheng Cheng Lineage* (Xiuning Gucheng Chengshi zongpu) contains a short front section honoring the kinsmen who had compiled the previous genealogies of the Gucheng Cheng lineage and its nearby related branches. For the pre-1570 Ming period, it lists twenty editions, fifteen of which were printed during a short span of forty-five years from 1521 to 1566.[52]

Also revealing is a comparison of two Ming dynasty versions of the prefectural gazetteer, compiled in 1502 and 1566, respectively. For the large independent lineage temples, or ancestral halls, key to kinship institutions and rituals, the 1502 gazetteer mentions just four *citang* (ancestral halls), three of which were for the Wang lineages, whereas the 1566 version lists over two hundred, all of which were called *zongci*, lineage temples honoring the apical ancestors.[53] Indicative of the explosion of building lineage temples around the mid-century, the compilers of the latter gazetteer proudly boasted: "The lineage temples built to conduct ancestral rites and gather kinspeople to inculcate Confucian codes of behavior are only present in our Huizhou while lacking in other prefectures, and therefore we note [the trend] and prepare this 'Halls and Temples' Record."[54]

It is no accident that the 1502 gazetteer depicts an idyllic life of literate men and small cultivators living off the land, interrupted only by the occasional trader, whereas the 1566 account describes a thoroughly commercialized atmosphere: "As the locals lack land, they take trade as the permanent source of wealth. During the spring months, they go out for trade with their savings, in the hope of making 20 percent profit for a year, and will not return until the winter. Some merchants return home only once every couple of years."[55] With political support from powerful kinsmen who were scholar-officials at various levels and financial support from home lineages, Huizhou men spread throughout the empire and began to enjoy enormous success in the commercial realm, especially in the middle and lower Yangzi valleys. As the prominent Jiangnan scholar Gui Youguang (1507–1571) noted, "Xin'an is filled with prominent lineages; they settled in a mountainous region, lacking flat fields to provide arable land. So even the families of scholar-officials have all nurtured merchants to go into trade by sojourning through the four directions." As a result, merchants who dominated commercial activities "in the metropolitan centers under Heaven" were "mostly Xin'an men."[56] Later, the famous scholar-official from a Shexian merchant family named Wang Daokun (1525–1593) reported, "seven or eight out of ten households" engaged in trade in his home region.[57]

The rise and success of Huizhou merchants were rooted in home lineages. In his classic study of Huizhou merchants, Fujii Hiroshi divides Huizhou merchant capital into seven types: joint capital, entrusted capital, marriage capital, supporting capital, bequeathed capital, labor-accumulated capital, and bureaucratic capital, most of which were kinship related in one way or another.[58] More focally, in a major new study on the socioeconomic history of the Huizhou lineage, Joseph McDermott sketches out in his concluding remarks on the role of ancestral halls in promoting both commercial ventures and lineage rituals:

> many Huizhou lineages and their branches used these halls' construction budgets, maintenance costs, membership fees, and spirit tablets' admission charges to accumulate considerable funds that their managers could proceed to lend out cheaply to lineage members or more expensively to non-lineage members. The ancestral halls, whose numbers soared over the last half of the Ming, provided financial backing not only to commercial and financial partnerships in Huizhou villages but also to smaller Huizhou merchants' expansion into the markets and pawnshop operations in the lower Yangzi delta. The profits that these ancestral halls accrued from interest payments helped to pay for the ancestral worship rituals that lineage elders practiced in part to please their ancestors and in part to retain the loyalty of fellow lineage members.

From the mid-Ming on, McDermott continues, Huizhou lineages resolved some of the threats that rampant commercialization posed to their collective property and ultimately their own survival, turning the "cause of their troubles into their solution" by making the ancestral hall serve "as a credit association."[59] In addition, Huizhou merchants tapped kinsmen for organizational support, drawing upon kinship ties for their practice of trade (including partnerships) and for the construction of their trading networks, thereby building a home-linked or kinship-bound infrastructure of market access channels out of the region.[60]

Socioeconomic facets aside, the home lineage gentry and gazetteer compilers also helped fashion a new code of mercantile ethics emphasizing honesty, righteousness, and generosity, key to Huizhou merchants' long-term success. The same 1566 prefectural gazetteer begins to include biographic sketches of contemporary merchants that celebrate their moral integrity while noting their Confucian deeds of making contributions to rebuilding county academies, repairing local waterways, and especially setting up lineage corporate estates or ritual land endowed for maintaining ancestral halls.[61] The inclusion of righteous merchants in the officially compiled gazetteer marked their improved status as well as local officials' efforts at moral inculcation to set examples for traders amid rapid commercialization.

And yet, this was a lagging reflection of what had already been attempted in the privately compiled Huizhou genealogies. Virtuous merchants are already featured in the *Anthology of Xin'an Documents*, mostly taken from local genealogies, with an emphasis on their care for and contributions to home lineages.[62] For another example, the 1501 edition of the composite genealogy of the Xin'an Huangs contained an epitaph praising a fellow merchant named Huang Zhongrong, notably referred to as a *chushi* (untitled gentryman, or scholar-turned-merchant), for his genteel lifestyle and for his generosity and righteousness in assisting other kinsmen.[63] More biographies of righteous merchants active in the first half of the sixteenth century, and even earlier, and mostly drafted before the mid-century, are included in the 1570 edition of the Shuaikou Cheng genealogy.

Most notably, as a collective representation of nearly eight hundred individual genealogies, the publicly available *Prominent Lineages* begins to note virtuous merchants. As will be demonstrated in chapter 5, the genealogical gazetteer was partially a product of power jockeying for symbolic capital among regional elite lineages. And yet local gentry compilers obviously agreed on one thing: this collective genealogical gazetteer, like the individual genealogies, was intended to maintain patrilineal kinship order by promoting Confucian social ethics. One guideline reads: "The real stories of each lineage, regarding *zhongxiao* [loyalty and filial devotion], *jieyi* [male integrity, female chastity, and righteousness], *xunye* [illustrious accomplishments in the political and military realms], *wenzhang* [publications], whatever [the accomplishments] that are relevant to [the promotion of] moral teaching, are all recorded, whether they are hidden or noted, still alive or long departed."[64] On the basis of this guideline, *Prominent Lineages* included in many lineage entries "righteous" merchants, as well as other male and female Confucian exemplars. According to a study by Huizhou specialist Zhao Huafu, just forty entries of village lineages in the genealogical gazetteer cover the following five groups of noteworthy men and women:

(1) 933 officials and exam degree winners;
(2) 61 filial sons and devoted grandsons;
(3) 96 devoted widows and martyred women;
(4) 415 scholars with significant publications;
(5) 258 kinsmen noted for virtue and righteous deeds, many of whom were merchants or landlords.[65]

Additional records of righteous merchants not covered in Zhao's list also exist. A short account for the Cheng lineage in the Xuanmingfang village, in Shexian, identifies four merchants, two of whom traded salt in the Lianghuai and Zhejiang areas (two of the most important salt business regions of the later empire), noting their integrity, generosity, and gentry comportment.[66] A rather lengthy entry on the Cheng branch in Wenchangfang, in Xiuning County, for whose genealogy Cheng Minzhang had written a preface (see chapter 1), mentions three righteous merchants. One student at the prefectural school, named Huan, upon the death of his father, quit Confucian learning for trade to support the family and became rich. While sojourning in Huguang, he built "righteous" graves (*yizhong*) to bury a large number of famine victims; he also donated grain in response to the call of the central government. Another named Zu preferred righteousness over profits. A third named En was noted in the Yangzhou salt trade for preferring kin over wealth.[67] A more detailed account of a righteous merchant concerns a certain Huang Zhengyuan of Ruiye Huangcun, in Shexian, who was orphaned at thirteen. Growing up, Huang traveled on business between Wu and Yue (Jiangsu and Zhejiang). He "traded fairly, supported the poor, and so elders and youth, men and women all called him 'Sir Huang.'" Local officials (in the places where he traveled and settled) all admired his virtue, and even offered him the official gentry status of the cap and sashes (*guandai*). In his home community he built a village worship association, promoted ancestral rites, set up ritual land, initiated the bimonthly village compact, honored local gentry, ordered strict family-lineage instructions, mediated local disputes and lawsuits, supported orphans and weak people, and hence was called a "pure gentryman" (*yiqing chushi*).[68]

With the image of merchants improved and elevated, we begin to see certain accounts that equalize trade with learning or merchants with scholars. An entry for a certain Huang lineage, in Shexian, notes that three brothers "either focus on Confucian learning or pursue trade, and their achievements are genteelly notable."[69] In another instance, in a short entry on the Yichuan Yus in Wuyuan, not one of the most commercialized counties of the prefecture, we see the identification of a certain Yu Fuhua, who, "excelling in trade, started a [great] undertaking glorifying his ancestors" (*shan gangu, chuangye guangqian*).[70] To my knowledge, this is one of the first instances in Ming China that celebrated a kinsman's business endeavor, like examination success, as the outstanding achievement that could glorify his ancestors, the highest praise for kinsmen in this stronghold of lineage settlements. Many single-lineage genealogies compiled in the late Ming (1550–1644) contained far more detailed biographies of righteous merchants with similar honors.[71] But as a collective gazetteer of all of the acknowledged regional elite lineages, and a unique Huizhou product in Ming times, *Prominent Lineages* not only marked the self-identification of Huizhou, but also represented the emergence of what can be termed "mercantile lineage culture" in the region, a culture that was kinship constituted and Confucian oriented, gentry led and merchant based, while containing sufficient space for incorporating local popular culture.

In all these accounts, it was the virtue, not the wealth, of Huizhou merchants that was highlighted. The coverage was not evenly represented in all lineage entries. Consider the two aforementioned Cheng settlements in Taitang and Shuaikou. Both lineages, located in Cheng Minzheng's ancestral county, were heavily engaged in commercial adventure in the Ming, even before 1500.[72] But the entries for these two mercantile lineages in *Prominent Lineages* do not touch upon merchants, focusing instead on the notable kinsmen in the ancestry with illustrious accomplishments in other areas, mostly in the civil service realm, even though neither the Chengs of Taitang nor of Shuaikou produced any higher exam degree holders prior to 1551.

Consider one case from Shuaikou. Cheng Wenjie (1459–1533), according to the epitaph contained in his home genealogy, was particularly good at literary studies in his youth, but upon orders from his father he turned to trade, traveling for business widely through Jiangnan, Hunan, Shandong, and Shanxi. The epitaph nevertheless emphasized his literary learning, gentility, and generosity. Even famed literati went to him for instructions. He was characteristically defined as "a merchant in name and scholarly gentryman in practice" (*shangming er shixing*).[73] Yet the *Prominent Lineages* used just four characters to identify him: *yishi haoming* (famed for his poems), not even mentioning his commercial career.[74]

In the Taitang case, whose remarkably short entry consisted of just five lines, the lack of mention of other Confucian men and women might be due to the lack of data, as their first genealogy had just been compiled in 1545, and it contained little else besides a descent line.[75] In contrast, the Shuaikou Chengs had compiled and expanded their genealogy numerous times in the Ming before the mid-sixteenth century, although only the 1570 edition is now extant, which contains many biographies or epitaphs on virtuous merchants. As a whole, however, the Shuaikou Cheng genealogy (even the merchant accounts) still emphasizes the lineage's scholarly tradition. One postscript to an earlier edition of the Shuaikou Cheng genealogy even quotes a still earlier statement that had since become a local idiom in Huizhou: "If a lineage does not compile a genealogy for three generations, does not produce an official for three generations, does not engage in learning for three generations, then [its kinsmen] will fall into [the category] of petty men [*xiaoren*]."[76] The *Prominent Lineages*, too, ends the entry with an emphasis on the scholarly tradition of the Shuaikou Chengs: "There were eminent Confucians and kinsmen with remarkable virtue in the past for each generation. Now, nearly three thousand kinspeople live together within the lineage, they love and practice the ancient way of life, reading books and honoring propriety; kinsmen who have studied for the civil service exam and excelled in the government schools succeed one after another with remarkable achievements."[77]

Here we see an apparent contradiction between reality and representation: some heavily commercial lineages were actually presented in a way that emphasized their scholarly practice even if these same lineages did not achieve great success in the exam hall. This contradiction points to the discrepancy between the projected identity of Huizhou and the actual working of mercantile lineages. The contradiction seems also to reveal a certain concern about their perceived status: the merchant-dominated lineages often acted in a way that made them look more Confucian than the scholar-gentry. As already noted, just as Huizhou merchants relied on home lineages for commercial ventures and success, they in return also made significant contributions to fashioning home lineage building in mid-Ming Huizhou. Cheng Nai (1438–1490), a commercial landlord and respected leader of the Cheng lineage of Shuaikou, urged his sons—including the eldest, Cheng Wenjie—to engage in trade while simultaneously supporting his own father's initiatives to revise the Cheng genealogy and repair the branch temple to Cheng Lingxi (which served as the Shuaikou Chengs' ancestral hall).[78] The merchant Cheng Wenjie, based on his father's work, started the compilation of the first printed version of the Shuaikou Cheng genealogy in the early 1500s. Cheng Minzheng, in a note added to Cao Jing's epitaph on the merchant Cheng Xinyu of Shuaikou (discussed in chapter 1), commended Cheng Xinyu's branch in building ancestral halls, compiling ritual covenants, and applying Zhu Xi's *Family Rituals* to the performance of the ancestral rites. The Shuaikou Cheng community, Minzheng concluded, led all the Huizhou Chengs in "honoring the descent line and harmonizing the lineage" (*jingzong muzu*).[79]

The Chengs of Shuaikou and Taitang are represented in *Prominent Lineages* in such a way that suggests that the compilers of the composite genealogical gazetteer most likely took whatever data the participating lineages provided them. The scholarly emphasis on gentility over commerce, however, certainly did not contradict their own overall compiling guidelines, even though they also took the latter into account whenever appropriate or available. Indeed, a similar consideration may have been at work in the collective mentality of Huizhou "prominent" lineages in the mid-sixteenth century and of the compilers and endorsers of the *Prominent Lineages*, and therefore may have played a significant role in the production of the unique genealogical genre in the first place.

Above all, *Prominent Lineages* was a genealogical gazetteer, with kinship matters at its core. Its function was to record (or, in some cases, reclaim) the illustrious ancestry of these "prominent" (and, to quote McDermott again, not-so-famous) lineages by highlighting the ancient roots of their pedigree and historical accomplishments in the most endearing Confucian realms of academic-official success and scholarly writing. Zhao Huafu's data of forty leading lineages, listing far more Confucian scholar-officials than commercial landlords or merchants, confirms the preferred focus. Why, then, the need to compile such a composite genealogical gazetteer to publicly boast their "prominence," obviously aimed at not just a home audience but also outsiders?

Hong Jueshan, the editor-in-chief (*zongcai*) of *Prominent Lineages*, in his 1550 preface to the genealogical gazetteer, seems to reveal something significant regarding the motivation for the compilation that nevertheless could not be openly broadcast. "This gazetteer," Hong wrote, "is to preserve the inherited custom and popular trend. Indeed, when kinship rules are established, kinspeople understand where they come from, thereby respecting the ancestors and honoring the descent line; when the sociopolitical institutions are properly erected, with the [dynastic] court being centered and prominent lineages prevailing, the kinspeople feel protected, obeying kinship order and ancestral power. [All of this] purifies local customs and advances imperial rule." He goes on to state that so long as the compilation of the composite genealogical gazetteer "benefits all under heaven, even if it [signals something that] normally should be avoided, the gentrymen understand that they must certainly do it."[80]

What exactly was that something that "normally should be avoided"? Was it the self-glorifying nature of such a massive genealogical gazetteer, and, more seriously, a collective (rather than an individual) project documenting the elite lineages of the entire prefecture that clearly distinguished Huizhou from other regions? If this was the case, why did the Huizhou gentrymen feel so compelled to create it? Publicly, it could be justified that such a gazetteer could work to both "purify local customs and advance imperial rule." Hong Jueshan was a notable follower of Wang Yangming, and herein he echoes, or resonates with, the latter's idea of erasing differences, whether between the dynastic center and local society or between the elites and ordinary people.[81] His justification for the gazetteer compilation was sincere, and it did fulfill the double role he specified, as will be further discussed later in this chapter. But were there other more mundane or practical concerns other than self-promotion and self-protection behind the publicly stated aims of the project?

The motivation for publishing a gazetteer of prominent lineages of the entire prefecture came from without as well as from within. For the collective community of Huizhou elite lineages, there seemed to exist a certain degree of anxiety over the regional image and its difference from Jiangnan, the economic and cultural heartland of the Ming empire—especially after the turn of the sixteenth century when these lineages produced increasingly large number of sojourning merchants. As Joseph McDermott insightfully suggests, the absence of any commercial wealth in the entries of *Prominent Lineages* and their stress on antiquity of residence (as well as Confucian accomplishments) were likely also meant to show Jiangnan literati that they were not *nouveaux riches*. Indeed, few Suzhou, Hangzhou, or Songjiang natives could boast such roots in their prefectures, and Huizhou men, often subject to barbs from these tastemakers for being mountain hicks and money-grubbers, were anxious to present themselves as the true living embodiments of earlier aristocratic elite culture.[82] This hypothesis is not pure speculation, as later, when the leading scholar-official from Jiangnan Wang Shizhen (1526–1590) toured Mount Huang, his Huizhou counterpart Wang Daokun (1525–1593) invited the best of Jiangnan's artists and artisans to engage in a friendly competition with the best of Shexian over the quality of the gentlemanly arts: poetry, calligraphy, chess, and music.[83]

In the mid-sixteenth century, even more urgent was a concern over the negative perception of these merchants outside of Huizhou. As the Chinese historian Wang Zhenzhong demonstrates, the term *Huishang* (Huizhou merchants) first appeared in the early sixteenth century; by the late sixteenth century it had become fixed in popular parlance, used by outsiders to refer to the powerful mercantile group.[84] But this was not the term Huizhou merchants used to identify themselves, and, indeed, it tended to connote negative meanings. A late Ming account from a Songjiang native reveals how merchants from Huizhou snatched away assets from local people: "Toward the end of the Chenghua (r. 1465–1487), a prominent official returned home full of accolades. One elder kept kneeling down at his door. Alarmed, the official asked why. [The elder] responded, 'the wealth of Songjiang people has mostly been taken by the Huishang, but now it's been returned with your homecoming. How could I not express my appreciation?'" Upon close examination, as discovered by Wang Zhenzhong, this anecdote was copied verbatim from an earlier sixteenth-century story, except that "Huishang" had been inserted in the place of "government" (*guanfu*).[85] A satire of a homecoming high official had been instantly turned into a satire of Huizhou merchants.

For outsiders, merchants from Huizhou were not just greedy, they were also profligates. Toward the end of the fifteenth century, a wealthy merchant from Huizhou named Wang Yang became involved in a notorious affair. While sojourning in Guichi, he committed adultery with a widow who attempted to coerce her widowed daughter-in-law, Tang Guimei, into developing an intimate relationship with the merchant, which ended with Tang hanging herself. By the late Ming, this tragedy came to be widely represented in various genres of publications, from literati jottings to popular fiction, and from handbooks of virtuous women to the official *Ming History*.[86] All of this might have been reason enough for the compilers of *Prominent Lineages*, and indeed for various individual-surnamed genealogies as well, to highlight the virtue and gentility of their fellow merchants.

Outside pressures aside, the genealogical gazetteer was fundamentally a product of Huizhou local society. The burst of compilations of individual-surnamed genealogies, including composite ones following Cheng Minzheng's *Composite Genealogy of the Xin'an Chengs*, had prepared the compilers of the *Prominent Lineages* to claim Huizhou as the sole place where medieval aristocratic culture was still alive and well in the mid-sixteenth century. Aside from collectively recording (or claiming) the ancient roots of these prominent lineages, the genealogical gazetteer set up a reliable reference book for a unique Huizhou institution—allegedly inherited from the medieval aristocracy—the intermarriage of local elite lineages.[87] Zheng Zuo, one of the two top endorsers of the *Prominent Lineages*, states in his 1549 preface:

> The Han and the Sui-Tang dynasties did not mete out fiefs, but emphasized the pedigree of aristocratic families. They set up a court bureau in charge of all genealogies under Heaven and selected erudite scholars to command matters of genealogical compilation. The bureau and its officials were not abolished until the Five Dynasties. Yet in our Xin'an, family status is checked when [selecting a] marriage partner, and genealogies are sought [to clarify] kinship branches, all of which have long become custom without losing the meanings handed down from ancient times. Thus it is

that in the making of kinship settlements, there is the flourishing growth of the one descent line in linked settlements in various counties or one surname settling in multiple villages; in the making of marriage, there is the noted distinction of the poor not marrying the rich and the debased [bondservants or "little surnames"] not pairing with the dignified [*jian bu ou gui*]. [In Xin'an], the surviving tombs of forebears can be traced as far back as the Qi and the Liang [in the fifth and sixth centuries] or as "recent" as those from the Tang and Song onward, not to mention the tombs of ten generations within one hundred years.

Zheng Zuo then proudly states that because of the development of Huizhou lineages and their notable traditions, "Hardly can any other prefecture come close to" Xin'an. He moves on to define the "prominent lineage" with the accomplishments by kinspeople, past and present, in "illuminating the Way as embodied in writings; fulfilling loyal and righteous deeds [in high politics], thereby standing out in historical records; practicing filial piety and friendship, thereby purifying customs and promoting benevolence; living happily in retirement while cultivating virtue and committing to moral rules."[88]

Zheng Zuo makes several important points in this passage. First, biased or not, no other prefecture could match his native place given the historical roots and unique characteristics of Huizhou kinship society. Second, the prominent lineage was defined in a way that made it possible to include ordinary kinspeople practicing Confucian ethics as well as those with notable accomplishments in politics and scholarship, which, again, resonated with the approach of Wang Yangmingism then in vogue. Such inclusiveness opened the door to incorporate righteous merchants in certain lineage entries, with their achievements in the commercial sector soon to be likened to exam success. Also relevant here is a notable marriage pattern, which paralleled and further substantiated the "aristocratic" tradition that the Huizhou gentry claimed.

Indeed, the pattern of intermarriage among local elite lineages was well established in Huizhou, as reported in the 1566 edition of the Huizhou gazetteer: "Marriage is arranged on the base of family/lineage pedigree, disregarding the wealth."[89] Cheng Minzheng, in a rather casual manner, mentioned numerous cases of elite lineage intermarriage. One reason that he actually maintained good personal relations with certain Wang kinsmen had to do with Cheng-Wang intermarriage, despite the competition between the two leading surnames in the symbolic realms.[90] In a preface Cheng Minzheng penned for a local Wang genealogy, he noted that certain Wang and Cheng branches in his ancestral county had been linked through marital relations for generations (*shiqi*).[91] In another preface to the genealogy of the Gulin Huangs in Xiuning, he notes that the Huangs intermarried with the "major families of the great surnames" (*dajia juxing*) of the Cheng, Wu, and Wang who "support each other to stand firm and tall" (*xiangfu erli*).[92]

In the aforementioned note to Cao Jing's (*jinshi* 1268) epitaph on the merchant Cheng Xinyu of Shuaikou, Cheng Minzheng indicates that the Shuaikou Chengs and Cao Jing's lineage were linked through intermarriage. This last case is particularly revealing, suggesting that merchant families were readily married into top gentry families so long as they belonged to local prominent lineages. Indeed, by the sixteenth century, merchant assimilation into the scholarly elite strata of their own lineages or of the partnered ones was no longer exceptional. Mercantile families married their sons and daughters into prestigious Huizhou gentry families and supported their sons and grandsons to sit for the civil service examinations. And yet, it was not the wealth of individual families but their lineage affiliation that was the key to making such marriages socially acceptable. In a long "Record of the Lineage Code" (Jiadian ji) of the Mingzhou Wus in Xiuning, penned around 1574, which recalls an earlier ancestral stipulation, there is an item concerning "Careful Selection of a Marriage Partner" (Jin hunpin):

> [The selection of a] marriage partner should not be concerned with [individual] wealth but with the commensurate status of the lineage. If one carelessly marries with a person [girl] from a lineage with which [we] have never had marriage ties, without equal social status, he will become the laughing stock of the local neighbors, as he treats himself as a slave, further treating his own son as debased. Our lineage should certainly not affiliate ourselves with him: he must not be allowed to enter the ancestral hall while alive, and his soul tablet must not be allowed to be erected there either.[93]

This elite-surname marriage institution worked to both maintain social hierarchy based on surname-kinship and promote social mobility regardless of the individual vocation among/between prominent lineages. From this perspective, *Prominent Lineages* offered a who's who handbook for the regional marriage market, and its publication worked favorably for merchant families of the covered prominent lineages, as the locals now had a public reference guide for selecting marriage partners. This function in part explains why at least twelve different versions of *Prominent Lineages* were published around the mid-sixteenth century. Clearly, the local lineages, being transformed into mercantile lineages, were eager to be covered in *Prominent Lineages*. All of this explains why, in part, the rise of Huizhou merchants in the sixteenth century did not destroy the old system of intermarriage among elite lineages (which would prevail up to the twentieth century), but instead further enhanced it through merging scholarly and commercial families as integrated units within mercantile lineages.

Assimilation of merchants into lineage establishment was urgent for lineage elders for other practical concerns in the mid-sixteenth century. One was to turn the wealth earned from commerce to good use. Commercial success raised the social status of Huizhou merchants, and at the same time enabled them to turn their hard-earned money into cultural capital, in particular by helping to strengthen home lineage institutions. Local gentry acknowledged their contributions in home genealogies, local gazetteers, and in *Prominent Lineages*. By way of example, around the mid-sixteenth century, Jin Deqing sojourned to several provinces and over a decade accumulated ten thousand taels of silver. Upon returning home, he contributed six hundred taels to building the ancestral hall for his home lineage in Qimen, and thus earned a biography in the home genealogy.[94] There is obviously a connection between accounts of the explosive construction of ancestral halls, the commercial boom, and the biographies of virtuous merchants in the same 1566 gazetteer of Huizhou.

The other side of the story about the strengthening economy was its corrupt effect on moral, or kinship, bonds. As the Huizhou specialist Zhao Huafu suggests, *Prominent Lineages* was compiled at a time when Huizhou lineage institutions flourished, but at the same time were facing challenges from rapid commercialization, the most notable of which was the disruptive power of money.[95] The concern over moral decay was among the most important reasons why the compilation of individual genealogies was booming (and at the same time was made possible with the support of merchants' wealth). The most radical or critical view of the moral decline that began in the early sixteenth century was presented retrospectively toward the end of the dynasty by the Shexian magistrate Zhang Tao (1554–1618) and Shexian gentryman Xie Bi (1547–1615). This view was made popular in English-language scholarship by Timothy Brook in his *Confusions of Pleasure*:

> The dynasty's winter of repose gave way to the bustle of spring. [Around the 1520s] the sedate certainty of agriculture was edged out by the hotter speculative world of commerce: "Those who went out as merchants became numerous and the ownership of land was no longer esteemed. Men matched wits using their assets, and fortunes rose and fell unpredictably." Polarizations of capability and class followed, with some families becoming rich and others impoverished. "The balance between the mighty and the lowly was lost as both competed for trifling amounts." As the prospect of wealth fueled avarice, the moral order that had held society together gave way. "Each exploited the other and everyone publicized himself." In this evil climate, "deception sprouted and litigation arose; purity was sullied and excess overflowed."[96]

Contemporary or slightly later local observers also noted the moral disorder. According to the 1570 preface to the Chen lineage code of Wentang in Qimen County, Wentang's customs used to be "pure and sincere," but "the present is unlike the past, which worries the lineage elders," and so the Chen elders prepared the lineage code to uphold the moral bonds among kinspeople.[97] Many other lineages did the same thing, even though they did not publish a similar code independently but instead included in their genealogies the lineage rules that had the same function of moral binding power. As early as 1494, Cheng Zengjie (1469–1542), the youngest brother of the merchant Cheng Wenjie, had crafted two sets of admonitions for his highly commercialized lineage (among the earliest commercialized in Huizhou): "Exhortation on Respecting Ancestors and Harmonizing the Lineage" (Zunzu muzu zhen) and "Exhortation on Establishing Self and Behaving Well"

(Lishen xingji zhen). The first exhortation highlights the significance of rituals held at both the ancestral tombs and ancestral halls, as the ancestors' virtue would enlighten their offspring. Severe violators at the lineage rituals would be "expelled from ancestral hall and removed from the genealogy" (*cipu liangchu*), the most serious punishment for kinspeople in Huizhou lineage culture. It also emphasizes that the prosperous lineage now had one thousand kinsmen who, all descended from the same ancestor, should be treated equally regardless of their status in terms of familial wealth or lack thereof. The strong must avoid being overbearing and the rich must avoid being arrogant. The violators in this regard, too, would be punished. The second exhortation urges the kinspeople to be filially devoted, to practice fraternal love, and to maintain a clear demarcation between men and women. Those who failed in the areas of men's integrity and women's chastity, again, would not be allowed to enter the ancestral hall and would be removed from the genealogy.[98]

The *Prominent Lineages*, as a collective document, could of necessity only use positive images to convey the same message of exhortation at a moment when virtually the entire prefecture was drawn into the commercial tide. Besides featuring Confucian men and women throughout the gazetteer, it carries prefaces by famed scholar-officials and representatives of local gentry. Zheng Zuo emphasized the noble tradition of Huizhou society; Hong Jueshan stressed the significance of kinship laws in purifying local customs and enhancing dynastic rule; Cheng Guang-xian promoted "the style of benevolence and self-effacement" (*renrang*) as the essence of Zhu Xi learning; while Wang Feng made a straightforward call to "use the *Gazetteer of Prominent Lineages* to remold Xin'an's customs."[99] Seemingly presenting different or even contradictory views of local customs at the mid-century, these prefaces convey one message: the genealogical gazetteer was meant to promote Confucian ethics and kinship values.

Also urgent, amid the rapid commercialization of the day, was to keep track of the increasing numbers of sojourning kinsmen so as to create, or further enhance, a sense of personal belonging to the home lineage. One such method of binding sojourning men was to compile or recompile a genealogy, which would generate a consciousness of common identity and prestige, and thus help bind sojourning men to their home lineages. The 1570 edition of the Shuaikou Cheng genealogy stipulates in one of its guidelines that the lateral branches from the previous generations that dwelled elsewhere would be "marked in red."[100] It was not directly concerned with tracking sojourning merchants, but nevertheless reflected the gentry compilers' concern for recording all kinspeople descended from the same apical ancestor or the first migrant ancestor so as to enhance the lineage consciousness or common identity. This lineage consciousness of tradesmen had a strong tradition in Huizhou even before the sixteenth century. We have seen how deeply those merchants featured in Cheng Minzheng's *Anthology of Xin'an Documents* cared about their lineages, and, more specifically, how merchants of the Shuaikou

Chengs contributed to the building of ancestral halls and the compilation of the branch genealogy at home. The first printed version of the Shuaikou Cheng branch genealogy had a good deal to do with the sojourning merchant Cheng Wenjie and his nephew Cheng Zuyuan.[101] Wenjie's younger brother, Zengjie, eventually completed the version that Wenjie had begun and had it printed in 1511.[102]

The 1570 edition of the Shuaikou Cheng genealogy, expanded from the 1511 edition, contains a long list of 230 household heads, each of which was assigned a corresponding number of printed copies of the genealogy.[103] The copy number and the household head who received the copy are also shown on a specifically printed sheet illustrated with a sacred Bell of Treasure and Harmony (Baohe Zhong); its bottom caption reads: "Upon the completion of the revised genealogy, we inform our kinsmen. You are each to treasure it forever and leave it to posterity. Do not be unfilial. If you demean or sell it, your name will be excluded from the ancestral hall and your wrongdoing will be reported to the officials."[104] The private genealogy was considered sacred. It contained all the names of ancestors as well as living kinsmen, illustrated with their glory and dreams, lineage regulations, and often records of ancestral tombs and corporate estates as well. It was a private history of the entire lineage and thus became the central reference point of identity for the lineage, including its sojourning merchants.

The sixteenth-century boom in building kinship identity through the compilation of individual genealogies led to the construction of the collective identity of Huizhou lineages with the publication of *Prominent Lineages*. If an individual genealogy was partially meant to keep track of sojourning men, then the composite genealogical gazetteer was meant to keep track of all the branches of the acknowledged elite surnames of the entire prefecture, which in part explains the multiple editions published in the mid-century. While the individual lineage identity was primarily blood-bound, the collective identity of Huizhou was regionally bound, but was nevertheless based on or comprised of the individual identity of the blood-bound descent lines.

Prominent Lineages, it should be emphasized again, was primarily concerned with establishing the pedigree of Huizhou lineages by noting the ancient roots of their aristocratic ancestors and illustrious achievements of their gentry kinsmen in official services, civil exams, and scholarly writings. These historical and social characteristics defined the prominent lineages and formed the Confucian and political foundation of the emerging mercantile lineage culture. While most preface-writers or endorsers of *Prominent Lineages* still chose to be silent on the merchant constituency of local lineages, the scholar-official Hu Xiao (*jinshi* 1544) of Jixi notably took sojourning merchants into account when describing Huizhou prominent lineages in his 1551 preface to the genealogical gazetteer. After noting the remarkable natural environment of Huizhou, and the illustrious ancestry and the social development of the local kinship communities, Hu wrote, "kinspeople live together in the lineage settlement, and sojourning merchants converge along the pathways."[105] This paired characterization of Huizhou kinship society succinctly marked the emerging mercantile lineage culture, which would blossom after the mid-century in the late Ming. *Prominent Lineages in Xin'an* signaled the collective identity of Huizhou that was partially predicated upon mercantile lineage culture.

Central to emerging mercantile lineage culture was gender. Unlike *Anthology of Xin'an Documents* that focuses on the glories of statesmen, Confucian literati, and local lineage leaders, *Prominent Lineages* became the first collective document with prefecture-wide coverage that systematically highlighted the trend of devotional widowhood. Zhao Huafu's study, discussed earlier, lists ninety-six chaste women out of just forty entries of kinship settlements in *Prominent Lineages*. I will enumerate some additional cases, generally not included in Zhao's data, to give a concrete sense of how dear the Confucian core value of female chastity, just like righteousness of merchants, was to the mid-century gentry compilers of the genealogical gazetteer. In the brief Xuanmingfang account covering four "righteous" merchants noted earlier, we see a commendation for a young woman who was "firmly devoted to widowhood."[106] For another Shexian Cheng lineage dwelling in Censhan, a short account in *Prominent Lineages* lists three living women, née Yin, Zhou, and Wang, who were widowed at the ages of twenty-two, twenty-seven, and twenty-four, respectively, praising them as "all devoted to widowhood, willingly living a deprived life while taking good care of their mothers-in-law and raising their children," and adding that the "local administration has requested imperial awards for them."[107]

Consider three more cases of devoted widows from other Cheng branches: One from Huaitang in Shexian, née Ling, who committed suicide upon the death of her husband, a student at the county academy, and received the official banner of "chastity martyr." The second from Chakou in Xiuning, née Sun, who became a widow at twenty-six following the death of her sojourning husband and raised her fatherless son. And the third case from Jinchuan in Xiuning, in which two wives of sojourning merchants were "committed to widowhood and raised the fatherless children."[108] Entries on other surnamed lineages highlight the same womanly virtue, too. Most notably, a remarkably short entry, three lines in total, on the Hu settlement in Zhongxinfang, in Yixian, lists little else but the names of three devoted widows. It uses the same term, which signified the highest accolade for women: "committed to widowhood and raising fatherless children" (*shoujie fugu*).[109]

Similar acknowledgements of Confucian widowhood can be easily located in numerous entries of lineage settlements in *Prominent Lineages in Xin'an*; most of these entries are short, but the compilers hardly ever missed a chance to record the cases of female chastity when available. The genealogical gazetteer, by systematically documenting the rise of the female chastity cult throughout the prefecture, played a role in elevating Huizhou as a center of devoted widowhood. The Huguang scholar-official Li Weizhen (1546–1626) would soon call Shexian (and

Huizhou as a whole) the "Confucian heartland of women" (*nüliu zhi Zou-Lu*).[110] This is the story that will be taken up in chapter 4.

CONCLUSION

Huizhou had self-identified as the "Zou-Lu of the southeast" (Zou-Lu refers to the native places of Mencius and Confucius) ever since the famed neo-Confucian Zhao Fang (1319–1369) first coined the term for his native place. This name came about after he observed that, beginning with Zhu Xi, Xin'an had produced an unusually high number of neo-Confucian scholars. The appellation was frequently repeated in local texts, such as the *Anthology of Xin'an Documents* and the 1566 edition of the prefectural gazetteer and 1693 edition of the gazetteer of the Xiuning county.[111] And yet this geographic term was not exclusive, as other places in southeastern China, such as Jinhua in Zhejiang, were also labeled thusly.

An equivalent yet uniquely Huizhou identity was "the ancestral place of Cheng-Zhu." Still, the term is a bit too elite when accounting for the social and demographic makeup of the region. Surely, the ninety different surnamed-lineages recorded in *Prominent Lineages* were not evenly developed in social terms. The Zhus of Zhu Xi, for instance, while illustrious for their intellectual pedigree, were not as socially and demographically developed as the leading surnames or descent lines of Huizhou. The most developed and prominent descent lines included the Chengs, Wangs, Huangs, Fangs, Wus, and Hus; this, in part, accounts for the Zhus relatively lower placement in three Huizhou genealogical gazetteers (placed sixteen, nineteen, and twenty-one, respectively).[112]

Taken together, however, these ninety descent lines were clearly dominant within Huizhou. Although demographic data is not available for the region in the mid-sixteenth century, by 1600, Huizhou would have a population of about 1.2 million, and by 1820, the population would surpass 2.4 million.[113] As noted in chapter 1, Cheng Minzheng's *Composite Genealogy of the Xin'an Chengs* covers over ten thousand kinsmen from forty-four branches. As Harriet Zurndorfer demonstrates in another example, based on the 1600 genealogy of the Xiuning Fans (not a particularly prominent or developed descent line in Huizhou), the number of males born into the lineage during the century from 1475 to 1564, with date of birth available, was 1,160, most of whom appear to have resided in three of nine Xiuning villages (along with 866 first wives identifiable with birth data).[114] Clearly, the ninety "famous" and "not-so-famous" descent lines (many of which had numerous settlements throughout the prefecture) recorded in *Prominent Lineages* account for the vast majority of the Huizhou population from the mid-sixteenth century onward.

Indeed, it was the gentrified lineages covering various social categories—including commoner kinspeople, righteous merchants and devoted women in particular—that formed the social fabric of "the Zou-Lu of the southeast" or "the ancestral place of Cheng-Zhu." With the publication of the *Prominent Lineages*,

Huizhou presented itself to the entire realm as a stronghold of the lineage settlement, the archetypical neo-Confucian social institution. From this perspective, the printing of *Prominent Lineages*, while deepening the Huizhou consciousness regarding local lineages, helped to spread Confucian values to other localities. As Cheng Guangxian, a metropolitan degree holder from Yixian, eloquently put it in his 1551 preface to *Prominent Lineages*:

> *The Gazetteer of Prominent Lineages* is meant to record prominent lineages. What is to be recorded? It is designed to show the virtue of ancestors, in which lies the key to inspiring our offspring. If the key to inspiring our offspring works well, the culture of benevolence and self-effacement [*renrang*] will not die out but endure. If the style of *renrang* spreads to other places, then the pedigree of Xin'an will be further enhanced throughout the realm. Xin'an is the native place of Ziyang [Zhu Xi], and the learning of Master Ziyang lies in using *renrang* to mold [all people] under heaven. Therefore, if one attempts to hold that key to extend its remolding power and widely apply it to promote Zhu Xi's teaching everywhere, this should be the responsibility of everyone born to the native place of Ziyang. Thus, this gazetteer, even though an expanded edition of Chen Dingyu's volume, is more or less also an asset in promoting the teaching of Ziyang [to all under heaven]. Why? Combining all different branches to show the meaning of one single ancestral root is to extend love to relatives [*guang qinqin*]. When one loves one's relatives, one also establishes self-love and shows benevolence. Noting the [local] people and examining their real contributions to society extends promotion of the worthies [*guang xianxian*]. When one promotes the worthies, one also establishes self-respect and practices self-effacement. Who does not have a heart full of "loving relatives and appreciating worthies" [*qinqin xianxian*]? I understand that different regions under heaven are endowed with different mountains and rivers, and their people with different characters of toughness and softness. The customs (of different regions) differ, but the Way of benevolence and self-effacement is rooted in human nature and therefore all the same. This is why [we should] encourage and promote it. Moreover, the state instructs society and guides the customs with codes and regulations, which, if taken from the genuine histories, are all based on people's traditions and habits.

Therefore, Cheng Guangxian continues, with the printing of the composite genealogical gazetteer, the molding power of *qinqin xianxian* will not just "end in Xin'an," but will "move on with divine force to robustly spread to the four seas" and thereby bring about "peace under heaven. Does this not further enhance the pedigree of Xin'an?!"[115] Sounding like a disciple of Wang Yangming or, perhaps more apropos, of Cheng Minzheng's idea of the *Oneness of the Way*, Cheng Guangxian saw in *Prominent Lineages* the potential empire-wide impact of the social values it conveyed, which in turn would further elevate the status of Huizhou within the Great Ming.

For Huizhou itself, the Confucian values promoted in *Prominent Lineages* may have contributed to facilitating the workings of local mercantile lineages: encouraging women to be more devoted and merchants to be more home loving, all the while shielding Huizhou merchants from outside criticism via their affiliation with prominent home lineages. Moreover, the composite genealogical gazetteer celebrated an accepted ordering of the major local surnames. It assured and facilitated their cooperation in important local matters such as elite surname intermarriage, which in turn paved the way for Huizhou to keep producing large numbers of scholar-officials and prominent merchants throughout late imperial times. Indeed, the localist turn of Huizhou gentrymen, from Cheng Minzheng to the producers of *Prominent Lineages*, served the empire well, while at the same time enabling them to maintain and develop their distinctive Huizhou identity.

PART II

Mercantile Lineage Culture

3

———

Wang Daokun and the Promotion of Mercantile Lineage Culture

Wang Daokun (1525–1593), only briefly identified in *Prominent Lineages in Xin'an* for having passed the metropolitan examination in 1547, would go on to become a top scholar-official and a literary luminary throughout the empire. He also made a major contribution to the development of Huizhou mercantile lineage culture. Although "mercantile lineage" is a modern concept, it was becoming increasingly essential to the land of "prominent lineages" during Wang Daokun's time. If *Prominent Lineages in Xin'an* delineates for the first time the new Huizhou identity, featuring the added elements of Confucian values for merchants and kinswomen, Wang Daokun substantiated it in several significant ways to greatly enrich a mercantile lineage discourse, both describing and prescribing the social development over the late sixteenth century and beyond.

Wang Daokun's contributions lay in three interrelated dimensions of Huizhou mercantile lineage culture. He promoted lineage institutions, compiling an innovative genealogy for his own lineage and supporting the compilation of genealogies and construction of ancestral halls for others; he became the leading champion for Huizhou merchants, crafting a large number of merchant biographies or epitaphs honoring their vocation, encoding their new mercantile ethics, complimenting their business acumen and devotion to home lineages, and advocating their social advancement strategy of alternating between learning and trade; and he honored the practice of female chastity, compiling a new *Biographies of Exemplary Women* (Lienü zhuan) and recording a large number of local chastity martyrs and devoted women, thereby helping to promote the cult of female chastity in late Ming Huizhou.

As with the case of Cheng Minzheng, Wang Daokun's empire-wide standing and accomplishments enhanced his work and achievements at home. He represents another instance of Confucian scholar-official engagement in local matters,

83

especially during the last eighteen years of his life, which he spent living at home in retirement. Wang Daokun was the most influential and productive scholar-official from and for late Ming Huizhou, as Cheng Minzheng had been in his time, even though neither Wang nor Cheng were the highest-ranked officials that the prefecture produced during the second half of the Ming dynasty.[1] These two eminent figures, perhaps not incidentally, were linked to the two most prestigious and populous lineages of the region; they left behind an enormous amount of writings from which we can learn a great deal about Huizhou culture and its transformation from the mid- to the late Ming. Roughly three generations apart, the two were faced with different issues and, not surprisingly, had different responses. Cheng Minzheng spent his entire life in the mid-Ming when farming and study still constituted the dominant way of life, even as the seeds of commercialization were being nurtured, whereas Wang Daokun spent his entire adult life in the commercialized sixteenth century. The top priorities for Cheng Minzheng were to establish the primacy of his Cheng descent line in Huizhou (along with his Xin'an roots) and the importance of Huizhou within the entire realm; for Wang Daokun, they were to remold mercantile lineage culture and Confucian womanhood. Cheng Minzheng's philosophical musings presaged the coming of Wang Yangming, whereas Wang Daokun firmly belonged in the camp of the School of the Mind, as was reflected in the inclusivity of coverage in his genealogy and his merchant biographies. Cheng Minzheng was noted for his scholarly erudition, always serving at the court, whereas Wang Daokun enjoyed an empire-wide reputation as a man of letters while serving at various regional posts before reaching the center.

Relatively speaking, Wang Daokun has received more scholarly attention than Cheng Minzheng, in large part because of his literary reputation and many records of Huizhou merchants. These studies of Wang Daokun, however, have not attempted to examine all of his writings in light of his fashioning of Huizhou mercantile lineage culture. Nor has anyone explicitly examined his genealogy or his accounts of women, including his *Biographies of Exemplary Women*.[2] A full understanding of Wang Daokun's contribution to Huizhou social history in the late sixteenth century requires a balanced inquiry into all of his writings, his merchant biographies, and, especially, his lineage documents (including the compilation of his unique home genealogy) and records of devoted women. A balanced analysis will also help illuminate his differences from Cheng Minzheng and the development of Huizhou society over the course of the sixteenth century: from a land of prominent lineages to one increasingly shaped by mercantile lineages and their interests.

I begin with a brief biographical sketch of Wang Daokun to pave the way for illustrating the Huizhou mercantile lineage culture of which he was both product and producer.

BIOGRAPHICAL SKETCH

In many ways, Wang Daokun personified the mercantile lineage culture of Huizhou; he was also emblematic of late Ming literati life. He was born into a wealthy merchant family descended from Wang Hua, and his family had intermarried for generations with the prominent mercantile lineages of the Wus, Chengs, Huangs, and Fangs. His Song dynasty ancestor had moved back to Huizhou from Zhejiang, settling in Songmingshan, Shexian. The Wangs of Songmingshan had engaged in farming until his grandfather, Wang Shouyi (1468–1548), first ventured out of Huizhou to engage in trade in the late fifteenth century. Notably, Shouyi's commercial endeavors were initially encouraged and financially supported by his wife, the daughter of a merchant from the Xi'nan Wu lineage, in Shexian, that dominated the highly profitable salt trade in the Ming. Following his father-in-law, Shouyi soon established himself in business. Shouyi was also well educated, and he began teaching poems to Daokun, his eldest grandson, when he was just three years old. Thanks to his education and righteous character, Shouyi succeeded in the salt business in Zhejiang (his secondary ancestral place where he had important kinship ties), being eventually promoted to the position of *jijiu* (the forerunner of the position of salt "head merchant" or *zongshang* under the Qing) who coordinated salt trade (the biggest state monopoly) between merchants and the official salt bureau. He passed away in 1548, one year after his grandson earned the metropolitan *jinshi* degree and was appointed as a magistrate in Zhejiang. On his death bed, the eighty-year-old man spoke to Daokun's father, saying: "Liangbin, I, your father, will soon be gone. Your younger brother Liangzhi engages in trade and your son serves as an official. Please kindly remind them not to disregard the unfinished accomplishments of their forefathers; now I can close my eyes." The "unfinished accomplishments," in this context, were to glorify the ancestors by succeeding in producing both "prominent scholars" and "good merchants." This deathbed injunction implied that Daokun as an official should help out his merchant uncle. Shouyi's exhortation clearly carried enormous weight for Wang Daokun, as he used it to conclude his biography for his grandfather.[3]

Also influential on the growth of Wang Daokun was his father, Wang Liangbin (1504–1581), who, along with more than ten of his cousins and nephews, followed his father east to the coast to engage in commerce, helping to chart the Huizhou model of family business. Liangbin had only one expectation for his eldest son—to pass the civil service exams. In his youth, Wang Daokun was, according to the biographies prepared by his own son and grandson, particularly fond of historical romances and vernacular literature, but his father banned him from reading anything that was deemed useless. At night he would hide and read for pleasure by the light of fireflies. Once he even composed a *chuanqi* play out of an unofficial historical account, but his father found it and burned it, crying, "If you do not work for your proper calling, how can you make progress?"[4] Yet Daokun's curiosity about popular literature had already been planted in his heart. Wang Daokun was remarkably gifted, good at both the classics and other genres, including history and belles lettres. And he was the first in his descent line to become an established scholar-official.[5] At twenty, his father took him to Hangzhou to study the classical learning of the rites with a famous scholar, and two years later, in 1547, he succeeded in passing the metropolitan exam and earned the *jinshi* degree. Among the class of students who passed the 1547 metropolitan exam were future Grand Secretariat Zhang Juzheng (1525–1582) and the literary luminary Wang Shizhen (1526–1590).

Unlike Wang Shizhen, who had earned his literary fame before climbing the official ladder, Wang Daokun had a successful career in officialdom before earning literary recognition. Known for his administrative talent and pragmatism, he rose quickly from county magistrate to prefect, governor, and eventually vice minister of war. In the end, however, due to disagreement with some of Zhang Juzheng's personnel policies, he was forced to retire in 1575. He moved back to his beloved home region, living in his villa Taihan, located about four hundred meters from the Shexian County yamen, for the final eighteen years of his life.[6]

His long retirement gave Wang Daokun firsthand access to local matters as well as the time to reflect upon changes in local society. Most of his Huizhou-related writings were crafted during this period, including two innovative genealogies of his home lineage and a large number of biographies or epitaphs of Huizhou merchants and devoted women. While most of his prose and poetry are included in his massive *Taihan Collection* (Taihan ji), a number of his biographies of merchants and women were initially written for genealogies, including those of the Wangs of Songmingshan and their kinswomen, which are printed in the genealogy he compiled for his home descent line, *The Genealogy of the Sixteen Branches of the Lingshanyuan Wangs* (Lingshanyuan Wangshi shiliu zu pu; 1592). In his retirement, he also organized several literati clubs, including the Baiyu Society in 1580 (named after a hill in Shexian). The Baiyu Society marked his emerging leadership in intellectual circles; its members included several celebrated literati and scholar-officials, including Tu Long (1543–1605), Hu Yinglin (1551–1602), Pan Zhiheng (1556–1622), Xie Bi (compiler of the 1609 *Gazetteer of Shexian*), and Li Weizhen (1546–1626). By now, Wang Daokun enjoyed a literary reputation equal to that of Wang Shizhen, and these two leading lights were hailed as the "Two Simas."[7]

Among Ming literati, Wang Daokun's prose was some of the most difficult to understand. He practiced the so-called restored style of ancient prose (*fugu*) that was in vogue at the time, and he was eventually recognized as a leader of the *fugu* movement together with Li Panlong (1514–1570) and Wang Shizhen. The prose styles Wang Daokun admired and imitated all came from the pre-Tang period, and one style that particularly appealed to him was that of Sima Qian's *Records of the Grand Historian*, especially its *jizhuan* (annals and biography) format.

Wang Daokun authored one of the best commentaries on the great Ming novel *Water Margin* (Shuihu zhuan). *Water Margin* is full of stories that both criticize corrupt officials—and even a Song emperor—and praise chivalrous heroes driven by a strong sense of justice and righteousness (*xiayi*). These were the same values he highlighted as central to the ethic of Huizhou merchants. Xu Shuofang believes that the *Water Margin* commentary, three pages in length, is more valuable than any other piece in his *Taihan Collection*.[8] Xu's appraisal is understandable from the perspective of Chinese literature, but the *Taihan Collection* also contains rich material for making sense of Huizhou social development in the second half of the sixteenth century.

Also notable is Wang Daokun's achievement as a playwright. In 1560, during his tenure as the Xiangyang prefect, Wang Daokun authored four one-act plays collectively titled *Plays of the Great Elegant Hall* (Da yatang zaju). These included *Dream of Gaotang* (Gaotang meng), *Tragedy of the Luo River* (Luoshui bei), *Drawing Eyebrows* (Huamei), and *Recluses on the Lakes* (Wuhu you), all based on stories first narrated in the ancient texts that Daokun so admired: the *Zhaoming Collection of Writings*, the poetry of Song Yu, Ban Gu's *History of the Han Dynasty*, and Sima Qian's *Records of the Grand Historian*, respectively. Wang Daokun was among the first Ming playwrights to attempt to transform the northern *zaju* play into the *nanxi* (southern drama) format.[9] The four works in *Plays of the Great Elegant Hall* all feature historical figures, but they also reflected the playwright's concerns about the domination of the imperial court by the clique surrounding the corrupt top official Yan Song (1480–1567). The most notable of the four is *Recluses on the Lakes*, which portrays the legendary beauty Xishi in a positive light, in contrast to earlier literature in which she was blamed as a typical femme fatal who brought down the kingdom.[10] The focus on romance within the four plays reflects Wang Daokun's overall theory that drama should be the artistic expression of human feeling or passion: "As for poetry, song, and dance, all three must be based on [feeling or passion of] the heart, thereby giving rise to musical composition."[11] With these four romances, Wang Daokun anticipated the popular themes of late Ming drama, which championed the cult of *qing* (passionate love) under the influence of Wang Yangming's School of the Mind, while at the same time emerging as a staunch advocate for female chastity.[12]

Wang Daokun was an enthusiastic follower of Wang Yangming, even though he grew up in a Huizhou cultural atmosphere infused with Zhu Xi's School of Principle. In an essay discussing the Huizhou discourse, Wang Daokun proudly pointed out what Cheng Minzheng had valued most: the region had nurtured Zhu Xi and the two Cheng brothers, while at the same time declaring that in the Ming dynasty it was Wang Yangming who clarified the Confucian Way (*mingdao*).[13] Wang Yangming provided mid- to late Ming literati with a moral philosophy during a time of unpredictable emperors, who were often surrounded by corrupt and devious courtiers and eunuch chiefs who were in control of imperial power. By concentrating on one's own mind and remaining indifferent to changes beyond oneself, Confucian literati could maintain their moral integrity, regardless of whether or not they served in office.[14] Even Zhu Xi's ancestral place was swept by the popular tide of Wang Yangming's teaching of innate moral worth, especially after Wang Yangming's disciple, Xiong Shifang, became the Huizhou prefect in 1512. Emphasizing "clarifying ethics and promoting schools" (*minglun jianxue*) in his administrative approach, Xiong rebuilt Huizhou's most important school, the Ziyang Academy, for which his master Wang Yangming authored an essay stating: "There is nothing outside of the heart, no principle outside of the heart [*xinwai wushi, xinwai wuli*]. Erudite scholars study for this; interrogators interrogate about this; deep thinkers think about this; clarifiers clarify this; doers practice this."[15] Virtually all of the leading scholars associated with Wang Yangming toured Huizhou, including Wang Gen, Qian Dehong, Zou Shouyi, Liu Bangcai, Luo Rufang, and Wang Ji (1498–1583); they lectured at Ziyang or other academies on how "the streets are full of sages" and why "people's daily practice is the Way," attracting large numbers of local literati.[16] In several biographic accounts of local literati, Wang Daokun praised how they pursued Wang Yangming's learning with utmost earnestness or followed the lecture tours of Huizhou by the famous Yangming disciples, noting that these Huizhou followers of Wang Yangmingism had "soundly established their names."[17] In late 1575, not long after settling at home in retirement, Wang Daokun hosted Wang Ji on his tour of Huizhou, composing two poems in honor of the visit and noting that Wang Yangming's teaching "has spread throughout the realm."[18] He also befriended the famed scholar Jiao Hong (1541–1620), largely on account of their shared philosophic position with regard to the learning of the mind.[19]

For Wang Daokun, Wang Yangming was the greatest hero of the Ming dynasty. He states in his preface to the *Taihan Collection*, "The Great Ming opened up heaven day and night, thoroughly rebuilding the empire. Human talents and literary endeavors peaked during the Hong-Zheng-Jia-Long (1491–1573) era. Wang Yangming quickly rose with force; he asserted that *liangzhi* [good intuitive knowledge] carried on the disrupted learning, directly approaching the [true learning of the] Three Dynasties [Xia-Shang-Zhou] and belittled the Six Classics. As for mastery of the mind, it does not look like the law and yet works like the law."[20] In one of Wang Daokun's first official biographies drafted by his friend Xie Bi, he is succinctly identified as firmly belonging to the Yangming camp: "As for literature, his prose followed Zuo and Ma [Zuo Qiuming and Sima Qian] and his poems followed Duling [Du Fu]; as for philosophic learning, he revered Xiangshan [Lu Jiuyuan] from the past and Dongyue [Wang Yangming] more recently."[21]

This explains why Wang Daokun viewed Wang Yangming's School of the Mind as "uniquely stunning learning" [*juexue*].[22] For Wang Daokun, a man capable of engaging in both civil and military tasks, no scholar-officials of the

Ming dynasty were as outstanding. As he put it, "Sir Yangming . . . is equipped with both civil and military talents."[23] This corresponds well with Wang Yangming's emphasis on the unification of knowledge and action, which also marked Wang Daokun's daily approach. Unlike Cheng Minzheng, Wang Daokun did not author any formal philosophic treatises to explore the historical transmission of Confucian learning or discourse on human nature. Rather, he conveyed his philosophic leaning through the meanings embodied in both his acts and his nonphilosophic writings about changing social life (especially in his home region) as well as his literary works articulating his philosophical bent. Under the influence of Wang Yangming's notion of inner moral knowledge, Wang Daokun could largely come to terms with being cast out of politics in his retirement, which further enabled his focus on local matters. Wang Yangming also provided Wang Daokun with a new class calculus: advocating equity in terms of moral integrity (at least within the same lineage), which thereby paved the way for uplifting the social status of merchants and, at the same time, promulgating the new social advancement strategy of alternating between learning and commerce within local lineages.

A ONE-OF-A-KIND GENEALOGY

Wang Daokun shared many views with Cheng Minzheng, but he often moved a step further than his eminent Huizhou predecessor, reflecting the socioeconomic and intellectual changes that had taken place over the sixteenth century. One of those shared views had to do with the relation between the family (local society) and the state. As a good student of the *Great Learning*, Cheng Minzheng stated that "the rule of the family is like the law of the state." Wang Daokun shared this view, but pushed this belief further by inventing a new, bold genealogy format modeled on official history, in particular the format of his favorite *Records of the Grand Historian*. But whereas Cheng Minzheng exerted significant impact upon later genealogical compilations in Huizhou, Wang Daokun's stylistic innovations did not have a similar lasting influence. Nevertheless, Wang Daokun's unique genealogical format was consequential on another front—it had the effect of uplifting the status of merchants within the lineage and promoting women's virtue, thereby illustrating and promoting mercantile lineage culture. As we will see, the part of his genealogy that did not have a lasting influence was his format linking his descent line to the Zhou royal family. His inclusion of commoner kinspeople, including both merchants and kinswomen, was shared by, or had impact on, many other late Ming Huizhou genealogies.

One highly revealing insight into Wang Daokun's view of genealogy as history comes from the preface he penned for the genealogy of the Xi'nan Jiangs in Shexian, which also hints at his Wang Yangming–like philosophical positioning. After underscoring the need to "respect the ancestors thereby honoring the descent line; honor the descent line thereby harmonizing the lineage" (a stock statement, echoing Cheng Minzheng, which he made again in the preface to his genealogy), Wang Daokun stated,

> Zhongni [Confucius] authored the *Spring and Autumn*, covering a multitude of states and yet highlighting [the state of] Lu. The rites of Zhou were [best] represented in Lu, because of this it stood out. When Lu is highlighted, all of the other states are presented. In ancient times, each state had its history, so should families [*guo you guoshi jia yi yiran*]. Indeed, genealogy falls into the category of history [*puzhe shi zhi liu ye*]. Thus it is that there are people who treat the county yamen as their own house, who treat heaven as their own ancestor, who treat [the peoples from] the four seas as their own brothers, and who even treat the birds and animals as their same beings—all of these combine into one. Who would disagree with this?![24]

In addition to his straightforward likening of genealogy with official history, Wang Daokun also reveals that his Wang Yangming–like leanings undergird his innovative genealogical style; he erases state-society and elite-commoner differences. This would have profound implications for his views on not just the lineage but also its merchants and kinswomen.

The "modern" lineage is often seen as a local expression of Song neo-Confucianism.[25] Whether or how Wang Yangmingism was factored into the upsurge of genealogy compilation in the sixteenth century is still an open question, but we can certainly see the influence of Cheng Minzheng's thinking on moral leveling in this practice. Here, I shall go into great detail of the genealogy Wang Daokun compiled for his home lineage and its directly related branches in Shexian, *The Genealogy of the Sixteen Branches of the Lingshanyuan Wangs*, partially to illustrate the philosophical premise of his work. In his first preface to the genealogy, Wang Daokun clearly states that he was following Sima Qian in terms of format.[26] *The Lingshanyuan Wangs* falls into the genre of *jizhuan* (chronological tables and biographies), first invented by the Grand Historian Sima Qian. It is composed of ten volumes:

1. "The Abbreviated Basic Annals of the Zhou" (Zhou benji lue)
2. "The Abbreviated Hereditary House of the Lu" (Lu shijia lue)
3. "The Hereditary House of Yueguo" (Yueguo shijia)
4. "The Hereditary Chronological Table from Longxiang Onward" (Longxiang yixia shibiao)
5. "The Hereditary Chronological Table of the Home Branch" (Benzhi shibiao)
6. "The Hereditary Chronological Table of Affiliate Branches" (Fenzhi shibiao)
7. "Brief Biographies of the Hereditary Descent Line" (Shixi xiaozhuan)
8. "Collective Biographies" (Liezhuan)
9. "Records of Ancestral Tombs" (Qiumu zhi)
10. "Gazetteer of Lineage Documents" (Dianji zhi)

Many of these volume subtitles are directly borrowed from Sima Qian's *Records of the Grand Historian*, including "Basic Annals," "Hereditary House," "Hereditary Chronological Table," and "Collective Biographies."[27] Most strikingly, indeed virtually unprecedented, the genealogist dared to adopt the title of "Basic Annals" that Sima Qian (and all later historians of official histories) used exclusively to apply to accounts of kings or emperors for biographies of those within his (assumed) apical ancestry dating back to the Zhou dynasty. Wang Daokun's "Basic Annals," already revealed in the subtitle, is an abbreviated version of Sima Qian's "Basic Annals of the Zhou." Similarly, his "Hereditary House of the Lu" is an abbreviated version of Sima Qian's "Hereditary House of Lu's Duke of Zhou" (Lu Zhougong shijia). This genealogical arrangement dramatically elevated the pedigree of the Huizhou Wangs, further justifying their descent from the ancient royal family (which had been claimed by other Wang notables). Also notable is the elevation of Yueguo (Wang Hua) to "Hereditary House," a subtitle Sima Qian used to cover the prime minister or other top state officials. Yueguo was placed in the third volume, immediately following the first two volumes covering the Zhou "Basic Annals" and the Lu "Hereditary House," whereas his Han dynasty ancestor, General Longxiang (Wang Wenhe), was placed in volume 4 to lead the first ancestral tree (Hereditary Chronological Table) of the Huizhou Wangs. This placement clearly indicates that Wang Hua was treated as the apical ancestor of the Shexian (and Huizhou) Wangs, even though his thirteenth-generational ancestor Wang Wenhe was the first to cross the Yangzi River in the Later Han, honored as "the apical ancestor of Jiangnan" (Jiangnan shizu).[28] Wang Hua was given greater priority than Wang Wenhe also because, as explained in Wang Daokun's own preface, "Yueguo was a lord of righteousness while alive and turned into an enlightened deity upon death. Throughout the Tang-Song-Yuan-Ming, he was consistently conferred with titles of nobility and [worshipped with] sacrifices, therefore he is more than qualified [to be covered in] 'Hereditary House.'"[29]

To further enhance the credibility of the deep ancestry, as well as to demonstrate the honoring of the ancestors, Wang Daokun details the ancestral tombs in Huizhou in volume 9, tracing back as far as Lord Wang of Lu, the marquis of Yingchuan, who was first given the surname of Wang and whose tomb "is located thirty-eight *li* south of the seat [of Shexian]." Two more notable examples concern Wang Wenhe and Wang Hua: (1) "Lord Wenhe: his tomb is located nine *li* west of the prefectural capital . . . numbered 1346910; the tax on its mountain field was initially placed under the two households headed by Wang Ruchu and Wang Tiequan. In the twenty-first year of the Wanli reign [1592–1593] when the tax was newly calculated, [all ritual land] was listed under the household of Wang Longxiang, numbered 1"; and (2) "Lord Hua: Lord Yueguo long lived in the town of Huayang; he died on the third day of the third month of the twenty-third year in Chang'an, aged sixty-four. His sons carried his coffin back home, which was buried in the Yunlan Mountain of Shexian. His successive wives, née Qian, Ji, and Zhang, were buried together there. His mausoleum has enjoyed godly sacrifice, and its ritual land is exempted from taxation."[30] As Wang Daokun notes in his second preface regarding the ancestral tombs of the Huizhou Wangs, "from the end of the Han to the Tang, seven or eight out of ten are permanently attended to. From the first migrant ancestor, Lord Sili, onward, there have been *shimuhu* (permanent tenant houses) assigned to take care of their ancestral tombs generation after generation."[31] Wang Sili, the eleventh generational descendant from Wang Hua, active toward the end of the Tang dynasty, married into a Cheng family in Shexian's Tangmo, and his descendants blossomed into the sixteen branches recorded in volumes 5 and 6.

In terms of contents, if not the innovation of format and its symbolic implications, the last volume on lineage documents (Dianji zhi) is the most important and also the richest. Constituting more than two-thirds of the entire genealogy, it is further divided into twelve sections: 1. "Edicts or Imperial Proclamations" (Gao); 2. "Memorials" (Biaoshu); 3. "Biographies" (Zhuan); 4. "Records" (Ji); 5. "Prefaces" (Xu); 6. "Covenants" (Yue); 7. "Life Descriptions" (Zhuang or Xingzhuang); 8. "Epitaphs and Inscriptions" (Zhiming); 9. "Tomb Inscriptions" (Mubei or/and Mubiao); 10. "Prayers" (Jiwen); 11. "Eulogies" (Zanlei); 12. "Verses" (Shi).

Notably, some of the most revealing biographies of Wang merchants and kinswomen are covered in this volume, in addition to nearly fifty other biographic accounts. The substantial biographies included here are virtually all about commoners of recent times (mostly penned by Wang Daokun himself), different from the brief ones on selected figures in the ancestry that are covered in volumes 7 and 8. This arrangement ensured that the symbolic uplifting of the Wang pedigree in the first two to three volumes extended to the commoners covered in volume 10, as they were all purportedly descended from the Duke of Zhou and hence related to the Zhou royal family. Other lineage-related documents in the last volume include imperial edicts highlighting Wang Hua, memorials or policy recommendations by ancestral kinsmen, and records, prefaces, local lineage contracts (on ritual performances), prayers, and poems. Many of these documents were authored by famous or powerful local figures, including Zhu Xi, Qiu Jun, Cheng Minzheng, Zheng Yu (1298–1358), Wang Shunmin, Bao Xiangxian (1496–1568, *jinshi* 1529), Zhang Juzheng, Fang Liangshu (*jinshi* 1553), Wang Shizhen, and Tao Chengxue (Huizhou prefect from 1556 to 1560, *jinshi* 1547).[32] Zhu Xi starts his 1188 preface to an old Wang genealogy justifying the illustrious ancestry of the Huizhou Wangs and the powerful rewards reaped by the remarkable virtue of their apical ancestors: "The Xin'an Wangs are so prominent and prosperous that no other lineages can match [their nobility and prosperity]. Looking into the reason, it is largely because Duke Cheng of Lu had accumulated vast virtue and had been further supported by his benevolent, filial, and kind wife née Si. Thus, it is that their benevolence and grace have been cast down among the people. Heaven has rewarded [the Wangs], specially demonstrating its distinguished efficacy."[33]

Wang Daokun secured a preface for the genealogy from his friend Li Weizhen, a rising star in both official and literary circles. In the preface, this future minister of rites likened Wang's genealogy to the Five Classics and provided detailed reasoning for his analogy.[34] Setting aside whether his reasoning was justified or not, the effect of his preface was achieved. It honored, and by extension, authorized and authenticated, both the content and format of the genealogy, which was handsomely cut and printed.

As with Cheng Minzheng, Wang Daokun's commitment to writing a genealogy appears to have dated to his youth, when he assisted his father in compiling a family genealogy and learned from the latter that genealogy was "key to harmonizing the lineage." His busy schedule after passing the metropolitan exam had delayed this passion, although he had never completely forgotten it.[35] Later, his Zhejiang kinsman, the posthumously anointed minister of rites Wang Tang (1512–1588), urged Daokun to compile a composite genealogy covering the Wangs from both Huizhou and Zhejiang, which the latter declined. He chose, instead, to fix his attention on the sixteen branches in Shexian descended from Lord Sili.[36] His stated reason for rejecting the compilation of a composite genealogy was that by providing his work with a narrow focus, he could guarantee credibility. But might there have been any other unstated reasons? Like Cheng Minzheng (whom he highly respected, as can be seen from his inclusion of seven of Minzheng's writings in the *Lingshanyuan Wangs*), Wang Daokun also wanted to be an innovative genealogist, which, ironically, would prevent him from copying Minzheng by compiling a composite genealogy. After all, there already had been a massive composite genealogy of the Huizhou Wangs printed in 1571.[37]

More importantly, in reflection of the social changes since Cheng Minzheng's death, namely rapid commercialization and the changes it had wrought on local lineage life (including gender relations), what was urgent for Wang Daokun was not just to further enhance lineage institutions (already well established in Huizhou), but to further build upon the new discourse of Huizhou mercantile lineage culture. In addition to numerous prefaces to Huizhou genealogies and commemorative records on the construction of local ancestral halls, Wang Daokun stood out for his passion for crafting biographic accounts of two commoner subgroups: merchants and kinswomen.[38] Some of the best of these narratives are included in the *Lingshanyuan Wangs*. Viewed from this perspective, his decision to focus on the sixteen branches of the Shexian Wangs, as well as his innovative genealogical format, was determined by the twofold related needs of illustrating his illustrious ancestry (claimed or real), and finding the best ways to enhance the social status of the two commoner kin subgroups, as merchants and kinswomen were becoming increasingly important for local lineages in the late sixteenth century. In other words, by the late sixteenth century, the compilation of genealogy per se was no longer the top agenda for Wang Daokun. What the genealogist felt most passionate about (or what he felt most needed elaboration) was the mercantile lineage discourse.[39] All of this may explain the innovative format of his genealogy and the narrow focus of the sixteen branches, which at once further authenticated the unmatchable pedigree of the entire Wang descent line and covered in great detail its commoner kinspeople. In its entirety, this format had the effect of shaping the lineage identity with greatly enriched elements of mercantile lineage culture. In this goal, Wang Daokun was successful, even though his innovative format did not have much impact on subsequent compilation of Huizhou genealogies.[40]

Leaving aside the uniqueness of his genealogical style, Wang Daokun appears to have been influenced to a certain degree by the earliest extant Wang genealogy from Huizhou, Wang Songtao's *Origins of the Wangs* (Wangshi yuanyuan lu). This Yuan dynasty genealogy is also composed of ten *juan*, but it differs from Wang Daokun's in terms of format, coverage, and contents.[41] Songtao's genealogy claims that the Wang descent line originated with the Yellow Emperor, distinguished itself from others with Houji, formed its lineage with Ji-Lu (referring to the Duke of Zhou), and gained its surname at Yingchuan, whose lord was the second son of Duke Cheng of Lu. This lord was named Wang, as the lines of his hands looked like the archaic character of Wang; he was later honored as the marquis of Wang after being enfeoffed at Yingchuan, and his descendants thereafter use Wang as their surname.[42] In addition, Wang Hua is highlighted in virtually every volume except the first one that focuses on the origins of the Wang surname (*Yuanxing*). These shared features noted, the Yuan version does not carry the governing titles for the first two volumes (even though it features subtitles for each section within the two volumes), and it clearly covers the Wangs from the entire prefecture (and even beyond). Variations of format and coverage aside, the contents differ even more sharply between Wang Daokun's and Wang Songtao's versions. We can look to Songtao's sixth volume as a telling example. Titled *Records of Famous (Kinsmen)* (Chuiming ji), it concentrates on recording scholar-officials. Starting with Wang Hua, the volume goes on to cover around two hundred *jinshi* degree holders from the Wang descendants (with a brief biography), mostly from the Song dynasty. The volume preface clearly states that it records only the kinsmen noted for virtuous deeds and accomplishments in both state service and scholarly writings, leaving unrecorded those who quickly succeeded in the various "miscellaneous skills" of sorcery, medicine, technology, and commerce" (*wuyigonggu zaji*).[43] In contrast, Wang Daokun's genealogy, in its lengthiest tenth volume, covers many detailed biographies of merchants and kinswomen, from one main descent line.[44]

Arguably, Wang Daokun's adoption of the Grand Historian's "royal" format to illuminate his ancestral pedigree and his narrowed coverage of the directly related sixteen branches in a local area of Shexian bespoke his Wang Yangming–like philosophic positioning of erasing distinctions between the central state and local society, between official history and family genealogy, and between elites and commoners. In the hands of Wang Daokun, Cheng Minzheng's localist approach went even deeper: a kinship community, and in this case, one prominent local mercantile lineage, was directly related to the ancient royal house symbolizing political authority. Here we see an outstanding case (quite exceptional even for a region filled with great families) illustrating that a state-society continuum was more or less organic in Confucian thinking, and not just in the thinking of Cheng Minzheng, Wang Yangming, and Wang Daokun. The more locally rooted a society was, the more prepared it was to reach up to the center.

The same format and localist coverage, however, also betrays an inherent dilemma. On the one hand, Wang Daokun tended to erase the elite-commoner divide in his writing, but on the other, he still tried to affiliate his lineage with the ancient royal house of Zhou that was beloved by the Confucians and arguably the most esteemed royal family in Chinese history, as if commoners alone were not sufficiently elevated or esteemed. The same contradictory premise, as will be discussed later in this chapter, also is inherent in his approach toward the merchant-gentry (and sojourning men and home lineage) relations. Still, Wang Daokun mostly fixed his attention on local matters, and especially the two commoner groups of merchants and kinswomen, as they constituted two key—and closely related—ingredients of new mercantile lineage society.

MERCHANTS AND MERCANTILE LINEAGE CULTURE

China historians, and especially Huizhou specialists, have claimed that Wang Daokun was "a powerful spokesman" for merchants or, more accurately, Huizhou merchants in late Ming China, as he produced more merchant biographies than any other late Ming literatus.[45] Reading these biographies thoroughly, and especially in the context of Wang Daokun's entire corpus of writings and of sixteenth-century Huizhou, I argue that he was more than a spokesman for Huizhou merchants. He was, more accurately, the spokesman for Huizhou mercantile lineage culture. I make this observation based on my reading of his merchant biographies as well as his Huizhou-related writings; this reading has significant implications for properly diagnosing the character of not just Huizhou merchants but of late Ming Huizhou kinship society as a whole: merchants were treated as integral to local prominent lineages.

The late sixteenth century marked the peak of commercialization under the Ming empire, undergirding an era of great social and cultural change. Huizhou was central to this transformative period, and its native son Wang Daokun happened to live at home in retirement where he gathered firsthand information and observation, thereby enabling him to produce most of his Huizhou-related writings. Of these, the most notable are his merchant accounts, including biographies (*zhuan*), life descriptions (*xingzhuang*), and epitaphs (*muzhiming* or *mubiao*). For the sake of convenience, I will simply call them biographies. In total, he penned 112 merchant biographies, seventy-one of which focus on Huizhou merchants (although only forty-five out of seventy-one contain sufficient narrative detail).[46] Thus far, historians have used these biographies, in addition to other contemporaneous materials, to understand some of the key aspects of the great transformative era of the late Ming, ranging from Huizhou merchant capital formation and types and the running of their businesses to the rise of merchant status and the new mercantile ethos.[47] What has not been fully explored is the social embedding of Huizhou merchants, especially in terms of their position within home lineages and family life, central to which was the husband-wife and mother-son relationships. As a whole, it should be noted, Wang Daokun's merchant biographies are particularly detailed in terms of these lineage- and family-related aspects. Integrating these details with previously observed features, we can see the ways in which Wang Daokun's literary production greatly enhanced Huizhou mercantile lineage culture.

To analyze these details such that they illustrate a larger pattern, I have prepared a summary of Wang Daokun's forty-five biographies of Huizhou merchants (see appendix, this volume).[48] Through these biographies we see Wand Daokun's efforts to raise the social status of Huizhou merchants. This was in accord with Wang Daokun's philosophic leanings, which, partially rooted in Wang Yangming–like belief in popular sagehood, tended to elevate the moral standing and social status of ordinary people. Wang Yangming famously stated, "The four categories of the people differ in vocations but share the same Way, as they all devote their hearts [to their work] the same way." He further rejected the conventional disdain for merchants: "Although engaging in trade all day long, [merchants] are not prevented from becoming sages or worthies."[49] By the late Ming, the sheer number of merchant biographies by Wang Daokun (and other literati) spoke to the socioeconomic significance Huizhou merchants had earned in local kinship communities.

Perusing these biographical accounts, however, we can read certain mixed messages. To begin with, the titles of these biographies never identify their subjects as merchants (shanggu); instead, they are called chushi ("untitled gentryman," a scholar without an exam degree), a respectful term that made them comparable to the local gentry who had succeeded in the civil service exams. This term indicates that a large percentage of Huizhou merchants that Wang Daokun recorded were indeed well educated, especially those who had switched from pursuit of the exams to sojourning trade (see appendix, this volume). Specifically, according to Zhu Wanshu, out of the more than seventy biographies that Wang Daokun penned for Huizhou merchants, forty-three had engaged in classical learning in preparation for the exams before switching to trade. Other late Ming records of Huizhou merchants, from literati such as Li Weizhen and Yuan Zhongdao (1570–1623), also indicate they were well educated.[50]

That merchants were frequently called chushi instead of shanggu suggests that they preferred this appellation, and this preference seems revealing of their self-image. After all, some Huizhou merchants who were recorded in Wang Daokun's accounts, including his own grandfather, still called themselves "mean traders" (gushu; see appendix, entry 23).[51] Even in the emerging commercial capital of Huizhou, the merchant stigma continued to linger. Part of the reason for this was that the era was noted for its "craze for money," and there was a critical response to this trend. As Timothy Brook has shown, late Ming scholar-officials such as the Shexian magistrate Zhang Tao decried the corruption of a transactional age.[52] Zheng Zhizhen (1518–1595), Wang Daokun's Huizhou contemporary, wrote a satirical song called "Ten Not So Dears" (*Shi buqin*) that captured such sentiments; it was based on a folk-ballad style known as *lianhua lao* (lotus petals fall) and was incorporated into the popular ritual opera *Mulian*.[53] The song starts with a complaint about the unfair treatment by "dearest" heaven and earth regarding the rich and poor; it proceeds next to human relations, calling attention to the capriciousness of those "dearest" of kin:

> Dearest parents sometimes are not so dear,
> Actually, parents are often not so kind.
> If their kids don't see to their every need,
> They mutter and grumble all the time.
> *Chorus*: Ah, lotus, lotus petals fall.

The song offers a running commentary on how money has undermined all kinds of "dear" human relationships, including those between parents and children, older and younger brothers, husbands and wives, and in-laws, relatives, and friends. The final verse underlines the corrupting influence of money:

> Dearest friends sometimes are not so dear,
> Actually, friends are often not so kind.
> When you're loaded with money and wine,
> Friends flock to you in droves,
> When you're down and out, there's not a soul to be found.
> *Chorus*: Ah, lotus, lotus petals fall.

In this cultural milieu, the preference for the appellation *chushi* (untitled gentrymen) instead of *shanggu* (merchants) makes perfect sense.

The image of Huizhou merchants outside of their home region was even more conflicted, as can be seen in a set of late Ming vernacular short stories. A recent study on Huizhou merchants in Ming-Qing literature notes that in fifteen late Ming short story collections, there are forty tales that feature Huizhou merchants. While some characters are generous and gentrified, the majority are depicted as greedy, stingy, litigious, or lecherous, as well as being subordinate to scholar-officials.[54] In the rest of the country, these negative images of Huizhou merchants overshadowed the positive ones, as can be seen in these popular stories. All of these collections were printed in the post–Wang Daokun era, but they were based on the popular stories in circulation during Wang's lifetime, an era when Huizhou merchants emerged as a dominant mercantile group. Within this cultural atmosphere, Huizhou merchants and their defenders responded to such sentiments by emphasizing their moral worth through biographic titles such as *chushi*, implicitly referring to their educated or culturally positive characteristics (and by implication also to their links to prominent local lineages).

Wang Daokun did not invent the term *chushi*. It had already appeared in *Prominent Lineages in Xin'an* and even earlier individual genealogies. During the mid-century, however, the official prefectural gazetteer still reserved the term for scholars or literati who were not titled (either because they had failed or had not participated in the exams); it was not used for righteous merchants.[55] A new and even loftier term was *sufeng*, literally meaning "enfeoffed without a noble title," which was used to refer to a successful merchant as gentleman-like, yet without a title or an examination degree. The term had first been coined by Sima Qian to refer to successful traders, but had fallen into disuse until, to the best of my knowledge, it reemerged in Huizhou documents during Wang Daokun's time with this new meaning. Fang Yulu, Wang Daokun's junior in-law, was a famous ink merchant and also a poet. One of his poems identifies great enterprise with *sufeng*: "In untitled nobility there is a great enterprise; inscrutable discourse brings out famed figures."[56] With the term *sufeng*, Huizhou merchants equated themselves with the local gentry. As the most important token of this change in status, especially given the kinship values in the region, the *sufeng* were now considered as pursuing a vocation that could enable them to "promote our lineages" (appendix, entries 29 and 31), which, along with "glorifying our ancestors," previously had been reserved only for kinsmen who had earned exam degrees.[57] Still, merchants in the late Ming were in no position to replace the gentry, which had replaced the aristocratic clans after the Tang-Song transition to become the new leading social class. Instead, it was a mutual penetration between the two social categories that took place in Huizhou.

Out of this mutual penetration emerged what can be called the Huizhou social strategy, alternating among brothers or generations between classical learning (*ru*) and trade (*gu*), which Wang Daokun promoted via his documentation of social practice in his biographies (appendix, entry 37):

> The capital of Xin'an, with one scholar for every three merchants, is indeed a land rich in literary traditions. Just as merchants seek handsome profits, scholars strive for high honor. Only after one has exhausted his effort on behalf of Confucian learning with no result does he let go of study and fasten on to trade. Once he has joined those who enjoy high profits, he prefers his descendants, for the sake of their future, to let go of trade and fasten on to study. Letting go and fastening on thus alternates so that one can enjoy either an income of ten thousand bushels of grain or the prestige of a retinue of one thousand horse carriages. This can be likened to the revolution of a wheel, with its spokes pointing to the ground in turn. We Xin'an people are never devoted to commerce alone, but are judicious in choosing our career path.[58]

It was in the context of describing two merchant families who had produced the two highest metropolitan *jinshi* degree holders, including the biographer himself, that Wang Daokun made his famous statement, "In what way is a good merchant inferior to a prominent scholar?!"[59] Historians have tended to invest much into this statement, seeing in it merchants' decisive climbing of the social ladder.[60] Although this assessment probably is not incorrect, it has sometimes been taken out of context. Wang Daokun was clearly speaking of the obviously successful Huizhou social strategy: merchant families strove to join gentry circles while the gentry accommodated to trade. In addition, the adamant tone of Wang's statement is itself revealing. He was massaging the collective ego of merchants, some of whom still viewed themselves as "mean traders," especially amid the late Ming atmosphere of condemning the craze for money. At the same time, he was assuaging those sojourning merchants who needed to engage in trade to support brothers pursuing exam success, or those students-turned-merchants who were homesick and frequently complained about the unfortunate fate of sojourning.[61]

Most importantly, the Huizhou social strategy was deeply rooted in the local kinship tradition, as the alternating pursuit of exam and commercial success would not have worked so effectively without local mercantile lineage investment practices. As a local saying put it: "Use [the wealth from] commerce to pursue literary studies, use literary studies to enter officialdom, use official posts to protect commercial adventures."[62] As seen in the appendix, Wang Daokun took pains to report the family life and kinship-related activities of Huizhou merchants, often with far more detail than business pursuits. Even in those sections of a biography that focus on business, we still learn a good deal about the working of kinship connections, including hiring poor kinsmen as workers (appendix, entry 32), or kinsmen who teamed up to trade outside of Huizhou, or wives who contributed their dowry for business start-up capital (appendix, entry 23). Why, then, was Wang Daokun so concerned with family-lineage aspects of merchant life?

Timothy Brook, in his beautifully crafted history of Ming commerce and culture, perceptively illustrates a convergence of the merchant and gentry by describing the former's mimicry of the latter's cultural gestures, while also briefly quoting Wang Daokun on Huizhou families that alternated between the two vocations.[63] The unstated assumption of this perspective of a shifting identity is still class-bound. But in Huizhou, quite simply, merchants and home lineages or mercantile lineages were inseparable. When Wang Daokun wrote about Huizhou merchants, he was reflecting not just merchants as individuals, but also local mercantile lineage culture as a whole; this coverage was both a reflection and reinforcement of the ongoing social practice. In Huizhou, personal identity was kinship defined, especially after the mid-sixteenth-century publication of *Prominent Lineages in Xin'an*. This is one of the reasons why spouse selection highlighted lineage affiliation without regard to wealth. By extension, class distinction was overshadowed by kinship distinction, especially for a prosperous and populous lineage that constituted a socially complicated community itself, including the various social groupings of gentry, merchants, peasants, and artisans (in addition to non-kin tenants or bondservants).[64] And in Huizhou, the demographic and social domination by those "prominent lineages" was overwhelming.

Here we see another potential reason for why Wang Daokun used the identity-blurring terms *chushi* and *sufeng* to refer to merchants, many of whom had once been examination students. The term *gu* (trade, trader) is only used in the biographic narratives, but more often than not it is used as a verb, indicating not an identity but the activity. At the same time, the biographer was often careful to underscore the previous pursuit of study or the continued love of book reading by these men. In a typical Huizhou expression, they "traded and yet loved being Confucian" (*gu'er haoru*; appendix, entry 45). Based on his own experience, as well as his observation of many local families and lineages, Wang Daokun wrote about merchants in their relations with gentry culture on the one hand and with home lineages on the other. This alternating or shifting gentry-merchant identity was key to the prosperous Huizhou mercantile lineage culture, which in turn shored up the capital for the successful pursuit of learning. Merchant status was indeed elevated, and yet this did not lead to the creation of a distinctive, or independent, merchant culture, due to the dominance of gentry culture or, in Huizhou, the gentrified mercantile lineage culture as a whole.[65]

Wang Daokun singled out one ingredient of Huizhou mercantile ethics, *jiexia* (chivalrous righteousness and generosity), to highlight virtually all of his merchant biographies (see appendix). Notably, Wang Daokun even used a failed merchant but a good family man named Shen Wenzhen to emphasize the significance of generous righteousness: no matter how much he had lost in business, Shen upheld the principle of righteousness (*dajie*) by being devoted to his mother and constantly urging his son to pursue Confucian learning (appendix, entry 4).[66] This emphasis may have been a reflection of Wang Daokun's personal character and predilections. Perhaps it was for the same reason that he loved the novel *Water Margin*, which features many righteous and generous outlaws. Wang Daokun also appears to have been a person of integrity and righteousness. Despite a dispute with Grand Secretariat Zhang Juzheng, which led to his early retirement, he still included Zhang's felicitation commemorating the seventieth birthday of Wang's father in his genealogy. In fact, this was a somewhat risky choice, as Zhang had by then been disgraced by the Wanli emperor.[67] A more notable example has to do with the different attitudes Wang Daokun and his good friend Wang Shizhen took toward the disgraced Zhang. Both Wangs wrote letters celebrating the seventieth birthday of Zhang's father. Wang Shizhen first published his letter in a collection of his essays, which became widely known. Six years later, after Zheng Juzheng had been condemned, Wang Shizhen excised the letter from his collection when it was reprinted. When Wang Daokun published his collection of essays toward the end of his life, however, he included his commemorative letter without changing a word.[68]

Personal character aside, Wang Daokun may have highlighted the merchant virtue of righteous generosity because it was not only good for assuring merchants long-term success in the outside commercial realm but also, more importantly, crucial to the fostering of home kinship communities. Wang Daokun occasionally mentions the righteous deeds of Huizhou merchants in business transactions (appendix, entry 33), but frequently features their righteous generosity in helping kinspeople (appendix, entries 7, 12, 21, 23, 30, 32, 38, 44) and contributions to consolidating home lineage institutions, ranging from setting up ritual land and building ancestral halls to reclaiming ancestral tomb land (appendix, entries 1, 15, 17, 18, 22, 31, 36, 40, 43, 44, 45).

Clearly, merchants' kinship-related activities, along with the alternating pursuit of commerce and exam success, were the central concerns of Wang Daokun's merchant accounts, and they were the main characteristics of Huizhou mercantile lineage culture. Simply put, especially at a time when it was widely claimed that local customs were in decline (appendix, entry 26) and increased numbers of sojourning merchants posed a threat to kinship cohesiveness, nothing was more important for local lineages—financially, at least—than securing support from the vast resources of these sojourning men. That importance could be realized only if they were steeped in the values of righteous generosity and care for their families and lineages. Highlighting and securing the financial contributions of merchants to enhancing home lineages certainly also raised their social status, further blurring the merchant-gentry boundary within the home community. As Joanna Handlin Smith has astutely noted, invoking Lewis Hyne, charity "is a way of negotiating the boundary of class . . . it is the 'tyranny of gift,' which uses the bonding power of generosity to manipulate people."[69]

Writing biographies of merchants thus was itself a part of constructing new mercantile lineage ethics. Moreover, these merchant accounts would most likely end up being reprinted in the genealogies of the profiled merchants' home lineages, again, a key lineage institution. In the late Ming, after all, the genealogy was the best, or most readily available, venue in which to publicize these accounts (in part explaining why merchants were eager to make contributions to home genealogy compilations).[70] Five of Wang Daokun's biographies on the Wang merchants were included in his own genealogy; eventually these accounts would also be included in his *Taihan Collection*. Wang Daokun, given his reputation as a famed scholar-official in retirement, was solicited as an author of merchant biographies because his name would glorify not just the profiled merchants, but also their home lineages when those biographies were printed in their genealogies.[71]

Most of the merchants Wang Daokun profiled dealt in salt, which makes sense given the Huizhou dominance in the salt trade and his own family's deeply involvement in that same trade. A most vivid expression of the relation of Huizhou merchants with their home lineages, again with a focus on salt merchants, is offered in an epitaph Wang Daokun penned in memory of a distant uncle who "traded salt in Huai [Yangzhou] while building an [ancestral] hall at home" (*Yanjia zai Huai, tanggou zai li*).[72]

Wang Daokun's focus on salt merchants may call into question the reliability or objectivity of his narratives (as does the fact that he only profiled "good," successful men). This nevertheless reflects the nature of virtually all literati narratives of social life in late imperial times. Literati always had their own preferred focus in their writings. They selected details and framed their stories to highlight or convey their preferred meanings or discourses. The merchant stories Wang Daokun chose to tell illuminated some key aspects of mercantile lineage culture, including alternating between trade and learning, sojourning men's contributions to home lineages, and ideal mercantile ethics. From other source materials as well as recent studies, however, we can be assured that his narratives reflected the larger pattern of local mercantile lineages as well as the deeds and passions of Huizhou merchants as a collective group (if not as individuals).[73] Moreover, they were also endowed with a prescriptive power of further enhancing the larger social pattern, influencing others to follow the suit. Wang Daokun's narratives undoubtedly played a role in contributing to the trends shown in the following numbers and records. His home county in the subsequent Qing dynasty produced five top examination graduates (*zhuangyuan*), 296 metropolitan *jinshi* degree holders, and nearly one thousand provincial *juren* degree holders (including Shexian natives registered at home and elsewhere) between 1664 and 1904.[74] From 1646 to 1802, during the second boom era of Huizhou merchants (the first one being in Wang Daokun's time), fewer than 250 Lianghuai salt merchant families, many of which were patrilineally linked to mercantile lineages back in Wang Daokun's home county, generated 139 *jinshi* and 208 *juren*.[75] The "glories" Huizhou mercantile lineages achieved in the post–Wang Daokun era should not be attributed to Wang alone; they had grown out of a strategy established in the late Ming era. In other words, what Wang Daokun promoted was a shared mercantile lineage discourse.

FEMALE CHASTITY AND RECORDING THE OTHER HALF OF MERCANTILE LINEAGE

As notable as Wang Daokun's attention to merchants is his profiling of Huizhou women. This is manifested not just in the sheer number of biographies on the two social groups, but also in his concentration on the social value they shared, with a gendered division key to making mercantile lineages work smoothly. In his *Taihan Collection* alone, we find at least sixty-six records on women, written in various formats including longevity tributes (*shouxu*), biographies (*zhuan*), life descriptions (*xingzhuang*), epitaphs (*muzhiming*), prayers (*jiwen*), and tomb inscriptions (*mubiao*). In addition, there are about thirty more pieces in the format of epitaphs or tomb inscriptions jointly covering both husband and wife. Many of the women profiled were linked to merchants or gentrymen (or scholar-officials) either as their wives, mothers, or daughters, and many were profiled for their role in maintaining harmonious and successful family relations within the larger mercantile lineage. Huizhou merchants' wives played an important role in assisting husbands' commercial careers beyond Huizhou, while they themselves lived extremely frugal lives back home taking care of parents-in-law and raising children. They also helped sustain the Huizhou social strategy by instructing or supporting sons in alternating between pursuit of examination and commercial success. Wang Daokun's many biographic accounts of Huizhou women deserve attention for their illumination of family life, gender relations, and other aspects of social life, but this section focuses on the biographic accounts of female chastity and integrity (*jielie*), as these female values help illustrate another key ingredient of Huizhou mercantile lineage culture in the late Ming: the formation of the cult of female chastity.

The value underlying *jielie* is firm integrity that calls for righteous and heroic deeds of self-sacrifice, such as lifelong widowhood or suicide upon being widowed, comparable to the *jiexia* Wang Daokun used to characterize good businessmen. Only eight pieces on *jielie* (in the forms of biographies, epitaphs, and prayers) are included in the *Taihan Collection*, one of which nevertheless covers seven chastity martyrs linked to Wang Daokun's own lineage. The limited number of *jielie* pieces included in the *Taihan Collection* does not matter much, given that Wang Daokun also covered many such women in his family genealogy and further compiled his own version of *Biographies of Exemplary Women* (Lienü zhuan), indicating his uppermost attention to the matter of female virtue, and *jielie* integrity above all.

Wang Daokun was among the first famous high-ranking scholar-officials to reinvigorate the *Biographies of Exemplary Women* tradition in the late Ming.[76] It not only expanded the collection to sixteen volumes, but also started the popular late Ming trend of illustrating such books for women. For those exemplars featuring Huizhou women, he added his characteristic comments after the narrative.[77] Of the sixteen volumes of Wang's expanded version, the last two cover female exemplars, mostly chastity martyrs, from the second half of the Ming (up to Wang's time), more than half of whom are from Huizhou, fourteen in total, including four chaste maidens (*zhenlie* or *zhennü*).[78]

One chastity story concerns a Ms. Fang Xizhang, the daughter of a local (gentry?) man named Fang Haozhi of Wuyuan (which explains, perhaps, the use of her given name; most female exemplars were simply identified by kinship terms). Ms. Fang lost her husband Hu Henghua almost immediately after their wedding. Upon recovering from fainting three times, she decided to use all of her dowry to finance Hu's funeral and also to build an empty tomb for herself, on the right side of Hu's grave. She served her mother-in-law well for a full day before she went to her husband's tomb, kneeling down in the company of her mother-in-law to tell the dead man that she had completed all she needed to do. She then hanged herself upon returning home. After the narrative, Wang Daokun noted that Wuyuan, as "the ancestral place of Zhu Xi," had no lack of exemplars of *zhongxiaojieyi* (loyalty, filial piety, chastity, and righteousness); he acclaimed Ms. Fang for being on a par with any of the ancient chastity martyrs.[79]

Another such biography is about a woman from the Shaxi Baos of Shexian, who was married to Wang Yingsu, a sojourning merchant who worked hard but had no success. Yingsu's family barely scraped by, and she alone took meticulous care of her parents-in-law for ten years until, in 1564, her husband returned home after having fallen terribly ill. Realizing he would soon die, Wang Yingsu suggested to his mother that Ms. Bao, still young and having endured hardships over the past ten years, be remarried to a proper man after his death. Overhearing the conversation, Ms. Bao felt deeply wounded. She first looked around for good physicians, talked to every kinsman for possible support, and prepared all the things needed for her husband's funeral. She then told Yingsu, "I've heard what you said to Mother. My only desire is to follow you in death!" After making all preparations for the funeral for her husband, she took poison and died, sitting with equanimity in the main bedroom, firm in her commitment "to serve her husband in the underworld." Three days later, Wang Yingsu passed away. In a separate comment after the narrative, Wang Daokun praised Ms. Bao for being as outstanding as any chastity martyr of medieval times (*zhonggu zhenlie*).[80]

Wang Daokun's renewed expansion of *Biographies of Exemplary Women* undoubtedly contributed to the rising cult of female chastity, a hallmark of late Ming culture (explored in depth in chapter 4). This female chastity cult was male-centered. It was also kinship-centered in the works of Wang Daokun; often lurking in the background of the stories he told of female martyrs was the patrilineal establishment of local lineages. Highly revealing is the tale of Maiden Fang of Qimen, who was engaged to the exam student Li Zongmin of Xiuning. She was "widowed" at sixteen before the marriage could be held. Devastated but devoted, she insisted on participating in Li's funeral, which would amount to publicly acknowledging her commitment to her dead fiancé. While her parents tried to talk her into selecting another suitable man to marry, Maiden Fang said that even though she had never met her husband, since she was engaged to Li, she would be "the wife of Li while alive and the ghost of Li in death." She refused to eat anything for several days before her parents realized that her commitment would not be altered. They prepared a sizable dowry and sent the chaste maiden to Li's home village. Several hundreds of the Li kinspeople, sad yet pleased, all came out to welcome Maiden Fang. Upon seeing Li's coffin, she threw herself to the ground and wailed. Wailing day and night in rags, she wanted to commit suicide. Her parents-in-law and Li's kinspeople tried in tears to calm her down. When she finally pulled herself together, she said, "my husband is my heaven; with heaven gone, I am dead." Eventually, realizing her duty to serve her fiancé's family, she gave up the plan to kill herself and lived a widowed life, taking good care of her parents-in-law.[81] More extreme than the kneeling, and even, perhaps, the suicide, of Widow Fang (Hu Henghua's wife) was the "widowed" Maiden Fang who performed a lifelong obeisance to her dead fiancé, his parents, and his kinspeople.

This male- and kinship-centered thread in Wang Daokun's *Biographies of Exemplary Women* also permeated the narratives included in his *Taihan Collection*. Characteristically, none of the women are given personal names, except the chaste widow Sun, née Fan, who is listed as having the revealing personal name, Jingui (Golden Inner Quarters), which was given to her by her mother-in-law. Her mother-in-law talked Jingui out of committing suicide upon being widowed and treated her as a daughter; the devoted widow treated her parents-in-law as her own parents. At the beginning of the narrative, Wang Daokun proudly noted that both the Caoshi Suns and Lintang Fans stood out in the booming town of Haiyang as two prominent lineages (actually mercantile lineages, as can be shown from other sources), and they intermarried for generations. Toward the end of the narrative, he further compares the way of being a wife as identical to the way of being an official (*qidao chendao yiye*); both lay in absolute devotion to the patriarch (*zhuanhu baozhu*).[82]

The most notable account of women exemplars in Wang's collection is "Biographies of the Seven Chastity Martyrs" (Qilie zhuan), which recounts the "heroic" deeds of seven women from his own lineage; these biographies are also covered in his genealogy.[83] Instead of supplying comments only at the end of the narrative, Wang Daokun also adds opening comments, which promote the characteristics of his descent line: "My lineage has stood out in our prefecture for a long time. Not only are the men talented; even our virtuous women are always notable. Since my coming of age, seven notable kinswomen among my relatives have martyred themselves to maintain their chastity. These chastity martyrs are either from or married into my lineage, and the martyring took place within the past thirty years." The first among them is the wife (again from the Caoshi Suns) of Wang Yongxi, a poor vendor from the prominent Songmingshan Wangs. As Wang Daokun tells it, Yongxi began to develop a serious disease a few years after marriage. Similar to the story of Wang Yingsu and his wife, Yongxi wanted his wife to remarry after he died, but his wife was committed to serving only one man in her life; she took poison and killed herself ten days before Yongxi died. Perhaps it was no coincidence that both Yingsu and Yongxi were equally unsuccessful in business, and that their wives met a similar fate.

The second of the biographies concerns the daughter of Wang Tiangui, whose husband died while sojourning to Luzhou only several months after their wedding. She fainted three times and wanted to die for her husband. But since her mother-in-law was ill, the woman continued to take care of her. Soon her mother-in-law passed away, however, she sought a moment of privacy during the Lantern Festival in 1553 to commit suicide. She was just twenty years old.

Two years later, a Wang woman threw herself into a river upon the death of her sick husband. Seven years after this, a woman née Cheng, the wife of Wang Yizhong, the deputy governor of Guangxi, committed suicide when Yizhong was killed by bandits during a local revolt. Upon committing suicide, she was honored with a spirit tablet in her husband's shrine. In 1565, Wang Yingsu's wife committed suicide. This story, also covered in Wang's *Biographies of Exemplary Women*, suggests the importance it signaled to the author, underscoring the kinship-centered values behind the martyred deeds of Wang's wife.

During the first year of the Longqing reign (1567), two more women martyred themselves for chastity. One was the daughter of Fang Wei, who was engaged to Wang Fengshi at two. Fifteen years later Wang died before the marriage could be consummated, so the girl committed suicide on her way to Wang's tomb. She was then buried with her fiancé in the same grave. The same story is also covered in *Biographies of Exemplary Women*, where Wang Daokun proudly notes, "the Wangs and Fangs have intermarried for generations."[84] The next biography concerns Ms. Li, who at nineteen became the second wife of Wang Yingxuan, who was wealthy but not in good health (and apparently much older than Ms. Li). Upon being widowed at twenty-two, she arranged for all of Wang's wealth and property to be divided among her two step-sons before committing suicide.[85] In the concluding remarks, Wang Daokun again boasts how outstanding his lineage was in producing virtuous women who maintained lifelong widowhood or martyred themselves for chastity (*qijie yilie*), whether poor or wealthy.

Another case features a second Maiden Fang. But in this case, what is notable is not just Wang Daokun's ultimate concern for his lineage as a whole but also his direct involvement and cold-blooded treatment of the martyred woman. Wang Daokun comments, "To starve to death is a small matter; but to lose one's chastity is a great matter," echoing the infamous statement by the Song dynasty neo-Confucian Cheng Yi. Maiden Fang was betrothed to Daoqi (Daokun's cousin) at age twelve. Five years later, in 1579, just months prior to the planned wedding, Daoqi fell ill and died. Kinspeople all tried to console Ms. Fang. Wang Daokun, too, showed up at Daoqi's house (where Ms. Fang was staying), doing nothing except hear out this not-yet-dead (*weiwangren*) woman on her reasoning for wanting to follow her betrothed in death. Wang Daokun, the most respected and powerful elder in the lineage at the time, signaled his endorsement of her decision through his silence. That night after bathing and dressing in her finest, Ms. Fang hanged herself and, as Wang Daokun notes with macabre delight, "an iridescence from her face illuminated the room." When she was encoffined the next day, "her face looked as if she were alive." Wang Daokun then led the entire lineage in presiding over a funeral for Ms. Fang.[86]

Other chastity martyr narratives included in *Taihan Collection* look largely similar in terms of emphasizing the kinship mooring of the martyrs as well as their determined integrity. Notably, Wang Daokun also included eight *jielie* records in his genealogy, including "Biographies of the Seven Chastity Martyrs." While female virtues included loving mothers or mothers-in-law, devoted daughters or daughters-in-law, and principled wives, it was the value of *jielie* that Wang Daokun's writings highlighted as central to the patrilineal lineage.

This era saw the formation of the female chastity cult, during which Huizhou emerged as a center of *jielie*. It is revealing to compare the region to another center of the female chastity cult, Quanzhou Prefecture in Fujian. From 1522 to 1644, Quanzhou recorded 152 female suicides (131 cases upon the death of the husband and twenty-one upon the death of a betrothed), whereas Shexian County alone generated 191 cases (174 cases upon the death of the husband and seventeen upon the death of a betrothed), as well as 596 lifelong widows.[87] Turning to sources internal to Huizhou, we see the intensification of chastity practice around the mid-sixteenth century, just at the time when Huizhou mercantile lineage culture took shape. Although the 1502 edition contains accounts of chaste women from the Tang dynasty onward, the 1566 edition expands them by roughly 25 percent, adding mostly devoted widows in the years between the two publications (meaning that Huizhou over the previous sixty-four years had produced about one-fourth of all devoted widows in the region over the past one thousand years).[88] The compilers of the 1566 gazetteer quoted Zhu Xi as saying that the Xin'an landscape of steep peaks and pure streams had helped nurture women's virtue as well as men's integrity, and then quickly added that local gentry's inculcation had also contributed to this moral molding.[89]

But it was in this stronghold of kinship settlements, as revealed in Wang Daokun's writings, that kinswomen's *jielie* practice reached a cultic level in the late Ming. This specific contextualization appears to shed new light upon the current interpretation of the chastity cult. Thus far, scholarship has tried to locate the impetus for this social trend in various causes from literati activism (or male anxiety in general terms) to changing state policies under the Ming and Qing dynasties, evolving property-status laws, and mounting demographic pressures.[90] The causal link between lineage institutions and the chastity cult has not been properly accounted for, or at best just assumed in terms of the apparent compatibility between women's virtues and Confucian kinship values. Moreover, scholars have not fully accounted for the reasons for the rise of the female chastity cult at a time when China enjoyed rapid commercialization with profound and wide-ranging impacts upon society and culture.

For Huizhou, how did the rise of local merchants in the late Ming factor in these concurrent trends? In other words, how was female chastity related to mercantile lineage culture? Wang Daokun does not explicitly comment on this question, although he authored several accounts of exemplary wives of merchants. Nevertheless, a parallel preoccupation with merchants and women clearly surfaces in his biographic writings. Was there an underlying cause for this joint emphasis? I will examine this question in the following chapter.

CONCLUSION

Wang Daokun is best known for having profiled a large number of Huizhou merchants, and these accounts have been used to explore Huizhou men's economic behavior and literary value. In my recounting of these merchant biographies, I have instead highlighted their social life. This reading exhibits new meanings, especially when observed in combination with Wang Daokun's genealogy on the one hand and his accounts of chaste women on the other. Out of this approach emerges a greatly enriched account of the mercantile lineage discourse first delineated in *Prominent Lineages in Xin'an*.

Wang Daokun's special format of genealogy in *The Genealogy of the Sixteen Branches of the Lingshanyuan Wangs* is almost unique, but this may be a case of the exception proving the rule in terms of Huizhou genealogies all aspiring to trace back to prominent historical figures. It claimed the utmost pedigree for the Huizhou Wangs as being descended from the Duke of Zhou, while at the same time covering and thereby elevating the commoner kinspeople. Here we see the close link between the symbolic center and local settlement of the lineage. This was certainly not in conflict with the moral-leveling in the thinking of Cheng Minzheng, which was now more notably embodied in the populist school of Wang Yangming, the greatest Ming dynasty hero for Wang Daokun.

In his biographies, Wang Daokun justified commercial activities while at the same time prescribing a Confucian mode of mercantile ethics through his descriptions of the righteous deeds of good merchants. He appeased Huizhou merchants by equating them with gentry, even as some Huizhou merchants, including his own successful grandfather, still referred to themselves as "mean traders." While highlighting the righteous conduct of Huizhou merchants, Wang Daokun also appears to have employed the tactic used in *Prominent Lineages in Xin'an* to ward off outside criticism, which had intensified in the late sixteenth century. The virtue of righteousness is highlighted in virtually every merchant biography Wang Daokun wrote, as it was key to keeping sojourning merchants bound to their home lineages during a time of rapid commercialization, which had the potential to erode the home bonds of sojourners.[91] All of this helps to explain why lineage identity, instead of class or vocational belonging, was critically important for Huizhou merchants. They were mostly *chushi*, untitled but educated gentrymen. More importantly, they were members of mercantile lineages, which had long been established as "prominent," with ancestral roots purportedly going back to medieval or older aristocratic families from the orthodox Confucian heartland of north China, and with their Xin'an ancestry further glorified by examination success and literati accomplishments. In the process of writing about merchants, Wang Daokun not only raised their status, he also eloquently described the practices among Huizhou mercantile lineages—that is, their strategy of alternating between the two most important vocations of learning and trade. Because of the staying power of higher gentry culture, or gentrified mercantile lineage culture, Huizhou merchants did not forge their own independent identity. Indeed, Wang Daokun never described a merchant who had disavowed the Huizhou social strategy of alternating between learning and trade or disassociated himself from his home lineage.

Huizhou women, of course, were also attached to their own or their husbands' lineages, and this, too, was reflected in Wang Daokun's biographies of women. He highlighted women's *jielie*, which paired with men's *jiexia*. This set of characteristics not only reflected but also helped to shape the emerging cult of chastity in the late Ming. As we shall see in the next chapter, this gender discourse so central to Huizhou kinship society was intimately intertwined with the material realities of mercantile lineages in a time of expanding commercialization.

In the post–Wang Daokun era, the narrative of worthy merchants and chaste women from Huizhou reached a new level. The official gazetteer of the Lianghuai salt region, compiled in the late seventeenth century, at which time a new commercial surge began to propel Huizhou merchants to even more remarkable financial success, features a large number of "good" merchants (mostly from the late Ming and contemporary Huizhou) in four lengthy *juan* chapters: "Filial and Friendly" (Xiaoyou), "Cultivated Behavior" (Zhixing), "Honest Behavior" (Duxing), and "Espousing Righteousness" (Shangyi). Concurring with (if not directly following) Wang Daokun's narratives, these chapters detail the righteous and trustworthy deeds of Huizhou merchants not just in business transactions but, especially, in their generous contributions to enhancing home lineage institutions and other public welfare endeavors.[92]

In a separate "Merchant Customs" (Shangsu) section, we find an entire paragraph paying tribute to Huizhou merchants. It glorifies their family backgrounds and the tradition of learning: "Salt dealers from Huizhou are mostly descendants from prominent lineages, with pure and glorious kinship and with a family life marked by ritual comity. [They] are versed in the classical books from the ancient sages that dwell on benevolence and righteousness, having long been immersed in the teachings of the Literary Master [Zhu Xi]." The passage goes on to note how "people from near and afar heartily" admired Huizhou merchants for their "forthrightness and integrity," "ingenuity and resolve," and "experience and acumen." Most importantly, they were "chivalrously righteous and generous" (*renxia kangkai*), especially when it came to making donations to set up schools and charities.[93]

Here we again see the essence of Huizhou mercantile lineage tradition, first conveyed, even if vaguely, through *Prominent Lineages in Xin'an* and further enhanced in the hands of Wang Daokun. Huizhou merchants were under pressure to act righteously as they came from local prominent lineages that were steeped in family traditions of studying the classics. Similar to Wang Daokun's own family practice, dating from the time prior to his grandfather, the family strategy was to alternate between farming and learning (*gengdu*); farming then turned into trade as commercialization accelerated in the sixteenth century. The causal relation between the righteousness of merchants and their prominent learned family backgrounds is not specified, but nevertheless is taken as a given.

It turns out that a leading compiler of and a chief financial contributor to the Lianghuai gazetteer was none other than a top salt merchant named Cheng Jun (1638–1704), who, now permanently settled in Yangzhou, was himself from a prominent mercantile lineage in Shexian, known as the Censhan Chengs.[94] Although a lower-exam degree holder (another *chushi* student-turned-merchant), he was widely respected as "thoroughly immersed in the salt dealing rules in combination with the learning of his family tradition," wrote the Lianghuai top administrator Cui Hua in his preface to the gazetteer. Cui Hua also commended Cheng Jun's inclusion of stories about the ordinary (degreeless) people covered in the gazetteer.[95] This editorship of the gazetteer, like Wang Daokun reporting on local Huizhou men in trade, calls attention to two new points.

First, it suggests the dual nature of the recording. On the one hand, Cheng Jun was an insider, having access to information about Huizhou merchants. But on the other, on account of his insider status, his insight was inherently biased or skewed. However, while the gazetteer narratives should not be taken at face value, the sheer number of good merchants recorded is still revealing. If we treat Huizhou merchants as a collective group, and as a group closely linked to their home lineages, and if we believe that their espoused business code of righteousness and honesty enhanced merchants' long-term profits, then the success of Huizhou merchants suggests that collectively they acted righteously. Their good deeds in other respects, such as contributions to enhancing home lineage institutions, are much easier to verify. What is recorded in the Lianghuai gazetteer, as well as by Wang Daokun, was not just prescriptive, but also descriptive, "describing" not only the individual deeds but also the collective behavior through the telling of individual stories. Indeed, in this case, the credibility of any individual story matters little if it reveals a larger historical pattern.

Second, Cheng Jun went one step further than Wang Daokun. By compiling the gazetteer of the Lianghuai salt region, he officially codified Huizhou mercantile lineage culture and promoted it to the entire realm (different from merchant accounts printed in the *Taihan Collection* or in local genealogies, both of which were privately produced documents). Here we see another case for the potential of the local culture to have an impact well beyond the home locale. The mercantile lineage culture that Wang Daokun promoted was deeply rooted in Huizhou, but it spread to Yangzhou and beyond. It produced a large number of higher-exam degree holders and merchants who were placed in official posts or succeeded in markets throughout the realm.

For the Lianghuai gazetteer, Cheng Jun also compiled a lengthy volume on virtuous women, most of whom came from his ancestral prefecture, placed immediately after the four volumes covering worthy mercantile figures.[96] This attentive, voluminous pairing of virtuous women with righteous merchants, the two key demographic groupings within Huizhou mercantile lineages, most notably started with Wang Daokun in the late Ming. Its full meaning will become apparent only after looking deeply into how commercialization altered local lineage-family structure so as to propel Huizhou into the center of the female chastity cult. Like Cheng Minzheng, who best represented his age by marking the rise of Huizhou consciousness, Wang Daokun best represented his age by promoting Huizhou mercantile lineage culture.

4

——

"A Confucian Heartland of Women"

Huizhou, the land of prominent "mercantile" lineages, emerged as the center of female chastity cult in the late Ming. Wang Daokun focused on the values of male *jiexia* and female *jielie*, although he did not directly link the two. From our perspective now, however, it becomes clear that there was a connection in Huizhou between mercantile lineage and what contemporary observer Li Weizhen called, "the Confucian heartland of women."[1] In this chapter I turn to the material reasons behind the causal links between the mercantile lineages and the female chastity cult in late Ming Huizhou.

As noted in the previous chapter, scholars have not reached a consensus regarding the reasons for the rise of the chastity cult in the Ming dynasty. Most recently, Siyen Fei has offered a provocative interpretation of the origins of the chastity cult in the Ming dynasty that argues against a simple causation between state indoctrination, socioeconomic change, and gender regimes. Instead, she places the beginning of the female chastity cult squarely with male literati activism. In recording chastity stories in the face of injustice in the state rewarding system and bureaucratic corruption, the literati, facing a collective identity crisis, found a space to assert themselves while at the same time acting on behalf of chaste women. As such, Fei argues, "contrary to what has been seen as a reflection of changed social attitude, the massive appearance of chastity biographies was in fact what triggered the social change"; the cult, she suggests, was hardly "a creation of Confucian patriarchal suppression."[2]

Fei's work represents a new interpretive approach suggesting that representations call into being social practice just as much as, if not more than, they reflect it, reminiscent of the enormously insightful perspective that Dorothy Ko developed in her widely acclaimed revisionist history of footbinding.[3] Fei's interpretation may make sense from the perspective of the empire-wide development of the chastity cult. However, it alone cannot be used to explain why certain regions were

111

particularly fervent in the practice and patronage of female chastity throughout late imperial times.[4] Nor can it account for an apparent paradox: the rise of the female chastity cult around the mid-sixteenth century coincided with dramatic commercialization that actually loosened normative moral bonds and generated a seemingly contradictory "cult" of *qing* (passionate love).

This chapter, drawing on Huizhou's rich sources, argues that the expanding money economy of the second half of the sixteenth century was intimately connected to the formation of the chastity cult. More specifically, it shows that commercialization altered the local social fabric and family life, which in turn shaped, or reshaped, gender relations and conditioned the rise and continuous popularity of the cult in certain regions. I do not just account for the cult, but also, more importantly, show how the social trend was an integral dimension of mercantile lineage culture, helping to define the emerging Huizhou identity.

It is worth reemphasizing that both the cult of female chastity and Huizhou mercantile lineage institutions emerged around the same time during the late sixteenth century and continued to develop in tandem thereafter. And yet, the links between the two still remain largely assumed, neither well documented nor explained. This chapter draws on demographic data from one particularly well-compiled Huizhou genealogy and many other genres of local sources to show that an important underlying factor in the formation of the cult of female marital fidelity in sixteenth-century Huizhou was the changing family-lineage structure, which was brought about by the high incidence of sojourning tradesmen in the region amid intensified commercialization. In this merchant hub of late imperial China, since the majority of young men left home for business, often leaving immediately after marriage and returning home only "once in three years," the age at which couples had their first son tended to be high. This demographic trend combined with a moderate average life span to form a small nuclear family (consisting of a couple with or without children), not the ideal three-generation family, even as the natural increase in population augmented the size of the kinship settlement.[5]

Situated in single-couple nuclear households, wives of sojourning husbands tended to be relatively free from the monitoring of their sexuality. The only effective way to assure the fidelity of these abandoned women was to appeal to the larger lineage. This, in part, accounts for Wang Daokun's profiling of so many righteous merchants and chaste women in the context of local patrilineal mercantile lineage culture, even if he himself did not explicitly mention or fully understand the underpinning factors for his dual emphasis. Furthermore, it helps explain why Huizhou merchants were so eager to consolidate home kinship institutions through the building of corporate estates (partially to take care of widows) and ancestral halls (including female shrines), alongside the construction of memorial archways (to honor chaste kinswomen).[6] By the eighteenth century, a prosperous mercantile lineage in Huizhou could accommodate several thousand kinspeople, though a significant portion of kinspeople might be living in places beyond Huizhou for business concerns. All of these trends started in the sixteenth century.

THE CENSHAN CHENG GENEALOGY AND ITS DEMOGRAPHIC DATA

I have selected demographic data from *The Branch Genealogy of the Censhandu Chengs in Xin'an* for three reasons.[7] First, it is one of the most detailed Huizhou genealogies. Second, the genealogy is focused on just one branch settlement covering a suitable chronology from its beginning during the Yuan-Ming transition up to 1741, which, in combination with sufficient numbers of kinspeople with demographic data, nicely shows historical trends. Third, the Censhan Chengs, though a relative latecomer among elite Huizhou kinship settlements, in many ways showcased the prominent and prosperous Huizhou mercantile lineages in late imperial times. The Censhan Chengs not only put into perfect use Wang Daokun's Huizhou social strategy of alternating between learning and commerce, but also highlighted the practice of female chastity (as recognized by *Prominent Lineages in Xin'an*, noted in chapter 2).

The Cheng lineage is listed first among the ninety elite surnames in *Prominent Lineages in Xin'an*, and the Censhan settlement originated from the prominent Cheng branch in nearby Huaitang village, the very first village-lineage settlement illustrated in *Prominent Lineages in Xin'an*. The first migrant ancestor of the Censhan Chengs, Cheng Cheng (fl. 1357), had five sons, and the branch began to take off demographically and socially after Cheng Cai of the sixth generation earned the metropolitan *jinshi* degree in 1496 (see fig. 2). After the turn of the sixteenth century and through the end of the Ming dynasty, the Censhan Chengs would produce five more *jinshi* and six *juren* degree holders, making it a new prominent kinship community in a region crowded with great families and renowned lineages.[8]

Amid their academic and political success in the mid-sixteenth century, the Censhan kinsmen began to take on commercial endeavors outside of Huizhou. Cheng Yingshe (1536–1591) of the eighth generation, probably along with his younger brother Yingbiao (1539–1603), apparently started his mercantile career at a young age, and the genealogy commends him as "sincere, honest, and considerate," and as having always "engaged in fair trade."[9] Yingbiao's son, Dagong (1565–1648), was the first Censhan kinsman who established himself in the Lianghuai salt business, one of the most competitive and lucrative trades in the realm. The Huaitang comprehensive genealogy commends his righteous deeds in "refurbishing the home ancestral hall and harmonizing kinspeople, [and] building river embankments to prevent flood" after making a fortune "in the salt trade." Toward the end of the Ming he also contributed a large amount of silver to feed the imperial army. He and his cousins' descendants "oversaw the [Lianghuai] salt business for five generations."[10]

His cousin, Yingshe's son, Dadian (1575–1652), also engaged in the Lianghuai salt business, but settled in Yangzhou, about two hundred miles northeast of Huizhou where the Lianghuai salt administration was headquartered. The home genealogy characterizes him as a filial son and a loving brother who "enjoyed giving" (*leshi*), a generic term used in local lineage documents to mean donating a handsome sum

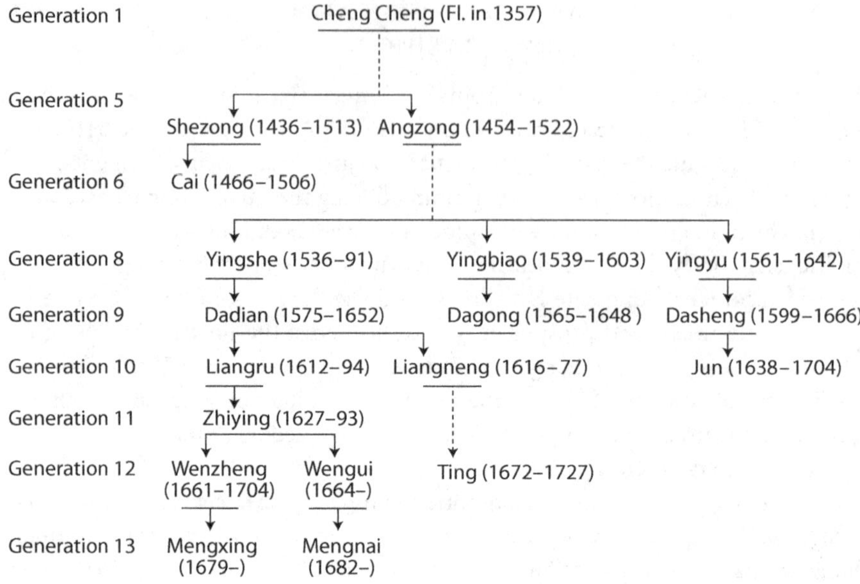

FIGURE 2. The key kinsmen of the Censhan Cheng lineage. *Xin'an Censhandu Chengshi zhipu* (1741).

of silver to building home kinship institutions and improving the surrounding infrastructure (such as repairing roads, canals, or local ritual establishments).[11] Most notable were the achievements of Dadian's five sons, especially his first and second, Liangru (1612–1694) and Liangneng (1616–1677), now permanently settled in Yangzhou. Liangru, and later his son Zhiying (1627–1693), became head merchant (*zongshang*) of the Lianghuai salt business after he successfully negotiated with the state to win back for the Lianghuai merchants the right to sell salt to three prefectures in southern Hunan, which had since Song times been controlled by the Guangdong salt administration. His grandson Wenzheng (1661–1704) and great grandson Mengxing (b. 1679) earned the metropolitan *jinshi* degree in 1691 and 1712, respectively, further boosting the prestige of the Censhan Chengs.[12] His younger brother, Liangneng, was noted for his contributions to building kinship institutions. He initiated the construction of the first ancestral hall for his kinspeople dwelling in Yangzhou, and for his ancestral lineage back home in Shexian he almost single-handedly financed the renewed compilation of the 1673 edition of the Huaitang Chengs' genealogy, which included the Censhan branch.[13]

Clearly, it was by no means accidental that in 1741 the Censhan Chengs produced one of the best Huizhou genealogies, given the branch's enormous success in both business and civil service. Compiled by Wenzheng's younger brother, Wengui (b. 1664), financed by Wengui's son, Mengnai (b. 1682), and prefaced by Mengxing, the seven-volume genealogy employs the state-of-the-art *tuzhuan* (ancestral tree plus biographic sketch for each kinsman) format to cover all kinsmen (not just prominent figures in the ancestry), a tradition first introduced by their famous

TABLE 2. Average age at birth of first son (ABFS) and average lifespans

Year Span	Age at Birth of First Son		Average Lifespan	
	Male	Female	Male	Female
1360–1380	23.5 (2)[a]	22 (1)	—	—
1381–1400	28.5 (2)	18 (1)	53 (1)	—
1401–1420	27.44 (9)	25.88 (8)	49.2 (5)	48.5 (2)
1421–1440	27.75 (12)	25.72 (11)	55.6 (5)	42.83 (6)
1441–1460	31.4 (5)	27.2 (5)	69 (1)	56 (7)
1461–1480	28.09 (11)	25 (7)	—	—
1481–1500	28.92 (14)	26.44 (9)	—	—
1501–1520	25.78 (23)	24.64 (17)	54.9 (10)	34.75 (4)
1521–1540	26.22 (35)	24.5 (32)	53.95 (21)	52.42 (12)
1541–1560	25.74 (47)	23.55 (38)	60.13 (30)	58.21 (33)
1561–1580	28.54 (46)	23.43 (37)	58.09 (35)	56.96 (24)
1581–1600	31.15 (46)	25.19 (36)	56.04 (23)	61.27 (15)
1601–1620	30.36 (85)	23.94 (69)	58.62 (34)	59.89 (27)
1621–1640	28.81 (108)	23.48 (92)	51.8 (60)	47.9 (49)
1641–1660	28.09 (146)	23.49 (129)	53.65 (116)	47.46 (84)
1661–1680	29.61 (205)	23.83 (188)	49.80 (96)	44.37 (122)
1681–1700	28.23 (270)	23.28 (239)	51.53 (151)	43.33 (171)

(Contd.)

TABLE 2 (*Continued*)

Year Span	Age at Birth of First Son		Average Lifespan	
	Male	Female	Male	Female
1701–1720	28.63	23.91	52.27	46.08
	(356)	(334)	(286)	(274)
1721–1740	30.12	25.06	51.84	48.16
	(524)	(486)	(447)	(531)
1741	27	22.83	62	70
	(6)	(6)	(3)	(3)
Total Average	29.02	24.15	52.60	47.58
Total Cases	(1952)	(1745)	(1324)	(1364)

SOURCE: *Xin'an Censhandu Chengshi zhipu* (1741).

[a] Numbers in parentheses indicate the total cases for which information is available.

[b] Ages given here refer to the actual years lived, not the Chinese *sui*. Women tended to have a shorter average lifespan than men largely because a significant portion of women died in childbirth.

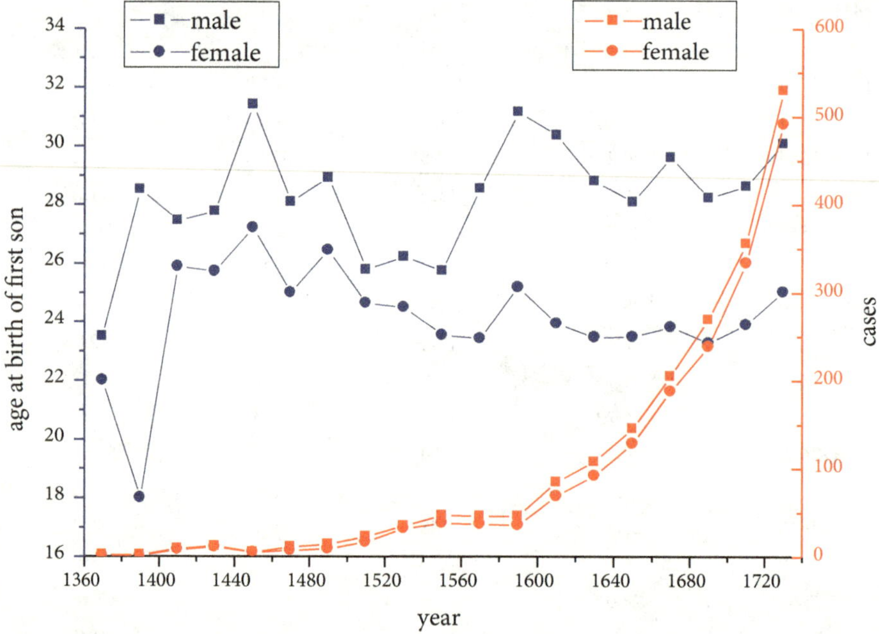

FIGURE 3. Average age at birth of first son among the Censhan Chengs. *Xin'an Censhandu Chengshi zhipu* (1741).

Ming dynasty kinsman from another branch, Cheng Minzheng.[14] Most important for my purposes is the rich demographic data in this branch genealogy. In addition to its brief life and career sketches, the biography section records all the available

TABLE 3. Number of kinsmen in each generation

Generation	Age difference[a]	Number of kinsmen[b]
2nd–4th[c]	1333/1442[d]	58
5th	1408/1480	50
6th	1437/1518	70
7th	1488/1567	115
8th	1513/1608	194
9th	1531/1637	295
10th	1535/1685	377
11th	1582/1721	627
12th	1614/1740	955
13th	1644/1741	1,141
14th	1666/1741[e]	726
15th	1686/1741	244
Total (including first ancestor)		**4,853**

SOURCE: *Xin'an Censhandu Chengshi zhipu* (1741).

[a] There were often considerable age differences between kinsmen of the same generation (except the first cohort covering three generations). The deeper the generation, the larger the gap. In this column, the designated years, separated by a slash, refer to the birth years of the oldest and youngest kinsmen within the same generation, respectively.

[b] Kinswives are not listed in the family tree section of the Censhan Chengs' genealogy, therefore total numbers are virtually impossible to calculate. There were probably more kinswives than kinsmen, as wealthy kinsmen often had concubines or remarried after their first wives passed away, though some poor kinsmen probably never married and still others died before marriage.

[c] As the first four generations did not have many kinsmen, they (minus the first migrant ancestor) are calculated in one cohort. From the fifth generation onward, each generation makes one calculating cohort.

[d] The year 1333 is when Cheng Cheng's first son, Yue, was born, and thus the oldest among the second generation, while 1442 refers to the year when the youngest among the fourth generation was born.

[e] As of 1741 (when the genealogy was compiled), many kinsmen of the fourteenth and fifteenth generations were still young and unmarried, or married without children, so the numbers of kinsmen in the last two generations declined.

or traceable birth and death dates of kinsmen and their wives and concubines from the first migrant ancestor Cheng Cheng down to 1741.[15]

The demographic data included in the branch genealogy yields table 2. The family tree sections in the Censhan Chengs' genealogy list 4,853 kinsmen in total (see table 3); from the biographical sketches we can glean and calculate the age at the birth of first son for 1,952 men and 1,745 women, and birth and death dates for 1,324 men and 1,364 women. Although not a perfect representation of the historical demographics of the Censhan Chengs, the pool of available cases is large enough to make sense of the demographic data presented in table 2, especially from the early sixteenth century onward.[16] The average lifespan is about 52.6 for men and 47.6 for women, and the average age at birth of the first son (ABFS) is about twenty-nine for men and twenty-four for women.[17] While meaningful in characterizing their impact upon local lineage-family structure (as will be discussed shortly), the average numbers of the demographics do not show a historical trend. Grouping the data by every two decades, however, we find that from around 1581 to 1620 the age at birth of the first son for men rose well above the average, to over thirty-one for the 1581–1600 cohort and over thirty for the 1601–1620 cohort. It shot up over thirty again for the 1721–1740 cohort. The data then shows the developing trajectory of historical variants (see fig. 3).[18] I will now turn to an interpretation of this change in demographic data, along with the data from the other two-decade cohorts shown in table 2.

COMMERCIALIZATION AND THE SMALL-FAMILY/LARGE-LINEAGE FABRIC

From table 2 we can conclude at least two points that must have had significant impacts upon local family life and family structure. First, we can link the demographic change in the period from 1581 to 1620 to contemporary commercialization, especially for the highly commercialized Censhan Chengs and Huizhou in general.[19] The period falls into what Timothy Brook has termed the "late summer" and "early fall" of the Ming dynasty—the most rapidly accelerating period in terms of the development of the money economy.[20] In terms of local lineage developments, it corresponds to the coming-of-age of Cheng Dadian and Cheng Dagong, who ventured out of Huizhou to engage in the Lianghuai salt business, by which time their fathers (Yingshe and Yingbiao, who represent the first generation of serious merchants in Censhan) had probably retired from their commercial careers. For Shexian and Huizhou as a whole, this was about the time when "seven or eight out of ten households" engaged in trade, as reported by Wang Daokun.[21]

In this intense mercantile atmosphere, Huizhou men normally started their sojourning business career at a young age, and often found it difficult to visit home given the limits of transportation (further compounded by Huizhou's mountainous landscape) as well as the vigorous demands of the competitive market. One popular source from the Qing dynasty notes "an established rule in Huizhou: men at sixteen must leave home to learn a trade."[22] Another age-old proverb from Yixian (which was not the most commercialized of the six Huizhou counties) went, "We didn't build up merit a lifetime ago, so we were born in Huizhou; at thirteen or fourteen, it's out we go."[23] The late Ming scholar from Yixian, Huang Shiqi, wrote eight casual verses portraying local customs in his home county, one of which, "Merchants," begins:

> The men set their ambitions on the four directions;
> they shirk not from traveling three thousand miles.
> Xin'an is full of traveling youths,
> who do nothing but pursue fly-head profits.

This spirit has gradually turned to custom;
abacuses in hand, they spread throughout the realm.[24]

These sojourning youths, according to the 1566 edition of the Huizhou prefectural gazetteer, "returned home only once every couple of years." This obviously had become a pattern, which was reconfirmed not only in later Huizhou gazetteers and other genres of documents but also reflected in additional Ming sources.[25] A late Ming literati account of two Huizhou brothers who were "deeply ashamed and depressed" after an unsuccessful business venture in the northeastern province of Liaoning noted "a Huizhou custom": "merchants all return home once every couple of years; their affines and kin all view them as worthy or worthless, and so either admire or despise them, based on what they have earned in trade."[26] Here we see a further cultural factor, in addition to the geographical impediments and economic reasons already mentioned, that hindered visits home for many sojourning youngsters. Wang Daokun, in one of the numerous biographies of Huizhou merchants he penned, noted that for every ten Huizhou households, seven engaged in trade but only "three out of ten succeeded."[27] Given this low success rate, we might wonder how many young traders never had the nerve to return home and might even have died outside of Huizhou. The demographic data of the Censhan Chengs presented in table 2, or rather the lack of it in many cases, especially the lack of kinsmen's death dates, may indirectly reflect the commercial hardship and cultural bias faced by sojourning youths.[28]

The long-term absence of sojourning men exerted a significant impact upon family life at home. Xu Guo (1527–1596), a future grand secretariat from Shexian mentioned in the previous chapter, did not meet his sojourning father until he was six.[29] Xu Guo was indeed lucky to have been conceived before his father left home on a business trip. In a region full of sojourning youths, who often left home not long after their wedding, having a child was a rare event. Early marriage appears to have been well established in Huizhou (and was probably further accentuated amid intense commercialization during the late Ming), as was the custom of young men leaving home immediately after the wedding.[30] As Gu Yanwu (1613–1682) noted, Huizhou merchants left home "a few months after marrying, often for as long as ten years at a time, so that if father and son met they would not recognize one another."[31]

This custom is also reflected in popular fiction. In *Slapping the Table in Astonishment* (Pai'an jingqi), a late Ming collection of popular short tales, we find a story about a Huizhou merchant by the name of Pan Jia (a gloss, perhaps, on two homophonic characters, *panjia*, meaning "longing for home"). This scholar-turned-merchant has just married the "delicately pretty" Yao Dizhu. Just two months after the wedding, Pan Jia's father bitterly scolds him, saying, "Look at the two of you, so lovey-dovey. Husband and wife can't just while away a lifetime doting on each other. Why don't you put your mind to going out to do business?" Pan Jia has no choice but to talk it over with Dizhu. The two of them weep and spend the whole night talking. The next morning, Father Pan forces his son to leave home. Yao Dizhu is left behind as if a "widow," "dropping pearl-like tears," echoing the literal meaning of her given name, every day. Later, the story goes, she runs away from home after being bitterly scolded by her parents-in-law and falls into the hands of a pimp and a procuress. She eventually loses her fidelity to another Huizhou merchant, leading to a two-year lawsuit and her eventual reunion with Pan Jia.[32]

This pattern of youths leaving home on business not long after their weddings, multiyear separations between sojourning men and their wives, plus high expectations placed upon the careers of young sojourners within an overall atmosphere of intensifying commercial competition, worked in tandem to alter local demographics in late Ming Huizhou. It was these new trends that likely account for the significant rise around 1580 in the ABFS in the Censhan Chengs data. This corresponds to the generation of Dagong and Dadian, with Dagong's ABFS being twenty-three and Dadian's thirty-seven.[33] A rigorous travel regime could not only raise the ABFS, it could even leave some sojourning men childless. A case in point is the story of Cheng Dajie (b. 1559) of the Censhan Chengs. In his youth, this elder cousin of Dadian was afflicted with a terrible disease on a business journey and died three years later at home without a descendant (we are left with a detailed account of him in the branch genealogy because he had a remarkable wife, as will be discussed later).[34]

What, then, does all of this have to do with family life and gender relations in Censhan? The second point we can draw from table 2 is that the rising ABFS, in combination with a moderate average lifespan, began to alter the fabric of family life in Censhan (and, by implication, in Huizhou at large). Taking into account margin of error and other factors, we can subtract two years from the male ABFS (twenty-nine) to arrive at the typical kinsman's average age at birth of the first *child* as approximately twenty-seven.[35] Not incidentally, the average generational years for the Censhan Chengs come out to be approximately twenty-seven.[36] When subtracting this number from the average lifespan of the Censhan Cheng kinsmen (52.6) and their wives (47.6), we get 25.6 for kinsmen and 20.6 for their wives. The implication of this is that on average three-generation households in Huizhou were not the norm.[37]

The combination of high age at the birth of the first son (or child) and a moderate lifespan made it almost impossible to maintain a three-generation family in Censhan (though in reality three-generation families certainly existed, as many kinsmen died young and others lived longer than the mean lifespan).[38] On average, the dominant family type for the Censhan Chengs was the nuclear family with or without children, and this trend became particularly notable in the late sixteenth century (and again in the early eighteenth century) when commercialization intensified. This appears to have also been reflected in the "virtuous women" section in the 1566 gazetteer of Huizhou prefecture. According to Katherine

Carlitz, the "virtuous women" section of the *Huizhou Gazetteer*, describing 290 exemplary women, mentions parents-in-law in the home in only 19 percent of Ming cases, while a quick survey of six late Ming gazetteers from Jiangsu, Zhejiang, and Fujian shows parent(s)-in-law present in, on average, 48 percent of Ming cases. This regional divergence supports the small-family/large lineage thesis in Huizhou.[39]

Other factors played into the shrinking family size in sixteenth-century Huizhou. Instead of living up to the Confucian ideal of sharing wealth under the same roof of a multigenerational house, brothers now tended to divide family property, some even when their parents were still alive. A large number of handwritten "drawing-lots" contracts (*jiushu*) of dividing property among brothers from Ming Huizhou are still extant. The following examples are revealing. One was prepared in 1543 by a widow, née Cheng, for her three sons upon the death of her husband. The latter had attempted several times to divide his estate while still alive, but his sons were unwilling to follow through with the division at the time.[40] Still another drawing-lots contract, signed in 1570 by two Su brothers, states that they were getting old so they decided to divide their property—including houses, land, ponds, mountainous slopes they had inherited and further expanded themselves—into two parts for their infant sons and had the division guaranteed by their relatives.[41] From yet another drawing-lots contract signed in 1561 by the merchant Sun Shi and supervised and handwritten by his son-in-law Wu Xizhi, we learn that Sun's father was a trader who, orphaned at the age of one, had worked hard and eventually amassed some fortune. However, he did not have a son until "middle age." Now, in 1561, Sun Shi's own sons, three in total, were all married, and so he decided to divide all of his property, including land estates and commercial shops, evenly among them.[42] In the brief introduction to the division contract, Sun Shi put forward his hope that all three sons would work diligently and live frugally so that the "enterprises" laid down by their ancestors would not fall apart. This statement appears to reflect a new Huizhou merchant tactic of dividing property for better management.[43] As the Sun Shi contract lists many plots of land and mountain slopes, along with tenants assigned to them, the story appears to confirm another pattern of investment by Huizhou merchants—they invested in property at home after getting rich while sojourning.[44]

Beyond practicing division of land through drawing-lots, some Huizhou proprietors even pondered the philosophical meanings of property division. The boldest account endorsing the moral value of property division came from the drawing-lots contract signed in 1572 by two Fang brothers, which declared in its introduction that family property "undivided is a big disaster under heaven, whereas that divided is a big benefit under heaven." Brutally honest, the statement defies the conventional wisdom of shared property within a multi-generational family. Its boldness reflects the changing mood in Huizhou, signaling how deeply commercialization had altered the local value system and family fabric.[45]

While property division was shrinking the family size, the property divided still remained within the same lineage so that the estate holdings of the larger kin community were not split up.[46] Meanwhile, as table 3 demonstrates, the size of the kinship settlement continued to expand as the population increased. Partially in response to the growth of kinspeople, and partially in response to the new challenges of the changing times, lineage institutions kept growing over the course of the sixteenth century (and afterward through the Qing dynasty), when we see an explosion of genealogy compilations, ancestral halls, corporate estates, perfection of lineage value systems (including the fashioning of new mercantile ethics and an emphasis on lineage identification), and the construction, or reorientation, of symbolic lineage resources such as ritual opera performance and religious beliefs. Led by gentry, and often financed by merchants, Huizhou kinship institutions matured during the sixteenth century, marked by the formation in the mid-century of mercantile lineages.[47] The small-family/large-lineage patterned the structural fabric of these Huizhou mercantile lineages.[48]

ENGENDERING MERCANTILE LINEAGE CULTURE

The emerging Huizhou mercantile lineage culture was male centered. Chinese lineage, which follows patrilineal descent, stressed the Confucian norm of female chastity and marital fidelity. Some recent studies have complicated the issue by, for instance, looking into actual lawsuits over women's "disgraceful matters" (adultery or suicides), which involved conflicts between patrilineal kin networks and affinal kin networks, to show that the promotion of female chastity was not always consistent with the promotion of patriarchal hierarchy.[49] But Huizhou was different, or differently complicated, as this kinship stronghold was marked throughout late imperial times by a long-established custom of intermarriage between local elite lineages so that patrilineal and affinal kin networks generally shared the same male "lineage" interests over female "gender" interests. We have seen how *Prominent Lineages in Xin'an* worked to enhance the Huizhou marriage pattern.

In this section I draw upon a handful of the many Huizhou writers who all admiringly commented on the custom of their homeland. Wang Xun (*jinshi* 1496) of Xiuning noted that his home canton was prominent for having four long-established *shijia* (prominent lineages)—the Fengcun Wangs, Shanhou Huangs, Zhangyuan Fangs, and Yupengyuan Wangs—who "intermarried for generations" (*shiwei hunyin*).[50] The rise of the Huizhou mercantile group in the mid-sixteenth century, instead of weakening this old custom, actually further enhanced it, as the ingredients of "elite lineage" now included not just ancestral pedigree (including exam degrees) but also commercial wealth. Given that wealthy merchants mostly came from prominent lineages and that kinship and affinal support was behind their success, there was no reason for Huizhou merchants to undo the elite intermarriage custom, whose continued popularity can be easily confirmed by late Ming sources. Fang Chengxun, a scholarly merchant from a prominent Shexian mercantile lineage who was active during the Wanli reign (1573–1620), noted that the Luntan Fangs (his home lineage) and the Dafo Pans were "bound in intermarriage for generations" (*shidi hunmeng*), and his own great grandmother and great great grandmother, "worthy and virtuous," were both from the Dafu Pans.[51] Fang Chengxun's contemporary Wu Ziyu, from the neighboring county of Xiuning, noted that in the county seat the Jins "intermarried for generations" with the Wang and Ye families.[52] Another elder contemporary, the renowned Wang Daokun, admired the deep-rooted intermarriage pattern of Huizhou elite lineages on numerous occasions.[53]

These general comments aside, a more concrete confirmation of the lineage intermarriage custom can be gleaned from the Censhan Chengs' genealogy. Table 4 shows the intermarriage patterns between the Censhan Chengs and other Shexian prominent mercantile lineages. In this land of kin communities, daughters from lineage A (first column) married into lineage B (the Censhan Chengs), while daughters from lineage B married into lineage A. In such an interconnected network, lineage A probably would not lodge a complaint against lineage B if one of their daughters wound up being mistreated—at least not in principle (perhaps with the exception of very special cases in practice), as these linked lineages needed to work together to protect patrilineal interests and secure the sources of future daughters-in-law for their sons. Given this logic, the local intermarriage system clearly played a significant role in enhancing the patriarchal rule of kinship communities by unifying them in practical interests as well as social values on the gender front.[54]

Given the intrakinship networks and patriarchal ideology, Huizhou genealogies, like their collective representation, *Prominent Lineages in Xin'an*, unanimously endorsed the value of female chastity, along with male loyalty, filial devotion, brotherly love, righteous generosity, and ancestral pedigree. Here, too, the mid-Ming represents a significant turning point when it comes to commenting on female chastity. Cheng Minzheng did not even touch upon gender matters in the kinship rules he formulated in the genealogy he compiled in the late fifteenth century for his ancestral lineage.[55] After the mid-sixteenth century, however, Huizhou genealogies began to formulate "lineage rules" (*zugui*) that included concerns over gender issues, in correlation with the boom in both genealogy compilation and officially endorsed biweekly "village-lectures" (*xiangyue*). A recent study by Chang Jianhua on Ming kinship examines several lineage rules from late Ming Xiuning genealogies, one of which is titled *Guimen dangsu* (The women's quarter must be strictly disciplined). The earliest of these *zugui* is the *Guidelines for the Lineage Temple* (Tongzong cigui) of the Xiuning Fans, dated 1566. Chang Jianhua further suggests that these lineage rules, given the remarkable similarity of their titles and contents, must have come from an earlier common source, most likely first formulated around the mid-sixteenth century.[56] He cites another lineage rule contained in a 1572 Huizhou genealogy in great detail, which sounds particularly

TABLE 4. Lineage intermarriage patterns

Village-lineage	Daughters married into Censhan Cheng lineage	Daughters married out of Censhan Cheng lineage
Primary wives		
Caoshi Sun	13	13
Changgai Bi	12	2
Chengkan Luo	15	10
Fudai Hong	19	6
Hangbu Cao	11	8
Hangbutou Cao	22	19
Hongkeng Hong	70	51
Hongkeng Wang	10	8
Hongyuan Hong	20	14
Huangbei Zhang	18	10
Huanshan Fang	37	6
Jielin Fang	83	60
Jielin Wang	17	8
Jielin Xu	15	2
Jingxing Liu	10	4
Juncheng Bi	17	7
Luotian Fang	14	14
Pancun Pan	37	22
Qiankou Wang	10	3
Shaocun Zhang	45	44
Tandu Huang	19	17
Wangcun Wang	41	19
Wucun Zhu	13	30
Xi'nan Wu	57	46
Xiongcun Cao	93	70
Xiongcun Hong	27	12
Xucun Xu	13	6
Yanzhen Fang	14	8
Yegan Ye	11	2
Yicheng Yang	15	6
Yicheng Zhu	36	31
Yu'an Wang	10	2
Zhangqi Wang	38	13
Zhengcun Zheng	10	8

TABLE 4 (*Continued*)

Village-lineage	Daughters married into Censhan Cheng lineage	Daughters married out of Censhan Cheng lineage
Second Wives (after remarriage)		
Hongkeng Hong	10	—
Shaocun Zhang	12	—
Xiongcun Cao	15	—

NOTE: The first column lists the village-lineages that married ten or more daughters into the Censhan Chengs; their numbers are listed in the second column. The third column lists the number of the daughters from the Censhan Chengs who were married into those same village-lineages. Data are limited to the county of Shexian. Only those lineages whose village settlements are identified are included in the table. For instance, the Pans married seventeen daughters into the Censhan Chengs, while the Pancun Pans married thirty-seven daughters into the Censhan Chengs. But since I cannot be sure if these first Pans hailed from Pancun, the first seventeen cases are not included.

SOURCE: *Xin'an Censhandu Chengshi zhipu* (1741).

harsh to daughters-in-law. It urges couples to maintain harmonious relations with each other and with other family members by urging husbands to refrain from listening to any of their wives' words that might harm the "harmonious atmosphere" at home, further stating that "one family's harmonious atmosphere, or lack of it, all depends on whether women are virtuous or not."[57]

To Chang Jianhua's list I add four more Huizhou genealogies that included a clause or two on gender or chastity issues. The recently uncovered genealogy compiled by Zheng Zhizhen (1518–1595) of Qimen County—who was best known for having authored the first (extant) Mulian opera that depicts the use of godly power to promote female chastity (and other Confucian values, including the new mercantile code of ethics)—states in its guidelines that "remarried women are not to be recorded" (*gaijia zhe bushu*).[58] This rule was more than just a practical matter of not entering the name of a remarried woman who now belonged to another lineage in the genealogy. It had the effect of serving as a warning—being excluded from the family genealogy (that is, being expelled from the lineage temple) was, like remarriage, a matter of shame.

Another lineage from Qimen County, the Wentang Chens, stood out in formulating an individually printed lineage code pamphlet that contained a number of rules concerning gender matters in 1572.[59] One rule concerning ancestral rites makes the penalty clear: "Whoever commits adultery, robbery, and deception that damages the family code will be exposed and openly expelled from the lineage temple; they will never be allowed to sneak into the ritual process to tarnish ancestral spirits." Another rule reads, "In cases of women who, arrogantly uncontrollable by nature, constantly threaten us with suicide by hanging or drowning that eventually lead to real death, they should be ignored; if their natal families make unreasonable demands, the head and deputy-head of the *xiangyue* community shall deal with and reject the demands."[60] Yet another urged the maintenance of a clear demarcation between men and women, as it was believed that youngsters who refused to study, instead spending their time drinking with others and then entering the women's quarters, are the reason for a variety of shameful matters; it went on to announce that severe cases must be dealt with harshly and never tolerated. The next rule concerns positive aspects of kin life, promising awards to kinsmen and kinswomen marked by integrity and chastity, whom the *xiangyue* leaders would report to officials for the coveted imperial banners so as to glorify ancestors.[61]

The 1570 genealogy of the Shuaikou Chengs in Xiuning put the promotion of female chastity and devoted widowhood in more specific terms. One of its guidelines states, "Good women's quarters generate good customs automatically. For kinswives who are widowed young and devoted to their departed husbands or who sacrifice themselves to follow their departed husbands, regardless of whether they have been bestowed imperial awards or not, their deeds will all be recorded. Married kinsdaughters who are committed to widowhood will also be recorded in attachments. The names of those [kinsmen] who married servants, those [kinswives] who remarried, and those kinsdaughters who married into debased families will all be erased without being recorded [in the genealogy]."[62] The Censhan and Huaitang Chengs, ancestrally related to the Shuaikou Cheng lineage, focused only on the reward side, without threatening punishment for unworthy women. One of their guidelines states, "According to the *Situ* genealogy, kinswives' life-long devotion to widowhood and chastity should be recorded with some praise [in the genealogy] so as to promote good customs. For those kinswives who meet the new requirements for the award of imperial banners, they should be recorded in a genealogical biography. Even those kinswives who do not meet the new requirement but are devoted to widowhood and chastity for many years should also be applauded [in the genealogy]."[63]

The Censhan Chengs, by focusing on positive commendation without appealing to punitive wording for unworthy women, appeared to exude confidence in regard to the practices of their women. In any event, they are known for having created other means or institutions to promote womanly virtue, and chastity in particular. In the late Ming they built a shrine honoring chaste women, a trend that current scholarship has assumed to have emerged in the late High Qing. As evidence, we can return to the story of Cheng Dajie in the mid-sixteenth century. This elder cousin of Cheng Dagong and Cheng Dadian became critically ill while on a business journey and so had to return home. His wife, née Wu (b. 1567), from a local prominent lineage, carefully attended to him for three years before he died without a descendant. After preparing a perfect funeral for her husband according to Confucian ritual norms, Ms. Wu fasted for seven days before taking some food, and then again refused to take food for two more days before dying (the genealogy does not indicate in what year). In the early Wanli period (1573–1620), the genealogy proudly noted, the imperial state awarded Ms. Wu with a "chastity martyr" plaque to build an archway in her honor, and she was accordingly glorified in the lineage shrine of female chastity (*jielie ci*), enjoying the spring and fall sacrifices. The Huizhou high-ranking official Luo Wanhua personally wrote the calligraphy for the commemorative arch, which read, "Choosing righteous death with grace" (Congrong jiuyi).[64]

Other mercantile lineages also built shrines to honor devoted women in the late Ming. Wang Daokun, at the request of his close friend Pan Zhiheng (1556–1621), who came from a wealthy merchant family known for having great taste in operatic performance, wrote a stele inscription for the ancestral hall of Zhiheng's clan, a prominent Shexian mercantile lineage. The construction of the Lineage Temple of the Pans started in 1587 and was completed in 1591. The magnificent central hall had two side wings: the west honored devoted kinswomen and chastity martyrs (*xici jielie*) and the east housed the Earth God (*dongci houtu*).[65]

Indeed, the construction of the lineage female shrine was a concrete embodiment of the intensified gendered demands of mercantile lineage culture in late Ming Huizhou, a material symbol of the rise of the female chastity cult. Also notable for the two *jielie* shrines was the involvement of merchants, one showcasing the value of a martyred wife of a sojourning man and the other showcasing the financial contribution by wealthy merchants to the construction of home lineage institutions. Pan Kui, who Wang Daokun referred to as a *chushi* (scholar-turned-merchant), began planning the Lineage Temple of the Pans in the mid-century. Kui had three sons, the eldest serving as a county magistrate, the second noted for his longevity, and the third noted for his wealth. At the request of the elder brother to fulfill their father's will to build the lineage temple, the youngest brother immediately contributed two thousand taels of silver. Pan Zhiheng, another son of a merchant, was also directly involved in the construction of the lineage temple.[66]

The most remarkable contribution to a lineage institution was from a couple from another Shexian prominent mercantile lineage, again reported by Wang Daokun. Wu Pei from the Xi'nan Wu's fourth branch, again referred to as a *chushi*, harbored great scholarly ambition but established his household as a merchant. Whenever he was at home, this sojourning man constantly said to his wife (née Wang, from another Shexian mercantile lineage in Qianchuan and related to Wang Daokun's ancestral clan), "My two younger brothers are devoted to mastering classics, and in the future they will surely glorify my ancestors. But as I am working in a lowly occupation, how can I promote my lineage? I certainly hope that I have special skills in making money, and [can] build an ancestral hall for my branch. I will not be fulfilled if I fail to make this happen." Ms. Wang always respectfully nodded in agreement. Before long, Wu Pei died in Kaifeng while on business; he had no sons. After the funeral, Ms. Wang wept saying, "My husband died; it's not that hard for [me as] one not-yet-dead [*weiwangren*] to follow him [by committing suicide]. But my husband had a will that has not yet been fulfilled." So she entrusted the wealth left by her husband to capable merchants to make money.

Within several years, after having accumulated one hundred taels of silver, she began to talk about, and soon initiated, the building of the ancestral hall. It took a couple of years to complete the construction. In the process, she first sold all of her dowry, and then took out loans, and then resumed and sold needlework to accumulate the additional funding needed to complete the project.[67] The story of Ms. Wang highlights the gendering of mercantile lineage culture in many ways. A young devoted widow of a sojourning merchant, she embodied the cult of female chastity while also making a direct contribution to augmenting the "home" lineage institution on behalf of her late husband.[68]

Huizhou merchants were eager to join lineage elders (often led by gentry) to play a significant role in enhancing kinship institutions for several reasons. In addition to the influence they received from home mercantile lineage culture, Huizhou merchants, often unsuccessful scholars turned *chushi*, wanted to seize any opportunity to assert themselves and demonstrate their worthiness in front of home kin—especially those who had failed in the exams but now succeeded in commerce. This was even more the case when a merchant, such as Wu Pei, had brothers focusing on exam studies with highly promising careers. This assertion made sense in both social and psychological terms in a place where merchants were still viewed as inferior to scholars despite their rising significance. General concerns aside, there were specific gendered reasons for Huizhou merchants to shore up home lineage institutions, especially when commercialization worked to change the local family structure and the negative public image of the sexual license of merchants in the sixteenth century.

Sojourning merchants were, quite naturally, concerned with their family members back home, especially their young wives. The aforementioned Fang Chengxun, a scholar-turned-merchant involved in the money lending business, for instance, complained about the length of his sojourning career in one of the many poems he wrote conveying his homesickness and longing for his wife back home: "I have been a stranger traveling long distances for ten years; how long it has been!"[69] Another poem titled, "Attempting a Reply to My Wife," began: "High in an alcove, my wife pines away; from dawn to dusk she heaves such heavy sighs. For whom does she sigh so heavily? Her heart is troubled by the man she holds so dear."[70]

Fang Chengxun also authored a number of merchant biographies. One was about a Shexian man named Huang Yu, calling him *fengjun* (literally meaning "gentleman with an officially bestowed title"), a more prestigious term than *chushi* to refer to a merchant. The biographer emphasized three things that *fengjun* Huang did after making a fortune from the Lianghuai salt trade: he helped out kinspeople, urged offspring to pursue scholarly careers by studying the classics, and "used the Confucian code of propriety to strictly discipline the women's quarter" (*yili yansu guimen*).[71] Indeed, all three became related ingredients of Huizhou mercantile lineage culture, showcasing the typical concerns of Huizhou merchants as a group, given the sojourning nature of their career, their ambiguous position in local society (rising significance versus deeply rooted—and newly emphasized—bias against the merchant vocation), and their social metamorphosis strategy (using wealth from commerce to support siblings or offspring who were pursuing a career in officialdom).

Huizhou merchants' strict disciplining of the women's quarters, often inflected by these sojourning men's longing for home, should be linked to their generous support of home lineage institutions, and indeed the former should be seen as an ingredient of the latter—that is, as part of what I have called the "engendering" of mercantile lineage culture. This became especially acute when intensified commercialization was placing downward population pressure on individual families within expanding lineages in the late Ming. Huizhou merchants formed a united front with lineage gentry out of concern over the loyalty of their wives. Situated in shrinking nuclear families, the young wives of sojourning men were vulnerable to sexual enticement or threat, both because they were lonely and because there were few family members watching over them.[72] Huizhou sojourning men were fully aware of this threat, as it often came from their fellow Huizhou merchants with deep pockets. An example of this can be seen in the aforementioned *Slapping the Table in Astonishment* story about the newlywed Pan Jia, whose young wife was later seduced by another Huizhou merchant. Little wonder, then, that in the popular "Hanged Woman" episode of the late Ming opera *Mulian*, the sojourning vendor is so sensitive about the sexual fidelity of his young wife that he beats her upon returning home after overhearing that she has given her earrings to two monks, which he mistakes as a token of love. After being beaten, she hangs herself, but is ultimately saved by a divinity as she turns out to be a genuinely devoted wife.[73]

More widely publicized in various genres over the course of the sixteenth century was the real tragedy of Tang Guimei, a young widow who chose to hang herself after the lover of her widowed mother-in-law sexually harassed her. As reported in a typical literati jotting by Yang Shen (1488–1559), the man implicated in the notorious scandal was none other than a merchant from Huizhou.[74] An illustration of Tang Guimei was also included in the famous *Records of Model Women* (Nüfan bian). This book was compiled by Huang Shangwen, a late Ming calligrapher from Shexian who specialized in woodblock cuts and printing.[75] Beautifully illustrated, *Records of Model Women* falls into the late Ming genre of moral handbooks such as *Biographies of Exemplary Women*, whose female exemplars became, as Katherine Carlitz insightfully notes, "simultaneously icons of virtue and objects of sensuous connoisseurship."[76]

The same twofold characterization can be said of Wang Daokun's illustrated edition of *Biographies of Exemplary Women*, which may also contain a clue to explaining the coexistence of the two seemingly contradictory cults of female chastity and romantic love. As shown in the previous chapter, Wang Daokun's support for and—in at least one instance—adamant encouragement of chastity martyrdom seems to fly in the face of his notable penchant for the cult of *qing*. And yet, the two trends combined perfectly in the persona of Wang Daokun. He had three formal wives in succession and loved all three women, in particular the last one, née Jiang. He took no concubines nor did he engage in any sexual liaisons outside of his marriages, except toward the end of his life when he was briefly attracted to a famous Nanjing courtesan named Xu Pianpian.[77] He penned "Biographies of the Seven Chastity Martyrs" in 1570 when he was forty-four years old, about ten years after he authored the four romance plays in 1560. His romances—though criticized as "nothing but florid prose" at the time—foreshadowed what was to become the cult of *qing*. This was most famously embodied in the plays of Tang Xianzu (1550–1616), whose writing style Wang Daokun admired for being "deeply erudite and astonishingly exquisite."[78] Wang's two seemingly different types of writing—biographies of female martyrs and romance plays—along with his personal history, reflect the emergence of two concurrent and seemingly opposing cults of female chastity and romantic passion.

That these two seemingly contradictory trends were combined in Wang Daokun can be partially explained through the complex intellectual influences of both Wang Yangmingism and the Cheng-Zhu School of Principle. Wang Daokun was an enthusiastic follower of Wang Yangming; at the same time, he also was immersed in a local mercantile lineage culture that mixed the philosophical stances of both the Cheng-Zhu school and Wang Yangming. The *xin* of Wang Yangming's school points to both the rational mind and affective heart, an intellectual and emotional harbinger for the cult of love.[79] Yet, as shown in his pieces on the female martyrdom, Wang Daokun could be cold-blooded in his treatment of widows and utterly demanding of kinswomen to maintain their chastity. The cults of female chastity and romantic passion were two facets of the same coin of engendered Huizhou mercantile lineage culture; it is thus no coincidence that the two trends were embodied in Wang Daokun.

Wang Daokun aside, the explanation of the coexistence of the two opposing cults of female chastity and romantic passion amid the commercialization of the late Ming may be found in a more mundane realm, which entailed, more or less, a gendered double standard: for men the emphasis was on "romance" (that is, fulfilling sexual desire); for women, it was on chastity (including, even in the case of high-class courtesans, "chaste romance"). Indeed, beneath the two opposing trajectories of the "beautiful images" of virtuous women embodied in Huang Shangwen's prints, we may discern another seemingly paradoxical dual projection of the gender politics of Huizhou mercantile lineage culture. Huizhou sojourning men held a notorious double standard in terms of their own sexual practices versus the expectations they demanded of their wives. As vividly represented in a popular late Ming collection of short stories, Huizhou merchants, extraordinarily parsimonious in normal times, were willing to spend whatever it would take to obtain their two most coveted "commodities": "red embroidered shoes" (beautiful women) and "a black chiffon cap" (official-gentry standing).[80] Huizhou merchants were infamous womanizers. One of the most notorious examples was Wu Tianxing, a fabulously wealthy businessman from a prominent Shexian mercantile lineage who, around the mid-sixteenth century, built gardens for over one hundred women and thereby earned the nickname, the "master of one hundred concubines" (*baiqie zhuren*).[81]

The subtlest representation of this double standard can be discerned in the symbolic transformation of one local variety of the popular God of Wealth. Huizhou was the original home of Wutong, a demonic mountain goblin who was, during Song-Ming times, transformed into a popular God of Wealth signaling warnings of both ill-gotten money and illicit sex.[82] Midway through the Ming dynasty, however, Wutong was replaced in Huizhou by another beastlike Five Fury (Wuchang) pentad spirit, partially as a result of the construction of the local pantheon headed by the famous historical hero, Wang Hua, who was widely honored as the apical ancestor of one of the most powerful and populous lineages in Huizhou (fully explored in the next chapter).

Located at the bottom of the hierarchical local pantheon, it was believed that Wuchang could convey riches to merchants who worshipped him—especially as he was commanded by the deified symbol of kinship authority, Wang Hua, and thus willingly participated in the religious hierarchy of the gentry-dominated lineage. At the same time, as played out in the popular ritual performance of the *Mulian* opera, the Wuchang pentad spirit was charged with catching the soul of Madame Liu, a disobedient widow. The conflation of the two popular deities of money (or, more accurately, the replacement of Wutong by Wuchang) also entailed a shift in their secondary role as guardians of local sexual politics, with a sexually insatiable goblin that symbolized men's ungovernable desires shading over into a beastlike fiend that was responsible for policing women's behavior. Indeed, what appealed to Huizhou merchants and lineage elders was a God of Wealth who policed the wives left behind at home (and also assisted the fertility deities, as well be illustrated in the following chapter)—not a God of Wealth who cautioned against male lust. Here we seem to see an undeclared symbolic pact reached between sojourning merchants and home-lineage elders in the Mulian-Wuchang performance: sojourning young men entrusted lineage elders back home to watch over their young wives; in return, they willingly channeled part of their profits back home to enhance the kinship institution.[83]

In other words, in Huizhou mercantile lineage culture, male desire was left unchecked while the female body was closely supervised. The changing family-lineage structure, spurred on by commercialization, underpinned the promotion of female chastity, and indeed helped it to grow to cultic proportions in late Ming Huizhou. But by tightening the Confucian yoke on their kinswomen, in the end Huizhou merchants constrained themselves as well, for this oppression reproduced not just the patriarchal order but also the entire hierarchical kinship regime. The gentrified mercantile lineage at home subordinated merchants to gentry leadership and values, even as their wealth in local society gave them substantial power and local gentry helped to uplift their social status.

CONCLUSION

In the spring of 1718, amid a new wave of commercialization during the High Qing, the grandson of Cheng Liangneng, named Ting, now a Yangzhou "native" noted for his poetry, took a long journey to visit his ancestral village of Censhan. On the day he was about to enter Shexian, he noted in his travel diary certain social characteristics of Huizhou:

> It is the custom in Huizhou that scholar-officials and prominent households settle in the countryside. Each village is occupied by a certain lineage whose members live together, with no men of other surnames dwelling there. In each village a temple is built for the Earth God and an ancestral hall for the descent line. Genealogies are written for lineage branches so that their origins and lineal order are not confused. . . . Men uphold integrity and righteousness, and women cherish uprightness and chastity. Even in straitened circumstances, they never abandon their [husbands'] villages. There are maidens whose husbands travel far [to do business] immediately after the wedding, and, in some cases, never return. But still they judiciously care for their parents-in-law, uphold high aspirations, and behave flawlessly. Throughout their lives they make no complaints.[84]

Many men—insiders and outsiders—made similar observations about this land of prominent mercantile lineages. But Cheng Ting specifically juxtaposed Huizhou women's (and men's) virtue with strong institutions of local prominent lineages and, more interestingly, used the cases of sojourning merchants' wives to illustrate his observation. Cheng Ting, in other words, paired devoted womanhood with the mercantile lineage. This pairing certainly was not new. The more famous Wang Daokun focused his Huizhou-related writings on these paired concerns when compiling his own family genealogy, providing prefaces to other lineages' genealogies, and writing biographies of righteous merchants and devoted widows. Many of the latter hanged themselves and served in the biographer's mind as the best exemplars of the female chastity cult. But neither Wang Daokun nor Cheng Ting had ever looked into the possible impact of commercialization upon the local lineage-family structure, understanding it as the link that paired the cult of female chastity with mercantile lineage culture.

Bernard Bailyn, in his presidential address to the 1981 AHA Conference, called for the integration of "manifest" and "latent" events in historical inquiry. Bailyn defines manifest history as "the story of events that contemporaries were clearly aware of, that were matters of conscious concern, were consciously struggled over, were, so to speak, headline events in their own time even if their causes and underlying determinants were buried below the level of contemporaries' understanding."

Whereas latent history, often discernible through the extraction of quantitative data, includes "events that contemporaries were not fully or clearly aware of, at times were not aware of at all, events that they did not consciously struggle over, however much they might have been forced unwittingly to grapple with their consequences, and events that were not recorded as events in the documentation of the time."[85]

Though four decades have passed, Bailyn's call is still highly relevant. Applying his approach to the study at hand, we may be able to make manifest the rise of the female chastity cult together with latent changes in the Huizhou family-lineage structure. The extraction of quantitative information from the *Branch Genealogy of the Censhan Chengs*, which was never compiled with the intent to provide such data, makes it possible to detect events in the population and kinship history of the late Ming years that profoundly affected local family life, gender relations, and mercantile lineage rules. Indeed, when seen in connection with the landscape of shrinking nuclear families within a growing lineage, the emphasis on female devotion becomes more meaningful than before.

The argument presented in this chapter, founded on work in one prefecture, and for its "latent" part, mostly on the quantitative analysis of one genealogy, must be taken as tentative, as a hypothesis for testing and elaboration elsewhere.[86] I cannot claim that my data have established a sole causal link between the rise of the chastity cult and commercialization's impacts on local demography and family-lineage life in late Ming Huizhou. And yet, we see that the two were connected. Indeed, we further see their connection to other concurrent socioeconomic and cultural changes. Commercialization, sojourning merchants, shrinking households, merchant contributions to the enhancement of home lineage institutions, including their "disciplining of women's quarters," various genres of publication ranging from literati reports, genealogies, and local gazetteers that paired biographies of virtuous merchants with that of chaste widows, cultural brokers who compiled the moral or liturgical handbooks illustrating female exemplars or the local pantheon, a popular God of Wealth also serving as a divine guardian of women's behavior, and a remolded *Mulian* ritual opera exhorting both mercantile ethics and conventional Confucian values including female chastity—none of these phenomena were isolated events. Indeed, these simultaneous developments were deeply connected, and they interacted to shape the unwieldy yet coherent entity of Huizhou mercantile lineage culture. The mercantile lineage set the conditions for the rising cult of female chastity, which in turn engendered the identity of Huizhou as a "Confucian heartland of women."

The Local Religious Order

Thus far, we have established the localist turn represented by Cheng Minzheng's impulses in promoting Huizhou and the Huizhou Chengs, the formation of Huizhou identity as embodied in *Prominent Lineages in Xin'an*, the deepening of Huizhou identity in the relationships between home lineages and sojourning traders and between the gentry and merchants, as well as the gender dynamics particular to mercantile lineage culture. All of these facets of Huizhou identity were manifested in the symbolic realm of ritual performance. In fact, no other dimension of Huizhou culture more saliently featured the Ming localist turn than its religious order, as best embodied in the patterned assembly of deities headed by Wang Hua.

Wang Hua was the leading patron deity of the region from the Song dynasty onward, and around the mid-Ming, this deified seventh-century hero emerged as the de facto head of the Huizhou pantheon. This was a result of the localized transformation of the Ming state religious system, as Wang Hua emerged as the local proxy of the official City God. In the process, a large number of popular and locally worshipped gods and spirits, as well as some powerful deities from the institutionalized religions of Buddhism and Daoism, were incorporated to make the regional pantheon. This was the religious expression of Huizhou consciousness and Huizhou identity.

By looking at the local pantheon, this chapter also develops a new perspective from which to analyze popular religion, at least for the Huizhou region. Examining the seemingly "messy" landscape of popular cults from the perspective of the local pantheon, rather than focusing on one specific deity or demon, has the advantage of better contextualizing and historicizing local cults. This enables us to make better sense of the various issues surrounding Chinese popular religion, such as the interaction between high and low cultures—as well as between empire-wide and local cultures—and exchange between cultural representations and social practices. The materials discussed here suggest a substantive integration of the local religious landscape; this cultural integration was not imposed by the state, but rather was orchestrated, or negotiated, by local lineage elites. Ultimately, my observations on local ritual performance speak to the concerns of social historians: this chapter deciphers the meanings of the local pantheon in light of both changing state-society relations and Huizhou mercantile lineage culture.

Merchants and kinswomen were some of the key members of kin groupings, and their relations with the larger lineage (as well as with each other) were expressed and negotiated via the Huizhou religious order. The Wang Hua pantheon was hierarchically structured and served to control the power of many popular deities that were incorporated into its symbolic network, including the collective God of Wealth, the Wuchang pentad spirit. The pantheon channeled the spirit's power—the symbolic representation of merchant money—to good use while averting its potential harmful impacts. This patron deity of Huizhou merchants also acquired a gendered role, helping to police kinswomen's sexuality and assure their well-being in childbirth, both critically important for sojourning merchants and their home mercantile lineages. Furthermore, as Wang Hua was also worshipped as the apical ancestor of all the Huizhou Wangs, this tutelary deity of the region was turned into the generic patron deity of all the Huizhou lineages. In this sense, the Wang Hua pantheon was an extension of Confucian ancestral worship. Indeed, the making of the Huizhou pantheon marked the rise of regional consciousness and reflected the dynamics of mercantile lineage culture in the ritual realm.

MODEL PRAYERS TO THE DEITIES *AND THE MAKING OF THE HUIZHOU PANTHEON*

The best source material on the Huizhou pantheon in Ming times is the newly uncovered rare book *Model Prayers to the Deities* (Qishen zouge). This is a vast ritual guidebook, comprised of six volumes, that contains encyclopedic data about Huizhou's local cults. Its most notable feature is the depiction of the regional pantheon, which was headed by the official City God and the "God of Xin'an," Wang Hua. *Model Prayers to the Deities* is undated, but internal evidence suggests it was a mid- to late Ming text.[1] Quite intriguingly, the original compilation of the handbook is attributed to Cheng Minzheng. This religious handbook was, most likely, first printed in the sixteenth century, after Cheng Minzheng had passed away (whether or not the attribution of authorship to Cheng is correct will be discussed later); it was frequently reprinted in Ming and Qing times and probably revised or "updated" in the process until it was finalized in the Ming version now available. It covers all kinds of prayers used in local popular communal and family rituals. It also reflects the triumph of the Huizhou printing industry, itself a key artifact of local mercantile lineage culture, in publishing the scripted versions of local prayers.

TABLE 5. The Wang Hua pantheon

Upper Register	Lower Register
City God	Attendants on the Left and Right
Wang Hua	Wang Hua's ninth son
Wuxian (Five Manifestations)	Bodhisattva Huaguang
Guan Dadi (Great Thearch Guan)	The Wen-Xiao Emperors
Great Thearchs Zhang and Li	Ministers Yang and Yao
Eastern Peak (Dongyue)	Our Lady Venerable Mother of Infinite Fortune (Shengmu Qianjin Furen)
Divine Emperors of the Four Peaks	Wenchang (Patron Deity of Letters)
Immortal Zhang who controlled childbirth	
Immortal Zhang	Third Prince (Zhang Xun)
Three Kings and Marquis	King Xuanling of the Zhou
Cheng Lingxi	Cheng Lingxi's son
Yue Fei's Deputy Marshals Gao and Du	Marshals Cheng and Ren
Generals Qian and Yuan	Secretary Yang San
Secretaries of Security and Fortune	Secretaries of Gentleness and Kindness
Guards of all local temples	Marshals Tang, Ge, and Zhou
Great Marshal Zhao	
The Five Furies (Wuchang)	The Hehe Deities of Fortune
Gods of Communities and Grains	Earth God (Tudi)
Earth God of the Eastern Districts	Earth God of the Postal Services
Bridge Agent	Communication Agents

Of utmost relevance here is the local pantheon featured in many of the prayers. Representative is one prayer in the first volume entitled "Offering Thanks to the Many Deities on New Year's Eve" (Chuye xie zhongshen), used on one of the most important annual ritual occasions. The prayer reveals a hierarchically arranged pantheon of deities led by the official City God and his Huizhou proxy, Wang Hua, called here "Imperially Conferred Lord Wang the Great Thearch of Yueguo" (Chifeng Yueguo Wanggong Dadi). Since Wang Hua was the de facto head of the hierarchically arranged list of gods, I call this the Wang Hua pantheon or, alternatively, the Huizhou pantheon (and not the City God pantheon). Table 5 lists the deities who made up the Huizhou pantheon invoked on New Year's Eve.[2] The pages of the text are split into upper and lower registers. Another prayer, invoking basically the same pantheon, is characteristically called the "Ritual Code of Xin'an" (Xin'an zhi sidian), which echoes the designation of Wang Hua as the God of Xin'an.[3]

Looking at table 5, we see that the top deity apparently was not Wang Hua, but the City God, which raises the question of why this should be called the Wang Hua pantheon and not the City God pantheon. The generic City God began as a nature deity, and was later recruited into the Daoist pantheon. In Tang-Song times, this regional tutelary deity was often embodied by famous historical figures, which varied by region; that is, the initially generic nature deity of the City God underwent an anthropomorphic transformation into a regional hero.[4] Then, in the late fourteenth century, the first Ming emperor enacted a thorough reform of the regional tutelary deities to unify the worshipping system within the new empire. As a result, a shrine to the Earth God was set up in each local community, while at higher administrative levels, from the county through the prefecture to the capital, a City God temple was built or rebuilt. The City God cult was placed in a hierarchical chain of authority mirroring the political order in this world, which ran from the emperor in the capital through the descending levels of princedom, prefecture, county, and, in this case, even down to the subcounty and village (in the form of the Earth God). The City God was subordinate to the Eastern Peak, who was in turn subordinate to the God on High (Shangdi), an official counterpart of the Daoist and popular Jade Emperor. The first Ming emperor also ordered the destruction of statues of the gods in the City God temples, which were to be replaced by wooden spirit tablets. This reform thoroughly unified the City God cult that had once had strong localized traditions.

These imperial policies appear to have been strictly carried out in the early Ming. For Huizhou, according to the 1502 prefectural gazetteer, the sacrifices to all local or popular deities except Wang Hua and Cheng Lingxi were abandoned after Zhu Yuanzhang's "massive rectification of the ritual code" (*dazheng cidian*) to unify the territorial deities (the City God and Earth God).[5] After several decades, however, the old localizing traditions began to resurface. One key development in the history of Chinese popular religion is the mid-Ming metamorphosis of the official City God within local society, through a strategy of "borrowing [official titles] to name [locally worshipped deities]" (*jie er mingzhi*). This change was partially inherent to the early Ming reform of the City God cult. As part of that reform, the City Gods acquired the authority of the *mingguan* (officials in charge of the dark realm), who presided over exorcisms conducted at the official *litan* (ghost altar).

The *litan* liturgy at local levels was staged three times a year on the fifth day of the third month, the fifteenth day of the seventh month, and the first day of the tenth month. These three dates were later popularly called the three "ghost festivals." The ghost altar was always located outside the city wall, while the City God temple was within. This meant that a City God replica needed to be paraded from its temple to the ghost altar to preside at the exorcising rituals. But the first Ming emperor had ordered the destruction of the City God statues, and their spirit tablets—lacking spectacle and awe—were hardly worthy of a procession. Gradually, over the course of the fifteenth century, as revealed in various sources, the locals restored the City God statues, thereby bringing back the anthropomorphic retransformation of the generic regional tutelary deities into regional heroes.[6] In Huizhou, it was Wang Hua who emerged as the City God's substitute or local proxy, which is directly verified by *Model Prayers to the Deities*. And their temples, along with the temple to the Eastern Peak, were constructed in the same complex on Fu Hill, as illustrated in one Huizhou Wang genealogy (fig. 4).

The same process, conceivably, coincided with the construction of the Wang Hua pantheon, as it was partially inherent in the early Ming reform policy

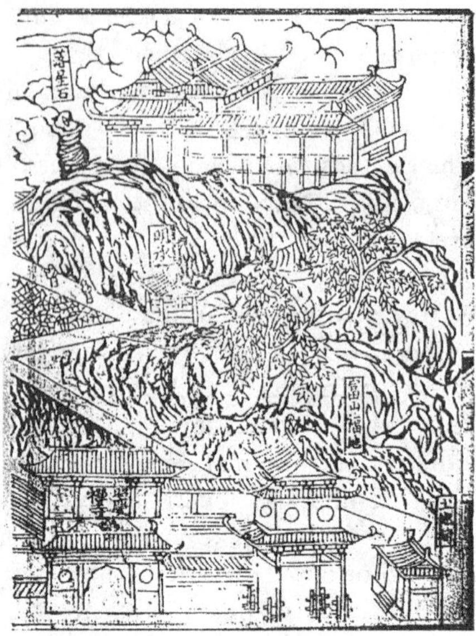

FIGURE 4. *Three Temples on Fu Hill*, left and right panels. Temple to the City God (far left), Temple of Loyalty and Integrity (Wang Hua; top left), and Temple to the Eastern Peak (top right). Wang Nanxuan, *Chongbian Xin'an Zhonglie miao shen jishi* (1460), illustration *juan*, 15b–16a.

assigning the City God to preside over the *litan* liturgy, thereby leading to the popular processions on the three "ghost festivals." Huizhou locals staged large-scale parades on these ritual occasions, and often held many other processions, including for temple festivals on deities' birthdays. Sources show that residents carried divine statues from local temples in these processions. Through the ordering of the deities in the procession, these deities were visibly structured into a pantheon.[7] This partially explains how the temples to the deities listed in the 1502 Huizhou prefectural gazetteer were linked to make the Wang Hua pantheon. Additional evidence for the making of the Wang Hua pantheon include two wings for Wang Hua's attendants already built into the Wang Hua mausoleum, along with a small Earth God hall built in front of the Wang Hua Branch Shrine no later than the 1460s.[8]

By the mid-Ming, a distinctive local pantheon headed by Wang Hua had emerged in Huizhou (naturally, there was a process of accretion and coming-into-being before the regional pantheon incorporating all of these deities became finalized as scripted in the *Model Prayers to the Deities*). We might also say that the Huizhou pantheon was two-headed, both symbolically in the form of the City God, who represented the presence of the state in local worship, and substantially in the form of Wang Hua, who represented the divine interest of local society. Still, this was a distinctive Huizhou religious order, and thus should be identified as the Wang Hua pantheon.

A RELIGIOUS PRAXIS

Was the Huizhou pantheon scripted in *Model Prayers to the Deities* truly worshipped in local ritual practices? There are three kinds of sources that suggest the pantheon is a faithful representation of local religious practice. First, most leading deities included in this Huizhou pantheon had their own individual temples in the local community. The main temples at the prefectural seat listed in order in the 1502 edition of the Huizhou prefectural gazetteer include:

> Temple to the City God
> Temple of Loyalty and Integrity (Wang Hua)
> Temple of Everlasting Loyalty (Cheng Lingxi)
> Shrine to Prefect Lord Sun
> Temple to General Lan
> Temple to the King of Righteous Bravery and Martial Security (Guandi)
> Temple to the Eastern Peak
> Temple to the Five Manifestations (Wuxian)
> Tongzhen Temple (Zhang Xun)
> Temple of the Black Altar (Marshal Zhao).[9]

There is no fundamental difference between the *Model Prayers* list and the gazetteer list in terms of the major deities and their ordered sequence ("subordinate" deities like Wuchang had altars, but not temples, and the structure holding the Earth God was often a small hall or altar as well).[10] Virtually every county and prefecture in late imperial China compiled its own gazetteer, and each gazetteer included a section on local temples and rituals. But we have yet to learn how to make sense of the temple lists in these official gazetteers from the perspective of forming a pantheon in local ritual practices. This correlation between the ritual handbook and the gazetteer sources suggests that local temples were listed in a certain order in the local histories for a reason and that the worship of these local temples was interconnected.

Official documents, of course, do not tell the whole story. Notably missing in the gazetteer list is the Wuchang pentad spirit, but this popular deity is missing in virtually all kinds of late imperial formal writings. Often, a complete picture can be reached only after piecing together various kinds of sources. For example, one map from the 1693 county gazetteer of Xiuning illustrates the locations of some key temples in Xiuning city, including those to the City God, Wang Hua, and Eastern Peak. It also marks popular Zhi Hill within the city wall. Hidden in Zhi Hill, not marked in the official gazetteer illustration but revealed in other sources, is a magnificent Wuxian Temple that includes a Wuchang Hall—that is, a shrine dedicated to the worship of the Five-Fury spirits. From other sources, too, we learn that the main temple to Wang Hua at the prefectural seat also hosted a shrine to Marshal Zhao, who, as shown in numerous liturgies contained in the *Daoist Canon*, had commanded the Wuchang furious soldiers since the Yuan dynasty.[11]

Nonofficial materials cover the pantheon list more completely than official ones. One such source confirming the practice of local pantheons comes from popular ritual opera performance, which in Huizhou also matured during the sixteenth century. An early twentieth-century handwritten liturgy from the remote Huizhou village of Limu, handed down from late imperial times, shows another pantheon invoked in a ritual staged before the performance of *Mulian*, arguably the most popular and down-to-earth ritual opera for Huizhou kinship society. The featured local pantheon, invoked in the *Mulian* ritual opera, is divided into five rows:[12]

First row of deities

> Local Lord (Tuzhu, which in this case refers not to Limu's Earth God but the proxy of the Earth God, Wang Hua)
> The Three Saintly Thearchs of Wang (Wang Hua and his eighth and ninth sons)
> The Wen-Xiao Emperors (of the Ming dynasty)
> Wuxian (The Great Thearchs and Divine Agents of Five Manifestations)
> The Fifth Saint Thearch Zhang (Zhang Xun)
> The Cardinal Master of Red Mountain, the Cardinal Master of Long Hair, and the Cardinal Master of Bringing Rains

Second row

> Guandi (The Saint Emperor Guan)
> Generals Zhou Cang and Guan Ping (Guandi's attendants)

Third row

> Marshal Ma, Marshal Zhao, Marshal Yin, and Marshal Liu (the Four Great Martial Attendants of the Buddha)
> Miss Golden Flower, Lady Plum Blossom, and Madame Snowflake
> The Divine Agents of Hehe and Lishi (popular variants of the God of Wealth)

Fourth row

> Boy of Opening Pure Voice (a Huizhou variant of an attendant to the tutelary deity of the theater, Master Laolang)
> Qu Yuan (the leading deity worshipped in the Dragon Boat Festival)

Fifth row

> Wuchang (Five Furies)

This Wang Hua pantheon includes virtually all of the leading deities we find in *Model Prayers*.[13] As for the *Mulian* ritual opera for which this liturgy was staged, we know that these performances lasted up until the early twentieth century, suggesting the longevity of the Wang Hua pantheon within Huizhou society.

Model Prayers constitutes the third kind of source that points to the popularity of the Wang Hua pantheon. This is a "how-to" primer for local prayers, designed for easy use. A supplicant (often leading his family or relatives) just needed to fill in his name and communal location and the date of prayer in the marked blank spaces and then chant the prayers. As an example, we can turn to the prayer invoking the multitude of the deities on New Year's Eve, which starts:

> We prostrate as the light of precious candles shines down from on high to illuminate the plum blossom nighttime festival and wine overflows the cups, imbuing the First Spring with the fragrance of bamboo leaves. This ritual concludes the whole year, paying our respect and requital to the ten temples. Now, I _____ [name], a believer worshipping the deities, hailing from _______ [location], accompanied by my family and dependents, in _____ [year] during the last month on the night of New Year's Eve, reverently prepare pure wine and a feast of meats and vegetables. I first petition his lordship deity the Earth God to ask the divine runners on duty to respectfully convey our prayers to [the City God and Wang Hua and all other deities in the Huizhou pantheon].

Adding to the easy format of the prayers is their catchall nature. There are prayers designed for various seasonal festivals, deities, and different kinds of supplicants, including students, merchants, shopkeepers, farmers, travelers wishing security, elders wishing for good health, and women wishing for sons or safe childbirth. The ritual handbook also includes rites resembling simplified or popularized versions of the four family rituals stipulated by Zhu Xi (cappings, weddings, funerals, and ancestral rites), but each prayer still ends procedurally with the "thrice-toast" (*sandian*) routinized in Zhu Xi's *Family Rituals*.

In terms of the book structure, volume 1 of *Model Prayers to the Deities* contains prayers on seasonal festivals, starting from New Year through Spring Request and Fall Requital to New Year's Eve (including "Invoking the Sages and Worthies on the Opening Day of School" for students). Volume 2 contains the individual prayer to each main deity in the Huizhou pantheon invoked in "Offering Thanks to the Many Deities on New Year's Eve." The remaining four volumes cover all other prayers. Whereas all prayers would have been useful for the local people, the most important part of the handbook clearly lay in the first two volumes, invoking the local pantheon and its various deities, with the individual prayers to each of the main deities also working to substantiate and enhance the pantheon. In most of the prayers covered in the handbook, it was with these divine beings, now firmly structured in a pantheon, that local supplicants communicated.

Most importantly, perhaps, this pantheon was now scripted, printed, and readily accessible to locals. The late Ming witnessed a publishing boom (from the 1570s to 1630s), and Huizhou was a center of the printing industry.[14] One genre of such printing was *leishu* (encyclopedias), to which *Model Prayers to the Deities* belongs. The encyclopedia-like ritual handbook was repeatedly printed; two other versions of *Model Prayers* are known to be extant.[15] There seems to have been remarkable stability in the printed prayers, as the two Ming and Qing versions of the handbook are virtually identical, which further suggests its usefulness and popularity. Although the scripted prayers are identical, the Ming imprint is of much higher quality than the Qing version. Most likely, the latter was hastily cut to meet the ritual needs of local people, which also suggests a growing local market for it by Qing times. And the frequency of its printing indicates that it likely sold for a profit. The preface that is included in a different version of *Model Prayers* is revealing. It reads: "the old texts [of *Model Prayers*] are full of unruly elements; they can hardly present the model prayers to the deities. This publishing house has made revisions in ways unlike the other versions. . . . Buyers should take a note of this."[16] Here we see the marks of local commercial interests, or rather the interests of local mercantile lineages. Indeed, frequent reprinting with assurances of the authenticity of its contents, as well as relying upon Cheng Minzheng's reputation to "sell" the religious handbook, was consonant with other merchant practices in Huizhou. Local mercantile lineage culture was characterized by a melding of Confucian values with business prowess and popular religious worship, the latter of which was best embodied in the Wang Hua pantheon.

The multiple sources discussed thus far suggest that the Wang Hua pantheon invoked in these model prayers represented the actual religious praxis of Huizhou people. As will be shown, it was constructed by local elites, but shared by all kinspeople. It was a constant, stable, long-term construction, a product not just of religious piety but also of Huizhou mercantile lineage culture.

THE WANG HUA PANTHEON AND MERCANTILE LINEAGE CULTURE

The Huizhou pantheon was defined by its de facto head. As noted in chapter 1, by the time of the Song dynasty, Wang Hua was worshipped as the God of Xin'an—that is, the single powerful patron deity of the entire prefecture. We can identify three dimensions of character combining in his persona. In addition to being a patron deity of the region, Wang Hua was a potent symbol linking the imperial state and local society, eventually also emerging as the apical ancestor of the Huizhou Wangs. A regional warlord during the Sui-Tang transition, Wang Hua turned over the six prefectures he controlled—including his native prefecture, Xin'an, and the part of Zhejiang known as Yue—to the Tang empire. In return, the Tang made him a top general in command of the military and political affairs of the six prefectures. For his loyalty, Wang Hua was further awarded two imperial jade tablets from emperors Gaozu (r. 618–627) and Taizong (r. 627–649) granting him the title of Duke of Yueguo (Yueguo Gong Gui). The Huizhou genealogists loved to include these testaments to honor and loyalty in the Wang genealogies.[17] The subsequent dynasties, the Song and the Yuan, granted him, his wives, his sons, and his grandsons many more honorable titles, both divine and secular, making him all the more powerful.[18] All of these were further authenticated in the subsequent Ming dynasty, being materialized in the steles erected on the two sides of the main temple to Wang Hua.[19]

The Ming dynasty appears to have treated Wang Hua particularly well, largely because, according to local legend, his spirit had protected Zhu Yuanzhang and his troops when they engaged in fierce fighting in Huizhou before the founding of the Ming dynasty. Acknowledging his efficacy, and to protect his main temple, Zhu Yuanzhang issued a dynastic public notice (*guochao bangwen*) in the seventh lunar month of the fourth year of the Hongwu reign (1371):

> Emperor's Edict to the Provincial Governors of Jiangnan and Other Places: The Local Lord [Tuzhu] of Huizhou, King Wang, has been recorded in the Ritual Code for his protection of the regional society. When the grand [Ming] army conquered the cities of the [Jiangnan] province, the divine soldiers repeatedly assisted in the process, efficaciously abetting powerful and notable accomplishments; [King Wang] deserves to be honored and worshipped. [I hereby order that] the spiritual tablet [of King Wang] be set up in the Tianxing Adjacent Shrine outside of the Main Temple [to Wang Hua] to enjoy sacrifices.

The edict goes on to forbid soldiers from staying in the Wang Hua Temple, cutting down trees, and stationing their horses on the grounds so as to avoid profaning against the divine spirit.[20]

From the Tang through the Ming, honoring Wang Hua was one method the imperial state used to appease the people of Huizhou. And the Huizhou Wangs clearly felt honored, evident in their recording of Wang Hua's imperially granted titles in lineage documents. Such honors were used by the center to enhance its symbolic presence in local society, but the Wang lineage also mobilized them to express loyalty and claim closeness to the center, which further legitimated their local power. The central state treated Wang Hua as a local leader turned regional patron deity, while the locals identified him as a Huizhou hero with ties to the dynastic center. Wang Hua thus became a symbol for the Huizhou people to proclaim the legitimacy of their local power. This might account for the shared nature of the Wang Hua cult in Huizhou. Huizhou dignitaries not affiliated with the Wang lineage also readily paid tribute. For instance, Cheng Minzheng penned verses celebrating him in addition to other commemorative pieces, such as the one recording the reconstruction of the lineage temple worshipping Wang Hua by the Wangs of Yanshan, Xiuning.[21] Bao Xiangxian (*jinshi* 1529) of Tangyue, Shexian, also paid tribute to him when commemorating the building of the Zhonglie (Wang Hua) Shrine in Tangmo.[22]

Well into the Ming dynasty, Wang Hua was universally recognized as the apical ancestor of the Huizhou Wangs. This, combined with his roles as the patron deity of the region and the symbolic link with the imperial state, completed his three-part persona. Wang Songtao's Yuan dynasty genealogy, which highlighted Wang Hua's glorious contributions, is the earliest extant lineage-related source marking the beginning of this evolution, but from the Song through the Yuan, Wang Hua

FIGURE 5. Wang Lineage Temple in Hongcun, front gate. The two couplets read: "The Tang dynasty enfeoffed Yueguo three thousand households strong" (*Tangfeng Yueguo sanqian hu*). "The Song dynasty granted this family the distinction of being number one in all of Jiangnan" (*Songci Jiangnan diyi jia*). Photograph by author, November 2018.

was primarily still seen as the patron deity of the region.[23] In the early Ming, an independent, large-scale lineage temple was built in Hongcun, Yixian, perhaps the first marker of Wang Hua as the apical ancestor of the Hongcun Wangs (fig. 5).

In the main hall of the Wang Lineage Temple, however, are three portraits of three different representative "apical" ancestors: in the middle is Marquis of Yingchuan, the first to gain the surname of Wang; to the left is Wang Hua and to the right is the first migrant ancestor to Hongcun, Wang Yanji (1085–1151).[24] Given the internal arrangements, and in spite of the front-gate couplets, it is still not clear as to whether the lineage temple was constructed to honor Wang Hua as the apical ancestor of the Hongcun Wangs. In any event, the construction of a lineage temple worshipping the apical ancestor was still rare at the time, and would remain so throughout the entire fifteenth century (even taking into account the lineage temple Cheng Minzheng commemorated in 1489). As a comparative reading of the 1502 and 1566 editions of the Huizhou gazetteer shows, the construction of lineage temples, like the compilation of lineage genealogies, did not become widespread until the sixteenth century. By the mid-century, even the remote village of Wuyuan, Fengsha, had built its own Yueguo lineage temple.[25]

The 1551 *Prominent Lineages in Xin'an* recognized Wang Wenhe as the first migrant ancestor, but Wang Hua stood out as the most glorious figure in the ancestry of the Huizhou Wangs.[26] Looking deeper into the Wang settlements listed in the composite genealogical gazetteer, we see that most of them claimed descent from Wang Hua's eight sons, which suggests that Wang Hua was by then collectively treated as the apical ancestor of the Huizhou Wangs.[27] Two decades later, their composite genealogy, *Authentic Lineage of the Composite Wang Descent Line*, compiled in 1571 by Wang Zhonglu and five other kinsmen, identified Wang Hua as their apical ancestor.[28] This timing appears to have coincided with the finalization of *Model Prayers to the Deities*—that is, when Wang Hua was formally scripted as the regional proxy of the City God, commanding a patterned assembly of deities that constituted the Huizhou pantheon. At the same time, as the patron god of Huizhou, the apical ancestor of the Huizhou Wangs also became the lineage tutelary deity of other kinspeople. In this way, the Wang Hua cult also became an extension of Confucian ancestral worship.[29]

That Wang Hua was also worshipped by non-Wang kinspeoples in lineage rituals is clearly borne out by one invaluable type of Huizhou *wenshu* (lineage document), the handwritten *Registers of the Sage-Worshipping Society* (Zhushenghui bu) from Xikou, Xiuning, ritual registers running from the late Ming to the early twentieth century. The first of the ritual documents contained in Registers of the Sage-Worshipping Society is a quasi-community covenant signed in 1602 by two lineage leaders of three villages, Wu Tianqing and Wang Zonggong, for all of their kinspeople. It states that the Wus and Wangs of the three villages, including all of the "gentry, farmers, artisans, and merchants" have had a profitable year because "we believe in divine protection." Three of their tutelary deities are identified: "Duke Wang of Yueguo, the Ninth Lord [Wang Hua's ninth son who was thought to have died young], and Marshal Hu." The community covenant then announces, "Although the Sage-Worshipping Society has been established to offer sacrifice [to our tutelary deities] for a long time, we have not yet organized the procession rite. Now we have decided to carry the deities in procession for the Spring Requesting Festival. This requires both money and labor." And thus, it stipulates, "The households of gentry and merchants shall provide money, prepare the carriages, paraphernalia, and so on. The households of farmers and craftsmen shall provide labor. The upper and lower villages shall take care of the emperor's carriage [for Wang Hua] and the lord's carriage [for the Ninth Lord], and the Shangzhuang village shall take care of the marshal sedan [for Marshal Hu]." This lineage document, in addition to verifying that the cult of Wang Hua was shared by the non-Wangs as well as the Wangs, shows that both gentry and merchant lineage elites engaged in worship of Wang Hua and his divine subordinates. It further demonstrates that they clearly recognized the religious hierarchy by preparing different kinds of paraphernalia for the three different deities.[30]

Wang Hua gained his godly puissance not just by commanding a hierarchically arranged pantheon; he was also Confucianized. As reflected in the name of his main temple, Zhonglie (loyal and righteous), Wang Hua was always a symbol of loyalty and integrity, similar to the most powerful symbol of loyalty and righteousness, Guandi, who was worshipped throughout the empire. Indeed, there was significant conflation of the two deities, especially given that Guandi was incorporated into the Huizhou pantheon to further empower its de facto leader.

In a portrait of Wang Hua included in a 1480 Wang genealogy, we can see that he was depicted as a warrior-statesman of integrity and courage (fig. 6).[31] Notably, he was visibly Confucianized: he is shown holding a book, which in this case was almost certainly the *Spring and Autumn Annals*, as the iconography was almost certainly fashioned after the popular image of Guandi holding the same Confucian classic.

This Confucianized head deity defined the character of the entire Huizhou pantheon: localized yet linked to the imperial center, kinship-oriented yet protective of all the lineages within the entire prefecture. Other deities incorporated into the pantheon, however, were also important. The incorporation of these powerful deities greatly boosted the authority of their commander, Wang Hua, but they also gained additional meanings by virtue of their position within the religious order, which was hierarchically structured. This divine system included thearchs, kings, marquises, ministers, marshals, generals, secretaries, agents, guardians, and soldiers, a mirror of the empire's bureaucratic machine. The pantheon was omnipotent, endowed with divine power overseeing virtually all aspects of human life, hidden or manifest, in the functions of the various incorporated deities. It was syncretic in nature, regionally bounded and yet exceeding the boundaries of Huizhou, open to divine influences from the entire realm. It embraced Daoist immortals and Buddhist bodhisattvas, local and national deities, and officially sanctioned gods and spirits of dubious, or even devious, character.

The most intriguing of the divine beings within the pantheon were the fearsome Wuchang Five-Fury Spirits, placed in the lowest rank. (The Hehe twin genii of concord balanced the frightening quality of the Five-Fury Spirits with auspiciousness, and the official Earth God was placed at the end to conclude the pantheon, parallel to the way in which the official City God headed it). The Wuchang pentad spirit was endowed with multiple roles; it acquired new meanings by being conflated with or sheltered under other deities. The Five-Fury Spirits were enormously popular, being the demon bailiffs in charge of the exorcistic rituals staged along with the *Mulian* operatic performance in Huizhou. And yet, unlike other pentad spirits, Wuchang were hardly ever recorded as independent deities in late imperial writings.[32] Indeed, the Wuchang pentad spirit never worked alone: in the Daoist tradition, it was subordinated to Marshal Zhao, and in Huizhou local worship, it was also sheltered under other deities, such as Wuxian on Zhi Hill and the fertility deities, and ultimately subsumed within the Wang Hua pantheon.[33]

The Wuchang pentad spirit was primarily a symbol of exorcism, and in late Ming Huizhou it emerged as a leading variant of the God of Wealth, partially through a process of cultural and mythological conflations with another diabolical pentad spirit, Wutong. Wutong, believed to be a mountain goblin who brought money to men in exchange for sex with their wives, was enormously popular as a

贊曰
越國汪王處
心忠良施偉
烈而保障六
州著名譽而
感慕萬邦懹
既佐唐朝之
主復助我
祖高皇宜其享
祀無窮以增
先後之光
大明宗室
遼王書

FIGURE 6. Portrait of Wang Hua. The caption reads: "Praising Commentary: Lord Wang of
Yueguo was possessed of loyal will. He acted decisively in protecting the six prefectures. His
fame attracted gratitude and admiration from all of the regions. O! He not only assisted the
Tang emperors, but further protected my ancestor, the First Ming Emperor. He deserves sacrificial rites forever to enhance the glory of the realm. Written by Lord Liao, prince of the royal
family of the Great Ming." Wang Daojin, *Wangshi zupu* (1480), *Fulu* (appendixes), 4b. Courtesy
of Shanghai Library.

"devious" God of Wealth in certain Jiangnan areas.[34] But in Huizhou, its place of origin, it came to be eclipsed by Wuchang over the course of the sixteenth century.[35] Other sources indicate that Huizhou merchants did indeed worship Wuchang, not Wutong, as their God of Wealth. Xu Zhuo, in his *Miscellaneous Matters of Xiuning*, an 1811 collection of anecdotal notes on daily life in Xiuning, includes a late Ming account detailing popular Wuxian/Wuchang worship in sixteenth-century Haiyang—the bustling county seat of Xiuning that emerged in the sixteenth century as a commercial center for the whole prefecture:

> On the [Zhi] Hill is the Wuxian King Temple. From the Jia-Long eras [the Jiajing-Longqing reigns, 1522–1566 and 1567–1572] onward, inhabitants from all five directions have made pilgrimages to the temple every year on the first day of the fourth month, offering incense and drawing lots. According to local lore, whoever draws the lot of one of the five deities [the Five Manifestations] will be blessed. Those who do not draw one of these lots dare not vie with each other [for the blessing]; the honor of inviting the deity down from the hill [to be carried in procession] is determined on the basis of the drawn lots. A day is chosen for the procession. [People from] the five directions participate in it in a random way, depending on their time of arrival. On the day of the procession, the paraded banners, weapons, and paraphernalia are as magnificent as those used for the king. Local benefactors provide the [carried] tableau stages [*taixi*]. The tableau stages are decorated with flashy and ornate yellow and white pearls and beads, each prepared to show uniqueness and ingenuity. Should any sector [of the procession] attempt to skimp on the preparations, it is cursed and mocked by all. In this manner, [each contingent] encourages the others in ever more splendid display: this is the so-called competition festival [*saihui* or temple festival of ritual operatic performance]. On the chosen day, colored flags block out the sun, drummed music deafens the heavens, and spectators from near and far gather thick as walls. After the procession, each household from the constituent communities is ordered to prepare a lantern, candle, and torches to escort the deities back up the hill. On this night, the torches light up the sky like daylight. In front of the temple is the Huaguang Tower, alongside which is a Wuchang Shrine. Prayers [to the Wuchang] during all four seasons are always efficaciously answered. At the end of the year, even more livestock and wine are sacrificed there. The deity has enjoyed blood offerings for many years. Legend has it that this is the Ancestral Palace of Zhi Hill.
>
> *Gazetteer of the Mountains and Rivers of Haiyang*[36]

Xu Zhuo included in his *Miscellaneous Matters* another account of the Wuxian cult associated with Zhi Hill from a different sourcebook called *Random Jottings from the Ren'an Hall*. It notes that "the Huaguang Temple lies in the east of Xiuning City, in which the Wuxian God is worshipped. In the Ming dynasty, the wealthy in the county offered rich sacrifices there. After the fall of the dynasty, the temple gradually fell into disuse."[37] The snippet in *Random Jottings* complements the earlier account, specifying who offered "rich sacrifices" to the Wuxian

Temple and its auxiliary Wuchang shrine. When read together, these two accounts clearly indicate that from the sixteenth century on the people of Haiyang, and especially wealthy merchants or wealthy households from local mercantile lineages, worshipped Wuxian/Wuchang.[38]

The temple or shrine layout on Zhi Hill also suggests that over the course of the sixteenth century, Wuchang had replaced Wutong as the popular variant of the Wuxian (which had been the official avatar of the sinister Wutong since Song times). There is additional evidence, especially *Model Prayers to the Deities*, to verify this process, which appears to have coincided with the coalescence of the Wang Hua pantheon.

Cheng Minzheng, while compiling the *Supplemented Heart Classic*, includes one statement by Zhu Xi regarding the Wutong cult in Xin'an: "Local customs worship ghosts. Places like Xin'an appear to live day and night in a ghost-dominated den. There are so-called Wutong temples, which are most efficacious."[39] And again, in *Xin'an Documents*, Cheng Minzheng includes a passage by Zhu Xi's second generation disciple, the notable Wuyuan native Hu Sheng (*jinshi* 1185), on clarifying some "facts" on Wuxian, wherein he rejects the equation of Wutong and Wusheng (Five Sages).[40] If in Cheng Minzheng's time, Wutong had already disappeared in Huizhou, or had been replaced by Wuchang in local worship, he most likely would not have bothered to include Zhu Xi's and Hu Sheng's passages on Wutong in his important compilations of historical and philosophical documents.

By Wang Daokun's time, however, we see something different. In one of his merchant biographies, Wang Daokun mentions that a sojourning Huizhou merchant encountered the cult of the Wutong mountain goblin in Jingzhou of Hubei, but once he returned home to Huizhou, he disavowed it.[41] The best source to directly verify the usurpation of Wutong by Wuchang in post–Cheng Minzheng Huizhou is *Model Prayers to the Deities*. The religious handbook does not mention Wutong (except once in passing in a prayer to its official variant, Wuxian), whereas Wuchang is everywhere, suggesting the complete eclipse of Wutong by Wuchang in Huizhou local worship by the late sixteenth century.

This replacement of Wutong, I suggest, reflects the collective—even if unconscious—engineering of local elites, who acted on behalf of the "class" interests of mercantile lineages by "patterning" (*ge* of *Qishen zouge*) local prayers, which were then codified in the late Ming *Model Prayers to the Deities*. Wuchang's replacement of Wutong came to be accepted and then fixed in the religious handbook as well as on Zhi Hill. I base this interpretation of the cultural politics of the Wutong-Wuchang switch on three factors.

First, Wuchang, while demonic like Wutong, were nevertheless controlled within the Wang Hua pantheon. Wuchang were believed to be good ghosts (*haogui*), even if their ghostly nature made them potentially dangerous and threatening. This characterization shadowed that of Huizhou merchants who had been characterized as good merchants (*lianggu*)—or good but still morally ambiguous merchants, suspect partly on account of their dealings with money.[42] This symbolic resemblance between Wuchang and *lianggu* is reinforced—if not mirrored—in Huizhou merchants' worship of Wuchang as a God of Wealth. These parallel hierarchies in the spiritual and social realms suggest that Huizhou merchants, collectively as a social group (though not necessarily as individuals), willingly submitted to their home gentry and identified with their home lineages. Similarly, the Wuchang pentad spirit was subordinated to the patron deity of lineages. This had the effect of sanctioning their money-making efforts, so long as they channeled a portion of that profit back home to enhance their ancestral lineages. Central to popular Wuchang imagery was the negotiation in the symbolic realm of gentry-merchant and lineage-sojourner relations.

Second, Wuchang's suppression of Wutong in Huizhou was also entwined with local gender dynamics. Since many young Huizhou merchants left home on business for long stretches of time, they were overly concerned with the chastity of their wives at home. Wutong symbolized both ill-gotten money and men's illicit sex, but local mercantile lineages did not need a sinister God of Wealth that cautioned against male sexual intemperance and characterized merchants as dishonest. Rather, what appealed to them (and their lineage elders) was a God of Wealth who could also police lonely kinswomen; this was precisely the role that Wuchang could perform. As shown in popular *Mulian* performance, the Wuchang demon bailiffs were charged with the heavenly duty to punish disloyal or evil women.[43]

Third, Wuchang's roles were more extensive than those of Wutong, partially because the pentad spirit was positioned within the Wang Hua pantheon, as fully displayed in *Model Prayers*. In a prayer to the Wuchang spirits, the Five Furies are invoked as such: "May we live well and prosper, may elders and youngsters be of healthy mind and body; may the four seasons remain free of disasters, may the eight festivals be marked with celebration; may those who seek fame rise as high as the clouds [pass the exams]; may those who seek profits succeed in all markets; let the five grains be richly harvested and the six [kinds of] domestic animals thrive; whether by boat or by cart, let those who go to and fro the rivers and roads stay safe and sound."[44] Here, the Wuchang pentad spirit was not just a God of Wealth, but a divine force protecting the main interests of the leading social groupings living within the mercantile lineages. The pentad spirit was given so much efficacious purview not because it had become a patron deity of the mercantile lineage, but because it was a popular and down-to-earth god, positioned at the bottom of the Wang Hua pantheon, which engendered a sense of closeness among the local people.[45] The Wuchang prayer further shows that its religious role became conflated with that of other deities within the same pantheon. The individual prayers to Guandi and the Three Kings and Marquis (of Shi, Bian, and Zhou), for instance, display similar broad purviews of efficaciousness that these deities had acquired.[46]

From *Model Prayers to the Deities*, moreover, we see an additional facet of Wuchang in relation to women. The deity served to protect and assist mothers in reproduction. To put it in divine terms, Wuchang were also subordinate to, or the guardians of, the patron deities of childbirth.[47] The third volume of *Model Prayers* includes at least four prayers concerning childbirth. The opening short prayer of the third volume, titled "Offering Candles to the Deities in Seeking Offspring" (Qiusi qingshen zhu), clearly concerns childbirth, although no deities are specified. The next prayer, "Offering Candles to Secure the Deities' [Blessing]" (Anshen zhu), appeals to the three deities of fertility, including Immortal Zhang who controlled childbirth (*zhangsheng*), Marshal Gao—here called Marshal Gao, Sender of Sons from the Ninth Heaven (Jiutian Songzi Gao Yuanshuai), and Our Lady Venerable Mother of Infinite Fortune from the Eastern Peak. These two prayers, without mentioning Wuchang directly, pave the way for the subsequent two prayers on the same subject, showing how significant this was to locals.[48] In the next two prayers concerning childbirth, "Invoking Deities for Expeditious Births" (Cuisheng qingshen) and "Invoking Deities for the Birth of Sons" (Shengzi qingshen), not only are the three deities of fertility (and an unspecified multitude of gods or *zhongshen*, that is, the Huizhou pantheon) invoked, but so are the Wuchang, who serve as the guardians of these deities, as well as the direct protectors of women seeking children (especially sons) or expectant women seeking safe delivery.[49]

Given that the Wuchang were conceived as guardians of childbirth, and especially the birth of sons, it is likely that Huizhou kinspeople, and merchants in particular, would have had little need to continue to worship Wutong as a popular variety of the God of Wealth. Successful childbirth was quite simply the dearest thing for both women and their sojourning husbands, as well as their larger lineages. This was especially important in an age of commercialization, as a large number of young men sojourned out of Huizhou for business immediately after completion of the nuptials.[50]

In general, then, Wuchang were sheltered under a variety of deities with variant roles, including Marshal Zhao, Wuxian, and the popular fertility deities. All of them, along with many other gods with different functions, were ultimately incorporated into the Huizhou pantheon to make its divine rule and role all purposeful and all powerful. This omnipotent regional pantheon was directed by its de facto head, Wang Hua, who channeled the power of all the mighty deities therein incorporated.

I suggest that this pantheon, with Wang Hua on top and Wuchang at the bottom, further represented the collective interests of local mercantile lineages. Both had special Huizhou characteristics. Wang Hua was a deified Huizhou hero, and the Wuchang pentad spirit completely eclipsed the demonic Wutong that had originated in the region. Both were multivocal. Wang Hua was an officially sanctioned deity and, as the local proxy for the City God and tutelary deity of Huizhou, served to link the locality to the state. Moreover, as the most notable apical ancestor of the Huizhou Wangs, his cult served as a virtual extension of Confucian ances-tral worship. Wuchang, originally a symbol of exorcism sheltered under the great Daoist guardian Marshal Zhao, underwent a transformation, partially through mythological conflation with Wutong, to emerge as a patron deity of Huizhou merchants. Most intriguing of all, this popular god of wealth garnered additional powers to both monitor and protect women, represented either as the Five Fury beast-like bailiffs who punished transgressive women or as the guardians of the fertility deities who assisted mothers in reproduction. Symbolically, the role of Wuchang within the Huizhou pantheon mirrored that of merchants within the lineage. Just as merchants as a social group were subordinated within the lineage, so too did the Wuchang come under the surveillance of the tutelary deity of the lineage. Similarly, not unlike the ways in which kinswomen were both policed and protected by the larger lineage, the Wuchang played this dual role of enforcer on a symbolic level. Through subscribing to the multiple powers of the full Huizhou pantheon, the soteriological needs of local mercantile lineages were fulfilled.

Model Prayers to the Deities, by fixing the pantheon in print, greatly facilitated this religious fulfillment. By scripting and printing prayers for all of the ritual occa-sions, the producers of the religious handbook provided the locals with prepared prayers, which put ritual knowledge into the hands of laymen, thereby snatching ritual authority away from local religious institutions. *Model Prayers to the Deities*, especially its printed pantheon, marked the final triumph of the lineage institution over local religious establishments in the symbolic realm of ritual performance. This completed the historical process of the rise of the lineage in Ming Huizhou that Joseph McDermott has so amply documented.[51] By the time *Model Prayers* was finalized, what was reflected in it was not just the kinship culture, but that of mercantile lineages. Their regional pantheon also marked the completion of the localist turn, a historical process that Cheng Minzheng had initiated in Huizhou.

THE AUTHORSHIP OF *MODEL PRAYERS* AND ITS LARGER MEANINGS

I turn now to the attributed authorship of *Model Prayers* and its larger meanings vis-à-vis Huizhou lineage politics and emerging mercantile lineage culture as a whole. Cheng Minzheng is singled out as the "original compiler" (*yuanbian*) for *Model Prayers to the Deities*, and further identified as "Minister of Rites, Bamboo Mound of Xin'an" (Da Zongbo Xin'an Huangdun), the respectful appellation for him that was used in Huizhou and beyond after his tragic death in 1499. This attri-bution is suspect, but nevertheless should be understood in light of late sixteenth-century Huizhou. It is unlikely that Lord Bamboo Mound would have been party to a publication that inserted his celebrated ancestor Cheng Lingxi into the Wang Hua pantheon as a subordinate. This attributed authorship was made, quite pos-sibly, to justify the subordination of Cheng Lingxi to Wang Hua, which had the effect of thereby achieving a power equilibrium among local big-name lineages in the symbolic realm.

Cheng Minzheng's 1478 tour to Huangdun, as noted in chapter 1, had been designed, in part, to promote the godly power of Cheng Lingxi. As a corollary, in the two Cheng genealogies he compiled, he emphasized Cheng Lingxi's status as the traceable apical ancestor of the Huizhou Chengs. In *Records of Bequeathed Glories*, Cheng Minzheng again gave Cheng Lingxi special treatment, reprinting all of the Song-Ming imperial edicts sanctioning local sacrifices to his deified ancestor.[52] This appeal to lineage preeminence was made in the context of the local religious landscape. Cheng Lingxi had since the Song been emerging as a popular deity in Huizhou, but he was no match for Wang Hua, "the God of Xin'an," who had dominated local communal liturgies during the same period. Cheng Minzheng himself paid visits to the main temple to Wang Hua on Fu Hill, leaving behind two verses acknowledging that "sacrificial incense to [Wang Hua] temples have flourished for a thousand years, [from which we] know that the hero loved his native place."[53] He also wrote several commemorative pieces honoring this patron deity of Huizhou, although he often used these as opportunities to sneak in stories about the glory and efficacy of his deified ancestor as well.[54] Elsewhere, in his essays on local religious beliefs in general, Minzheng always put Cheng Lingxi ahead of Wang Hua, a practice also repeated in their ordered placement in his *Anthology of Xin'an Documents* and *Gazetteer of Xiuning*.[55]

Still, this consideration alone should not justify a complete write-off of Cheng Minzheng's role in the production of the religious handbook. After all, he had interest in the matter of local cults and communal rituals. He authored several essays on domestic and popular cults. One concerns the archaic Wusi—the five rituals to the deities of the stove, the cistern, the gate, the path, and the *li* (the spirits of those who died unnatural deaths)—in which Minzheng argued for the replacement of the path by the stove and of the generic *li* by the "lineage *li*" (another example showing Minzheng's localist focus through honoring kinspeople's spirits).[56] Another focuses on deified historical figures, listing four of them in the order of Guandi, Cheng Lingxi, Wang Hua, and Zhang Xun.[57] In yet another, Minzheng links rituals to his father to the Wusi as well as to the four deified historical figures.[58] In ritual practice, he selected a Buddhist chapel for the site of the shrine honoring his father, where he was to be worshipped along with Guandi, Zhang Xun, and the Buddha (see chapter 1).

For Cheng Minzheng, obviously, proper rituals to popular cults played an important role in maintaining order within local society. And in Huizhou, the Wang Hua pantheon was an important aspect of lineage institution, supplementing and strengthening ancestral worship. In light of these considerations, it is quite possible that Cheng Minzheng might have composed similar prayers upon which the later editors of *Model Prayers* drew. In fact, he did compose prayers on various ritual occasions. One enlists Cheng Lingxi's protection for the birth of his second son; a second prays for the peace of his father's spirit in the wake of a fire at home; and a third prays to the Wusi, Guandi, Cheng Lingxi, Wang Hua, and Zhang Xun on the occasion of rebuilding his father's shrine.[59]

It is conceivable that the editors of *Model Prayers* may have borrowed some of Cheng Minzheng's ritual writings in culling together local liturgies for the religious handbook. It should be noted that the six volumes of the handbook are titled by the six characters referring to the six arts that a gentryman was supposed to master in the Confucian tradition: "Rites" (Li), "Music" (Yue), "Mounted Archery (She), "Chariot Driving" (Yu), "Calligraphy" (Shu), and "Math" (Shu). This titling provides a classical luster as well as a Confucian façade to the handbook. More likely, though, the producers of this text were borrowing the fame of Cheng Minzheng to increase the authority of *Model Prayers*. The frontispiece of the Qing version lists, after Cheng Minzheng, five later editors or reprinters, including: Zhu Yishi as authenticator (*jianding*); Dai Tianpei, Dai Wei, and Huang Yuanbi as copyeditors (*jiaozi*); and Dai Qida as the reprinter (*chongkan*). Except Zhu Yishi, a noted Xiuning gentryman-artist who earned the provincial *juren* degree in 1642, the four others are unidentifiable figures. Given the background of the group leader Zhu Yishi, however, the other four most likely fall into the similar category of local gentry specializing in ritual matters.[60] Other sources indicate that Zhu Yishi ran away from Huizhou and hid himself in Wuxi (the heartland of Jiangnan) after the Qing conquest in 1644, which suggests that Zhu must have compiled the Ming version of *Model Prayers* before passing the *juren* degree, and the Qing version is a reprint of the former Zhu version by other "ritual specialists" (perhaps by someone like the "reprinter" Dai Qida?) who then replaced veneration of the Ming with the Qing in various prayers.[61]

In the late Ming, relying upon Cheng Minzheng's reputation to "sell" this text would surely have been consonant with other practices of Huizhou merchants or mercantile lineages, characterized by a melding of Confucian values with popular religious worship, which was furthered by a booming printing industry as well as ritual and opera performance. In the process, these ritual specialists further promoted the Wang Hua pantheon. In this instance, then, the name "Bamboo Mound" was used in a way that mimicked the strategy Cheng Minzheng had so skillfully employed in rewriting the philological origins of Huangdun in order to boost the prestige of the Huizhou Chengs.

Model Prayers may have been attributed to Cheng Minzheng not only to enhance its market value, but also to reconfirm Wang Hua's ritual authority over Cheng Lingxi, thereby increasing Wang Hua's divine power to balance the genealogical pedigree of the Chengs, which Cheng Minzheng had so skillfully promoted. No one could have worked more effectively than Cheng Minzheng to justify this localized religious order in which Cheng Lingxi is rather far down on the descending list of godly puissance. Looking through the vast inventory of Huizhou lineage-related documents, it is clear that the Wangs, while sharing with other surnames a strong interest in compiling genealogies, had since the Yuan dynasty developed an intense interest in documenting Wang Hua's religious power (which was built on the identification of the God of Xin'an in the Song by Luo Yuan, a non-Wang compiler of the *Xin'an Gazetteer*). This trend started with the Yuan-era *Wangshi yuanyuan lu* by Wang Songtao and was further enhanced with the reprinting in the 1460s of the expanded *Revised Records of Xin'an's Zhonglie Temple and Its Deities* (Chongbian Xin'an Zhonglie miao shen jishi) by Wang Nanxuan of Shexian's Huaitang. In the subsequent Ming and Qing, the Wangs continued to compile numerous works on the cult of their apical ancestor, including, for instance, the aforementioned *Briefs on the Ancestral Tombs of the Xixi Wang* (Xixi Wangshi xianying bianlan, 1539) and *Records on the Shrine and Tomb of Lord Wang of Yueguo* (Yueguo Wanggong cimu zhi, 1852). One way or another, the Wangs may have exerted influence upon *Model Prayers*.

Still, demonstrating Wang influence (or lack thereof) on this particular handbook is not necessary to establish the likely appropriation of Cheng Minzheng for the purpose of promoting the Wang Hua pantheon.[62] Concern with subordinating Cheng Lingxi to Wang Hua can be seen in other Huizhou anecdotes—for example, the story titled "Lord Wang Makes a Divine Appearance," which is recorded in the Xiuning county gazetteer. According to a local myth, when the Qing army entered Huizhou in 1646, General Zhang Tianlu had a dream in which he saw a deity with a red face and full beard, accompanied by two white-faced attendants. The deity admonished Zhang, saying: "You must take heed during this campaign. Do not kill people. Otherwise, I will see to it that you die a terrible death." Zhang woke up with a fright, figuring that he had seen Guandi. Upon seeing the images in the King Wang temple, he realized the deity in his dream was, in fact, Wang Hua, and he kept his troops disciplined throughout the campaign. One of the Wang attendants in Zhang's dream, the gazetteer account continues, was none other than Cheng Lingxi.[63] Thus, local texts and ritual practices are replete with examples of a lesser Cheng deity vis-à-vis the all-powerful Wang Hua.

Some of the fiercest resistance to Cheng Minzheng's self-glorifying endeavors, in fact, came not from the Wangs, but from other surnames, most notably from branches internal to the Chengs and from the Huangs.[64] In 1483, for instance, not long after the printing of the *Composite Genealogy of the Xin'an Chengs*, Cheng Wenji of the Xiuning Xiguan branch (an offshoot of Minzheng's Peiguo branch) wrote his own *pubian* (genealogical clarification) to refute Minzheng's *pubian*. Wenji complained: "The Academician, a northerner coming to the south to acquaint himself with his ancestral lineage, arbitrarily altered generational sequence and randomly cut off kin branches. This is absurd in the extreme. Therefore, my branch has no desire to be in agreement with him."[65]

Long after Cheng Minzheng had passed from the scene, his *Composite Genealogy* continued to cause controversy within the local Cheng community. In the mid-sixteenth century, Cheng Xu from Wuyuan County compiled a massive new

Xin'an Cheng composite genealogy, clarifying with detailed notations the authentic Cheng branches and their migration history. It includes eight essays identifying the errors of *Composite Genealogy*. In his 1563 preface, Cheng Xu reprimands Minzheng for having wanted to "be grandfather to others' grandfathers and father to others' fathers," a response to *Composite Genealogy* having raised the seniority of the Peiguo Chengs by adding or excising certain generations from other Cheng branches.[66]

Cheng Chang from Qimen County attacked Cheng Minzheng in the mid-sixteenth century for largely the same reasons. Cheng Chang compiled the massive *Genealogy of the Shanhe Chengs in Qimen*, with its opening guideline declaring that Cheng Minzheng's "*Composite Genealogy* was mostly false." He also prepared a substantive "genealogical clarifications" of his own, accusing Cheng Minzheng of altering the Cheng generational sequence for "self-glorification."[67] In an additional critique, Cheng Chang even rejected as groundless his famous kinsman's notorious alteration of "Yellow Mound" to "Bamboo Mound."[68]

If the Huangdun episode added additional fuel to Cheng Chang's rejection of Lord Bamboo Mound's arrogance and phony philology, the renaming surely would have been considered an insult among the Huizhou Huangs. Although no concurrent evidence for Huang umbrage has been uncovered, later sources may shed light back upon mid-Ming tension over Minzheng's arbitrary reinterpretation of the meaning of Huangdun. Both the editorial board of the *Complete Writings of the Four Treasuries* and Xu Chengyao criticized Minzheng's renaming, characterizing it as a "fabrication" and a sign of his "clan chauvinism."[69]

Even more powerful criticism has been preserved in earlier sources from a Shexian Huang gentryman. In the early seventeenth century, Huang Guan wrote two essays entitled "Clarifying Yellow Mound," his beloved ancestral settlement. To counter Minzheng's debranding of Huangdun as the Huangs' original settlement, the two pieces emphasize that the Huangs moved to Huangdun first and that "even women and kids also know Huangdun was the original settlement of the Huangs." The second clarification also notes criticism of Minzheng's Huangdun claim by his contemporaries and unwillingness on the part of Lord Bamboo Mound to take heed of it. Using Huang genealogical evidence to show Minzheng's mistaken history of Huangdun, Huang Guan calls his "bamboo-yellow-bamboo" renaming nothing but "fabricated nonsense."[70]

The rebukes of Cheng Minzheng from both within and without signaled the intensity of power jockeying over local symbolic resources among status-sensitive lineages. As intralineage disputes among the Chengs suggest, even various branches could be involved in these competitions for local prestige. All of this may very well suggest that Cheng Minzheng's name was used to justify the subordination of Cheng Lingxi to Wang Hua within the Huizhou pantheon, so as to offset the elite genealogical preeminence that Cheng Minzheng had worked so hard to build.[71] In effect, a power equilibrium in the symbolic realm was reached between

Huizhou's two most populous and prominent lineages, which at the same time could also comfort other kin groups with the assurance that no one single surname would achieve complete dominance in the local symbolic landscape. After all, Huizhou was a land with a multitude of prominent lineages. By the time the extant late Ming version of *Model Prayers* was finalized and printed, of course, these kinship communities had long turned into mercantile lineages, with fully developed concerns over merchants' virtue and kinswomen's fidelity. This development is clearly embodied in the local religious order as scripted in *Model Prayers to the Deities*. This religious representation also suggests that Cheng Minzheng himself could not have been the compiler of *Model Prayers to the Deities*, and yet at the same time the identification of him as its "original" compiler made perfect sense given the new mercantile lineage culture in the sixteenth century.

CONCLUSION

It is fitting to conclude the last chapter of this book by returning to the figure with whom we started this journey into exploring regional consciousness and local identity. Cheng Minzheng was publicly attributed as the author of *Model Prayers to the Deities*. Arguably, the appropriation of the name of Cheng Minzheng, who was himself masterful in using appropriation to promote his lineage, was in part to legitimate a localized religious order. This order fixed his eminent ancestor Cheng Lingxi as an attendant to Wang Hua in order to achieve a balance of the symbolic power shared by local prominent lineages. Wang Hua's divine power was used to offset the prominence of Cheng's genealogical pedigree as fixed in Huizhou composite genealogical gazetteers. This power jockeying in the local arena enriches the concept of the Ming "localist turn." First, there was competition for prominence among local lineages. Second, this competition ultimately reached a power balance, thereby paving the way for cooperation between elite lineages so as to assure their continuous generation of scholar-officials and top merchants. Third, in the end, the local religious order scripted in *Model Prayers to the Deities* complemented *Prominent Lineages in Huizhou* to enrich the local identity of Huizhou.

The making of the Wang Hua pantheon, however, was itself also part of the larger social and religious changes that were taking place empire-wide from the mid-fifteenth to the mid-sixteenth centuries. It was a historical process, coinciding with the rise of regional consciousness on the one hand and with the localized transformation of the official City God cult on the other. This process was likely not finalized until the late Ming, as reflected in the extant version of *Model Prayers to the Deities*. Cheng Minzheng may have had some impact on the ritual handbook, but the patterning of a local religious order was a collective product of local elites in response to changing state-society relations and the ritual needs of local people living under mercantile lineages.

Here we begin to see the theoretical implications of focusing on the regional pantheon. It was local elites, not the state, who were responsible for the "patterning" of local cults, and their integration into the Huizhou pantheon was remarkably stable, prevailing from the sixteenth century down through the early decades of the twentieth century.[72] The mid-Ming era was marked by the retreat of the state from society and increased activism by local gentry. The best embodiment of the historical process of the "localist turn" was located in the symbolic realm of ritual performance, especially evident in the making of the Huizhou pantheon. And yet, the state was still present in local worship, in the City God's symbolic heading of the pantheon. Even the pantheon's de facto head, Wang Hua, was a symbol of loyalty and righteousness that, while representing local interests, helped the dynastic center penetrate local society in Huizhou.

Once again, the Huizhou local pantheon embodied a mode of state-society relations that was not zero-sum, but mutually enhancing. This is not to say that tension did not exist, but that the tension was embodied in the rise of the Huizhou pantheon, with Wang Hua fulfilling the authority of the territory deity on behalf of the official City God. Moreover, the Wang Hua pantheon was a local variant of the official pantheon and the pantheons of the institutional religions, even though it was not as neatly constructed. It was a religious mirror of the imperial system, including an emperor, ministers, marshals, secretaries, agents, and soldiers in its hierarchy. It combined bureaucratic and personal modes of worship into one. For example, Wang Hua was also worshipped as the apical ancestor of the Huizhou Wangs and Our Lady Venerable Mother of Infinite Fortune as the fertility goddess.[73] The perspective and practicing of the local pantheon helps to illuminate some key issues in the study of Chinese religious history, ranging from the relationship between state and society to the interaction between highbrow and lowbrow interests in the making of cultural integration and diversity.

The concept of the local pantheon, furthermore, enables us to genuinely study religious culture as history. Ethnographic historians of Chinese popular religion seem to always find it difficult to develop a historical perspective while focusing on one particular deity, especially the popular ones, such as Wuchang. This is partly due to a scarcity of sources. When studied within a pantheon, Wuchang, for instance, can be traced historically; in this way, its religious and social meanings can be more fully illuminated. In addition, the local pantheon sheds new light upon the positioning of the various deities within a nested religious hierarchy. We are simply unable to make full sense of local deities in isolation, especially the seemingly demonic or "unruly" ones, as they acquired new meanings from their positioning within the local pantheon and from their relations to other deities through conflation or replacement. As such, the Wang Hua pantheon demonstrates a dialectical process of interaction between local and extra-regional (and secular and ideological) forces in shaping local rituals. *Model Prayers to the Deities* exhibits this pattern of integration and diversity. In other words, the process of "patterning," or integration, also allowed for the perseverance of cultural diversity embodied in the co-opted sinister spirits.[74] Only when contextualized in terms of their relationships within a larger network of deities can we properly understand how the locals made use of them. And in Huizhou, only then can we weave the symbolic meanings of various local deities, as well as the Wang Hua pantheon, into the social history of mercantile lineage culture.

Through studying the making of the Huizhou pantheon, we see not only how history transformed the symbolic order of local worship, but also how history itself was symbolically ordered and reordered. As the Wang Hua pantheon was hierarchically structured, it served to control the power of many popular deities that were incorporated into its symbolic network, including the dubious God of Wealth, Wuchang, channeling its power to good use while averting its potential harmful impacts. Wuchang as a "good ghost" as positioned with the Huizhou pantheon was the best symbolic analogy of Huishang as "good merchants" as positioned in the social order of local prominent lineages. Moreover, this Huizhou variant of the God of Wealth also played a role in shaping gender dynamics in local society, helping to police kinswomen's sexuality and protect them in childbirth, both key concerns for sojourning merchants and their home lineages. The de facto leader of the Huizhou pantheon, Wang Hua, while personifying the official City God, was also worshipped as the apical ancestor of all of the Huizhou Wangs. This tutelary deity of the region was thus turned into a generic patron deity of all of the Huizhou lineages, thereby extending and empowering Confucian ancestral worship. Indeed, the Wang Hua pantheon not only marked the rise of regional consciousness, but also became the religious representation of Huizhou mercantile lineage culture.

Conclusion

In 1626, *Prominent Lineages in Xiuning* (Xiuning mingzu zhi), the last of the three Huizhou genealogical gazetteers, was published. It was compiled by the Xiuning gentryman, Cao Sixuan, who fulfilled his father's will to update *Prominent Lineages in Xin'an*.[1] It was intended as one of six volumes of the new, expanded version of the 1551 prefecture-wide genealogical gazetteer, with the other five volumes projected to cover the other five counties of Huizhou.[2] In other words, *Prominent Lineages in Xiuning* was attempted as a separate set of six volumes of a new edition of *Prominent Lineages in Xin'an*, not as a county-wide genealogical gazetteer alone. Still, this Xiuning volume suggests that the localist turn went even deeper. Some new features of the Xiuning genealogical gazetteer turned out to enhance the Huizhou identity—with its camouflaged core of mercantile lineages—first established in the *Prominent Lineages in Xin'an*.

One notable feature of *Prominent Lineages in Xiuning* lies in its opening list of various social categories.[3] Fifteen categories are listed in total (the numbers refer to the historical figures recorded in each category):

Shuoru (Prominent Confucians): 12
Xunxian (Eminent Officials and Worthies): 6
Zhongchen (Loyal Officials): 11
Xiaozi (Filial Sons): 36
Wenyuan (Men of Letters): 24
Huanye (Successful Bureaucrats): 107
Fengya (Men of Elegance): 39
Fengjie (Men of Refined and Righteous Manners): 14
Yinyi (Recluses): 42
Duxing (Devoted Men): 47
Xiangshan (Local Philanthropists): 117
Qishou (Men of Longevity): 32
Caiwu (Men of Martial Genius): 55

Xuelin (Scholars): 56

Zhenlie (Faithful Maidens and Chastity Martyrs): 256[4]

As the list illustrates, the prominent lineage was still defined by the aristocratic or gentrified kinsmen in the political and scholarly realms, which suggests the accommodating orientation between the local society and state even as the focus of regional representation was further localized from the prefecture to county level. Confucian chastity martyrs and faithful maidens were the largest category, numbering 256 in total for the county of Xiuning alone, reflecting the peak of the chastity cult.[5] Also notable are the various categories of mundane accomplishments in lifestyle or philanthropy, additions since the 1551 *Prominent Lineages in Xin'an*, furthering the inclusiveness that resonated with the moral leveling of social distinctions of Wang Yangmingism.

What makes this outline of categories most notable, however, is not what it covers, but what it leaves out. In an age of mercantile lineage culture in Huizhou, there is no category for "merchants," especially given that so many of them are covered in various lineage entries. In fact, merchants were now honored with more socially elevated terms than in the 1551 genealogical gazetteer. For instance, Cheng Tingzhou of the Xiguan Chengs (an off-branch of Cheng Minzheng's ancestral lineage in Peiguo), sojourned to Jiangxi on trade, eventually settling there. His three sons worked together in the pawnshop business and salt trade, and "started a great enterprise and thereby built a lasting tradition" (*chuangye chuitong*).

This term, reserved in official historiography specifically for the founding emperors of dynasties, recalls the way in which Wang Daokun linked his descent line to the Zhou royal family. When looking further, however, we find that Tingzhou's second son, Jinan, is highlighted for having taken good care of his orphaned nephews as well as his own aging parents after his two brothers passed away. Indeed, we are told, the entire family lived "harmoniously and happily under the same roof."[6] This kinship-centered appreciation of merchant merits is central to the genealogical gazetteers of Xin'an and Xiuning.[7] And so, without an overall category in which they could be featured, Huizhou merchants are covered in other categories. Cheng Tingzhou, for instance, is honored in "Shanxing" (an alternative for Xiangshan or Local Philanthropists) and Cheng Jinan in "Dajie" (an alternative for Fengjie or Men of Refined and Righteous Manners).[8]

This textual arrangement makes the "conspicuously unmarked identity" of Huizhou merchants look even more pronounced than in the "category-less" *Prominent Lineages in Xin'an*. The key development in Huizhou local discourse from the 1551 Xin'an genealogical gazetteer through Wang Daokun to the 1626 *Prominent Lineages in Xiuning* was an increasing discrepancy between the rising importance of merchants and the decreasing visibility of them as a distinct category. The more socially elevated Huizhou merchants became in local writings, the deeper their lack of singular identity. This can be seen as the culmination of the historical pattern that began with Cheng Minzheng's focus on local kinship values, carried through the Huizhou self-identification in *Prominent Lineages in Xin'an*, and developed into the gentrified mercantile lineage culture in the age of Wang Daokun.

Throughout this study, I delineate the historical formation of the Huizhou identity as a land of prominent lineages, while at the same time illuminating its evolving core, which consisted of mercantile lineages. That core, however, was consciously elided in the regional self-identification. This distinction between the Huizhou identification in self-representation and its sublimated core in practice was significant. The identification with prominent lineages was one of the key factors that made Huizhou merchants enormously successful in the specific political and sociocultural environment of late imperial China. Ironically, however, it further hindered the formation of their own so-called class consciousness.[9] Merchants, in general, were looked down upon in Confucian gentry discourse; Huizhou merchants, in particular, were condemned by outsiders as overly dominant and overly shrewd, if not downright immoral or dishonest. The prominent lineages that sustained Huizhou merchants, however, lent them a sheen of cultural decorousness and moral worth, which shielded their mercantile activities outside of Huizhou. Home lineages also promulgated a strict gender regime to ensure kinswives' devotion to their absent husbands. One of the most important logistical supports sojourning men enjoyed, this regime nevertheless also worked to restrain Huizhou merchants, as it kept regenerating the mercantile lineage. The hierarchical social dynamics of Huizhou mercantile lineages was further embodied in the local religious order and enhanced through local ritual performance.

Understanding this Huizhou story is important not just for its intrinsic historical value. Rather, the practice of sublimating prodigious mercantile activity under the banner of dominant hierarchies and moral systems had tenacious staying power well beyond the Ming and well beyond the borders of Huizhou. The particulars have changed over time, but certain telltale patterns—the embrace of conservative social values and the collusion of business capital with both local power and state ideology—have persisted in China into modern times.

Summary of Wang Daokun's Huizhou Merchant Biographies

The numbers following each entry correspond to the page numbers in the original source, Wang Daokun's *Taihan Collection* (Taihan ji). I also consulted his *Genealogy of the Sixteen Branches of the Lingshanyuan Wangs* (Lingshanyuan Wangshi shiliu zu pu): 10.3.15b–18a; 10.3.6a–7b; 10.3.19a–21a; 10.7.17a–22b.

1. Wang Tongbao, Daokun's kinsman, was a successful self-made businessman. He was noted for his big-heartedness, righteousness, and generosity, especially reflected in his love and support for his kinspeople. Among his lineage-centered activities was the reclaiming of the land formally belonging to the Lingshan ancestral hall of the Wangs and some ancestral tombs that had been encroached upon by local strongmen (598–600).
2. Cha Nai, nicknamed Bashi (Eighty), once followed his father and brother to engage in trade, but eventually emerged as a famous *pipa* (lute) musician noted for his righteous chivalry (601–3).
3. Wang Zhong, who followed his father to Zhejiang for business, studied calligraphy. Called a *chushi* (untitled gentryman, generally referring to a student-turned-merchant), Wang Zhong was noted for his hospitality, *jiexia* (chivalrous righteousness), and love for cleanliness. His son engaged in trade (603–4).
4. Shen Wenzhen was a merchant who failed at whatever he did in business, whether selling liquor or fish, but he was generous and able to uphold the principle of righteousness (*dajie*). He was devoted to his mother and urged his son to pursue Confucian learning (605–6).
5. Zhu Jiefu, whose father dealt salt in Changzhou, enrolled in the county school in Changzhou at the age of fourteen. After his father died, he gave up classical learning to continue to trade in salt. Noted for his chivalrous righteousness, he still used a local debased term, *gushuzi* (mean trader), to refer to merchants (612–14).

6. Zhan Jie came from a family with many Confucian scholars in its ancestry who had been recorded in the prefectural gazetteers. A typical *chushi*, Zhan Jie engaged in trade along the southeast coast of China (Zhejiang and Fujian). He was noted for his ability to hold his liquor (like Wang Daokun) and his generous chivalry (*renxia*) (614–16).

7. Xu Fu, along with his father and uncle, engaged in the salt trade in eastern Jiangnan. His family had intermarried with the Wang Daokun lineage for three generations. He was widely respected within the Xu lineage. Particularly notable was his virtuous wife, who lived frugally and was completely devoted to supporting her husband and raising two sons. One of her sons was Xu Guo, the future grand secretariat, who did not see his sojourning father until age seven (635–37).

8. Fan Changjun was noted for successfully shaping the career selection for his two sons based on his reading of their characters: the elder son went into business and the younger one concentrated on Confucian learning (638–39).

9. Cheng the honorable ("Changgong," his given name is not mentioned) gave up Confucian learning (to which he had been devoted in youth) to engage in the salt trade. With support from his lineage, he eventually became the head salt merchant (*jijiu*). As he led the way in success as a businessman, he urged his younger kinsmen to switch from trade to devoting themselves to Confucian learning (694–96).

10. Cao Wenxiu gave up Confucian learning to engage in trade (723–24).

11. Pan Tingzhou was noted for having first engaged in trade in salt and clothes; he later returned to study for the civil service examinations. He eventually earned the highest metropolitan degree. His father urged his eldest son to concentrate on studying for the exams and the second to engage in trade. Pan turned the priority around, urging his sons to be good merchants and his grandsons to be prominent scholars (one of his grandsons, Pan Zhiheng, a close friend of Wang Daokun's, became a famous literatus and a drama aficionado; the Pans and Wangs were linked through generational marriages). This top merchant-scholar was also noted for his obsession with Chinese chess in his retirement, and he proudly stated, "Being a scholar you are in the market for a top exam degree; being a merchant you are in the market for untitled nobility [*sufeng*]; and being a chess player you enter the market for empire-wide champion" (737–41).

12. Ruan Bi, after becoming dominant in the paper-making industry in Wuhu, still referred to himself as a mean trader (*gushuzi*). This self-made top merchant was known for his faithfulness and generosity. In addition to taking good care of his parents, brothers, and their offspring, he supported other younger acquaintances (kinsmen or friends) for their career pursuits, either learning or trading (762–66).

13. Wang Songshan, Daokun's granduncle, specialized in the salt trade in Zhejiang, was devoted to his lineage, and supported his offspring so that they could study the Confucian classics, while himself often consulting Daokun about his specialty, the three classics on the rites (785–87).

14. Wu Ruzhuo was widely praised by the people from the four directions for his righteous deeds (*songyi sifang*) (788–90).

15. Cheng Weiqing, from the long-commercialized lineage in Xiuning's Shuaikou, engaged in Confucian learning before conducting salt trade and moneylending. He was oriented to his lineage and particularly devoted to the ancestral rites at the lineage temple. He also prepared a special ancestral hall, worshipping his immediate ancestors from his great grandfather downward (presumably based on Zhu Xi's model in *Family Rituals*). His family was noted for having long alternated between Confucian learning and commerce over the generations (800–802).

16. Wu Boju, from a commercialized family of the prominent Xi'nan Wus, gave up study of the classics after failing the examination several times. He then became a collector of books and paintings. His cultivation of Confucian virtue was constantly manifested through his generous and righteous (*xiajie*) activities (808–11).

17. Wang Huishou, Daokun's kinsman whose biography is included in the genealogy (*jiacheng zaizhi*), was notably attentive to lineage matters. He took good care of five of his nephews; when a Wang Hua temple suffered a conflagration, he contributed a large sum to repair it; he also built an ancestral hall based on Zhu Xi's model, setting up ritual land for it. The biography also notes the saying that Xin'an "is like Qi-Lu, noted empire-wide for its rich cultural traditions; as for its people, for every two who are engaging in trade, there is one engaging in Confucian learning (*qimin ergu yiru*). Its merchants are very rich . . . using learning to support commerce" (830–32).

18. Wang Liangrong, his mother from the Xi'nan Wus, was Daokun's uncle. He engaged in salt trade. The account notes that Daokun's family engaged in farming before his great grandfather. Liangrong resettled back home after making money outside of Huizhou, purchasing land, building houses, consolidating ancestral tombs, and engaging in other righteous deeds serving local communities. He gave financial support to his nephew Daokun as well as his own son Daoye for their Confucian schooling (847–49).

19. Wang Liangquan, a distant uncle of Daokun, also engaged in salt trade. A down-to-earth man, he once claimed that he would not trade for high profit and would not overreach for a high reputation (850–51).

20. Fang Jingzhen turned from a Confucian student into a merchant, and was noted for his Confucian chivalry (*ruxia*) with an exceptional sense of righteousness. He singlehandedly repaired a Buddhist chapel in Jingzhou, Hubei, where he was also disturbed by the worship of a popular "little spirit" (*xiaoshen*), which turned out to be a mountain goblin (i.e., Wutong). He acted as a generous benefactor and had no interest in gaining reputation for his righteous acts (856–60).

21. Cheng Yu of Huaitang studied for the exams in his youth, but then gave it up to become a merchant. Two of his sons passed the exams, with the eldest, Sigong, even earning the *jinshi* metropolitan degree. Sigong, who became friends with Wang Daokun (the two families established friendship for three generations), asked Daokun to write the biography. Cheng Yu was attentive to his kin and he was generous to the entire lineage of over one thousand

kinspeople, earning wide admiration for his generosity in local community (878–80).

22. Wang Kun, a close kinsman of the biographer, was noted for his assistance to his lineage, having built an ancestral hall, along with taking care of other matters relating to ancestral rites (including setting up ritual land). He took good care of kinswomen, and, in addition to practicing kinship-centered values such as filial devotion, brotherly love, respectfulness and frugality (*xiaodi gongjian*), and benevolence and righteousness (*renyi*), he preferred righteousness over wealth (*zhongyi er qingcai*). At the beginning of the biographic account, Daokun notes that the prefecture has been noted for having produced "gentrified merchants for generations," but in the end Kun is still depicted as urging his first grandson to pursue an exam degree to "elevate our lineage" (*gao wumen*) (903–6).

23. Wang Shouyi was Daokun's grandfather. Supported by his wife (through her dowry) and in-laws from the prominent Xi'nan Wus, he became the first in his family to engage in commerce, and eventually became a leading salt merchant active in the late fifteenth and early sixteenth centuries. As the first to engage in trade in the lineage, he often humbly called himself a mean trader (*gushu*). By Wang Daokun's time, over ten of his cousins engaged in commerce (919–21).

24. Wang Liangkai, a son of Daokun's grand-uncle, followed Daokun's grandfather (and his own father) to deal in salt. His father was intensely engaged in the construction of home lineage institutions, key to the prosperity of the Lingshanyuan Wangs. Like Daokun's grandfather, Liangkai's wife played a key role in supporting his business (923–24).

25. Wang Liangbin (1504–1581) was Wang Daokun's father who, along with more than ten of his cousins and nephews, followed his own father to the eastern seaboard to engage in commerce, helping to chart the Huizhou model of family/lineage business. Along with his interest in medicine, merchant Liangbin also practiced horseback riding and archery, and he was particularly fond of military strategy. For his son, however, he had only one expectation—a complete focus on studying to pass the civil service exams (935–41).

26. Wang Liangzhi, also involved in salt trade, was noted for his chivalrous generosity and his daughter-in-law being a chastity martyr. Liangzhi once said to Daokun, his nephew, "Our lineage became glorified because of your [exam success]. Now, local customs are increasingly deteriorating." Liangzhi thus urged Daokun to take some measures to uphold the lineage culture, saying, "At office you serve the state, and at home you contribute to the lineage—both are marks of accomplishment" (941–44).

27. Wang Quan, close to Daokun's family for two generations, was a leading salt merchant and a collector of antiques, noted for maintaining a large number of friends and for educating his sons in the spirit of righteousness and chivalry (950–51).

28. Jin Tang, who gave up Confucian learning to continue his father's pursuit in the salt trade, was noted for his brotherly love and for his devotion to his legal mother (the first wife of his father, not his biological mother). He hired schol-

ars to teach his sons about Confucian classics (969–71).

29. Hong Shi, a student turned merchant (*chushi*), is recorded in an epitaph that covers both him and his wife. His mother was widowed at twenty, and her chastity and motherhood was officially recorded in the prefectural gazetteer. Hong Shi followed his mother's order to select trade as his vocation, and owed a great deal to his wife's support for his commercial success. Daokun praised Hong Shi for his righteous chivalry (*jiexia*) and for having "promoted the lineage and harmonized kinspeople" (*kangzong shouzu*) and for modestly disavowing "untitled nobility" (*sufeng*) despite his commercial success (971–74).

30. Zheng Tianzhen, a kinsman of Zheng Zuo (who wrote a preface for *Prominent Lineages in Xin'an*), was noted for his attentiveness to lineage matters and for his devotion to his stepmother. He served his entire lineage of over a hundred kinspeople well. Each of his four sons won the accolade of *sufeng* for commercial success (975–76).

31. Cheng Zhengkui, another Confucian student turned merchant (*chushi*), was noted for his advocacy for reforming the salt trade regulations set up by the first Ming emperor. At age twenty, he was able to forcefully prevent a local strongman from encroaching upon the land of his ancestral tombs. His sons and grandsons all returned to exam studies, and he is characterized as having obtained "untitled nobility" (*sufeng*) and "elevated the lineage" (*kangzong*) (989–92).

32. Wu Rongrang, from the prominent Xi'nan Wu lineage, was orphaned at eight (his father, a sojourning trader, died in Hubei) and, at sixteen, after moving his father's coffin back to Huizhou, he followed his kinsmen to Songjiang on business. Having succeeded in trade, he hired a personal teacher for instruction. He grasped the moral principles from books and began to put them into practice. Admiring the *Record of Charity Land* by Fan Zhongyan (989–1052), he erected a lineage temple worshipping his ancestors and set up ritual land. He called together and hired for his business several dozen poor kin youth, who, twice each month, convened to listen to the famous *Yan Family Instructions*, read aloud by their caring boss (997–99).

33. Zhu Yunzhan, noted for his filial devotion and brotherly love (*xiaoti*), disregarded his business to take care of his ill father and, after his brother also fell ill, did the same thing again. He was noted for his generosity in giving a large amount of money to his employees (1001–3).

34. Chen Jing was another salt merchant who had studied Confucian classics in his youth and continued the pursuit with support from his wife after marriage; his two sons continued to pursue classical learning. He was good at calligraphy and poetry. Interestingly, in this case, Wang Daokun records a variety of his righteous stories without referring to the term *jiexia* (1032–35).

35. Pan Shi, Pan Tingzhou's cousin from the Yanzhen lineage, which was very close to Wang Daokun, switched from learning to commerce twice over the course of his life. He was good at trading in several commodities, including salt, food, and earthenware. His wife, while young, cut a piece of flesh from her thigh to cure her mother's illness, and the family was noted for having

produced four chaste women. Most offspring returned to pursue Confucian learning (1083–88).

36. Sun Congli, from the prominent and populous Caoshi Sun mercantile lineage, obeyed the order of his father (a merchant) to switch from learning to commerce. He was a typical *chushi* (untitled gentryman). He was devoted to his father's main wife (not his biological mother). His sons switched back to Confucian learning. His daughter was betrothed to Wang Zongshun (Daokun's kinsman), but died before the wedding. Sun *chushi* treated Zongshun as a nephew and his subsequent wife as daughter. He led the local community in repairing roads and set up ritual land for the ancestral hall. He treated visitors particularly well, another example that illustrates his character of generous chivalry. Wang Daokun ends the account with a revealing statement regarding the relation between fame and fortune: "If a person is not intended to work for high honor, he will be a person of great fame. What a *chushi* does is his chosen vocation, not work for high profit. Rich but acting morally, he earns high honor. If you do not work for high profit, then the profit you earn will be high; if you do not work for high honor, then the fame you earn will be great" (1096–98).

37. Jin She, a merchant's son who switched from study to trade, was filial, righteous, and devoted to his lineage. Notably, his wife played a key role in not only supporting his pursuit in commerce but also their two sons' pursuit of learning. Wang Daokun opens this account with a revealing statement about what might be called the "Huizhou social strategy" that was widely practiced regarding accruing fame and fortune: "The capital of Xin'an, with one scholar for every three merchants, is indeed a land rich in literary traditions. Just as merchants seek handsome profits, scholars strive for high honor. Only after one has exhausted his effort on behalf of Confucian learning with no result does he let go of study and fasten on to trade. Once he has joined those who enjoy high profits, he prefers his descendants, for the sake of their future, to let go of trade and fasten on to study. Letting go and fastening on thus alternate with each other so that one can enjoy either an income of ten thousand bushels of grain or the prestige of a retinue of one thousand horse carriages. This can be likened to the revolution of a wheel, with its spokes pointing to the ground in turn. We Xin'an people are never devoted to commerce alone, but are judicious in choosing our career path" (1099–1101).

38. Wang Boling, Daokun's kinsman (two generations senior) from Qianchuan in Shexian, earned enough wealth from the tea trade to become a *sufeng* (untitled nobleman). He was remarkably generous, giving half of his estate to his orphaned nephew, which was fully supported by his wife, née Yuan. Ms. Yuan, while extremely frugal for her own matters, took good care of her father-in-law, assisted her husband and sons, and treated over one hundred retainers well on a daily basis. Their sons all returned to the pursuit of Confucian learning. Wang Boling treated ancestral worship seriously. According to lineage rule, setting up a spirit tablet for one's ancestor at the Wang Hua Shrine in Qianchuan costs fifty taels; he paid five hundred taels to set up ten spiritual

tablets. As for his kinspeople, he was always happy to assist whomever needed financial assistance for important matters, such as marriages or funerals (1116–19).

39. Wu Liangru, another scholar-turned-merchant, eventually became the head salt merchant (*jijiu*). It was his "mother" (i.e., legal, not biological) who "ordered" his switch of vocation, and he obeyed her instructions as he realized that "scholars are obsessed with high fame, but fame is the same as profit [*ming yi li ye*]; if I follow [my mother's] will, I won't be able to glorify my family and promote my name, but profit is the same as fame [*li yi ming ye*]." In the end, all of his sons returned to the pursuit of classical learning to fulfill their ancestors' aspirations (1142–45).

40. Cheng Sheng, from Linhe in Shexian, teamed up with his kinsman Cheng Yu from Huaitang (for whom Daokun also penned a biography; see entry 21) and Daokun's father to deal in salt in Zhejiang. They ordered their sons and offspring all to return to the pursuit of Confucian learning (*guiru*), the result of which was two successful *jinshi* degree holders, Cheng Sigong and Wang Daokun. Cheng Sheng was notably full of the spirit of righteous chivalry (*jiexia*), leading kinsmen to build an ancestral hall and setting up ritual land. His wife was devoted to her parents-in-law and took good care of their sons. Wang Daokun opens this account with the following famous statement: "South of the Great [Yangzi] River, the capital of Xin'an is noted for its cultural traditions. Its custom is to pursue either study or trade, alternating with generations. In essence, in what way is a good merchant [*lianggu*] inferior to a prominent scholar [*hongru*]?!" (1146–49).

41. Wang Hai, from the Yanshan Wangs in Xiuning (who had intermarried with the nearby Caoshi Suns for generations), was descended from Wang Hua. He was widely known as an honest merchant (*liangu*). Wang Hai and his wife both were frugal. As he frequently left home on business, his wife took care of his parents and raised two sons. One son continued his father's business, whereas the other pursued classical learning in the hope of "glorifying our family-lineage" (*da wumen*) (1154–57).

42. Huang Zhong, whose mother was Daokun's kinswoman from Qianchuan, followed his own brother in business. He was a frugal man, even after having accumulated a large amount of wealth. And yet he was also generous, winning praise for his righteous acts in the local communities. His mother oversaw family matters while her sons sojourned for business (1180–83).

43. Wu Zhengzhong, whose great grandson married Daokun's granddaughter, came from the Xi'nan Wus who dominated the salt trade in the middle and lower Yangzi valley. His eldest son pursued the study of Confucian classics, whereas the second son engaged in the salt trade. Wu Zhengzhong supported "righteous acts" such as his son's running the lineage temple and feeding the homeless. Both Wu Zhengzhong and his wife were extremely frugal, setting examples for their offspring (1191–94).

44. Cheng Yi, another student-turned-merchant, was noted for taking care of lineage matters. Many of his kinsmen followed him into business and all made

money. He observed proper ritual protocol when building an ancestral hall and conducting ancestral rites; he also took good care of poor widows within his lineage (1210–14).

45. Cheng Suo, descended from the Huangdun branch, switched from studying to trade following his mother's injunction. Teaming up with ten kinsmen, he worked hard and lived frugally, succeeding as a moneylender. He reclaimed the ritual land attached to his ancestors' tombs from local strongmen. Three of his sons (and grandsons) all followed his injunction to return to the pursuit of Confucian learning. Wang Daokun called Cheng Suo as a *lianggu* (good merchant) who easily earned the status of an untitled gentryman (*sufeng*), as he was a real *rugu* (Confucianized merchant), not a *guru* (a merchant putting on a Confucian face without actually behaving as a Confucian). In a typical terminology, Cheng Suo "traded and yet loved being Confucian" (*gu'er haoru*) (1265–69).

ABBREVIATIONS

CSYFJ	Cheng Minzheng 程敏政, comp. *Chengshi yifan ji* 程氏貽范集. 1482. Library of Congress.
CZQLZ	Zhao Pang 趙滂, comp. *Cheng-Zhu queli zhi* 程朱闕里志. 1612. Anhui Provincial Library.
HDWJ	Cheng Minzheng 程敏政. *Huangdun wenji* 篁墩文集. *Siku* edition.
HZF	Peng Ze 彭澤, comp. *Huizhou fuzhi* 徽州府志. 1502. Reprint, Taipei: Xuesheng shuju, 1965.
HZMZZ	Yu Chenghua 余成華, comp. *Huizhou mingzu zhi* 徽州名族志, 2 vols. Beijing: Quanguo tushuguan wenxian suowei fuzhi zhongxin, 2003.
HZZ	*Huizhou fuzhi* 徽州府志. 1566.
LSW	Wang Daokun 汪道昆, comp. *Lingshanyuan Wangshi shiliu zu pu* 靈山院汪氏十六族譜. 1592. Beijing National Library.
MDJP	Wang Qiang 王強, comp. *Zhongguozhenxi jiapu congkan: Mingdai jiapu* 中國珍稀家譜叢刊：明代家譜, 32 vols. Nanjing: Fenghuang chuban chuanmei, 2013.
MS	*Mingshi* 明史. Beijing: Zhonghua shuju, 1974.
QS-M; QS-Q	*Qishen zouge* 祈神奏格. Shanghai Library. Ming print cited as *QS-M*; Qing print cited as *QS-Q*.
SKCM	Siku quanshu cunmu congshu bianzuan weiyuanhui四庫全書存目叢書編纂委員會, comp. *Siku quanmu cunmu congshu* 四庫全書存目叢書. Jinan: Qilu shushe, 1996.
SZ	Xie Bi 謝陛, comp. *Shezhi* 歙志, 1609. Reprint, Hefei: Huangshan shushe, 2014.
THJ	Wang Daokun 汪道昆. *Taihan ji* 太函集, 1591. Reprint, Hefei: Huangshan shushe, 2004.

XACST   Cheng Minzheng 程敏政, comp. *Xin'an Chengshi tongzong shipu* 新安程氏統宗世譜. 1482. Shanghai Library.

XAMII   Dai Tingming 戴廷明 and Cheng Shangkuan 程尚寬, comps. *Xin'an mingzu zhi* 新安名族志, compiled by Zhu Wanshu 朱萬曙 and Hu Yimin 胡益民. 1551. Reprint, Hefei: Huangshan shushe, 2004.

XAMZZ   Cheng Shangkuan 程尚寬, comp. *Xin'an mingzu zhi* 新安名族志. 1551. Library of Congress.

XAWXZ   Cheng Minzheng 程敏政, comp. *Xin'an wenxian zhi* 新安文獻志. 1497. Reprint, Hefei: Huangshan shushe, 2004.

XAZ   Luo Yuan 羅願, comp. *Xin'an zhi* 新安志. 1175. Reprint, Taipei: Shangwu yinshu guan, 1983.

XNMZZ   Cao Sixuan 曹嗣軒, comp., *Xiuning mingzu zhi* 休寧名族志, 1626. Reprint, Hefei: Huangshan shushe, 2007

XNPGC   Cheng Minzheng 程敏政, comp. *Xiuning Peiguo Chengshi benzong pu* 休寧陪郭程氏本宗譜. 1497. Shanghai Library.

XNSKC   *Xiuning Shuaikou Chengshi xubian benzong pu* 休寧率口程氏續編本宗譜. 1570. Shanghai Library.

XNZ   Cheng Minzheng 程敏政, comp. *Xiuning zhi* 休寧志. 1497.

XXZ   *Xiuningxian zhi* 休寧縣志. 1693. Reprint, Taipei: Chengwen, 1970.

NOTES

INTRODUCTION

1. Timothy Brook, *The Confusions of Pleasure: Commerce and Culture in Ming China*, chaps. 1 and 2.

2. The socioeconomic history of Huizhou has been studied in detail. See Fujii Hiroshi, "Shinan shōnin no kenkyū," *Tōyō gakuhō* 36, no. 1 (1953): 1–44, 36, no. 2 (1953): 180–208, 36, no. 3 (1953): 335–88, 36, no. 4 (1954): 533–63; Ye Xian'en, *Ming-Qing Huizhou nongcun shehui yu dianpu zhi*; Wang Tingyuan and Wang Shihua, *Huishang*; and especially Joseph McDermott, *The Making of a New Rural Order in South China*, vols. 1 and 2.

3. Qitao Guo, *Ritual Opera and Mercantile Lineage: The Confucian Transformation of Popular Culture in Late Imperial Huizhou*.

4. Brook, *The Confusions of Pleasure*, chap. 2.

5. Characteristic works include: Harriet Zurndorfer, *Change and Continuity in Chinese Local History: The Development of Hui-chou Prefecture 800–1800*; Yongtao Du, *The Order of Places: Translocal Practices of the Huizhou Merchants in Late Imperial China*.

6. Guo, *Ritual Opera and Mercantile Lineage*.

7. McDermott, *The Making of a New Rural Order in South China*, 1:1.

8. Philip A. Kuhn, *Rebellion and Its Enemies in Late Imperial China: Militarization and Social Structure, 1796–1864*.

9. See Michael Szonyi, *Practicing Kinship: Lineage and Descent in Late Imperial China* and *The Art of Being Governed: Everyday Politics in Late Imperial China*. There is debate in the anthropological and historical literature about the definition of the lineage in late imperial China, highlighting either ancestral rites or corporate estates as the defining feature. This is amply addressed in Szonyi's *Practicing Kinship*.

10. Peter Bol, "The 'Localist Turn' and 'Local Identity' in Later Imperial China," 1–50.

11. Robert Hymes, *Statesmen and Gentlemen: The Elite of Fu-chou, Chiang-hsi, in Northern and Southern Sung*. For Robert Hartwell, see his "Demographic, Political, and Social Transformations of China, 750–1550," 365–422.

12. See Paul Jakov Smith and Richard von Glahn, eds., *The Song-Yuan-Ming Transition in Chinese History*.

13. Bol, "The 'Localist Turn' and 'Local Identity' in Later Imperial China." Two new studies on literati also highlight the dialectic relationship between the state and local elites: Anne Gerritsen, *Ji'an Literati and the Local in Song-Yuan-Ming China*; Chang Woei Ong, *Men of Letters within the Passes: Guanzhong Literati in Chinese History, 907–1911*. See also John W. Dardess, *A Ming Society: T'ai-ho County, Kiangsi, in the Fourteenth to Seventeen Centuries*.

14. Cheng was a contemporary of Zhang Mou (1437–1522), a high-ranking scholar-official and leading local gentry who authored *The Gazetteer of the Shrine of Wu Worthies*, thereby initiating the Ming-dynasty renewal of the localist trend in Jinhua. Bol, "The 'Localist Turn' and 'Local Identity' in Later Imperial China," 26–27.

15. For local gazetteers as venues for regional consciousness, see Joseph Dennis, *Writing, Publishing, and Reading Local Gazetteers in Imperial China, 1100–1700*.

16. His forebears in the early Ming were on a punitive military assignment and moved from Xiuning to a relatively unknown place in the north. This may in part explain why Cheng Minzheng was so devoted to Huizhou, a place full of great families marked with historical achievements.

17. Going local for literati also could be a way to achieve national fame; see Beverly Bossler, *Powerful Relations: Kinship, Status, and the State in Sung China (960–1279)*.

18. Timothy Brook touches in passing upon the "conservative" response to late Ming commercialization, although his study does not approach this issue from the perspective of local lineages. See Brook, *The Confusions of Pleasure*.

19. Guo, *Ritual Opera and Mercantile Lineage*.

20. By devoting two chapters to Cheng Minzheng and Wang Daokun, this study represents a pioneering foray into a biographic history of the two prominent scholar-officials of Ming Huizhou. This approach accords with an emerging trend that again pays close attention to the micro-history of important (but unexplored) figures in the midst of the overwhelmingly dominant macro-societal history. But my account weaves their lives into the colorful historical development of Ming Huizhou.

1. CHENG MINZHENG AND THE RISE OF HUIZHOU CONSCIOUSNESS

1. *HDWJ*, 1252.169, 1252.389, 1253.462–63; *XNZ*, 36.26a–28a. For the official biography of Cheng Lingxi, see Yao Silian, *Chenshu*, 171–73; Li Yanshou, *Nanshi*, 1632–33.

2. "Huangdun shushe ji," in *HDWJ*, 1252.229–30.

3. *HDWJ*, 1252.512. The verse collection is no longer extant; for the poems and essays mentioned earlier, see *XAMZZ*, 1b–2a; *XNZ*, 19.32a–33b, 36.23b–25b; Peng Hua, *Peng Wensi gong wenji*, 332–36.

4. Bol, *Neo-Confucianism in History*, 219.

5. See Wing-tsit Chan, "The Ch'eng Chu School of Early Ming," in *Self and Society in Ming Thought*, ed. Wm. Theodore de Bary, 29–51.

6. Ying-shih Yu, *Song Ming lixue yu zhengzhi wenhua*, 250–332. Consult also Yin Zhi's (1427–1511) assault on the revival of the Learning of the Mind in the local context of Jiangxi in the mid-Ming. John W. Dardess, *A Ming Society*, 207–11.

7. Unlike his contemporary prominent neo-Confucian from Zhejiang, Zhang Mou, Cheng Minzheng's localist engagement did not lead to the building of new local academies, although like Zhang Mou, he did endorse the building of local shrines. Bol, *Neo-Confucianism in History*, 262.

8. *XAMZZ*, 73a.

9. *HDWJ*, 1252.601–3.

10. The inscription is included in both *CSYFJ, yiji*, 1.8a–10a and *XAWXZ*, 954–55.

11. *XAMZZ*, 1a.

12. *HDWJ*, 1252.473. Cheng Minzheng was always evenhanded in balancing the two most prominent surnames, Cheng and Wang. He later wrote in a postscript to yet another Wang genealogy: "Xin'an is located in a multitude of mountains and rarely affected by wars; it is noted for having a large number of deep-rooted lineages. The two surnames Cheng and Wang are particularly illustrious." *HDWJ*, 1252.673–4.

13. *Xin'an Wangshi chongxiu bagong pu* (1535, Shanghai Library), n.p.; *XAMZZ*, 88a. Cheng Minzheng acknowledges in a preface to a Wang genealogy that Wang Wenhe was prefect of Xin'an. *HDWJ*, 1252.473–74.

14. *XAMZZ*, 94b. The 1223 imperial edict is included in *CSYFJ, jiaji*, 1.8a.

15. Wang Daojin, *Wangshi zupu* (1480), preface.

16. Wang Shanghe, *Xiuning Ximen Wangshi zupu* (1527), 1.6b.

17. *XAMII*, 18.

18. "Wuyuan Chayuan Zhushi shipu houxu," in *XAWXZ*, 426–27; also included in *CZQLZ*, 3.33a.

19. The Huizhou Zhus, illustrious as the surname was, were in no position to compete for the top genealogical pedigree on two accounts: they did not migrate to Huangdun or Xin'an until the mid-Tang, and they were not nearly as developed—either socially or demographically—as the Chengs, the Wangs, or the Huangs. See *XAMII*, 432–45.

20. *CZQLZ*, preface.

21. *CZQLZ*, 1.1b–6a. The story of the "rainbow well" has it that when Zhu Xi's father was born, a white rainbow emerged from a well and, at the time of Zhu Xi's birth, a purple rainbow emerged from the same well. *CZQLZ*, 1.6a.

22. *XNPGC, shixi*, 16a, *shiluo*, 38a, 46a. Cheng Minzheng's forebears appear to have belonged to a military household. On the various strategies military households used to form and advance their lineages in the Ming, see Szonyi, *The Art of Being Governed*. Cheng Minzheng appears to fit the case that Chang Woei Ong has illustrated—that is, those literati who emigrated "from a place for an extended period of time or . . . moved from elsewhere to the place" often "still consider the locality as a source of pride and made effort to construct their identity based on it." Ong further defines one way of being local as "a consciousness that historical actors display in constructing the tradition, history, and identity of a place," which does not have to be in conflict with the state. Ong, *Men of Letters within the Passes*, 16.

23. *MS*, 4593–95.

24. *MS*, 7343–44; *Xiuning xianzhi* (1548), 6.26b; *GCLQJ*, 1053–68; Zhu Baojiong et al., *Ming-Qing jinshi timing beilu suoyin*, 2461–63. The couplet is quoted in Zhang Jian, "Lun

Mingdai Huizhou wenxianxuejia Cheng Minzheng," *Anhui sifan daxue xuebao*, 31, no. 5 (2003): 514.

25. *MS*, 7343–44. For details of the exam scandal, see *GCLQJ*, 2597–98; Xia Xie (1799–1875), *Ming tongjian*, 1061–63.

26. *MS*, 7343.

27. *HDWJ* (93 *juan*). Some of Cheng Minzheng's works are touched upon in Jennifer W. Jay, "Memoirs and Official Accounts: The Historiography of the Song Loyalists," 593, 605; Thomas Wilson, "Genealogy and History in Neo-Confucian Sectarian Uses of the Confucian Past," 19.

28. *XNZ* (38 *juan); XACST* (20 *juan); CSYFJ* (30 *juan); XNPGC* (3 *juan* plus one thick appendix volume).

29. Wu Changgeng, comp., *Zhu Lu xueshu kaobian wuzhong*, 10–11; Bol, *Neo-Confucianism in History*, 89.

30. Cheng Minzheng included in *Xin'an wenxian zhi* an epitaph on Cheng Shaokai (1212–1280), whose ancestors moved from Shexian to Jiangxi, where he headed the Xiang-shan Academy (named after Lu Jiuyuan). This neo-Confucian schoolmaster strove to balance Zhu and Lu learning in his teaching; Wu Cheng was among his disciples. Notably, Cheng Shaokai named his private school Daoyi (Oneness of the Way), which might have inspired the title of Cheng Minzheng's *Daoyi bian. XAWXZ*, 1715–18.

31. This refers to Confucius's instructions to his disciple Yan Yuan: "Do not look unless it is in accordance with the rites; do not listen unless it is in accordance with the rites; do not speak unless it is in accordance with the rites; do not move unless it is in accordance with the rites." Confucius, *The Analects*, trans. D. C. Lau, 112.

32. This refers to Confucius's disciple Zengzi's comment: "Every day I examine myself on three counts. In what I have undertaken on another's behalf, have I failed to do my best? In my dealings with my friends have I failed to be trustworthy in what I say? Have I passed on to others anything that I have not tried out myself?" Confucius, *The Analects*, 59.

33. Cheng Minzheng, comp., *Daoyi bian*, 6.616–17.

34. See the lengthy passage by Zhen on the transmission of the Way in Wm. Theodore de Bary, *Neo-Confucian Orthodoxy and the Learning of the Mind-and-Heart*, 9–10. The view of orthodox tradition (*daotong*) starting from archaic sages is an important one, and it was first articulated by Zhu Xi. It is not clear why Cheng Minzheng in this case omitted the beginning of the orthodox tradition, which he would pick up later in his annotation of Zhen's *Classic of the Mind-and-Heart*. Zhen appears to have rephrased Zhu Xi's view, but Zhen's version of the orthodox tradition was endowed with possibility of creation to "make new discoveries, rather than depend on received opinion" (de Bary, *Neo-Confucian Orthodoxy*, 9–10, 98–100). For Zhu's vision, see Bol, *Neo-Confucianism in History*, 204–9. Zhen also held elsewhere that, as de Bary notes, Zhu and Lu did not necessarily harbor the irreconcilably opposite views on the mind (*Neo-Confucian Orthodoxy*, 177).

35. Cheng, *Daoyi bian*, 6.646.

36. Cheng, *Daoyi bian*, 6.653.

37. Chen Jian, *Xuepou tongbian*, in *Zhu Lu xueshu kaobian wuzhong*, comp. Wu Chang-gen, 110–284, esp. 110, 284; Wm. Theodore de Bary and Irene Bloom, comps., *Sources of Chinese Tradition* (second ed.), 884–86. Chen Jian (*Xuepou tongbian*, 110) also pointed out that Cheng Minzheng misplaced the timing of some of Zhu's letters to give the false impression

that Zhu and Lu conflicted initially but came to an accord later in life. Chen, in contrast, offered the reverse argument; that is, the two agreed while young but departed later in life. See also Ho Wei Hsuan, "Cheng Minzheng jiqi xueshu sixiang." Compilation and interpretation of Zhu Xi's letters in this regard continued to be a concern in the early Qing; see Thomas A. Wilson, *Genealogy of the Way: The Construction and Uses of the Confucian Tradition in Late Imperial China*, chap. 6.

38. Quote is from Bol, *Neo-Confucianism in History*, 210.

39. *HDWJ*, 1252.2–3.

40. *HDWJ*, 1253.283. Cheng Minzheng himself had already made it clear in his Postscript to *Oneness of the Way Collection* that he was trying to balance Zhu Xi with Lu Jiuyuan to promote oneness of the Way. Cheng, *Daoyi bian*, 6.659.

41. *HDWJ*, 1253.284.

42. Bol, *Neo-Confucianism in History*, 210.

43. De Bary, *Neo-Confucian Orthodoxy*, 68, 70.

44. As Cheng Minzheng admirably notes in the preface to the *Supplemented*, *HDWJ*, 1252.521.

45. De Bary, *Neo-Confucian Orthodoxy*, 73–74. Consult also Bol, *Neo-Confucianism in History*, 205–6.

46. See Cheng Minzheng's preface to *Xinjing fuzhu*, in *HDWJ* (1252.521), in which Cheng quotes Zhu Xi as saying that Master Cheng's most notable contribution to learning lies in "the one word *jing*" (reverence) before noting that the *Heart Classic* focuses on nothing other than sayings on *jing*, thus prompting his effort to further expound upon this through additional classic passages and commentaries. Zhen Dexiu made a similar assessment regarding Cheng Yi's (and Zhu Xi's) greatest contribution to sagehood: the elaboration on *jing* as the foundation of learning. This, he maintained, had been lost since Mencius's times. Cheng Minzheng, *Xinjing fuzhu*, 4.847.

47. De Bary, *Neo-Confucian Orthodoxy*, 73–83.

48. Cheng, *Xinjing fuzhu*, 4.830. Zhen made a similar remark in his memoir of Cheng Hao, quoted in de Bary, *Neo-Confucian Orthodoxy*, 99.

49. Cheng, *Xinjing fuzhu*, 4.848.

50. *HDWJ*, 1252.520.

51. Cheng, *Xinjing fuzhu*, 4.867.

52. This is a rephrasing of a passage in Zhen Dexiu's memoir of Cheng Hao, in de Bary, *Neo-Confucian Orthodoxy*, 100. There is a logical development from here to the statement Wang Yangming made in his "Inquiry on the *Great Learning*": "The great man regards heaven-and-earth and the myriad things as one body. He regards the world as one family and the country as one person. As for those who make a cleavage between objects and distinguish between the self and others, they are small men. That the great man can regard heaven-and-earth and the myriad things as one body is not because he deliberately wants to do so, but because it is natural to the human nature of his mind to do so. Forming one body with heaven-and-earth and myriad things is not only true of the great man. Even the mind of the small man is no different. Only he himself makes it small." Trans. in Bol, *Neo-Confucianism in History*, 215.

53. Cheng Minzheng's original version of *Anthology of Xin'an Documents* covered the Huizhou documents down to the Yongle reign (1403–1424), but Shexian scholar Wang

Zongzhi and his cohort expanded the coverage, adding fifty-one essays and fifty-nine poems, all from the Xuande reign (1426–1435) to 1497. See Wang Zongzhi's 1497 postface, *XAWXZ*, 2613.

54. *XAWXZ*, 3.

55. Yong Rong, comp., *Siku quanshu zongmu*, 1685.

56. *XAWXZ*, 4. *Origins of the Yi-Luo Learning* is an anthology of the sayings of Song neo-Confucian masters, and especially the two Cheng brothers, and their disciples. It marked the formation of the orthodox tradition of the Learning of the Way.

57. *XAWXZ*, 2631.

58. About thirty years earlier than the compilation of *Xin'an wenxian zhi*, in 1460, a similar anthology titled *Xin'an wencui* (Essential writings of Xin'an) was printed (in *SKCM*, 4.292: 394–562). It was compiled by Jin Dexuan, another Xiuning native noted for his devotion to Confucian learning. Acknowledging Jin Dexuan's contribution, Cheng Minzheng included a short biography of Jin in *Xin'an wenxian zhi* (*XAWXZ*, 2432). Being about 170 pages in length, *Essential Writings of Xin'an* was far shorter than *Xin'an wenxian zhi*, although the former covers certain works and individuals that the latter omits (Jin Dexuan, *Xin'an wencui*, 562), and is thus of some value.

59. *XAWXZ*, 1–2.

60. *XAWXZ*, 983–84, 539–40.

61. *XAWXZ*, 1004; see also Cheng, *Daoyi bian*, 6.659.

62. Cited in Ho Wei Hsuan, "Cheng Minzheng jiqi xueshu sixiang," 204. Cheng Minzheng also compiled records of the Song adherents (*Song yimin lu*), which, like the *Xin'an Documents*, records "the traces of prosperity or chaos, gains or losses of the past and present."

63. *HZZ*, 20.1a.

64. According to legend, Mount Huang was "named after" Huangdi (the Yellow Emperor), the mythic progenitor of Chinese civilization who "was immortalized on the mountain." *XAWXX*, 381–83, 751.

65. See also Joseph Dennis, *Publishing, Writing, and Reading Local Gazetteers in Imperial China, 1100–1700* and Pu Xia, *Ming-Qing yilai Huizhou fangzhi bianzuan chengjiu*.

66. *XAWXZ*, 2587–90; *XAZ*, 8.3b–7b.

67. *XAWXZ*, 2295–98.

68. *XAWXZ*, 2162–64.

69. *XAWXZ*, 2193–95.

70. Zheng Yu, *Shishan ji*, 7.4b–7a. See also Zhang Yi, *Lixue, shishen he zongzu: Song-Ming shiqi Huizhou de wenhua yu shehui*, 152–54.

71. *XAWXZ*, 752–54. For Wu Yingzi, see *XAWXZ*, 29–30.

72. *XAWXZ*, 782–84.

73. *XAWXZ*, 2443–44.

74. *XAWXZ*, 2306–8. As it turns out, Cheng Jinghua, also known as Doushan, rose to a prominent position in Ming Huizhou by setting up the Doushan trust for the Shanhe Chengs. See *Doushan gong jiayi jiaozhu*, compiled by his great grandson, a prominent scholar official named Cheng Chang (1475–1551). The Doushan trust figures notably in McDermott's analysis of Huizhou lineage estates in his *The Making of a New Rural Order*, vol. 1.

75. *XAWXZ*, 2149–51, 1725–26. There are two more biographies on two local scholarly notables whose commercial endeavors were touched upon in *XAWXZ*, 2144–46, 2174–76.

76. *XAWXZ*, 2158–61.

77. *XAWXZ*, 2256–60. The *Xin'an Documents* includes another epitaph on a merchant, Cheng Xinyu (1239–1310) of Shuaikou, by the leading Xin'an neo-Confucian Cao Jing, which again emphasizes not his commercial adventures but his virtue and scholarly demeanor. *XAWXZ*, 2158–61.

78. Two of the very few accounts on Huizhou merchants or commercialized landlords that Cheng Minzheng penned himself will be discussed in chap. 2.

79. *XAWXZ*, 2302–6. Another grand secretariat, Peng Shi, also authored an epitaph jointly commemorating Cheng Minzheng's grandfather and grandmother. See *XNPGC, fulu* (appendixes), 47b–49b.

80. Cheng Minzheng authored several pieces on devoted women. See, for instance, "Shou Wu jiefu Wang ruren bashi yu" (Congratulate chaste woman Wu, née Lady Wang, on her eightieth birthday) and "Wang jiefu zhuan" (Biography of chaste woman Wang), in *HDWJ*, 1252.484; 1253.199–200.

81. In fact, as early as 1482, Cheng Minzheng should have appreciated the financial support from Huizhou merchants in building the Cheng Shrine (in honor of the two Cheng brothers) in Xiuning, a central piece of his Huizhou endeavor. For merchants' contributions to the Cheng Shrine, see Zhang Yi, *Lixue, shishen he zongzu*, 196–99.

82. *XAWXZ*, 2616–23.

83. They were Cheng Zuyuan (1447–1519), Cheng Xuan (1442–1505), Cheng Wenjie (1459–1533), and Cheng Fuxi (1455–?). See various biographies that cover these merchants or their families in *XNSKC*, 6.8a–9a, 6.13b–14b, 6.43a–44a.

84. Cheng Minzheng, "Shuaikou Chengshi Shizhong xingci ji" (Commemorative record on the Shuaikou Chengs' [reconstruction of] the branch shrine of Permanent Loyalty), in *XNSKC*, 5.3a–b.

85. *HDWJ*, 1252.696.

86. "Wenchangfang Chengshi zupu xu," in *HDWJ*, 1252.420–21.

87. According to Cheng Minzheng's postface, his assistant in the *Anthology* project, Wang Zuo, first suggested that he appeal to the descendants of former worthies (covered in the *Anthology*) for financial support, but Wang Zongzhi noted in his postface that the Huizhou prefect simply "ordered the descendants of the former worthies from six counties to contribute to the publication cost, and many happily followed" the demand. *XAWXZ*, 2613–14. As already mentioned, the whole process started with the endorsement of the governor of Southern Zhili after Cheng Minzheng was called back to service by the emperor.

88. Xu goes on to say, "Minzheng switched Yellow Mound for Bamboo Mound, which is a notable instance of his clan chauvinism. He simply did not want another surname to monopolize the Mound." Xu Chengyao, *Sheshi xiantan*, 859–60. Here, Xu Chengyao seems to have echoed the opinion of Ji Yun (1724–1805) and his editorial cohort when they summarized *Collected Essays of Bamboo Mound* for *the Four Treasuries* (*HDWJ*, 1252.1–2), but their summary of *Anthology of Xin'an Documents* is almost completely positive.

89. Jin Dexuan, *Xin'an wencui* (292.404–6), which opens the first *juan* with a record on the Song reconstruction of the Wang Hua Temple; the third entry is a record on the Cheng Lingxi Temple.

90. *XAWXZ* (Author Index, 2640–42, 2648–51).

91. *XAWXZ*, 1450–66. Cheng Minzheng reorders the sequence of placement, although both deified ancestors are still entered in *juan* 61, "Shenji" (Divine Traces), the first *juan* of collection 2.

92. *XAWXZ*, 1467–559. Also note that Cheng Minzheng includes two biographies on Cheng Lingxi and just one on Wang Hua.

93. "Shu Henan Shang Cheng shi *Yizhenlu* hou," in *XAWXZ*, 525–26. For Cheng Wen, vice director of a bureau in the Board of Rites, see Song Lian, *Yuanshi*, 4348.

94. Cheng Minzheng's preface to *CSYFJ*, 1a.

95. Bol, *Neo-Confucianism in History*, chap. 7.

96. McDermott, *The Making of a New Rural Order in South China*, vol. 1, chap. 3.

97. *XACST*, Cheng Minzheng's preface, 1a–6a; *Timing* (Names acknowledged), 1a–b for a long list of assistants. Besides acknowledging the kinsmen assistants, the short *Timing* section also sends out a warning: whoever sells his copy of the genealogy would be fined twenty taels of silver, which would be contributed to the corporate fund owned by a branch shrine to Cheng Lingxi to cover ancestral rites; violators would be reported to local officials and removed from the home genealogy.

98. Qian Hang, *Zongzu de shixixue yanjiu*.

99. The *Composite Genealogy* does not contain a separate biographic section, as many later Huizhou genealogies do; rather it covers the basic biographic data in the ancestral tree (see fig. 1). But the companion anthology of the Cheng documents fills this gap, even though the biographies are limited to important figures of the Cheng descent line. Cheng Minzheng's *Genealogy of My Peiguo Cheng Branch in Xiuning* (1497), composed of the three volumes of *shixi* (tree charts of descent), *xiaozhuan* (biographic sketches), and *fulu* (appendixes) of lineage documents, is closer to later genealogies in terms of its constituent parts than the *Composite Genealogy*. Nevertheless, it was the *Composite Genealogy* that first established the *tuzhuan* format, which the Peiguo genealogy mimicked.

100. As claimed by the late Ming Wanli edition of *Xin'an Xushi shipu*, cited in Xu Bin, "Wanli *Lingshanyuan Wangshi shiliuzu pu* de bianzhuan tedian jiqi jiazhi," 7.

101. *XACST*, Jiuxu (Former prefaces), 1a–26b, including prefaces to the three previous composite versions by Cheng Tao of the Tang, Cheng Qi of the Song, and Cheng Meng. Of the thirty-nine prefaces included, twenty-five are dated to pre-Ming times.

102. Cheng Meng's edition is much shorter than Cheng Minzheng's *Composite Genealogy*. It looks quite rough and disorganized, as implied, perhaps, in its title. According to Cheng Minzheng's preface to *Composite Genealogy*, Cheng Meng's composite version was "incomplete." *XACST*, 4b.

103. Both the composite genealogy and its companion *Records of Bequeathed Glories of the Chengs* are skillfully crafted and beautifully printed. I have examined their original versions, stored in Shanghai Library and US Congress Library, respectively. The *Records of Bequeathed Glories of the Chengs*, composed of five books, is a gigantic project. Many documents first compiled in the *Records* are later also covered in the *Anthology of Xin'an Documents*.

104. See Cheng Yi, "Yinming" (Seal inscription), in *CSYFJ, jiaji*, 1.1. See also Cheng Yi, "Mingdao xiansheng xingzhuang," cited in *Chengshi xungen cankao*, comp. Chengshi wenhua liangyihui jiapu weiyuanhui, 1:35.

105. Cheng Ying was central to the legend of "Zhaoshi gu'er" (Orphan of the Zhao Clan), which has been repeatedly chronicled, staged, and filmed. He was a retainer of Zhao Shuo, a top official of the state of Jin who was wronged and whose entire clan was killed except for his baby boy, later named Wu. According to legend, Cheng Ying managed to save the orphan, and later helped Zhao Wu avenge the family enemies; he then committed suicide to fulfill his promise to another retainer of the Zhao clan who had died to save

the orphan. Cheng Ying was posthumously bestowed the title of Marquis Chengxin (fulfilling the promise).

106. This ancient ancestry was first outlined in Cheng Meng's 1451 composite genealogy.

107. *XAWXZ*, 375–76.

108. *XACST, pubian*, 1a–14a; also included in one whole volume of *CSYFJ, dingji*, 1a–28b. The *Records of Bequeathed Glories of the Chengs* also covers a large number of imperial conferments of honorary titles to notable members in the Cheng ancestry. Many historical documents collected in the *Records*, as well as the detailed generational charts in *XACST*, further supplement and support the *pubian* claims. Some modern scholars, like their Ming contemporaries, question the claims of blood affiliation between the Cheng brothers and the Huizhou Chengs. See, for example, Ye Xian'en, *Ming-Qing Huizhou nongcun shehui yu dianpu zhi*, 199. And yet, a composite genealogy of all the Cheng branches in Henan also traces the ancestry of the Cheng brothers to Cheng Lingxi and Cheng Yuantan, and the genealogy, notably, carries a foreword by Cheng Minzheng. *Henan Chengshi tongzong pulüe* (1868).

109. *XACST*, 1a–6a. Cheng made a similar statement in his 1482 foreword to the *Records of Bequeathed Glories of the Chengs*: "The rule of the family is like the law of the state. For an official, obedience to the law of the state is loyalty. For an offspring, upholding the rule of the family/lineage is filial piety. The remaining men are all outcasts of society. The ancestry of our Cheng descent line is marked by the virtues of benevolence and righteousness [Xiufu and Cheng Ying], contributions to civil and military governing [Cheng Yuantan and Cheng Lingxi], and writings on human nature and the Way and Virtue [the Cheng brothers], and these are what they have passed on to the offspring [to assure the descent line] to last for so long. Even other places and different surnames read and followed them. Should not the descendants of their spirits and bodies in their tombs and shrines do so even more!" *CSYFJ*, 1.1b–2a.

110. Cheng Yizhi, in *Chengdian* (The code of the Taitang Cheng lineage), compiled in 1582, prepares a *Zongyue sanzhang* (three clauses for descent-line rules), explaining each of the three terms (*zunzu jingzong muzu*) in a long paragraph. Reprinted in Bian Li, comp., *Ming-Qing Huizhou zugui jiafa xuanbian*, 222–24.

111. In total, twenty-nine are included in *HDWJ*, three of which are about the *Composite Genealogy* and four of which are about non-Huizhou genealogies.

112. *XNZ*, 5.2a; see also Peng Hua's record commemorating the construction of the Cheng Xin shrine ("Cheng Xiangyigong ci ji"), and especially Cheng Minzheng's "Chongxiu Nanshan an ji" (Record of the reconstruction of the Chapel of Southern Hill), both in *XNPGC, fulu* (appendix), 59a–60a, 62b–63b. Guan Yu (or Guandi), a famous general from the Three Kingdoms period who became a symbol of righteousness, was popular throughout China, while Zhang Xun, who tried to protect central China during the An Lushan rebellion (755–763), was especially popular in Huizhou.

113. As Cheng Minzheng noted in "Chongxiu Nanshan an ji," in *XNPGC, fulu*, 62b.

114. Cheng Minzheng was quite friendly to local monks and Buddhism; see his "Dui fo wen" (Responses to questions about Buddhism), in *HDWJ*, 1253.352–57; see also Han Jiegen, *Mingdai Huizhou wenxue yanjiu*, 95–105. During the transitional period of the mid Ming, it was common practice for Huizhou lineages to situate their ancestral halls in a Buddhist temple. See McDermott, *The Making of a New Rural Order*, 1:105.

115. See *XNPGC, Fulu*, 60a–68a, for "burned prayers" (*shu*) to Guan Yu as well as Cheng Xin, and various contracts of ritual lands and the covenants of the Worship Societies.

116. Modern scholars consider these features the mature expression of lineage solidarity. See Patricia Ebrey and James Watson, "Introduction," in *Kinship Organization in Late Imperial China*, ed. Ebrey and Watson, 1–13.

117. Whether or not Xiufu and Qiaobo were the same person is a controversial issue. See Chengshi wenhua liangyihui jiapu weiyuanhui, comp., *Chengshi xungen cankao*, 1.57–58.

118. *XNPGC*, 11a–b. See also *CSYFJ, jiaji*, 1.1a–b (for the two inscriptions; the actual seals are not included here, possibly because Minzheng had not acquired them by 1482).

119. Cheng Minzheng was accompanied on the tour by Cheng Hong (*jinshi* 1466), another kinsman from Shanhe who was Touring Censorial Inspector of Henan. *CSYFJ, yiji*, 7.8a–12a.

120. *XNZ*, 4.3b–4a; *XAWXZ*, 375.

121. *CSYFJ, yiji*, 7.12a–17a; *XNPGC, fulu*, 25b–26b.

122. *XNZ*, 4.3a–4b, 31.16b–18b, 34.12a–13b, the last of which is Ouyang Dan's commemoratory piece on completing the construction of the Cheng Shrine, reemphasizing what had been emphasized in the correspondence between Cheng Minzheng and Lou Qian. See also *HZF*, 5.22a–23a, and a more detailed account in *XXZ*, 265–67. The compilation of *Gazetteer of Xiuning* also gave Cheng Minzheng an opportunity to pay public tribute to his father, furthering his illustrious ancestry. He incorporated into the text the imperial edict bestowing an honorary title on Cheng Xin and the funeral orations for Cheng Xin by Qiu Jun and himself. *XNZ*, 31.38b–40b.

123. *XNZ*, 3b.

124. *HDWJ*, 1252.169–74. See also Thomas A. Wilson, *Genealogy of the Way: The Construction and Uses of the Confucian Tradition in Late Imperial China*, 55; and especially Ho Wei Hsuan, "Cheng Minzheng jiqi xueshu sixiang," chap. 4.

125. *Ming xiaozong shilu*, 19.452. Cited in Ho Wei Hsuan, "Cheng Minzheng jiqi xueshu sixiang," 68.

126. See Ho Wei Hsuan, "Cheng Minzheng jiqi xueshu sixiang," 73–74.

127. "Qingzhou ji," in *XNZ*, 19.28a–29a; a slightly different version also included in *XAWXZ*, 412–13. Cheng Xin's writings are also printed in a collection titled after his style name, *Qingzhou ji*. See *XAMII*, 47.

128. *XAWXZ*, 2305–6.

129. As Cheng Minzheng revealed in an afternote to his father's will, "Shu xiangong Jianhe zhuang yizhu hou," *HDWJ*, 1252.695. For Cheng Xin's establishment of a lineage estate for the Peiguo Chengs, see *XNMZZ*, 83.

130. According to written documentation, 1478 was the first time Cheng Minzheng visited Huizhou, but his love for his ancestral place must have started much earlier, as indicated in his aforementioned 1490 statement that it took "thirty years" for him to accumulate source materials for the *Anthology of Xin'an Document*.

131. For Zhen and Qiu, see also Bol, *Neo-Confucianism in History*, 106.

2. A LAND OF PROMINENT LINEAGES

1. Taga Akigōrō, "Shin-an meizoku-shi ni tsuite," 79–102; David Johnson, *The Medieval Chinese Oligarchy*.

2. Joseph McDermott translates the same text as *The Famous Lineages of Huizhou*, which covers "all the famous (and not-so-famous) lineages of Huizhou prefecture." McDermott,

The Making of a New Rural Order in South China, 1:178. McDermott also characterizes the text as a historical "survey of Huizhou lineages," but for convenience of expression, I will call it a genealogical gazetteer.

3. *XAMII*. As Zhu Wanshu's foreword to *XAMII* notes (1–2), there are at least twelve different editions of *Prominent Lineages in Xin'an*, with various formats composed of two, four, or eight *ji* or *juan*. Different versions of this prefecture-wide genealogical gazetteer cover different numbers of surnames with different numbers of lineage branches, but they were all printed around the mid-sixteenth century. Personal communication with Zhu Wanshu. The Library of Congress holds an original copy of *Xin'an mingzu zhi*, in two *ji* volumes covering eighty-nine surnames, which was printed in 1551 and attributed to Cheng Shuangkuan.

4. It is also different from the composite genealogy covering all members of one single surname from one region (like Cheng Minzheng's *Composite Genealogy of the Xin'an Chengs*) or even throughout the empire, such as the late Ming edition of the massive *Zhangshi tongzong shipu* (Composite genealogy of the Zhangs), encompassing 117 Zhang branches from fifteen provinces. For the latter, see Xu Jianhua, *Zhongguo de jiapu*, 30.

5. Ye Xian'en, *Ming-Qing Huizhou nongcun shehui yu dianpu zhi*; Harriet Zurndorfer, *Change and Continuity in Chinese Local History*.

6. McDermott, *The Making of a New Rural Order*, vol. 1.

7. These claims bespoke the public function of Huizhou "private" genealogies. They were aimed at an audience composed of both kin and non-kin communities. Local lineages competed with each other in boosting prestige via genealogical compilations, although they also supported each other in their claims by providing prefaces to neighboring lineage publications. This competition accounts for numerous genealogical prefaces written by empire-wide luminaries, from both within Huizhou and without. Outsiders started to provide genealogical prefaces during Song-Yuan times, but the phenomenon, as well as genealogical compilation per se, did not become a trend in Huizhou until around the mid-Ming. See also Keith Hazelton, "Patrilines and the Development of Localized Lineages: The Wu of Hsiu-ning City, Hui-chou, to 1528," in *Kinship Organization in Late Imperial China, 1000–1940*, ed. Ebrey and Watson, 148–49.

8. The Xiuning Shuaikou Cheng genealogy included five prefaces dating 1390, 1437, 1454, 1468, and 1475, respectively. *XNSKC*, preface.

9. *HDWJ*, 1252.245–46, 247–48, 281–82. The Chakou Chengs had by then also compiled their branch genealogy. See *XAMII*, 41–42.

10. *XAMII*, 54.

11. *XAZ*, 50.

12. *LSW*.

13. In *LSW*, 10 (preface), 1a.

14. "Chengbei Wangshi pu xu," *HDWJ*, 1252.473.

15. Wang Rang, comp., *Chengbei Wangshi zupu* (1487), preface. See also Wang Daojin, *Wangshi zupu*, carrying Qiu Jun's 1480 preface; Wang Shanghe, *Xiuning Ximen Wangshi zupu*, carrying a 1385 preface to its previous edition, as well as Li Dongyang's 1488 preface to *Wangshi jiacheng*.

16. The version of *Wangshi yuanyuan lu* I have examined is a 1518 reprint, 1.2a–4a. See also Taga Akigōrō, *Chūugoku sōfu no kenkyū*, 214.

17. See a lengthy account on the Wang Hua cult, in thirteen sheets, in *XAZ* (66–79), which does not include a similar account on Cheng Lingxi, who nevertheless is covered in

a note on Lake Huangdun and earns a brief biography in the section on Xin'an governors, *XAZ*, 172–73, 577–78.

18. For the Huizhou Wangs, the earliest extant composite genealogy is Wang Tingfeng's *Wangshi tongzong pu*, compiled during the Jiajing era (1522–1566); see also Wang Zhonglu et al., *Wangshi tongzong zhengmai* (1571). For the Huizhou Huangs, see Huang Yunsu, *Xin'an Huangshi huitong zongpu* (1501), 16 vols., for which Cheng Minzheng wrote a foreword (1491). Other important surnames also compiled their composite genealogies, including the Zhu, Hu, Yu, Yu (different character), Wang (different Wang than Wang Hua), Wu, Li, Hong, Bi, Cao, Xu, Zhang, and Zhan. See Chen Rui, "Mingdai Huizhou jiapu de bianxiu jiqi neirong yu tili de fazhan," 24–27.

19. See the Tōyō Bunko edition of Chen Dingyu's *Xin'an dazu zhi* (Great lineages in Xin'an), which Taga Akigōrō argues was a Yuan print in his "Shin-an meizoku-shi ni tsuite," 79–102. I have through Zhu Wanshu acquired a copy of Tōyō Bunko's *Xin'an dazu zhi*.

20. *XAMII*, 15.

21. Another surname that had settled in Xin'an before the Chengs was the Fangs, whose first migrant ancestor to the region could be dated back to the Wang Mang era (23–40). *XAMII*, 98–99. The first county gazetteer of Shexian was not printed until 1609, which devotes a short section to "Surnames and Lineages" (Shizu). It lists the important regional surnames according to the order of their first migrant ancestor's settlement in Xin'an. The first seven surnames are, in order, Fang, Wang, Cheng, Huang, Bao, Yu, and Zhan. *SZ*, 84.

22. *XAZ*, 49–53.

23. The next three important surnames that produced the most metropolitan degree holders are the Wus (thirty in the Ming and sixty-one in the Qing); the Fangs (twenty-seven in the Ming and thirteen in the Qing); and the Hus (twenty-three in the Ming and eighteen in the Qing). Li Linqi, "Ming-Qing Huizhou jinshi shuliang, fenbu tedian jiqi yuanyin fenxi," 35. For the Song and Ming periods, see also Zurndorfer, *Change and Continuity*, 38 (table 4.3) and 53 (table 5.1).

24. *XAMII*, 15.

25. See Cheng Tong, *Xin'an xuexi lu*, 90.103–4.

26. The Chen genealogy compiled by Chen Dingyu is no longer extant, but a postface by Cao Jing is reprinted in the revised version, *Xin'an Chenshi zongpu* (1507, n.p.). For the forewords or postfaces Chen Dingyu wrote for other lineage genealogies, see Wang Rang, *Chengbei Wangshi zupu*; Chen Dingyu, *Dingyu ji*, 2.5a–6b, 3.2b–4a, 3.9b–11a.

27. Taga Akigōrō, "Shin-an meizoku-shi ni tsuite," 79–102.

28. See, e.g., Cheng Minzheng, "Dingyu xiansheng citang ji" (*HDWJ*, 1252.297–98); Jie Xisi, "Dingyu Chen xiansheng Li muzhiming" (*XAWXZ*, 1739–41). Chen's biography in *HZF* (7.44a–b) also does not mention *Great Lineages in Xin'an*.

29. The first modern scholar to have addressed this problem is Taga Akigōrō, who argued that the *Xin'an dazu zhi* he saw in the Tōyō Bunko was a Yuan print compiled by Chen Dingyu ("Shin-an meizoku-shi ni tsuite," 79–102). The Tōyō Bunko edition, however, is actually a Qing print (Zurndorfer, *Change and Continuity*, 15). More damaging to Taga's claim is a substantive essay by the Huizhou specialist Zheng Limin, who convincingly points out numerous evidential errors in Taga's piece. Names of some villages listed in the Tōyō Bunko edition for various elite lineage branch settlements, for instance, did not even exist until Ming times. See Zheng Limin, "*Xin'an dazu zhi* kaobian."

30. See Zhu Wanshu's preface to *XAMII*, 3–5.

31. *XAMII*, 16.

32. In Yu Chenghua, comp., *Huizhou mingzu zhi*, 1.7–8.

33. Zheng Limin, "*Xin'an dazu zhi* kaobian."

34. Wu Bosen, comp., *Ming shilu leizuan—Wenjiao keji juan*, 172; *Hunan tongzhi* (1885), 2768; *Changsha fuzhi* (1747), 639. *HZF*, 7.68a; *HZZ*, 16.18b–19a.

35. *Changsha Qingshan Pengshi hui zongpu* (1520), 1a. See also *HZF*, 4.34a for Peng Ze's official registration at Changsha.

36. *Changsha Pengshi dunxu xupu* (1915), 4b. For Ji'an literati, see Gerritsen, *Ji'an Literati and the Local in Song-Yuan-Ming China*.

37. *HZZ*, 3.7a, 3.12b; *HZF*, 1a–4a.

38. Also in *Peng Wensigong wenji* (which was first compiled by Peng Li and printed in Anfu in 1503), 324–28.

39. *XNPGC, fulu*, 47b.

40. *HDWJ*, 1253.212–13, 1253.421. Minzheng later noted that he had been a student of Peng Shi while studying in the Imperial Academy (*XNPGC, fulu*, 47b).

41. We might also read into these literary exchanges mechanisms for career advancement. The commemorative note, or preface or postface, was a medium that forged relationships and opened doors; I cannot help but wonder if the path that led Peng Ze to the post of Huizhou prefect might not have been paved with just such intangible favors to Minzheng.

42. *Xiuning Shuaikou Chengshi xubian benzong pu* (preface, n.p.), in which Peng Ze also mentioned, with passion, his own experience of compiling the aforementioned Changsha Peng genealogy.

43. Peng Ze's preface, in *HZMZZ*, 1.7–8.

44. See prefaces by Lin Han and Wang Shunmin to *HZF*.

45. Wang Zongjin, (*Shexian*) *Xixi Wangshi xianying bianlan* (1539, no page number); *Yueguo Wanggong cimu zhi* (1852), *Yuanxu* (original prefaces), 3b, 4.1b, 4.9b–10b. See also *HZF*, 2.18a; *HZZ*, 21.13a–b.

46. In all likelihood, *Great Lineages in Xin'an*, "based and further expanded" on Chen Dingyu's manuscript, was not cut until the mid-sixteenth century; this could be the print Zheng Shuangxi and Hong Jueshan endorsed. *XAMII*, 14. Zheng Shuangxi's 1549 preface (*XAMII*, 1–2) gave the credit for its compilation to Dai Tingming, along with several other local gentrymen surnamed Wang, Cheng, Fang, and Wu. Interestingly, the deferral of the publication of *Xin'an dazu zhi* seems to parallel the deferral, until 1530, of putting into practice Cheng Minzheng's 1488 proposal to reform the Confucian Temple in the "Memorial on the Assessment and Correction of the Ritual Code."

47. See also Cheng Tong's 1508 preface to his *Xin'an xuexi lu*, 90.24. The text starts with the two Cheng brothers.

48. *XAMII*, 13.

49. Timothy Brook, *The Confusions of Pleasure: Commerce and Culture in Ming China*. Brook, notably, uses a seasonal metaphor to discuss the burgeoning Ming economy, which is drawn from the views of Zhang Tao, the late Ming magistrate of Shexian.

50. McDermott, *The Making of a New Rural Order*, vol. 1, chap. 3.

51. Zhu's preface to *XAMII*, 10.

52. *Xiuning Gucheng Chengshi zongpu* (1570), 1a–2b. While many Ming dynasty Huizhou genealogies are no longer extant, many prefaces to them are still available, reprinted in later editions. Another example, as noted earlier, is the 1570 revised edition of another Cheng

branch's genealogy, *Xiuning Shuaikou Chengshi xubian benzong pu*, which reprints over a dozen prefaces and postfaces to the previous Huizhou (mostly Shuaikou) Chengs' genealogies compiled in the Ming dynasty, including Cheng Minzheng's preface to his composite genealogy, *Xin'an Chengshi tongzong shipu*. Consult also Taga Akigōrō, *Chūgoku sōfu no kenkyū*, 165–277; Wu Xuande and Zong Yun, comp., *Mingren pudie xuba jilue*, 2 vols.

53. *HZF* (1502), 10.41b, 10.46b (5.33a–49b for eleven large temples mostly set up to worship deified local heroes who were considered apical ancestors of Huizhou powerful lineages, including Wang Hua and Cheng Lingxi); *HZF* (1566), 21.5b–12b.

54. *HZZ* (1566), 21.4a.

55. *HZF*, 1.10a–b; *HZZ*, 2.39b–40a.

56. Compiled in Zhang Haipeng et al., comps., *Ming-Qing Huishang ziliao xuanbian*, 42–43 (no. 123).

57. *THJ*, 372.

58. Fujii Hiroshi, "Shinan shōnin no kenkyū."

59. McDermott, *The Making of a New Rural Order*, 1:432 and vol. 2.

60. See also McDermott, "The Rise of Huizhou Merchants: Kinship and Commerce in Ming China," 233–65; Wang Tingyuan and Wang Shihua, *Huishang*, 36–50.

61. See, for example, *HZZ*, 19.35a–36b for the biographic entries for Wang Qiong, She Wenyi, and Ma Lu.

62. In a commemorative record on a Shexian merchant that Cheng Minzheng wrote, he highlights the virtue of a trader named She Yanghao; in this case, it was the "righteous house" (*yizhai*) She Yanghao built in 1494 to accommodate his kinspeople that distinguished him as virtuous. See "Sheshi yizhai ji" in She Huarui, *Yanzhen zhicao* (1738), 186.

63. See "Huang chushi Zhongrong muzhiming" (Epitaph on untitled gentryman Huang Zhongrong), in Huang Yunsu, comp., *Xin'an Huangshi huitong zongpu*, 9652–54.

64. *XAMII*, 15.

65. Zhao Huafu, *Liangyi ji* (1999), 377–78.

66. *XAMII*, 24.

67. *XAMII*, 61–63.

68. *XAMII*, 161.

69. *XAMII*, 157.

70. *XAMII*, 150.

71. See, for instance, *LSW*.

72. For the Taitang Chengs, see McDermott, "The Rise of Huizhou Merchants," 249–60; for the Shuaikou Chengs, see also Zhang Yi, *Lixue shishen he zongzu*, 178–89.

73. *XNSKC*, 6.13b–14b: "*Hushan Chenggong fufu muzhiming*" (Epitaph on the couple of Sir Hushan [Wenjie]), penned in 1542 by a high-ranking official named Gu Dingchen.

74. *XAMII*, 54. Another notable example is the short entry for the Songmingshan Wang lineage, in Shexian. After a brief account of the ancestry, it turns to noting some notable contemporaries, including the young Wang Daokun, identified as a 1547 *jinshi*, completely leaving out his merchant father and even his grandfather, a leading salt merchant. *XAMII*, 191. Nevertheless, for other Wang branches in Shexian, their entries note the worthiness of merchants: some contemporary Wang men from Gutang either sojourned for business in eastern Jiangnan or practiced the scholarly profession at home; other Wang men from Yanzhen "committed to a scholarly or commercial career, with lofty commitment" (*weiru weishang lizhi bufan*); still other young contemporaries from Etian or Huanshan either "are able to continue the father's will by successfully engaging in trade" (*kecheng fuzhi, gangu*

yousheng) or "establish their households by engaging in trade" (*gangu qijia*). *XAWII*, 185, 193, 195.

75. McDermott, "The Rise of Huizhou Merchants," 260.

76. *XNSKC, Xu* (prefaces) section, 13b.

77. *XAMII*, 54.

78. See Cheng Minzheng's epitaph on Cheng Nai (styled Yongjian), in *XNSKC*, 6.3b–4b.

79. *XAWXZ*, 2160.

80. *XAMII*, 2–3. For Hong, later identified as the editor-in-chief, see *XNMZZ*, 20.

81. Hong Jueshan, unlike Cheng Minzheng, is covered in Huang Zongxi's *Case Studies on Ming Confucians*. He believed that "ten thousand differences are united in one root, which is the *li* principle; one principle is differentiated into functions." Huang Zongxi, *Mingru xue'an*, 3.26.98.

82. Joseph McDermott, personal communication. However, there were few elite families in Jiangnan who could not just claim aristocratic roots but also represented a culture of nobility in the Ming. Suzhou in the sixteenth century claimed to have the great Wen family that was composed of "a powerful mixture of ancient lineage, cultural achievements in the most esteemed fields, great wealth founded on the most socially acceptable form of riches, namely landholding, and the political leadership of the elite on the regional level." The Suzhou Wens traced a connection to a famous thirteenth-century prime minister, and beyond that to the "hoary" antiquity of the Han dynasty. Clunas, *Superfluous Things: Material Culture and Social Status in Early Modern China*, 20–21.

83. Zhang Chao, "*Shewen* xiaoyin," in Zhang Chao, comp., *Zhaodai congshu*, 1a–1b; also cited in Guo, *Ritual Opera and Mercantile Lineage*, 18.

84. Wang Zhenzhong, "Ming-Qing wenxian zhong 'Huishang' yici de chubu kaocha," 170–73.

85. Wang Zhenzhong, "Ming-Qing wenxian zhong 'Huishang' yici de chubu kaocha." See also Yongtao Du, *The Order of Places: Translocal Practices of the Huizhou Merchants in Late Imperial China*, 55.

86. The tragedy of Tang Guimei will be fully discussed in chap. 4. Timothy Brook also discusses the image of Huizhou merchants, perhaps distorted but popular, as "the grasping pawnbroker who sued anyone he disagreed with and spent vast amounts of money on commercial sex." Brook, *Confusions of Pleasure*, 127.

87. It is clear that this claim cannot be taken at its face value. We know that the strategy of intermarriage of local elite families started during the Southern Song and was reflective of the medieval transformation. Hymes, *Statesmen and Gentlemen*.

88. *XAMII*, 1.

89. *HZZ*, 2.41a. See also *Xiuning xianzhi* (1548), 1.1a.

90. The local gentryman that Cheng Minzheng singled out as most helpful in his compilation of the *Anthology of Xin'an Documents* was Wang Zuo, for whom he wrote a heartfelt epitaph. For this piece, along with three additional epitaphs he penned for Wang Zuo, see *LSW, Zhiming* (epitaphs) section, 4a–5a, 5a–6b, 6b–8b, 8b–9b. He also wrote two complimentary pieces for the elderly Wang Kejing of the Wangs of Chengbei (Xiuning) on the occasion of the longevity party for the latter's sixtieth anniversary; it turned out that Wang Kejing was the father-in-law of Cheng Minzheng's cousin Cheng Zongbi. See Wang Rang, comp., *Chengbei Wangshi zupu* (1487), 2.21a–22a, 26b.

91. Cheng Minzheng, "Shu Yanshan Wangshi zupu hou," *HDWJ*, 1252.674.

92. Cheng Minzheng, "Gulin Huangshi xupu xu," *HDWJ*, 1252.557.

93. Compiled in Bian Li, comp., *Ming-Qing Huizhou zugui jiafa xuanbian*, 202.

94. Ye Xian'en, *Ming-Qing Huizhou nongcun shehui yu dianpu zhi*, 138.

95. Zhao Huafu, "*Xin'an mingzu zhi* bianzuan de beijing he zongzhi," 369–75.

96. Brook, *Confusions of Pleasure*, 2–4; see also Xie Bi, comp., *Shezhi*, 99.

97. Chen Zhaoxiang, *Wentang Xiangyue jiafa* (1572), 3b–4a.

98. *XNSKC*, 5.7a–7b.

99. *XAMII*, 6–12, 13–14.

100. *XNSKC, Fanli* (Guidelines), 1a.

101. Both also contributed to the printing of the *Anthology of Xin'an Documents*, as noted in chapter 1. Cheng Zuyuan himself was purely a gentryman, "noted for his filial piety" (*XAMII*, 54), but his sons were all engaged in commercial ventures.

102. *XNSKC, Xu* (Prefaces), 1a–2a. Cheng Zengjie was one of a few Shuaikou Cheng kinsmen earning a lower *shengyuan* exam degree and one of Cheng Minzheng's most devoted disciples in Xiuning, and he encouraged his sons to embark on sojourning trade ventures. *XNSKC*, 6.50a–51b.

103. *XNSKC, Puhao* (Genealogy numbers), 1a–6a.

104. *XNSKC*, n.p. (front page of vol. 5). Again, this strict regulation may show some influence from Cheng Minzheng, who clearly stipulates in his postscript to the *Composite Genealogy of the Xin'an Chengs*: for any kinsman who "desires power and benefits to sell [the composite genealogy]," "the lineage head would publicize his misconduct to all kinspeople, trace back to the original copy, and fine the violator twenty taels of silver," which would be sent to the branch temple of Cheng Lingxi. Also reprinted in *HDWJ*, 1252.635.

105. *XAMII*, 4.

106. *XAMII*, 24.

107. *XAMII*, 39–40.

108. *XAMII*, 20–21; 42, 58.

109. *XAMII*, 315.

110. *Jiangnan tongzhi* (1737), 19.6a.

111. *XAWXZ*, 1763; *HZZ*, 2.39a; *Xiuning xianzhi* (1693), 237.

112. Another more dramatic example has to do with the Nies, who produced a number of *jinshi* degree holders and high-ranking officials in the Song (see Zhang Yi, *Lixue, shishen he zongzu*), and yet was not even included in *Prominent Lineages in Xin'an*. It is not clear what caused the absence of the Nies in the genealogical gazetteer. Was it because of the social and demographic decline of the descent line or their migration out of Huizhou? We know that Wang Daokun in the late sixteenth century penned a biography for the Priest Nie. *THJ*, 791–96.

113. Ye Xian'en, *Ming-Qing Huizhou*, 40–41; Zurndorfer, *Change and Continuity*, 170.

114. Zurndorfer, *Change and Continuity*, 175–81.

115. *XAMII*, 13.

3. WANG DAOKUN AND THE PROMOTION OF MERCANTILE LINEAGE CULTURE

1. Two of Wang Daokun's Huizhou contemporaries, Hu Zongxian (1512–1565) and Xu Guo (1527–1596), ended up becoming the minister of war and minister of rites (and a grand secretariat), respectively. *MS*, 5410–11, 5773–74.

2. The earliest treatment of Wang Daokun is found in Fujii Hiroshi's influential treatise on Huizhou merchants, citing numerous merchant biographies in Wang Daokun's *Taihan ji*. Fujii, "Shinan shōnin no kenkyū." A leading authority on Ming drama, Xu Shuofang, compiled a highly useful "annual annals" of Wang Daokun, which focuses on his literary works. Xu Shuofang, "Wang Daokun nianpu," in *Wan Ming qujia nianpu*, Xu Shuofang, 3:1–104. Zhu Wanshu examines the literary value of Wang Daokun's (and other literati's) merchant biographies in *Huishang yu Ming-Qing wenxue*, chap. 6.

3. Wang Daokun, "*Xian dafu zhuang* (Portrait of my departed grandfather)," in *THJ*, 919–21; "*Xian damu zhuang* (Portrait of my departed grandmother)," in *THJ*, 921–23.

4. Xu Shuofang, "Wang Daokun nianpu," 14.

5. Wang Daokun, "Ji shishu shiyi fujun wen (Elegiac address to my uncle, Sir Eleven)," in *THJ*, 1720–21.

6. Xu Shuofang, "Wang Daokun nianpu," 6, 12; *THJ*, 1092.

7. Sima was an ancient title for the vice minister of war, as both Wangs had once occupied that position, but the accolade also implied that the two were as talented in literary skill as the two Han dynasty literary greats, Sima Xiangru and Sima Qian. *MS*, 7382.

8. Xu, "Wang Daokun nianpu," 10. For Wang Daokun and his commentary on *Water Margin*, see also Andrew Plaks, *The Four Masterworks of the Ming Novel*, 286–87.

9. Another attempt was made around the same time by the Ming dramatist Xu Wei (1521–93) in his famous *Cries of the Four Gibbons*. Together, Wang and Xu anticipated the flowering of southern *chuanqi* drama in the late Ming. Xu Shuofang, "Wang Daokun nianpu," 11.

10. Yang Jin, "Wang Daokun liulun."

11. *THJ*, 145.

12. For the emotional dimension of Wang Yangming's moral philosophy, see Wm. Theodore de Bary, "Individualism and Humanitarianism in Late Ming Thought," in *Self and Society in Ming Thought*, ed. de Bary, 145–247. The cult of *qing* was marked by Tang Xianzu's (1550–1616) *Peony Pavilion*; Wang Daokun highly admired the writing of the young Tang Xianzu. *THJ*, 2201; Xu Shuofang, "Wang Daokun nianpu," 86; Xu Shuofang, "Tang Xianzu nianpu," in *Wan Ming qujia nianpu*, Xu Shuofang, 3:201–495. See also Dorothy Ko, *Teachers of the Inner Chambers: Women and Culture in Seventeenth-Century China*, chap. 2.

13. *THJ*, 330–31.

14. See Zuo Dongling, *Wangxue yu zhong wan Ming shiren xintai*.

15. Cited in Zhou Xiaoguang, *Xin'an lixue*, 196.

16. Zhou Xiaoguang, *Xin'an lixue*, 192–97.

17. See, for instance, three epitaphs on local literati and their spouses in *THJ*, 593–95; 993–97; 1187–91.

18. *THJ*, 2541–42.

19. *THJ*, 946–47.

20. *THJ*, 4.

21. Xie Bi ended the biographic account noting that Wang Daokun adhered to Confucius and Mencius for their moral teaching, although he supplemented it with the Daoist proclivities of Laozi and Zhuangzi. *SZ*, 296.

22. *THJ*, 1187.

23. *THJ*, 435.

24. *THJ*, 441–42. For the Xin'an Jiangs, who were related to the commercially successful Jiangcun Jiangs, see *XAMII*, 522–23 (highlighting their prominent ancestry and devoted women); see also McDermott, *The Making of a New Rural Order in South China*, 1:192; *Shexian zhi* (1937), 16a.

25. See, for instance, Ke Dawei (David Faure) and Liu Zhiwei, "Zongzu yu difang shehui de guojia rentong: Ming-Qing Huanan diqu zongzu fazhan de yishi xingtai jichu," 3–14; Patricia Ebrey, *Confucianism and Family Rituals in Imperial China: A Social History of Writing about Rites*; Bol, *Neo-Confucianism in History*.

26. *LSW*, Wang's preface. See also the postface by his cousin, Wang Daohui.

27. See Sima Qian, *Shiji*, and the English version, Burton Watson, trans., *Records of the Grand Historian of China*.

28. *LSW*, 4.1a.

29. *LSW*, Wang Daokun, "Xiaoxu (Brief [second] preface)."

30. *LSW*, 9.3b; 9.5a; 9.7b.

31. *LSW*, Wang Daokun, "Xiaoxu."

32. Included are a preface to eulogy verses by Qiu Jun, *LSW*, 10.5.12a–13a; prefaces by Zhang Juzheng and Wang Shizhen honoring the seventieth anniversary of Wang Daokun's parents, *LSW*, 10.5.2a-3b, 3b–5a; one biography by Fang Liangshu (a high-ranking official from Shexian) on Daokun's kinsman, Wang Shou'an (1491–1527), a *chushi* (untitled gentryman) who was "a scholar in name and merchant in practice" (*ruming shangxing*) and whose son and daughter became "exemplars of righteousness and chastity" (*yijie biaoshuai*), *LSW*, 10.3.22b–23b; a commemoration on the refurbished Wang Hua temple by Zheng Yu (a famous scholar from Xin'an), *LSW*, 10.4.1a; seven pieces by Cheng Minzheng, including a commemorative record on a Wang Hua shrine on Xiuning's Wulong Mountain, *LSW*, 10.4.1b–2b; an inscription on the Lingshanyuan lineage temple named after Wang Hua by Tao Chengxue, *LSW*, 10.8.1a–2b; and another commemorative record on a Wang Hua shrine in Tangmo by Bao Xiangxian, *LSW*, 10.4.4a–5a.

33. *LSW*, 10 *Xu* 1a.

34. *LSW*, Li's preface, 1a–5b.

35. *LSW*, Wang's first preface, 1a.

36. *LSW*, Wang's first preface; *THJ*, 2105–6. Wang Tang earned the *jinshi* degree in 1547 (the same year as Wang Daokun); he was from Yin County, Zhejiang.

37. Wang Zhonglu, comp., *Wangshi tongzong zhengmai*, 28 vols.

38. Here I also consider wives, mothers, and daughters of the gentry as commoners for two reasons. First, while these "gentry women" enjoyed certain privileges, they were not gentry themselves; and second, Wang Daokun covered them in a way that was similar to how he wrote about commoner women.

39. Wang Daokun penned at least ten prefaces to local genealogies; see Wu Xuande and Zong Yun, *Mingren pudie xuba jilue*, 1041–53. The *Lingshanyuan Wangs* also includes the following "covenants" related to the lineage's ancestral tombs and rituals (and one on a literary association), all drafted by Wang Daokun: (1) *Jian muci yue* (Covenant on [maintaining and building] the ancestral tombs and hall); (2) *Shimuhu congyue* (Contract on the hereditary tenant houses [care for] the inherited tombs); (3) *Jian jiaci yue* (Covenant on building the ancestral hall); (4) *Jiaci siyue* (Covenant on rituals at the ancestral hall). *LSW*, 10.6.1a–3b. The last covenant, penned in 1592, notes that the new ancestral hall "has not been built, as kinspeople are not in agreement." But the *Jian jiaci yue* was penned in 1576,

which appears to be the year when Wang Daokun led the construction, or reconstruction, of the ancestral hall for the sixteen Wang branches, which was located adjacent to Shanquan Temple. See Xu Chengyao, *Sheshi xiantan*, 980–82.

40. Huizhou genealogists dared not copy Wang Daokun's format, I believe, mainly because he "usurped" the "Basic Annals" and "Hereditary House" subtitle sections, previously reserved for royal households, to catalog his ancestors. Even just over two decades earlier, the Xin'an Wus in their *Chongxiu Xin'an Qidong Wushi zupu yaolue* (1568) had not dared to invent a new format to claim their outstanding descent line, even though they, too, claimed descent from the same apical ancestor as the founding king of the Zhou, Houji. *MDJP*, 3:819. Wang Daokun's boldness may have been rooted in the liberal atmosphere of the late sixteenth century. To my knowledge, only one Wang genealogy, a massive twenty-six volumes, compiled during the High Qing by a leading mercantile lineage, continued to use Wang Daokun's genealogical format: *Hongcun Wangshi jiapu* (1747).

41. The version of Wang Songtao's genealogy now available was reprinted in 1518.

42. Wang Songtao, *Wangshi yuanyuan lu*, 1.2a; 3.1a; 4.1a–b.

43. Quotation from Wang Songtao, *Wangshi yuanyuan lu*, 6.1a.

44. In this regard, Wang Daokun also differs from Cheng Minzheng. Cheng Minzheng compiled a separate book of the Cheng documents for his composite genealogy, whereas Wang Daokun incorporated all of the lineage documents he thought important or relevant into the same genealogy in its tenth volume. Different formats aside, more fundamentally, Cheng Minzheng's *Chengshi yifan ji* covers all elite documents, whereas Wang Daokun expanded to cover commoners, including in particular righteous merchants and devoted kinswomen.

45. Yu Ying-shih, *Rujia lunli yu shangren jingshen*, 299.

46. Geng Chuanyou, "Wang Daokun shangren zhuanji yanjiu," 2–3. In total, Wang Daokun penned 235 biographies (including many on women). Zhu Wanshu, *Huishang yu Ming-Qing wenxue*, 152 (several other late Ming literati also produced a large number of Huishang biographies). As in the case of Geng Chuanyou, Zhu Wanshu focuses on the literary value of Wang Daokun's merchant biographies.

47. Fujii Hiroshi, "Shinan shōnin no kenkyū"; Yu Ying-shih, *Rujia lunli yu shangren jingshen*; Tang Lixing, *Shangren yu Zhongguo jinshi shehui*; Wang Tingyuan and Wang Shihua, *Huishang*; Timothy Brook, *Confusions of Pleasure*.

48. I have selected forty-five out of seventy-one of Wang Daokun's biographies of Huizhou merchants because they contain sufficient detail for illustrating their social life.

49. Cited in Ying-shih Yu, *Rujia lunli yu shangren jingshen*, 290, 296.

50. Zhu Wanshu, *Huishang yu Ming-Qing wenxue*, 151–52.

51. Cf. Richard Lufrano, *Honorable Merchants: Commerce and Self-Cultivation in Late Imperial China*, and to a degree also Ying-shih Yu, *Rujia lunli yu shangren jingshen*.

52. For the money craze, see also Brook, *Confusions of Pleasure*; Guo, *Ritual Opera and Mercantile Lineage*, 70–71.

53. Zheng Zhizhen, *Mulian jiumu quanshan xiwen*, 1.63a–64b.

54. Zhu Wanshu, *Huishang yu Ming-Qing wenxue*, 168–74.

55. See *XAMII*, 161; Huang Yunsu, comp., *Xin'an Huangshi huitong zongpu* (1501), 9652–54; *HZZ*, 19.22a (for Huang Yiqing) and 19.35a–36b (for three merchants).

56. Cited in Zhu Wanshu, *Huishang yu Ming-Qing wenxue*, 458. The children of Fang and Wang were married, and the two wrote poems to each other. See Shen Defu (Ming),

Wanli yehuo bian, 707–8, 720. On the precedent for the term *sufeng*, see also, Sima Qian, *Shiji*, 3272: "Now there are men who receive no ranks or emoluments from the government and who have no revenue from titles or fiefs, and yet they enjoy just as much ease as those who have all these; they may be called the 'untitled nobility.'" Translation from Watson, *Records of the Grand Historian of China*, 2:492.

57. This was often still the case in the hands of Wang Daokun; see appendix, entries 22, 41.

58. This statement also appears to have been an attempt to refute the outside image of Huizhou where "trade is the number one career path, while the civil service exam is rather secondary," as conveyed in the famous late Ming collection of short stories, *Slapping the Table in Astonishment* (Pai'an jingqi).

59. Appendix, entry 40.

60. Ying-shih Yu, *Rujia lunli yu shangren jingshen*, 299, where Yu suggests merchants had developed a competitive mindset against the gentry.

61. Wang Daokun also profiled an unusual merchant-scholar, Pan Tingzhou, who was noted for having first engaged in trade before returning to study for the civil service examinations. He eventually earned the highest metropolitan degree. Appendix, entry 11.

62. This local saying most likely started circulation during the High Qing, but given Huizhou's social practice, it must have had a late Ming version in the making. Hu Shibin and Shu Yiling, *Xidi: Zhongguo Ming-Qing minju bowuguan*, 5.

63. Brook, *Confusions of Pleasure*, 212–15.

64. For class blurring even in the Republican era, see Henrietta Harrison, *The Man Awakened from Dreams*. For non-kin tenants or bondservants attached to Huizhou leading lineages, see Ye Xian'en, *Ming-Qing Huizhou nongcun shehui yu dianpu zhi*.

65. On the blurring of gentry and mercantile culture in the realm of taste in the late Ming, see Craig Clunas, *Superfluous Things*; for a peasant perspective on merchants as late as the nineteenth century, see *The Cult of Happiness: Nianhua, Art, and History in Rural North China* by James A. Flath, who shows that peasant producers of *nianhua* (New Year's prints) visualized merchants as nearly interchangeable with gentry-scholars; the former were depicted in visual culture as being carried in sedan-chairs while reading books.

66. In another case (appendix, entry 34), even though Wang Daokun does not explicitly use the term *jiexia*, he profiled a variety of Chen Jing's righteous deeds.

67. *LSW*, 10.5.2a–3b.

68. Shen Defu, *Wanli yehuo bian*, 630.

69. Joanna Handlin Smith, *The Art of Doing Good: Charity in Late Ming China*, 10, 285–86. Huizhou merchants' *yixing* (charitable or righteous deeds) started well before the High Qing.

70. See, for instance, the merchant biographies printed in full in *XNSKC*. Merchant epitaphs could also be publicized in tomb engravings, similar to having spirit tablets set up in ancestral halls.

71. According to the famous early Qing poet Zhu Yizun (1629–1709), who participated in the writing of the official *Ming History*, Wang Daokun, in his later years, needed to prepare numbered cards to keep a waitlist of the people who "filled his house to seek his poems and essays"; he enjoyed such popularity that he "nearly surpassed" the fame of Wang Shizhen. Cited in Hu Xiaoshan, "Wang Daokun beizhuanwen yanjiu," 44.

72. *THJ*, 1721.

73. See Guo, *Ritual Opera and Mercantile Lineage*, chap. 2.

74. Xu Chengyao, *Sheshi xiantan*, 348–55.

75. Ping-ti Ho, *Ladder of Success*, 83–84; *Shexian zhi* (1937), 159.

76. A similar handbook, *Exemplars in the Female Quarters* (*Guifan*), comp. Lü Kun (1536–1618), has received far more attention than Wang's work on women. See Joanna Handlin, *Action in Late Ming Thought: The Reorientation of Lü K'un and Other Scholar-Officials*; Ko, *Teachers of the Inner Chambers*, 55. By the mid-sixteenth century, virtually every local gazetteer included a chapter on virtuous women. Katherine Carlitz, "Desire, Danger, and the Body: Stories of Women's Virtue in Late Ming China," 106.

77. Michela Bussotti's "Images of Women in Late Ming Huizhou-Printed Editions of *Lienü zhuan*" (82) touches upon Wang Daokun's edition and the famous Huizhou painter-cum-woodblock cutter Qiu Ying who created the illustrations. As Bussotti (101) also notes, Huizhou was "an important center for the production of luxury illustrated publications" of the late-Ming empire.

78. On the cult of faithful maidens (betrothed women maintaining their "chastity" or martyring themselves) in late imperial China, see Weijing Lu, *True to Her Word: The Faithful Maiden Cult in Late Imperial China*.

79. Wang Daokun, *Lienü zhuang*, 15.5b–7a (including the beautiful illustration showing Widow Fang kneeling before her husband's tomb).

80. Wang Daokun, *Lienü zhuang*, 16.6a–b. For another Huizhou case involving a chaste maiden marrying into a merchant family, see chaste Maiden Wang. Wang Daokun, *Lienü zhuang*, 16.14b–15a.

81. Wang Daokun, *Lienü zhuang*, 16.19b–21b (including beautiful illustrations showing kinspeople lined up to comfort Maiden Fang).

82. "Sun jiefu Fanshi zhuan," *THJ*, 691–92. See also Katherine Carlitz on the influence of honoring loyal men on the rise of the female chastity cult in her "Shrines, Governing-Class, Identity, and the Cult of Widow Fidelity in Mid-Ming Jiangnan," 612–40.

83. *THJ*, 628–33; *LSW*, 10.3.11a–14a. Wang Daokun's "Qilie zhuan," along with Li Mengyang's "Liu lienü zhuan" (Biographies of the six chastity martyrs), was selected to be included in Qinhuai Yuke, comp., *Lüchuang nüshi* (1621) in the volume titled "Jiexia" (Chastity and chivalry), suggesting a perceived equivalency of female chastity and male righteousness.

84. Wang Daokun, *Lienü zhuan*, 16.24a.

85. This story is also covered in Wang Daokun, *Lienü zhuan*, 16.11a–11b.

86. See Wang Daokun's biography of Ms. Fang and joint epitaph on Wang Daoqi and Ms. Fang in *THJ*, 697–98, 1947–49.

87. Ju-k'ang T'ien, *Male Anxiety and Female Chastity: A Comparative Study of Chinese Ethical Values in Ming-Ch'ing Times*, 46, 51–52. Both Huizhou and Fujian were highly commercialized and successful in producing exam candidates in late imperial times. For a comparison of the two regions in late imperial times, see Harriet Zurndorfer, "Learning, Lineage, and Locality in Late Imperial China: A Comparative Study of Education in Huichow (Anhwei) and Foochow (Fukien), 1600–1800." For Fujian's commercial history, see also Billy So, *Prosperity, Region, and Institutions in Maritime China: The South Fukien Pattern, 946–1368*; for Fujian lineages, see Szonyi, *Practicing Kinship* and *The Art of Being Governed*.

88. *HZF*, 10.5a–20b; *HZZ*, 20.1a–20b. Cheng Minzheng's *Xiuning zhi* (1497) contains a very short section on Confucian women (17.1a–3b), though it also includes ten detailed

memorials or epitaphs on virtuous wives of Xiuning notables as well as commoners' widows of remarkable character (*XNZ*, 30.1a–13.b).

89. *HZZ, 20.1a.*

90. Some representative works include Mark Elvin, "Female Virtue and the State in China," 111–52; Ju-k'ang T'ien, *Male Anxiety and Female Chastity*; Bettine Birge, *Marriage and the Law in the Age of Khubilai Khan: Cases from the Yuan dianzhang*; Birge, "Levirate Marriage and the Revival of Widow Chastity in Yuan China," 107–46; Fangqin Du and Susan Mann, "Competing Claims on Womanly Virtue in Late Imperial China," 219–47; Siyen Fei, "Writing for Justice: An Activist Beginning of the Cult of Female Chastity in Late Imperial China," 991–1012. For a critique of T'ien's book, see Susan Mann, "Suicide and Survival: Exemplary Widows in the Late Empire," 23–39. For a later era, consult also Matthew Sommer, *Sex, Law, and Society in Late Imperial China*, and Janet Theiss, *Disgraceful Matters: The Politics of Chastity in Eighteenth-Century China.*

91. On the Huizhou salt merchants in Yangzhou, many of whose descendants never returned to their native place, see Antonia Finnane, *Speaking of Yangzhou: A Chinese City 1550–1850.*

92. Xie Kaichong, *Lianghui yanfa zhi* (1693), 1409–65, 1467–82, 1483–1526, 1527–90.

93. Xie Kaichong, *Lianghui yanfa zhi* (1693), 1186.

94. For Huizhou merchants who settled outside the region and yet were still emotionally attached to their ancestral place, like Cheng Jun, see also Yongtao Du, *The Order of Places: Translocal Practices of the Huizhou Merchants in Late Imperial China.*

95. Xie Kaichong, *Lianghui yanfa zhi* (1693), 3–4. The official editor-in-chief was an official named Xie Kaichong, but Cui Hua's preface indicates that Cheng Jun was the de-facto editor of the gazetteer and a leading financial contributor to the project.

96. Xie Kaichong, *Lianghui yanfa zhi* (1693), 1591–717.

4. "A CONFUCIAN HEARTLAND OF WOMEN"

1. Quoted in chap. 2.

2. Siyen Fei, "Writing for Justice: An Activist Beginning of the Cult of Female Chastity in Late Imperial China," 991–1012.

3. Dorothy Ko, *Cinderella's Sisters: A Revisionist History of Footbinding.*

4. Susan Mann has called for looking into particular social and cultural factors in different regions to account for different performances of gender. Mann, "Suicide and Survival."

5. Tang Lixing, a leading social historian of Huizhou, first developed the concept of "small family and large lineage" to characterize the social structure of late imperial Huizhou in his "Ming Qing Huizhou de jiating yu zongzu jiegou," 147–59. My work here is in a sense a critical refinement of Tang's concept. It is "critical" in two aspects: first, the demographic data Tang gleaned from the four Fang genealogies are relatively sketchy, only several dozen cases in total; and second, as the majority of Tang's demographic cases (and much of his other primary sources) are from after the eighteenth century, his work does not address the questions of when the Huizhou small-family-and-large-lineage structure took shape and the role of the sixteenth century commercialization in its development.

6. Viewed from another perspective, the Huizhou lineage was often strengthened by diaspora, as evidenced by the experiences of Cheng Wenjie and many other Huizhou merchants. For this phenomenon, see also Du, *The Order of Places: Translocal Practices of the Huizhou Merchants for the Qing dynasty.* Similarly, the role of diasporic men in funding

and organizing localist projects in Huizhou resembles the experiences of overseas Chinese; see, for instance, Shelly Chan, *Diaspora's Homeland: Modern China in the Age of Global Migration*. And the mercantile lineage also appears to have emerged in the homelands of the Hokkien maritime trade diaspora. See Lucille Chia, "The Butcher, the Baker, and the Carpenter: Chinese Sojourners in the Spanish Philippines and Their Impact on Southern Fujian (Sixteenth-Eighteenth Centuries)."

7. *Xin'an Censhandu Chengshi zhipu* (1741).

8. Xie Kaichong, *Lianghuai yanfa zhi* (1693), 16.1a–22b.

9. *Xin'an Censhandu Chengshi zhipu*, 4.32a. The branch genealogy begins from the Yingshe generation onward to commend good and successful merchants in their short biographic sketches. For another example, Yingshe's nephew, Cheng Youzi (1585–1639), is described as "talented at many arts and skilled at trade, starting his business" far away from home. *Xin'an Censhandu Chengshi zhipu*, 4.70a.

10. *Huaitang Chengshi Xianchengtang chongxu zongpu* (1673), 13.74a; Xie, *Lianghuai yanfa zhi* (1693), 23.14a.

11. *Xin'an Censhandu Chengshi zhipu*, 4.59a.

12. Xie, *Lianghuai yanfa zhi* (1693), 23.15b–16a, 27.11a–13a. For Wenzheng's birth and death dates, see *Xin'an Censhandu Chengshi zhipu*, 5.38a; his son, Mengxing, was still alive in 1741 and wrote a preface for the Censhan Chengs' genealogy.

13. *Xin'an Censhandu Chengshi zhipu*, 5.24b.

14. Information on kinswives comes from these kinsmen's biographies (*zhuan*). Kinswomen are not included in the family tree (*tu*) section of the genealogy.

15. Unfortunately full information on daughters is not included, although the names of daughters and their husbands and husbands' family backgrounds are often noted.

16. For the significance of Chinese genealogies as sources for demographic history and calculating methods, see Harriet Zurndorfer, *Change and Continuity in Chinese Local History*, chap. 4. My method is straightforward compared to Zurndorfer's more sophisticated approach, as I just need to calculate two sets of data: the age at birth of the first son for kinsmen and their wives (including some concubines or second or third wives) and the average lifespan for kinsmen and kinswives.

17. The average male ABFS of the Censhan Chengs over three hundred years is about 2.5 years higher than the mean male ABFS of the Xiuning Fans, which is about 26.45, based on 234 available cases (including data for twenty-eight first sons born by second wives) from about one hundred years, from 1475 to 1574. Zurndorfer, *Change and Continuity in Chinese Local History*, 192. I have reworked Zurndorfer's data to get the overall average male ABFS for the Xiuning Fans. One major reason for this discrepancy, I believe, lies in the fact that the Censhan Chengs were far more socially prominent and commercially successful (and therefore more commercialized with more young sojourning merchants) than the Xiuning Fans.

18. Ts'ui-jung Liu, the pioneering scholar working on kinship demographics using late imperial genealogies, has discovered similar data in terms of the mean male and female ABFS of fifteen lineages in the middle and lower Yangzi regions, ranging from 27.62 to 30.78 for males and from 24.71 to 24.92 for females. See Ts'ui-jung Liu, "Ming-Qing renkou zhi zengzhi yu qianyi: Changjiang zhongxia you diqu zupu ziliao zhi fenxi," 294. See also Ts'ui-jung Liu, "The Demography of Two Chinese Clans in Hsiao-shan, Chekiang, 1650–1850," 13–61. Liu's data of the overall *mean* ABFSs are revealing, but they do not show historical trends of kinship demographics over the course of late imperial times. For demographic

data that do demonstrate a historically developing trajectory of the ABFS, see James Lee, Wang Feng, and Danching Ruan, "Nuptiality among the Qing Nobility, 1640–1900," 353–73, esp. 364, table 16.4.

19. Table 2 shows that for the 1441–1460 period, the male ABFS was also over thirty-one, but as this average is based on only five cases, it could very well be an anomaly. And yet for the 1721–1740 cohort when the male ABFS rose above thirty again, this demographic change, based on 524 cases, makes perfect sense, as the High Qing era was highly commercialized and was when Huizhou merchants' dominance in commerce peaked.

20. Brook, *The Confusions of Pleasure: Commerce and Culture in Ming China*.

21. *THJ*, 372.

22. Compiled in Zhang Haipeng et al., comp., *Ming-Qing Huishang ziliao xuanbian*, 46 (entry 137).

23. Yu Zhihuai, *Yixian: Taohuayuan li renjia*, 139.

24. *Yixian zhi* (1812), 16.16b–17a.

25. This pattern is confirmed again in the early Qing gazetteers of Shexian and Huizhou Prefecture. Another Qing writer noted that Huizhou men "immediately after the wedding go out on a business trip for ten, twenty, or thirty years without visiting home once; upon returning home [they see that] their grandsons are married or that their sons cannot even recognize fathers." All three are compiled in Zhang Haipen et al., comp., *Ming-Qing Huishang ziliao xuanbian*, 46–47, 51 (entries 139, 140, and 154). *Huishang bianlan* (A convenient guidebook for Huizhou merchants), published in the early twentieth century, coined the term *sannian yigui* (visiting home once in three years) as an "established social system" (*jiuzhi*) for Huizhou sojourning traders. Quoted in Tang Lixing, *Huizhou zongzu shehui*, 52. On Huizhou merchants in Yangzhou, see Antonia Finnane, *Speaking of Yangzhou*, especially chap. 10.

26. Cai Yu, *Liaoyang haishen zhuan*, 3.1a.

27. *THJ*, 349.

28. Taking this into account, we can be fairly confident that the actual ABFS for the Censhan Chengs must have been even higher than what table 2 shows.

29. Ping-ti Ho, *The Ladder of Success in Imperial China: Aspects of Social Mobility, 1368–1911*, 275.

30. Wang Shixing (1577 *jinshi*) noted, "Fashion in Sichuan favors childhood wedding, males getting married at twelve or thirteen, marrying older females; so does the custom in Huizhou. But as Huizhou men engage in trade, after the wedding they can travel on business through the four directions." Wang Shixing, *Guangzhiyi* (preface dated 1597), 109.

31. Quoted in Paolo Santangelo, "Urban Society in Late Imperial Suzhou," 222.

32. Ling Mengchu (1580–1644), *Pai'an jingqi*, 26–51. Dizhu literally means "Sweet Pearl" or "Dropping Pearl-like Tears." In late imperial times, the same two characters also formed a technical term meaning "a small round lump of silver." The second meaning, together with the homophonic reading of the surname, becomes a pun: "Desiring Silver." This reading is mine, but I believe a significant portion of the readership of Ling's collection would have been able to decipher the meaning. It suggests the commodification of Yao Dizhu, and, together with the homophonic reading of Pan Jia, sets up the central conflict of the story (and, for that matter, of sojourning merchants in general)—desire for fortune versus desire for family. See also Guo, *Ritual Opera and Mercantile Lineage*, 168.

33. One factor that may have caused the ABFS disparity between the two cousins could have been that Dagong was financially better off than Dadian—or at least financially

established at an earlier age. Yet Dadian's descendants, having two Lianghuai "head merchants" and then two *jinshi* degree holders, would eventually overshadow Dagong's. His illustrious offspring, in fact, was a key factor in the branch genealogy giving him a fairly detailed account, noting that he was widely admired in local society for his generosity and had a virtuous wife who "works diligently and lives frugally in supporting her husband and teaching her sons the Confucian classics." *Xin'an Censhandu Chengshi zhipu*, 4.59a. Dadian's own business career, except for the fact that he eventually settled in Yangzhou, was probably not that notable. Many more of his cousins or contemporary kinsmen who were mediocre sojourning traders or small vendors simply went unnoted except for their basic demographic data when available.

34. As a late-blooming branch of the lineage (starting in the late Yuan and early Ming), the Censhan Chengs were commercialized slightly later than other prominent kinship communities. This is perhaps the reason why Censhan is not included in Zhao Huafu's forty prominent kinship communities when he calculates Confucian men and women in *Prominent Lineages in Xin'an*. If data were available, I would expect the collective ABFS of those forty elite mercantile lineages to rise around the mid-sixteenth century, about one generation ahead of what the Censhan Chengs' data suggests. We know that Yingbiao's ABFS (with Dagong) was twenty-six and Yingshe's (with Daxing, 1564–1610) was twenty-eight, and Yingbiao and Yingshe were among the first generation in Censhan engaging in sojourning commercial activities.

35. One other factor to take into consideration is that the first child might be of either gender. But since a daughter's birth date was not recorded in the branch genealogy, we have to calculate the age at birth of the first son, not that of the first child. Buy why a reduction of two years? Tang Lixing suggests that because merchants of Huizhou normally returned home once every three years; if we take into account the almost one year of pregnancy, and add the two numbers (three plus one) and then divide this number (four) by two (the two possible genders of the first child), we get the number of reduction from the mean ABFS, that is, two. See Tang Lixing, *Huizhou zongzu shehui*, 48. I have also consulted with China demographer and sociologist Feng Wang about this methodology. He thinks that my method is reasonably sound, given the imperfect features of premodern data.

36. The first son of Cheng Cheng, Yue, was born in 1333, and thus was the eldest kinsman in the second generation of the Censhan Chengs; the eldest kinsman of the fifteenth generation was born in 1686. If we subtract 1333 from 1686 and then divide by thirteen (fourteen generations minus one), we get 27.15 years. See table 3.

37. If we were to again subtract 27 from 25.6 for men and 20.6 for women, we would get -1.4 and -6.4.

38. It should be noted that in determining the size of a three-generation family, only the husband's, not the wife's, age at birth of the first son (ABFS), and not the age at birth of the first child (if the first child was a daughter), matters for two reasons. First, the age of a daughter-in-law was not biologically linked to the age of her in-laws. Let me illustrate this with a hypothetical three-generation family in which the husband was ten years older than his wife for two consecutive generations. When the husband had the first son at thirty, his wife was twenty. When their first son had his first child (either gender) at thirty, the grandfather was sixty and the grandmother was fifty. Second, in the case of determining the family size, only the first son matters, because if the first child was a daughter, by the time her eldest younger brother had his first child (either gender), she would have long

since been married out. (I have found only five cases where kinsmen were married into and lived with their brides' families out of 4,853 kinsmen of the Censhan Chengs for the entire period of over four hundred years covered in the 1741 branch genealogy, not including the first migrating ancestor, Cheng Cheng, who married into and lived with the family of his bride, surnamed Fang, in the village of Dacheng, from where he later resettled in nearby Censhan village. *Xin'an Censhandu Chengshi zhipu*, 2.32b.) So for this hypothetical three-generation family, the factors that determined the years for which grandparents lived with their first grandchild include the grandfather's age at birth of his first *son* and the son's age at birth of his first *child*. In other words, the average age at birth of the first son played a far more important role than the average age at birth of the first child in determining the family size. If this was the case for any one hypothetical three-generation family, this tendency would be enhanced even more so over the long run, because for the next generation only the father's (now himself becoming a grandfather) age at birth of the first son mattered, and progressively so moving down the generations.

39. Carlitz also notes a conflicting phenomenon: another Huizhou product, namely the illustrated and expanded edition of *Lienü zhuan*, continues to honor the ideal of the three-generational family. I believe this revealingly embodied a discrepancy between the description and prescription. I am indebted to Katherine Carlitz for her thoughtful comments on this chapter, first presented at the Association for Asian Studies in 2014; see also Katherine Carlitz, "The Social Uses of Female Virtue in Late Ming Editions of *Lienü zhuan*."

40. Zhongguo shehui kexueyuan lishi yanjiusuo, comp., *Huizhou qiannian qiyue wenshu*, 5:209–15.

41. Zhongguo shehui kexueyuan lishi yanjiusuo, comp., *Huizhou qiannian qiyue wenshu*, 6:215.

42. Zhongguo shehui kexueyuan lishi yanjiusuo, comp., *Huizhou qiannian qiyue wenshu*, 5:415–35.

43. See also Tang Lixing, *Huizhou zongzu shehui*, 55–56.

44. See also Zhang Haipeng et al., comp., *Ming-Qing Huishang ziliao xuanbian*, 292–303.

45. Zhongguo shehui kexueyuan lishi yanjiusuo, comp., *Huizhou qiannian qiyue wenshu*, 5:451.

46. Not just property division among brothers—even land transactions tended to be conducted within lineages. According to Harriet Zurndorfer, land transactions in Huizhou were frequently conducted among lineage members in the Ming dynasty, especially during the latter half of the sixteenth century, as "economic competition propelled producers and traders into a 'frantic press.'" This tendency assured that lineages would not split up by rapid commercialization. Zurndorfer, "Contracts, Property, and Litigation: Intermediation and Adjudication in the Huizhou Region (Anhui) in Sixteenth-Century China," 100–101.

47. See the previous two chapters and the following chapter on the Huizhou local pantheon.

48. The effect of male sojourning on family structure can be found among overseas Chinese. See, for instance, Philip Kuhn, *Chinese Among Others: Emigration in Modern Times*.

49. See Janet Theiss, *Disgraceful Matters: The Politics of Chastity in Eighteenth-Century China*.

50. Wang Xun, *Renfeng wenji*, 331. Wang Xun's contemporary Cheng Minzheng made similar comments on elite intermarriage, as noted in chap. 2.

51. Fang Chengxun, *Fuchu ji*, 188:155.

52. Wu Ziyu, *Dazhang shanren ji*, 141:728, 789. Wu is better known for having authored a thick handbook of kinship rules for his home lineage, *Mingzhou Wushi jiaji*.

53. See, for instance, *THJ*, 633, 691, 820, 1065, 1126, 1154. The intermarriage pattern of local elite lineages appears to be part of the localist trend that started in Song times; see Robert Hymes, *Statesmen and Gentlemen*.

54. That said, we probably should also note that lineage intermarriage at the same time had the potential to enhance women's position, or protect their interests, given well-established affinal ties. Some late Ming Huizhou genealogies contain a lineage rule that reads: "affinal relatives and neighbors must be treated generously" (*yinli danghou*). See Chang Jianhua, *Mingdai zongzu yanjiu*, 313.

55. Cheng Minzheng, comp., *Xiuning Peiguo Chengshi benzong pu*; see the appendix (*Fulu*, 66a–b, 67b–68a) for regulations that focus on the organization of ancestral and religious rites and setting up of corporate estates of ritual land.

56. Chang Jianhua, *Mingdai zongzu yanjiu*, 313–19.

57. As it turns out, this lineage rule from *Shexian Zefu Wangshi zongpu* looks remarkably similar to an earlier one contained in the 1548 edition of the Hong genealogy from neighboring Poyang County, *Poyang Hongshi tongzongpu*. See Chang Jianhua, *Mingdai zongzu yanjiu*, 319–28.

58. Zheng Zhizhen, *Qimen Qingxi Zhengshi jiacheng* (1583), front section, the page numbers are not identifiable. The guidelines on women's matters appear to be fairly detailed, but only the five characters quoted here are legible or meaningful.

59. The code was prepared for the Wentang Chens' organization of the biweekly "village lecture," which was encouraged by the state and gained popularity over the course of the sixteenth century. According to the preface to the Chens' lineage code, Wentang's customs used to be "pure and sincere," but "the present is unlike the past, which worries the lineage elders." *Wentang Xiangyue jiafa* (1572), 3b–4a.

60. Read between the lines, this might also be evidence to prove precisely what Janet Theiss contends in *Disgraceful Matters*, suggesting that women were indeed making these kinds of "unreasonable demands," which was why lineage elders needed to protect against the practice.

61. *Wentang Xiangyue jiafa*, 8b, 11a, 10a.

62. *Xiuning Shuaikou Chengshi xubian benzong pu*, the *fanli* (guidelines) section, 1b–2a.

63. *Xin'an Censhandu Chengshi zhipu*, 1.3a. The *Situ* genealogy in the quotation refers to the *Huaitang Chengshi zongpu*, compiled in 1586 by the kinsman Cheng Sigong, a high-ranking official (and therefore referred to here as *Situ*, the Han dynasty title for minister of education). The Censhan Chengs' genealogy simply copied part of the guideline of the *Situ* genealogy, which covers the Censhan branch. This, in part, explains why the Censhan Chengs did not compile their own branch genealogy until 1741.

64. *Xin'an Censhandu Chengshi zhipu*, 4.56b.

65. Wang Daokun, "*Panshi zongci beiji*," *THJ*, 1435–36.

66. Wang Daokun, "*Panshi zongci beiji*," in *THJ*, 1435.

67. Wang Daokun, "*Xi'nan Wushi citing ji*," *THJ*, 1462–63. Toward the end of the record, Wang Daokun notes that his Wang lineage and several Xi'nan Wu branches had "intermarried for generations."

68. In addition to Wang Daokun, many contemporary Huizhou writers noted the generous contributions enthusiastically made by Huizhou merchants toward enhancing home

lineage institutions. For instance, in a record on the construction of a magnificent lineage temple by another prominent Shexian mercantile lineage, the Shaxi Lings, the aforementioned Wu Ziyu noted that Huizhou was most notable empire-wide for having built the largest number of ancestral halls, and that wealthy merchants "tended to single-handedly offer money for quickly building" ancestral halls. *Dazhang shanren ji*, 141, 511. See two other examples of merchant contributions to lineage institutions in Zhang Haipeng, comp., *Ming-Qing Huizhou ziliao xuanbian*, 312 (entries 993 and 994).

69. Fang Chengxun, *Fuchu ji*, 187, 615. He once noted that he traveled to Yangzhou "on lending business." Fang Chengxun, *Fuchu ji*, 188, 129.

70. Fang Chengxun, *Fuchu ji*, 187, 609–10.

71. Fang Chengxun, *Fuchu ji*, 188, 214.

72. Mothers-in-law normally lived longer than fathers-in-law in Chinese multigenerational families, and the actual monitoring of women's sexuality often fell to mothers-in-law. For this phenomenon, see, for instance, Susan Mann, *The Talented Women in the Zhang Family*. As shown in table 2, however, women's lifespan, on average, was about five years shorter than men in Censhan. Another possible scenario that could have had different impacts upon the left-behind wife may have had to do with younger siblings staying in the household of the eldest brother after both parents died. Depending on their age, they would not have held sway over the eldest sister-in-law, who, instead of being watched over, needed to take care of them on behalf of her sojourning husband, especially if they were young. But if they were already grown, brothers likely would have been married and separately settled; sisters likely would have been married out, and thus the wife of the sojourning man was still left virtually unchecked.

73. See Guo, *Ritual Opera and Mercantile Lineage*, 162–64.

74. Yang Shen, *Sheng'an ji*, 11.6–7. The story was also represented in the late Ming collection of short stories called *Xingshi yan*, recently discovered in Korea and reprinted in Taiwan; see Tang Lixing, *Shangren yu wenhua de shuangchong bianzou*, 109. The story appears to be incorporated into Zheng Zhizhen's 1582 *Mulian* script, under the fictional name of Chen Guiying. See Guo, *Ritual Opera and Mercantile Lineage*, 175. Also covered in *Mingshi*, see Zhu Wanshu, *Huishang yu Ming-Qing wenxue*, 180. The Tang Guimei tragedy, implicating not just a Huizhou merchant but also corrupt local officials, generated much agitation in the sixteenth century, one of the phenomena Siyen Fei draws upon to develop her argument about the literati fight against injustice and bureaucratic corruption in the state award system of chaste widows. Fei, "Writing for Justice."

75. Huang Shangwen, *Nüfan bian*, 702–3. For Huang Shangwen, see Xu Chengyao, *Sheshi xiantan*, 444. Huang also participated in the cutting of the 1566 version of the Huizhou prefectural gazetteer.

In addition to making financial contributions, Huizhou merchants, especially those who specialized in cultural products like Huang Shangwen, also contributed to enhancing mercantile lineage culture. Of additional relevance is a comparison of the accounts on virtuous women in two Ming and Qing versions of *Gazetteer of the Lianghuai Salt Administration* (Lianghuai yanfa zhi). The 1551 edition includes no individual *juan* volume on women and only lists sixteen notable women toward the end of the "Noteworthy Figures" volume (8.11a–13a), whereas the 1693 edition includes one long section on notable women (24.1a–64a), many of whom were widows of Huizhou sojourning men, as well as a large number of righteous Huizhou merchants themselves. One difference certainly has to do with the timing of the different editions, reflecting different phases of the female chastity cult, but another clearly also has to do with the fact that the later version, as noted in the previous chapter, was partially financed and edited by none other than Cheng Jun, a leading Lianghuai salt merchant from Censhan who was a cousin of Cheng Liangru and Cheng Liangneng. In 1693, the Censhan Chengs' domination of the Lianghuai salt business was about to peak.

76. Carlitz, "Desire, Danger, and the Body: Stories of Women's Virtue in Late Ming China," 104.

77. Xie Bi, *Shezhi*, 296; Shen Defu, *Wanli yehuo bian*, 630.

78. Quoted in Xu Shuofang, *Wan Ming qujia nianpu*, 3:11, 290. For the influence of Wang Yangming on Tang Xianzu and his literary contributions to the cult of *qing*, see Dorothy Ko, *Teachers of the Inner Chamber: Women and Culture in Seventeenth-Century China*.

79. As Maram Epstein tries to show, the cult of *qing* could also become a new moral discourse to revitalize the Confucian ethics in the late Ming. Epstein, *Competing Discourses: Orthodoxy, Authenticity, and Engendered Meanings in Late Imperial Chinese Fiction*.

80. Ling Mengchu, *Erke Pai'an jingqi*, 331.

81. Xu Chengyao, *Sheshi xiantan*, 504.

82. See Richard von Glahn, *The Sinister Way: The Divine and the Demonic in Chinese Religious Culture*.

83. See Qitao Guo, *Exorcism and Money: The Symbolic World of the Five-Fury Spirits in Late Imperial Huizhou*.

84. Cheng Ting, *Chunfan jicheng*, 1a–2b; first quoted in Guo, *Ritual Opera and Mercantile Lineage*, 9–10. The diary entry (*Chunfan jicheng*, 4a) on the eighth day of the third month of 1718 also notes the staging that night of the "folksy" *Mulian* ritual opera in Censhan. For Cheng Ting, see also *Xin'an Censhandu Chengshi zhipu*, 5.190a–b.

85. Bernard Bailyn, "The Challenge of Modern Historiography," 9–10.

86. Different regions surely had different demographics. Mark Elvin, based on the demographic data drawn from local gazetteers in three different regions, warns against talking about "any single Chinese demographic pattern in late imperial times." Mark Elvin, "Blood and Statistics: Reconstructing the Population Dynamics of Late Imperial China from the Biographies of Virtuous Women in Local Gazetteers," in Harriet Zurndorfer, ed., *Chinese Women in the Imperial Past: New Perspectives*, 195.

5. THE LOCAL RELIGIOUS ORDER

1. I have acquired two virtually identical versions of *Qishen zouge*, one printed in the Ming and the other printed in the Qing (Shanghai Library). The Ming print (hereafter abbreviated as QS-M) lacks the front section of the first *juan*, which fortunately can be filled in by the Qing print (hereafter abbreviated as QS-Q). Nevertheless, many prayers in the Ming version use terms indicating the age of their circulation, such as "Da Ming guo" (Great Ming kingdom) or "Huang Ming" (August Ming), which are replaced by "Da Qing guo" (Great Qing kingdom) in the Qing version.

2. QS-M, 1.20b–23a. See also the identical prayer (number 18) in the first *juan* of QS-Q (the Qing version lacks pagination, but most of the prayers are numbered). A similarly structured pantheon is also presented in "Jie Baihu" (Exorcizing the white tiger), QS-M, 4.21a–25a; QS-Q, prayer 20, *juan* 4.

3. "Qing zhongshen" (Invoking the multiple deities), *QS-M*, 2.28a–30a; *QS-Q*, prayer 25, *juan* 2. The Wang Hua pantheon codified in the *Model Prayers* looks remarkably similar to the local pantheon first introduced in Guo's *Exorcism and Money: The Symbolic World of the Five-Fury Spirits in Late Imperial China*. At the time, without access to *Model Prayers to the Deities* (and some other primary sources used in this chapter), Guo used a variety of indirect source materials to demonstrate the formation of the regional pantheons in southern Anhui around the mid-Ming, as a process of localization of the official City God worship. This historical process is now directly verified by the religious handbook.

4. David Johnson, "The City-God Cults in Tang-Song China," 363–457.

5. *HZF*, 5.35a.

6. For the early Ming City God reforms and especially subsequent changes in local worship in the Ming dynasty, see Guo, *Exorcism and Money*, chaps. 2 and 3.

7. See Guo, *Exorcism and Money*, part 1.

8. Wang Nanxuan, *Chongbian Xin'an Zhongliemiao shen jishi* (1460), *Tu* (Illustrations) section, 23b–24a (illustrating two wings of Wang Hua attendants); in the illustration on 29b–30a, there is a small Earth God hall built in front of the Wang Hua branch shrine (*xingci*) in Chikan, Tangmo.

9. *HZF*, 5.34b–37b.

10. The exception here was probably for Cheng Lingxi, who as a local hero is officially listed above other popular deities that were worshipped empire-wide.

11. See Guo, *Exorcism and Money*.

12. *Qing tan chang zou* (Incantation Invoking [the Deities] at the Altar-Ground).

13. In terms of the positioning of deities, this Huizhou pantheon looks remarkably similar to a visual representation of a multilayered Cishan pantheon worshipped in the neighboring county of Guangde, which is also divided into five rows. The deities are mostly shared in the two regional pantheons, with the exception of the head of the Guangde pantheon in Cishan. Cishan refers to a Han dynasty hero who was later deified for having led a popular campaign to "dredge waterways" in and around the region. Like Wang Hua, Cishan functioned as the proxy of the City God in Guangde. See Guo, *Exorcism and Money*, chap. 3.

14. See Yuming He, *Home and the World: Editing the "Glorious Ming" in Woodblock-Printed Books of the Sixteenth and Seventeenth Centuries*. For scholarly observations of woodblock publishing in the late imperial period in general, see Cynthia Brokaw and Kai-Wing Chow, eds., *Printing and Book Culture in Late Imperial China*, 23–34; Tobie Meyer-Fong, "The Printed World: Books, Publishing Culture, and Society in Late Imperial China," 787–817. Consult also Joseph McDermott, "How to Succeed Commercially as a Huizhou Book Publisher, 1500–1644," and Joseph McDermott, *A Social History of the Chinese Book*.

15. See Wang Zhenzhong, *Huizhou shehui wenhua shi tanwei*, 168–72.

16. Quoted in Wang Zhenzhong, *Huizhou shehui wenhua shi tanwei*, 168.

17. Wang Nanxuan, *Chongbian Xin'an Zhonglie miao shen jishi* (1460), 3.5a–b (including the illustrations of two imperial jade tablets). See also Wang Songtao, *Wangshi yuanyuan lu*, 10.3a–b; *LSW*, 10.1.1b–2a.

18. Wang Nanxuan, *Chongbian Xin'an Zhonglie miao shen jishi*, *juan* 3A and *juan* 3B. Many other Wang genealogies also cover these records; see, for instance, Wang Zhonglu et al., comps., *Wangshi tongzong zhengmai*, 6776–811.

19. *HZF*, 5.35a.

20. *LSW* 10.1.3a–b; *HZF*, 5.34b–35a.

21. Wang Daojin, comp., *Wangshi zupu* (1480), *fulu* (appendixes), 8a–10b: "Yanshan Wangshi chongjian citang ji."

22. *LSW*, 10.4.4a–b.

23. For the murky beginning of Wang Hua being worshipped as an ancestral spirit (an outstanding apical ancestor) by a Wuyuan Wang branch during the Yuan-Ming transition era, see Chang Jianhua, *Mingdai zongzu zuzhihua yanjiu*, 76–80; Zhang Yi, *Lixue, shishen he zongzu*, 108–12.

24. I looked through the massive genealogy of the Hongcun Wangs, *Hongcun Wangshi jiapu* (1747), but was unable to come up with any information about the Lineage Temple of the Wangs, allegedly built in 1403 according to a plaque in front of the building. It looks more like a late Ming construction, but it was conceivably rebuilt, or refurbished, later in the dynasty. The genealogy does contain the portraits of the three outstanding ancestors displayed within the main hall of the lineage temple: Marquis of Yingchuan, Wang Hua, and Wang Yanji.

25. *XAMII*, 222; and "Fengsha Yueguo zongci ji," by the kinsman named Wang Si (a *jinshi* degree holder and an imperial academician), in Wang Ji, *Wangshi tongzong shipu* (1787), 46.37a–b.

26. *XAMII*, 182–83.

27. *XAMII*, 182–249.

28. Wang Zhonglu et al., comp., *Wangshi tongzong zhengmai* (1571), *MDJP*, 6739. At the beginning of each *juan*, the six compilers of the Wang composite genealogy, apparently from different branches of the Huizhou Wangs, identified themselves as the descendants of Wang Hua (*Yueguo yisun*).

29. Due to immediate conflicts of interests, however, certain non-Wang fellow villagers could be prevented from performing rituals in a Wang Hua shrine. See McDermott, *The Making of a New Rural Order in South China*, 1:199.

30. Yuko Shibuya. "Min Shin jidai, kishū kōnan nōson shakai ni okeru saishi soshiki ni tsuite—'Shukuseikaibo' no shōkai," 105. Marshal Hu was most likely a Xikou variant of Marshal Zhao or Marshal Ma (Wuxian). See Guo, *Exorcism and Money*, 126–27.

31. A variety of historical documents commemorating Wang Hua, ranging from records on the Zhonglie Temple to prayers to Lord Wang for protection and assorted poems are also reprinted in Wang Zhonglu et al., comps., *Wangshi tongzong zhengmai* (1571), *MDJP*, 18, 6825–45 (including the laudatory commentary by Lord Liao, in Wang Zhonglu et al., comps., *Wangshi tongzong zhengmai*, 18.6833).

32. In volume 2 of *Model Prayers to the Deities*, there is a separate prayer invoking Wuchang (or Five Chang), which is simply titled "Qing Changshen" (Invoking the Chang spirits).

33. In the neighboring Guangde, Wuchang were conceptualized as five divine soldiers commanded by Zhang Bo. In the summer of 2016, I attended a Wuchang ritual performance in Xinhua County, Hunan, where the *Mulian* performance was popular in late imperial times and the Five Furies were subordinated to Han Xin, a Han dynasty general who most likely acted as the local proxy of the City God in that region.

34. On Wutong, see Richard Von Glahn, "The Enchantment of Wealth: The God Wutong in the Social History of Jiangnan," 651–714, and his *The Sinister Way: The Divine and Demonic in Chinese Religious Culture*.

35. This Wuchang-Wutong conflation is fully explored in Guo, *Exorcism and Money*, chap. 5. Wutong worship originated from Wuyuan, one of the six counties of Huizhou in late imperial times, which is now part of Jiangxi Province.

36. Xu Zhuo, *Xiuning suishi*, 1.17a–b.

37. Xu Zhuo, *Xiuning suishi*, 1.14b.

38. For Huizhou merchants worshipping Wuchang as their God of Wealth throughout late imperial times, see Guo, *Exorcism and Money*, chap. 6.

39. Cheng Minzheng, *Xinjing fuzhu*, 4.829.

40. *XAWXZ*, 512.

41. *THJ*, 859.

42. See Guo, *Exorcism and Money*, chap. 6.

43. Guo, *Ritual Opera and Mercantile Lineage*, 186–94.

44. *QS-M*, 2.24a; *QS-Q*, prayer 20, *juan* 2.

45. For the Wuchang pentad spirit as a small deity, see Guo, *Exorcism and Money*.

46. *QS-M*, 2.4b–6a, 14a–15a; *QS-Q*, prayers 4 and 12, *juan* 2.

47. For the sociocultural significance of childbirth, see also Yi-li Wu, *Reproducing Women: Medicine, Metaphor, and Childbirth in Late Imperial China*.

48. *QS-M*, 3.1a; 3.1a–2a. In the table of contents of the Qing version (the last four volumes of which are no longer extant), the two characters *qiusi* (seeking offspring) are added to the title of the second prayer to make the two titles look parallel. These two prayers were obviously paired.

49. *QS-M*,3.14b–16a; 3.16a–17a. In another prayer, "Banxi qingshen" (Invoking Deities for an Opera Staging), a multitude of deities including Wuchang are invoked, not just to assure a good performance but also to realize the sponsors' wish to have sons or gain fame (most likely a reference to passing the exams). *QS-M*, 3.4a.

50. In the southeast coast (where the *Mulian* performance was also popular in late imperial times), the Wuchang pentad was sheltered under Our Lady of Ample Bosom (Danai Furen), a goddess of fertility who was often conflated with the northern Goddess of Taishan and the southern Empress of Heaven. See the late Ming handbook on the deities of the Three Teachings, Queming (Anonymous). *Huitu sanjiao yuanliu soushen daquan*, 183–84; 186–87; Zong Li and Liu Qun, *Zhongguo minjian zhushen*, 389–406. For Empress of Heaven, see James Watson, "Standardizing the Gods: The Promotion of T'ien-Hou (Empress of Heaven) along the South China Coast, 960–1960," 292–324.

51. McDermott, *The Making of a New Rural Order in South China*, vol. 1.

52. *CSYFJ*, 1.7b–14b.

53. *LSW*, 10. *Shi* (poems) section, 3a; *HDWJ*, 1253.499.

54. See, e.g., *HDWJ*, 1252.284–85; 1252.673–74.

55. *XAWXZ*, 1450–66, *XNZ*, 4.2b.

56. *HDWJ*, 1252.200–201.

57. *HDWJ*, 1252.201–2.

58. *HDWJ*, 1252.200.

59. *HDWJ*, 1252.216–17. There are many other prayers he wrote on other ritual occasions in *HDWJ*, 1252.212–30. One prayer to Guandi and Cheng Xin is included in *XNPGC*.

60. For Zhu Yishi, see Wan Zhengzhong, *Huizhou renwu zhi*, 517. These five local elites, unlike literati who consciously identified themselves as neo-Confucians, fall into the

category of the local gentrymen who accepted Confucian teachings as morally correct without necessarily devoting their lives to being neo-Confucians. For the distinction between the two, see Peter Bol, "Neo-Confucianism and Local Society, Twelfth to Sixteenth Century: A Case Study," 242. Consult also David Johnson's *Spectacle and Sacrifice* for local experts on ritual performance.

61. Wan Zhengzhong, *Huizhou renwu zhi*, 517. Looking through the Qing version, we find some printing errors and the font is not nearly as good as that in the Ming version.

62. It should be noted that the original version of *Records of Xin'an's Zhonglie Temple and Its Deities* was first compiled in the Yuan (printed in 1339) by a non-Wang local gentryman named Zheng Hongzu, well before Cheng Minzheng's Huizhou activities, and the version now extant also carries a preface by another non-Wang named Fang Mian (*jinshi* 1415) and another preface penned by Jiang Bochen. This non-Wang compilation of the Wang Hua-focused text testifies to the shared nature of the God of Xin'an cult by all Huizhou people.

63. *XXZ*, 1422–23. As further evidence of the popularity of Wang Hua, the account also notes that local opera festivals in honor of King Wang were "extremely lavish." See also Guo, *Ritual Opera and Mercantile Lineage*, chap. 6.

64. It appears that Cheng Minzheng maintained good relations with certain members of the Wang lineages. The local gentryman he singled out as most helpful in his compilation of *Xin'an Documents* was Wang Zuo, for whom he wrote a heartfelt epitaph. This piece, along with three additional epitaphs Minzheng penned for Wang Zuo's kinsmen, is included in *LSW*, 10. *Zhiming* (epitaphs) section, 4a–5a, 5a–6b, 6b–8b, 8b–9b. He also wrote two complimentary pieces for the elderly Wang Kejing of the Xiuning Chengbei Wangs on the occasion of the longevity party for the latter's sixtieth birthday; Kejing, it turns out, was the father-in-law of Cheng Minzheng's cousin Cheng Zongbi. See Wang Rang, *Chengbei Wangshi zupu*, 2.21a–22a, 26b. Elsewhere, Minzheng noted that certain Wang and Cheng branches in Xiuning had been linked through marital relations for generations. *HDWJ*, 1252.674.

65. In Cheng Xu, comp., *Xin'an Chengshi shipu zhengzong qianxi zhujiao zuan* (1563; reprint 1670), 10a.

66. Ibid., 1a. Cheng Xu's composite genealogy was recut, expanded, and reedited many times in the Qing and Republican eras. The Shanghai Library holds at least eight different Cheng composite genealogies based on Cheng Xu's version. See Wang Heming, comp., *Shanghai tushuguan guancang jiapu tiyao*, 824.

67. Cheng Chang, *Qimen Shanhe Chengshi pu, fanli* (guideline), 1a; *Chengpu bian* (Clarification of the Cheng genealogies), 1a–18b.

68. See Cheng Chang, "Hexi gong bian Cheng Minzheng Tongzong shi pu houshuo," in the revised *Shanhe Chengshi zongpu* (1907), *fulu* (appendix), 1b. The Shanhe Chengs, like the Peiguo Chengs, originated from Huangdun.

69. See the summary of *Collected Essays of Bamboo Mound* for *The Complete Writings of the Four Treasuries* (*HDWJ*, 1252.1–2).

70. Huang Guan's two pieces are in Xu Chengyao, *Sheshi xiantan*, 1133–37.

71. Local lineages must have felt the pressure Cheng Minzheng presented with his promotion of his surname as they also attempted to emphasize their origins or surnames in the realm of genealogical compilation, even if all of these efforts did not end up changing the surname order eventually publicized in the *Prominent Lineages in Xin'an*. For

instance, at the beginning of the sixteenth century—that is, not long after the death of Cheng Minzheng—the early Tang list of the top surnames was reemphasized in local Wang genealogies. The surname of Hexi Wangs, the ancestral surname of the Huizhou Wangs, was listed as one of the ten top surnames, the so-called *guozhizhu* (pillars of the state). Number one was none other than the surname of the royal family, Li. See Wang Kui, comp., *Chongxiu Wangshi jiacheng* (1508), in *MDJP*, 11263. This was again reemphasized in later Wang genealogies, such as *LSW*, 10.1.2b.

72. Cf. Watson, "Standardizing the Gods"; Szonyi, "Illusion of Standardizing the Gods."

73. For the two modes of divinity in China, see Robert P. Hymes, *Way and Byway: Taoism, Local Religion, and Models of Divinity in Sung and Modern China*.

74. See also Robert Weller, *Unities and Diversities in Chinese Religion*; Meir Shahar and Robert P. Weller, eds., *Unruly Gods: Divinity and Society in China*.

CONCLUSION

1. His father, Cao Gao (*jinshi* 1571), was a close friend of Hong Jueshan, the editor-in-chief of *Prominent Lineages in Xin'an* and an ardent follower of Wang Yangmingism; in 1579 Hong entrusted Cao Gao to update the old genealogical gazetteer. It was finally completed by Sixuan, albeit only in part, featuring just the volume on Xiuning.

2. Separate genealogical gazetteers for the other five Huizhou counties, however, were not compiled (perhaps due to the turbulence of the late Ming). There are some new prefaces written for the 1626 *Xiuning mingzu zhi*, the most notable of which was penned by the famous late Ming scholar-official Li Weizhen and revealingly called *Xin'an mingzu zhi zongxu* (Composite preface to the *Prominent Lineages in Xin'an* [not in Xiuning]). *XNMZZ*, 3–4. *Prominent Lineages in Xiuning* further includes a table of contents covering the major surnames of all six counties (*XNMZZ*, 25–31).

3. There is another difference in terms of the format: "The old [genealogical] gazetteer puts [the prominent lineages] of the same surname in six counties in one chapter, divided accordingly into six counties. Viewed today, this format seems inconvenient to read and check. Now [the prefecture-wide genealogical gazetteer is] divided into six counties, with each county having a separate book to make checking easier." *XNMZZ, fanli* (guidelines), 23.

4. *XNMZZ*, 47–68. These became the subtitles in each village-lineage entry wherever kinspeople fitting the categories were worth being recorded.

5. This number does not include other kinds of virtuous women. Reading through the genealogical gazetteer, we encounter devoted or virtuous women in virtually every lineage entry.

6. *XNMZZ*, 155.

7. The old pattern established in the former Xin'an genealogical gazetteer persisted in another fashion. The more gentrified lineages (which produced higher-examination degree holders like Wang Daokun) tended to be more willing to record righteous merchants than the lineages heavily engaged in trade who had not produced any higher-exam degree holders. For instance, as in the 1551 Xin'an gazetteer, the entries for the Shuaikou and Taitang Chengs list no merchants whatsoever (see also chap. 2). *XNMZZ*, 98–103; 126–27.

8. *XNMZZ* (1–2) is a combination of the four different versions of *Xiuning mingzu zhi*, which may account for the discrepancy in these Chinese subtitles or categories. This categorization of local people is largely similar to the categorization (without that of merchants)

used in local gazetteers. See, for instance, *HZF, juan* 7–10; *HZZ, juan* 16–20. Following Sima Qian's format, Xie Bi included one short section on trade (*huozhi*) in the first county gazetteer of Shexian, but it was tempered by dramatic anticommercial, antimonetization denunciation, which was presented in the section on the changing local customs in the same gazetteer that Timothy Brook (in *Confusions of Pleasure*) attributes to the Shexian magistrate, Zhang Tao. *SZ*, 99–100, 412–16.

9. It also helps, perhaps, to explain why Huizhou ultimately went into decline after the turn of the nineteenth century as China was forced into the global, modern political economy. Consult also Kenneth Pomeranz, *The Great Divergence: China, Europe, and the Making of the Modern World Economy*; R. Bin Wong, *China Transformed: Historical Change and the Limits of European Experience*. See also McDermott, *The Making of a New Rural Order in South China*, 1:15–16.

Anding 安定
Anfu 安福
Anshen zhu 安神燭

baiqie zhuren 百妾主人
Baiyu 白榆
Banxi qingshen 搬戲請神
Bao Chun 鮑椿
Bao Jingzeng 鮑景曾
Bao Xiangxian 鮑象賢
Bao Yuankang 鮑元康
Baohe Zhong 寶和鐘
Bashi 八十
Benzhi shibiao 本支世表
Biaoshu 表疏

Caiwu 材武
Cao Gao 曹誥
Cao Jing 曹涇
Cao Sixuan 曹嗣軒
Cao Wenxiu 曹文修
Caoshi 草市
Caoshi Suns 草市孫
Censhan 岑山
Cha Nai 查鼐
Chakou 汉口

Changgai Bi 長垓畢
chaoben 抄本
chaoran duqi benxin 超然獨契本心
Chen Dingyu 陳定宇
Chen Guiying 陳癸英
Chen Jian 陳建
Chen Jing 陳經
Cheng Cai 程材
Cheng Chang 程昌
Cheng Changgong 程長公
Cheng Cheng 程晟 (of Hejian or Peiguo)
Cheng Cheng 程誠 (of Censhan)
Cheng Dadian 程大典
Cheng Dagong 程大功
Cheng Dajie 程大節
Cheng Daxing 程大興
Cheng Decui 程德萃
Cheng En 程恩
Cheng Fuxi 程福熙
Cheng Guangxian 程光顯
Cheng Hong 程宏
Cheng Huan 程懽
Cheng Jinan 程繼南
Cheng Jinghua 程景華
Cheng Jun 程浚
Cheng Kentang 程肯堂
Cheng Liangneng 程量能
Cheng Liangru 程量入
Cheng Lingxi 程靈洗
Cheng Meng 程孟
Cheng Mengnai 程夢鼐
Cheng Mengxing 程夢星
Cheng Minzheng 程敏政
Cheng Nai 程鼐
Cheng Qi 程祁
Cheng Ruoyong 程若庸
Cheng Shaokai 程紹開
Cheng Sheng 程昇
Cheng Sigong 程嗣功
Cheng Suo 程鎖
Cheng Tai 程泰
Cheng Tao 程淘
Cheng Tingzhou 程廷周
Cheng Weiqing 程惟清
Cheng Wen 程文
Cheng Wengui 程文桂

Cheng Wenji 程文吉
Cheng Wenjie 程文傑
Cheng Wenzheng 程文正
Cheng Xiangyigong ci ji 程襄毅公祠記
Cheng Xin 程信
Cheng Xinyu 程心宇
Cheng Xuan 程炫
Cheng Yi 程沂
Cheng Ying 程嬰
Cheng Yingbiao 程應表
Cheng Yingshe 程應赦
Cheng Yitong 程以通
Cheng Yizhi 程一枝
Cheng Youzi 程有資
Cheng Yu 程昱 (merchant from Hejian)
Cheng Yu 程儩 (merchant from Huaitang)
Cheng Yuantan 程元譚
Cheng Yue 程月
Cheng Zhengkui 程正奎
Cheng Zhiying 程之韺
Cheng Zongbi 程宗弼
Cheng Zu 程祖
Cheng Zuyuan 程祖瑗
Chengbei Wangshi pu xu 城北汪氏譜序
Chengbo 程伯
Chengbo zhihou 程伯之後
Chengdian 程典
Chengkan Luo 呈坎羅
Chengxin 成信
chengyi fengjiao suoxi 誠以風教所繫
Chifeng Yueguo Wanggong Dadi 勅封越國汪公大帝
Chikan 赤坎
Chizhou 池州
chongde baogong 崇德報功
chongkan 重刊
Chongxiu Nanshan an ji 重修南山庵記
chuangye chuitong 創業垂統
chuanzong yinming 傳宗印銘
Chuiming ji 垂名記
chushi 處士
Chuye xie zhongshen 除夜謝眾神
Cimiao 祠廟
cipu liangchu 祠譜兩出
Cishan 祠山
citang 祠堂
congrong jiuyi 從容就義

Cui Hua 崔華
Cuisheng qingshen 催生請神

Da Ming guo 大明國
Da Qing guo 大清國
da wumen 大吾門
Da yatang zaju 大雅堂雜劇
Da Zongbo Huangdun Gong 大宗伯篁墩公
Da Zongbo Xin'an Huangdun 大宗伯新安篁墩
Dacheng Fang大程方
Dafo Pans 大佛潘
Dai Qida 戴啟達
Dai Tianpei 戴天培,
Dai Tingming 戴廷明
Dai Wei 戴煒
dajia juxing 大家巨姓
Dajie 大節
Danai Furen 大奶夫人
daotong 道統
daowenxue 道問學
daoxin 道心
Daoyuan 道原
dazheng cidian 大正祀典
dazong 大宗
dejun xingdao 得君行道
dianji wenxian 典籍文獻
Dianji zhi 典籍志
Diling zhi 地靈志
dingji 丁集
Dingyu Chen xiansheng Li muzhiming 定宇陳先生櫟墓誌銘
Dingyu xiansheng citang ji 定宇先生祠堂記
dongci houtu 東祠后土
Dongyue 東越 (of Zhejiang)
Dongyue 東嶽 (Eastern Peak)
Doushan 竇山
Du Fu 杜甫
Duanzhong 端中
Dui fo wen 對佛問
Duling 杜陵
Duxing 篤行

Fan Changjun 范長君
Fan Zhongyan 范仲淹
Fang Haozhi 方浩之
Fang Jingzhen 方景真
Fang Liangshu 方良曙

Fang Wei 方渭
Fang Xizhang 方細章
Fang Yulu 方于魯
fangqi deyi 放棄德義
fangzhi 方志
fanli 凡例
Fei Yin 費闇
Fengcun Wangs 馮村王
Fengjie 風節
fengjun 封君
Fengsha 鳳砂
Fengsha Yueguo zongci ji 鳳砂越國宗祠記
Fengya 風雅
Fenzhi shibiao 分支世表
Fu Han 傅瀚
Fudai Hong 富岱洪
fugu 復古
fulu 附錄

gaijia zhe bushu 改嫁者不書
gangu qijia 幹蠱起家
Gao 誥
gao wumen 高吾門
Gaotang meng 高唐夢
gengdu 耕讀
gewu zhizhi 格物致知
gu 賈
Gu Dingchen 顧鼎臣
Gu Yanwu 顧炎武
Gui Youguang 歸有光
Guan Dadi 關大帝
Guan Yu 關羽
guandai 冠帶
Guandi 關帝
guanfu 官府
guang qinqin 廣親親
guang xianxian 廣賢賢
Guangxin 廣信
Guanzhi 觀之
gu'er haoru 賈而好儒
Guifan 閨範
guimen dangsu 閨門當肅
guiru 歸儒
guo you guoshi jia yi yiran 國有國史家亦宜然
guochao bangwen 國朝榜文
guozhizhu 國之柱

guru 賈儒
gushu賈豎
gushuzi 賈豎子
Gutang 古唐

Haiyang 海陽
Hangbu Cao 杭埠曹
Hangbutou Cao 杭埠頭曹
haogui 好鬼
Hehe 和合
Hejian 河間
Hexi Wangs 河西汪
Hong Jueshan 洪覺山
Hong Shi 洪什
Hongcun 宏村
Hongkeng Hong 洪坑洪
Hongkeng Wang 洪坑王
hongru 閎儒
Hongyuan Hong 洪源洪
Hou Jing 侯景
Houji 后稷
Hu Bingwen 胡炳文
Hu Henghua 胡亨華
Hu Sheng 胡昇
Hu Xiao 胡曉
Hu Yinglin 胡應麟
Hu Zongxian 胡宗憲
Huaguang 華光
Huaitang 槐塘
Huamei 畫眉
huang 篁 (bamboo)
Huang 黃 (yellow or surname)
Huang Chao 黃巢
Huang chushi Zhongrong muzhiming 黃處士仲榮墓誌銘
Huang Gan 黃幹
Huang Ji 黃積
Huang Ming 皇明
Huang Shangwen 黃尚文
Huang Shiqi 黃士琪
Huang Yiqing 黃一清
Huang Yu 黃裕
Huang Yuanbi 黃元弼
Huang Zhengyuan 黃政淵
Huang Zhong 黃鐘
Huangbei Zhang 黃備張
Huangdi 黃帝

Huangdun 黃墩
Huangdun shushe ji 篁墩書舍記
Huanshan Fang 環山方
Huanye 宦業
Huishang 徽商
Huishang bianlan 徽商便覽
Huixue 徽學
Huozhi 貨殖
Huozhi zhuan 貨殖傳
Hushan Chenggong fufu muzhiming 湖山程公夫婦墓誌銘
Huzhou 湖州

ji 集 (volume)
Ji 記 (Records)
Ji shishu shiyi fujun wen 祭世叔十一府君文
Ji Yun 紀昀
jiacheng zaizhi 家乘載之
Jiaci siyue 家祠祀約
Jiadian ji 家典記
Ji'an 吉安
jian bu ou gui 賤不偶貴
Jian jiaci yue 建家祠約
Jian muci yue 建墓祠約
jianding 鑒定
Jiangcun Jiangs 江村江
Jiangnan shizu 江南始祖
Jiankang 建康
Jiao Hong 焦竑
jiaozi 校梓
Jie Baihu 解白虎
jie er mingzhi 籍而名之
Jie Xisi 揭傒斯
Jielie 節烈
jielie ci 節烈祠
Jielin Fang 結林方
Jielin Wang 結林王
Jielin Xu 結林徐
jiexia 節俠
jiexiao 節孝
jieyi 節義
jijiu 祭酒
Ji-Lu 姬魯
Jin Deqing 金德清
Jin Dexuan 金德玹
Jin hunpin 謹婚聘
Jin She 金赦

Jin Tang 金瑭
jing 敬
Jingui 金匱
Jingxing Liu 敬興劉
jingzong muzu 敬宗睦族
jinshi 進士
jiuben 舊本
jiushu 闓書
Jiutian Songzi Gao Yuanshuai 九天送子高元帥
Jiuxu 舊序
jiuzhi 舊制
Jiwen 祭文
Jixi 績溪
jizhuan 紀傳
juan 卷
juemin xingdao 覺民行道
juexue 絕學
jujing 居敬
Juncheng Bi 郡城畢
juren 舉人

kangzong shouzu 亢宗收族
kecheng fuzhi, gangu yousheng 克承父志，幹蠱有聲
Keqin 克勤
Kong Yuanfang 孔元方
kongshu 空疏
kuangdai zhenru 曠代真儒

leishu 類書
leshi 樂施
li 理 (principle)
li 厲 (ghost spirit)
li 禮 (rites)
Li Dongyang 李東陽
Li Mengyang 李夢陽
Li Panlong 李攀龍
Li Weizhen 李維楨
Li Xian 李賢
li yi ming ye 利亦名也
Li Zongmin 李宗敏
Liangbin 良彬
lianggu 良賈
liangu 廉賈
Liangzhi 良植
liangzhi 良知
Lianhua lao 蓮花落
Lienü zhuan 列女傳

Liezhuan 列傳
lijia 里甲
Linhe 臨河
Lintang Fans 林塘范
Lishen xingji zhen 立身行己箴
litan 厲壇
Liu Bangcai 劉邦采
Liu lienü zhuan 六烈女傳
Liu Shen 劉伸
Liu Zhen 劉震
Longxiang yixia shibiao 龍驤以下世表
Lou Qian 婁謙
Lu Jiuyuan (Xiangshan) 陸九淵 (象山)
Lü Kun 呂坤
Lu shijia lue 魯世家略
Lu Zhougong shijia 魯周公世家
Luntan Fangs 淪潭方
Luo Qi 羅綺
Luo Rufang 羅汝芳
Luo Wanhua 羅萬化
Luoshui bei 洛水悲
Luotian Fang 羅田方

Ma Lu 馬祿
Ming Wenheng 明文衡
ming yi li ye 名亦利也
mingdao 明道
mingguan 冥官
minglun jianxue 明倫建學
Mingzhou Wus 茗洲吳
Mingzhou Wushi jiaji 茗洲吳氏家記
Mubei 墓碑
Mubiao 墓表

Nanshan An 南山庵
Ni Yue 倪岳
Nianhua 年畫
nianpu 年譜
Nie Shidao 聶師道
nüliu zhi Zou-Lu 女流之鄒魯

Ouyang Dan 歐陽旦
Ouyang Xiu 歐陽修

Pan Jia 潘甲
Pan Kui 潘逵
Pan Shi 潘什

Pan Tingzhou 潘汀州
Pan Zhiheng 潘之恆
Pancun Pan 潘村潘
panjia 盼家
Panshi zongci beiji 潘氏宗祠碑記
Peiguo 陪郭
Peng Hua 彭華
Peng Li 彭禮
Peng Shi 彭時
Peng Ze 彭澤
Poyang Hongshi tongzongpu 鄱陽洪氏統宗譜
pubian 譜辨
Puhao 譜號
putu 譜圖
puzhe shi zhi liu ye 譜者史之流也

Qian Dehong 錢德洪
Qianchuan 潛川
Qiankou Wang 潛口汪
Qiaobo 喬伯
qidao chendao yiye 妻道臣道一也
qijie yilie 奇節異烈
Qilie zhuan 七烈傳
Qimen 祁門
qimin ergu yiru 其民二賈一儒
qing 情
Qing Changshen 請猖神
Qing zhongshen 請眾神
Qingzhou 晴洲
Qingzhou ji 晴洲記
Qingzhou ji 晴洲集
qinqin xianxian 親親賢賢
qiongli 窮理
Qishen zouge 祈神奏格
Qisheng wang 啟聖王
Qishou 期壽
Qiu fangxin 求放心
Qiu Jun 丘濬
Qiu Tong 仇潼
Qiu Ying 仇英
Qiumu zhi 丘墓志
Qiusi 求嗣
Qiusi qingshen zhu 求嗣請神燭

Rao Shuangfeng 饒雙峰
Raozhou 饒州

renrang 仁讓
renxia 任俠
renxia kangkai 任俠慷慨
renxin 人心
renyi 仁義
renyu 人慾
riyong gongfu 日用功夫
ru 儒
Ruan Bi 阮弼
rugu 儒賈
Ruiye Huangcun 瑞野黃村
ruming shangxing 儒名商行
ruxia 儒俠

saihui 賽會
sandian 三奠
sannian yigui 三年一歸
shan gangu, chuangye guangqian 善幹蠱，創業光前
Shandou 山斗
shanggu 商賈
shangming er shixing 商名而士行
Shangsu 商俗
Shangyi 尚義
Shanhe 善和
Shanhou Huangs 山後黃
Shanquan 山泉
Shanxing 善行
Shaocun Zhang 紹村張
Shaxi Baos 沙溪鮑
Shaxi Lings 沙溪凌
She 射
She Wenyi 佘文義
She Yanghao 佘養浩
Shen Wenzhen 沈文楨
shengdai ruzong 盛代儒宗
Shengmu qianjin furen 聖母千金夫人
Shengzi qingshen 生子請神
Shenji 神蹟
Sheshi yizhai ji 佘氏義宅記
shetian 社田
Shexian 歙縣
Shexian Zefu Wangshi zongpu 歙縣澤富王氏宗譜
Shi 詩
Shi buqin 十不親
shidi hunmeng 世締婚盟
shijia 世家

shiluo 事略
shimuhu 世墓戶
Shimuhu congyue 世墓戶從約
shiqi 世戚
shiwei hunyin 世為婚姻
shixi 世係
Shixi xiaozhuan 世系小傳
Shizhong 世忠
Shizu 氏族
Shou Wu jiefu Wang ruren bashi yu 壽吳節婦汪孺人八十序
shoujie fugu 守節撫孤
shouxu 壽序
shu 疏 (prayers)
Shu 數 (Math)
Shu 書 (Calligraphy)
Shu Henan Shang Chengshi *Yizhenlu* hou 書河南上程氏宜振錄後
Shu xiangong Jianhezhuang yizhu hou 書先公澗河莊遺囑後
Shuaikou 率口
Shuaikou Chengshi Shizhong xingci ji 率口程氏世忠行祠記
Shuntian 順天
Shuoru 碩儒
shusheng jiaoduan 書生腳短
Si 姒
Sili 思立
Sima Qian 司馬遷
Sima Xiangru 司馬相如
Situ 司徒
siwen 斯文
Song yimin lu 宋遺民錄
Songci Jiangnan diyi jia 宋賜江南第一家
Songmingshan Wang 松明山汪
songyi sifang 诵义四方
Su Xun 蘇洵
sufeng 素封
Sun Congli 孫從理
Sun Shi 孫時

Taihan 太函
Taitang 泰塘
taixi 臺戲
Tandu Huang 潭渡黃
Tang Guimei 唐貴梅
Tang Xianzu 湯顯祖
Tang Yin 唐寅
Tangfeng Yueguo sanqian hu 唐封越國三千戶
Tangmo 唐模

Tangyue 棠樾
Tao Chengxue 陶承学
tianli 天理
Tianxing 天興
tianzi mengao 天子門高
tongnian 同年
tongzong cigui 統宗祠規
Tu 圖
Tu Long 屠隆
Tudi 土地
Tuzhu 土主
tuzhuan 圖傳

Wang Boling 汪伯齡
Wang Daohui 汪道暉
Wang Daokun 汪道昆
Wang Daoye 汪道曄
Wang Fengshi 汪鳳時
Wang Gaoyuan 汪高元
Wang Gen 王艮
Wang Hai 汪海
Wang Hua 汪華
Wang Hui 汪煇
Wang Huishou 汪徽壽
Wang Ji 王畿
Wang jiefu zhuan 汪節婦傳
Wang Kejing 汪克敬
Wang Kun 汪琨
Wang Liangbin 汪良彬
Wang Liangkai 汪良楷
Wang Liangrong 汪良權
Wang Liangrong 汪良榕
Wang Liangzhi 汪良植
Wang Quan 王全
Wang Qiong 汪瓊
Wang Shixing 王士性
Wang Shizhen 王世貞
Wang Shou'an 汪守菴
Wang Shouyi 汪守義
Wang Shunmin 汪舜民
Wang Si 汪思
Wang Songshan 汪松山
Wang Tang 汪鐜
Wang Tiangui 汪天貴
Wang Tongbao 汪通保
Wang Wei 汪暐

Wang Wenhe 汪文和
Wang Yang 汪洋
Wang Yanji 汪彥濟
Wang Yingsu 汪應宿
Wang Yingxuan 汪應玄
Wang Yizhong 汪一中
Wang Yongxi 汪永錫
Wang Zhong 汪仲
Wang Zonggong 汪宗公
Wang Zongshun 汪宗舜
Wang Zongzhi 王宗植
Wang Zuo 汪祚
Wangcun Wang 王村王
Wangshi zongci 汪氏宗祠
wei shengxing zhe 未盛行者
weijing 惟精
weiru weishang lizhi bufan 為儒為商立志不凡
weiwangren 未亡人
weiyi 惟一
Wenchang 文昌
Wenchangfang Chengshi zupu xu 文昌坊程氏族譜序
wenshu 文書
Wenxi 紋溪
Wen-Xiao 文孝
Wenyuan 文苑
wenzhang 文章
Wenzhang zhengzong 文章正宗
Wu Bogang 吳伯岡
Wu Boju 吳伯舉
Wu Cheng 吳澄
Wu Kuan 吳寬
Wu Liangru 吳良儒
Wu Pei 吳佩
Wu Rongrang 吳榮讓
Wu Ruzhuo 吳汝拙
Wu Tianqing 吳天慶
Wu Tianxing 吳天行
Wu Xizhi 吳錫之
Wu Yingzi 吳應紫
Wu Zhengzhong 吳正中
Wuchang 五猖
Wucun Zhu 浯村朱
Wuhu you 五湖游
Wusheng 五聖
Wusi 五祀
Wutong 五通

Wuxian 五顯
Wuyi 武夷
wuyigonggu zaji 巫醫工賈雜伎
Wuyuan 婺源
Wuyuan Chayuan Zhushi shipu houxu 婺源茶院朱氏世譜後序

Xi'nan Jiangs 溪南江
Xi'nan Wus 溪南吳
Xi'nan Wushi citing ji 溪南吳氏祠堂記
xiajie 俠節
Xian dafu zhuang 先大父狀
Xian damu zhuang 先大母狀
xiangdao zhixin 向道之心
xiangfu erli 相輔而立
Xiangshan 鄉善
xiangyue 鄉約
xianzhi xianjue zhe 先知先覺者
xiaodi gongjian 孝弟恭儉
xiaoren 小人
xiaoshen 小神
xiaoti 孝悌
Xiaoxu 小序
Xiaoyou 孝友
xiaozhuan 小傳
Xiaozi 孝子
xiaozong 小宗
xiayi 俠義
xici jielie 西祠節烈
Xie Bi 謝陛
Xie Qian 謝遷
Xiguan 西館
Xikou 溪口
xin 心
Xin'an 新安
Xin'an mingzu zhi zongxu 新安名族志總序
Xin'an Xushi shipu 新安許氏世譜
Xin'an Zhi Shen 新安之神
Xin'an zhi sidian 新安之祀典
xingci 行祠
xingshi 行實
Xingshi yan 型世言
xingzhuang 行狀
xinwai wushi, xinwai wuli 心外無事, 心外無理
Xiong Shifang 熊世芳
Xiongcun Cao 雄村曹
Xiongcun Hong 雄村洪

Xishan 西山
Xiufu休父
Xiuning 休寧
Xu 序
Xu Fu許鈇
Xu Guo 許國
Xu Pianpian 徐翩翩
Xu Wei 徐渭
Xu Wenzhang zhengzong 續文章正宗
Xuanmingfang 宣明坊
Xucun Xu 徐村徐
Xuelin 學林
Xuepou tongbian 學蔀通辨
Xunxian 勳賢
xunye 勳業

Yan Song嚴嵩
Yang San 楊三
Yang Shen 楊慎
yanjia zai Huai, tanggou zai li鹽筴在淮，堂搆在里
Yanshan 兗山
Yanshan Wangshi chongjian citang ji 兗山汪氏重建祠堂記
Yanzhen 巖鎮
Yanzhen Fang 巖鎮方
Yao Dizhu 姚滴珠
Yaojiadun 姚家墩
Ye Benjing 葉本靜
Yegan Ye 葉干葉
Yicheng Yang 義城杨
Yicheng Zhu 義城朱
Yichuan houren 伊川後人
Yichuan Yus 綺川余
yijie biaoshuai 義節表率
yilao 遺老
yili yansu guimen 以禮嚴肅閨門
Yi-Luo yuanyuan 伊洛淵源 (原)
yimin 遺民
Yin 鄞
Yin Zhi 尹直
Yingchuan Wangs 潁川汪
Yingtian 應天
yinli danghou 姻里當厚
Yinming印銘
Yinyi 隱逸
yiqing chushi一清處士
yishi haoming 以詩豪名

Yixian 黟縣
yixing 义行
yizhai 義宅
yizhong 義塚
yizhuang 義莊
Yu 御
Yu Fuhua 余福華
Yu'an Wang 余岸王
Yuan Zhongdao 袁中道
yuanbian 原編
Yuanxing 原姓
Yuanxu 原序
Yue 約 (Covenants)
Yue 樂 (Music)
Yue 越 (Zhejiang)
Yueguo 越國
Yueguo gong gui 越國公圭
Yueguo shijia 越國世家
Yueguo yisun 越國裔孫
Yunhui 雲麾
Yunlan 雲嵐
Yupengyuan Wangs 予鵬源汪

Zanlei 贊誄
Zhan Jie 詹傑
Zhang Jiugong 張九功
Zhang Juzheng 張居正
Zhang Mou 章懋
Zhang Tao 張濤
Zhang Xun 張巡
Zhangqi Wang 章岐汪
zhangsheng 掌生
Zhangshi tongzong shipu 張氏統宗世譜
Zhangyuan Fangs 張源方
Zhao Fang 趙汸
Zhao Pang 趙滂
Zhao Shuo 趙朔
Zhao Wu 趙武
Zhaoshi gu'er 趙氏孤兒
Zhen Dexiu 真德秀
Zheng Shishan 鄭師山
Zheng Shuangxi 鄭雙溪
Zheng Tianzhen 鄭天鎮
Zheng Yixiao 鄭以孝
Zheng Yu 鄭玉
Zhengcun Zheng 鄭村鄭

Zhenlie 貞烈
zhennü 貞女
zhenyuan 貞媛
Zhi 芝
zhili 支離
Zhiming 誌銘
Zhixing 治行
Zhongchen 忠臣
zhonggu zhenlie 中古貞烈
Zhonglie 忠烈
zhongshen 眾神
zhongxiao 忠孝
zhongxiaojieyi 忠孝節義
Zhongxinfang 忠信坊
zhongyi er qingcai 重義而輕財
Zhongzhuang 忠壯
zhou 洲
Zhou benji lue 周本紀略
Zhu Jiefu 朱介夫
Zhu Que 祝確
Zhu Sen 朱森
Zhu Song 朱松
Zhu Tong 朱同
Zhu Yishi 朱一是
Zhu Yizun 朱彝尊
Zhu Yunzhan 朱雲沾
Zhuan 傳
Zhuang 狀
zhuangyuan 狀元
zhuanhu baozhu 專乎報主
Zhushenghui bu 祝聖會簿
Zijing 子靜
Ziling 子齡
zongcai 總裁
zongci 宗祠
zongshang 總商
Zongyue sanzhang 宗約三章
Zou kaozheng cidian 奏考正祀典
Zou Shouyi 鄒守益
zugui 族規
zundexing 尊德性
zunzu jingzong muzu 尊祖敬宗睦族
Zunzu muzu zhen 尊祖睦族箴
Zuo Qiuming 左丘明

Bailyn, Bernard. "The Challenge of Modern Historiography." *American Historical Review*, 87, no. 1 (February 1982): 1–24.

Beattie, Hilary. *Land and Lineage in China: A Study of T'ung-cheng County, Anhwei, in the Ming and Ch'ing Dynasties*. Cambridge: Cambridge University Press, 1979.

Bian Li 卞利, comp. *Ming-Qing Huizhou zugui jiafa xuanbian* 明清徽州族規家法選編. Hefei: Huangshan shushe, 2014.

Birge, Bettine. "Levirate Marriage and the Revival of Widow Chastity in Yuan China." *Asia Major* 8, no. 2 (1995): 107–46.

———. *Marriage and the Law in the Age of Khubilai Khan: Cases from the Yuan dianzhang*. Cambridge, Mass.: Harvard University Press, 2017.

Bol, Peter K. "The 'Localist Turn' and 'Local Identity' in Later Imperial China." *Late Imperial China* 24, no. 2 (December 2003): 1–50.

———. "Neo-Confucianism and Local Society, Twelfth to Sixteenth Century: A Case Study." In *The Song-Yuan-Ming Transition in Chinese History*, edited by Paul Smith and Richard von Glahn, 241–83. Cambridge, Mass: Harvard University Asia Center, 2003.

———. *Neo-Confucianism in History*. Cambridge, Mass.: Harvard University Asia Center, 2010.

———. *"This Culture of Ours": Intellectual Transformations in T'ang and Sung China*. Stanford: Stanford University Press, 1992.

Bossler, Beverly. *Powerful Relations: Kinship, Status, and the State in Sung China (960–1279)*. Cambridge, Mass.: Harvard University Asia Center, 1998.

Brokaw, Cynthia, and Kai-Wing Chow, eds. *Printing and Book Culture in Late Imperial China*. Berkeley: University of California Press, 2005.

Brook, Timothy. *The Confusions of Pleasure: Commerce and Culture in Ming China*. Berkeley: University of California Press, 1998.

———. *Praying for Power: Buddhism and the Formation of Gentry Society in Late Ming China*. Cambridge, Mass.: Council on East Asian Studies, Harvard University, 1993.

———. "Weber, Mencius, and the History of Chinese Capitalism." *Asia Perspective* 19, no. 1 (1995): 79–97.

Bussotti, Michela. "Images of Women in Late Ming Huizhou-Printed Editions of *Lienü zhuan*." *Nan Nü: Men, Women and Gender in China* 17, no. 1 (2015): 54–116.

Cai Yu 蔡羽. *Liaoyang haishen zhuan* 遼陽海神傳. In *Xiangyan congshu* 香艷叢書, compiled by Chong Tianzi 虫天子. Shanghai: Guoxue fulunshe, 1910.

Cao Sixuan 曹嗣軒. *Xiuning mingzu zhi* 休寧名族志. 1626. Compiled by Zhu Wanshu 朱萬曙. Hefei: Huangshan shushe, 2007.

Carlitz, Katherine. "Desire, Danger, and the Body: Stories of Women's Virtue in Late Ming China." In *Engendering China: Women, Culture, and the State*, edited by Christina K. Gilmartin, Gail Hershatter, Lisa Rofel, and Tyrene White, 101–24. Cambridge, Mass.: Harvard University Press, 1994.

———. "Shrines, Governing-Class, Identity, and the Cult of Widow Fidelity in Mid-Ming Jiangnan." *Journal of Asian Studies* 56, no. 3 (1997): 612–40.

———. "The Social Uses of Female Virtue in Late Ming Editions of *Lienü zhuan*." *Late Imperial China* 12, no. 2 (December 1991): 117–48.

Chan, Shelly. *Diaspora's Homeland: Modern China in the Age of Global Migration* (Durham, N.C.: Duke University Press, 2018).

Chang Jianhua 常建華. *Mingdai zongzu yanjiu* 明代宗族研究. Shanghai: Renmin chubanshe, 2005.

———. *Mingdai zongzu zuzhihua yanjiu* 明代宗族組織化研究. Beijing: Gugong chubanshe, 2012.

Changsha fuzhi 長沙府志. 1747. Reprint, Taipei: Chengwen chubanshe, 1976.

Changsha Pengshi Dunxu xupu 長沙彭氏惇敘續譜. 1915. Shanghai Library.

Changsha Qingshan Pengshi hui zongpu 長沙青山彭氏會宗譜. 1520. Shanghai Library.

Chen Dingyu 陳定宇. *Dingyu ji* 定宇集. In *Siku quanshu zhenben erji* 四庫全書珍本二集, compiled by Wang Yunwu 王雲五. Taipei: Shangwu yinshu guan, 1971.

———. *Xin'an dazu zhi* 新安大族志. Manuscript, no date.

Chen Rui 陳瑞. "Mingdai Huizhou jiapu de bianxiu jiqi neirong yu tili de fazhan" 明代徽州家譜的編修及其內容與體例的發展. *Anhui shixue* 安徽史學 (2000.4): 24–27.

Chen Zhaoxiang 陳昭祥. *Wentang Xiangyue jiafa* 文堂鄉約家法. 1572. Anhui Provincial Library.

Cheng Chang 程昌. *Doushan gong jiayi jiaozhu* 竇山公家議校注. 1545. Reprint, Hefei: Huangshan shushe, 1993.

———, comp. *Qimen Shanhe Chengshi pu* 祁門善和程氏譜. 1541. Shanghai Library.

Cheng Meng 程孟, comp. *Xin'an Chengshi zhupu huitong* 新安程氏諸譜會通. 1451. Shanghai Library.

Cheng Minzheng 程敏政, comp. *Chengshi yifan ji* 程氏貽范集. 1482. Library of Congress.

———, comp. *Daoyi bian* 道一編. *Siku* edition.

———. *Huangdun wenji* 篁墩文集. *Siku* edition.

———, comp. *Xin'an Chengshi tongzong shipu* 新安程氏統宗世譜. 1482. Shanghai Library.

———, comp. *Xin'an wenxian zhi* 新安文獻志. 1497. Reprint, Hefei: Huangshan shushe, 2004.

———, comp. *Xinjing fuzhu* 心經附註. *Siku* edition.

———, comp. *Xiuning Peiguo Chengshi benzong pu* 休寧陪郭程氏本宗譜. 1497. Anhui Provincial Library.

———, comp. *Xiuning zhi* 休寧志. 1497. In *Beijing tushuguan guji zhenben congkan, shibu* 29. Beijing: Shumu wenxian, 1988.

Cheng Qidong 程啟東, comp. *Huaitang Chengshi Xianchengtang chongxu zongpu* 槐塘程氏顯承堂重續宗譜. 1673. Shanghai Library.

Cheng Shangkuan 程尚寬, comp. *Xin'an mingzu zhi* 新安名族志. 1551. Library of Congress.

Cheng Sigong 程嗣功. *Huaitang Chengshi zongpu* 槐塘程氏宗譜. 1586. Shanghai Library.

Cheng Ting 程庭, *Chunfan jicheng* 春帆紀程. In *Xiao fanghu zhai yudi congchao* 小方壺齊輿地叢鈔, compiled by Wang Xiqi 王錫祺, 1877.

Cheng Tong 程潼 (fl. mid-16th c.). *Xin'an xuexi lu* 新安學系錄 (*Siku*).

Cheng Xu 程頊, comp. *Xin'an Chengshi shipu zhengzong qianxi zhujiao zuan* 新安程氏世譜正宗遷徙註腳纂. 1563. Shanghai Library.

Cheng Zeng 程曾 and Dai Xian 戴銑, comp. *Huangdun Cheng xiansheng wencui* 篁墩程先生文萃. 25 *juan*. 1505. Beijing National Library.

Chengshi wenhua liangyihui jiapu weiyuanhui 程氏文化聯誼會家譜委員會, comp. *Chengshi xungen cankao yi* 程氏尋根參考 1. Huai'an: Huaiyin dangxiao, 2005.

Chia, Lucille. "The Butcher, the Baker, and the Carpenter: Chinese Sojourners in the Spanish Philippines and Their Impact on Southern Fujian (Sixteenth to Eighteenth Centuries)." *Journal of the Economic and Social History of the Orient* 49, no. 4 (2006): 509–34.

Chongxiu Xin'an Qidong Wushi zupu yaolue 重修新安祁東吳氏族譜要略. 1568. *MDJP*, vol 2.

Chow, Kai-wing. *The Rise of Confucian Ritualism in Late Imperial China: Ethics, Classics, and Lineage Discourse.* Stanford: Stanford University Press, 1994.

Clunas, Craig. *Superfluous Things: Material Culture and Social Status in Early Modern China.* Honolulu: University of Hawai{okina}i Press, 2004.

Confucius. *The Analects.* Translated by D. C. Lau. London: Penguin Books, 1979.

Dai Tingming 戴廷明 and Cheng Shangkuan 程尚寬, comps. *Xin'an mingzu zhi* 新安名族志. 1551. Edited by Zhu Wanshu. Hefei: Huangshan shushe, 2004.

Dardess, John W. *A Ming Society: T'ai-ho County, Kiangsi, in the Fourteenth to Seventeen Centuries.* Berkeley: University of California Press, 1996.

De Bary, Wm. Theodore. "Individualism and Humanitarianism in Late Ming Thought." In *Self and Society in Ming Thought*, edited by Wm. Theodore de Bary, 145–247. New York: Columbia University Press, 1970.

———. *Neo-Confucian Orthodoxy and the Learning of the Mind-and-Heart.* New York: Columbia University Press, 1981.

———, ed. *Self and Society in Ming Thought.* New York: Columbia University Press, 1970.

De Bary, Wm. Theodore, and Irene Bloom, comps. *Sources of Chinese Tradition*, 2nd ed. New York: Columbia University Press, 1999.

Dennis, Joseph. *Writing, Publishing, and Reading Local Gazetteers in Imperial China, 1100–1700.* Cambridge, Mass.: Harvard University Press, 2015.

Ding Xiqin 丁希勤. *Gudai Huizhou zongjiao xinyang yanjiu* 古代徽州宗教信仰研究. Wuhu: Anhui shifan daxue chubanshe, 2013.

Du, Fangqin, and Susan Mann. "Competing Claims on Womanly Virtue in Late Imperial China." In *Women and Confucian Cultures in Premodern China, Korea, and Japan*, edited by Dorothy Ko, Jahyun Kim Haboush, and Joan R. Piggott, 219–47. Berkeley: University of California Press, 2003.

Du, Yongtao. *The Order of Places: Translocal Practices of the Huizhou Merchants in Late Imperial China*. Leiden: Brill, 2015.

Duara, Prasenjit. "Superscribing Symbols: The Myth of Guandi, the Chinese God of War." *Journal of Asian Studies* 47, no. 4 (November 1988): 778–95.

Ebrey, Patricia. *Confucianism and Family Rituals in Imperial China: A Social History of Writing about Rites*. Princeton: Princeton University Press, 1991.

Ebrey, Patricia, and James Watson, eds. *Kinship Organization in Late Imperial China, 1000–1940*. Berkeley: University of California Press, 1986.

Elvin, Mark. "Blood and Statistics: Reconstructing the Population Dynamics of Late Imperial China from the Biographies of Virtuous Women in Local Gazetteers." In *Chinese Women in the Imperial Past: New Perspectives*, edited by Harriet Zurndorfer, 135–222. Leiden: E. J. Brill, 1999.

Epstein, Maram. *Competing Discourses: Orthodoxy, Authenticity, and Engendered Meanings in Late Imperial Chinese Fiction*. Cambridge, Mass.: Harvard University Press, 2001.

Fang Chengxun 方承訓. *Fuchu ji* 復初集. In *Siku quanshu cunmu congshu* 四庫全書存目叢書, compiled by Siku quanshu cunmu congshu bianzuan weiyuanhui. Jinan: Qilu shushe, 1997, series 4.

Fei, Siyen. "Writing for Justice: An Activist Beginning of the Cult of Female Chastity in Late Imperial China." *Journal of Asian Studies* 71, no. 4 (November 2012): 991–1012.

Finnane, Antonia. *Speaking of Yangzhou: A Chinese City 1550–1850*. Cambridge, Mass.: Harvard University Asia Center, 2004.

Flath, James A. *The Cult of Happiness: Nianhua, Art, and History in Rural North China*. Vancouver: University of British Columbia Press, 2004.

Freedman, Maurice. *Chinese Lineage and Society: Fukien and Kwangtung*. London: Athlone, 1966.

Fujii Hiroshi 藤井宏. "Shinan shōnin no kenkyū" 新安商人の研究. *Tōyō gakuhō* 東洋學報 36, no. 1 (1953): 1–44; 36, no. 2 (1953): 180–208; 36, no. 3 (1953): 335–88; 36, no. 4 (1954): 533–63.

Geng Chuanyou 耿傳友. "Wang Daokun shangren zhuanji yanjiu" 汪道昆商人傳記研究. Master's thesis, Anhui University, 2002.

Gerritsen, Anne. *Ji'an Literati and the Local in Song-Yuan-Ming China*. Leiden: Brill, 2007.

Guo, Qitao. "Engendering the Mercantile Lineage: The Rise of the Female Chastity Cult in Late Ming Huizhou." *Nan Nü: Men, Women and Gender in China* (Brill, Leiden) 17, no. 1 (2015): 9–53.

———. *Exorcism and Money: The Symbolic World of the Five-Fury Spirits in Late Imperial China*. Berkeley: Institute of East Asian Studies, University of California, 2003.

———. "Genealogical Pedigree versus Godly Power: Cheng Minzheng and Lineage Politics in Mid-Ming Huizhou." *Late Imperial China* 31, no. 1 (June 2010): 28–61.

———. *Ritual Opera and Mercantile Lineage: The Confucian Transformation of Popular Culture in Late Imperial Huizhou*. Stanford: Stanford University Press, 2005.

Han Jiegen 韓結根. *Mingdai Huizhou wenxue yanjiu* 明代徽州文學研究. Shanghai: Fudan daxue chubanshe, 2006.

Handlin, Joanna. *Action in Late Ming Thought: The Reorientation of Lü K'un and Other Scholar-Officials*. Berkeley: University of California Press, 1983.

———. *The Art of Doing Good: Charity in Late Ming China*. Berkeley: University of California Press, 2009.

Harrison, Henrietta. *The Man Awakened from Dreams*. Stanford: Stanford University Press, 2005.

Hartwell, Robert. "Demographic, Political, and Social Transformations of China, 750–1550." *Harvard Journal of Asiatic Studies* 42, no. 2 (1982): 365–422.

Hazelton, Keith. "Patrilines and the Development of Localized Lineages: The Wu of Hsiu-ning City, Hui-chou, to 1528." In *Kinship Organization in Late Imperial China*, edited by Ebrey and Watson, 137–69. Berkeley: University of California Press, 1986.

He, Yuming. *Home and the World: Editing the "Glorious Ming" in Woodblock-Printed Books of the Sixteenth and Seventeenth Centuries*. Cambridge, Mass.: Harvard University Press, 2013.

Henan Chengshi tongzong pulüe 河南程氏統宗譜略. 1868. Columbia University.

Ho, Ping-ti. *The Ladder of Success in Imperial China: Aspects of Social Mobility, 1368–1911*. New York: Columbia University Press, 1962.

Ho Wei Hsuan 何威萱. "Cheng Minzheng jiqi xueshu sixiang" 程敏政及其學術思想. PhD diss., Hong Kong Polytechnic University, 2013.

Hongcun Wangshi jiapu 弘村汪氏家譜. 1747. Anhui Provincial Library and the Center for Huizhou Studies Library, University of Anhui.

Hu Shibin 胡時濱 and Shu Yuling 舒育玲. *Xidi: Zhongguo Ming-Qing minju bowuguan* 西遞：中國明清民居博物館. Hefei: Huangshan shushe, 1993.

Hu Xiaoshan 胡小姍. "Wang Daokun beizhuanwen yanjiu" 汪道昆碑傳文研究. Master's thesis, Anhui University, 2014.

Huaitang Chengshi Xianchengtang chongxu zongpu 槐塘程氏顯承堂重續宗譜. 1673. Shanghai Library.

Huang Shangwen 黃尚文. *Nüfan bian* 女範編. In *Beijing Tushuguan Guji Zhenben Congkan* 北京圖書館古籍珍本叢刊, vol. 14. Beijing: Shumu wenxian chubanshe, 1988.

Huang Yunsu 黃雲蘇, comp. *Xin'an Huangshi huitong zongpu* 新安黃氏會通宗譜, 1501. In *MDJP*, vols. 23–24.

Huang Zongxi 黃宗羲. *Mingru xue'an* 明儒學案. In *Ruzang* 儒藏, compiled by Sichuan daxue guji zhengli yanjiusuo 四川大學古籍整理研究所, ser. 3, vols. 25–26. Chengdu: Sichuan daxue chubanshe, 2005.

Huizhou fuzhi 徽州府志. 1566.

Hunan tongzhi 湖南通志. 1885. Reprint, Shanghai: Shanghai guji chubanshe, 1990.

Hymes, Robert P. "Marriage, Descent Groups, and the Localist Strategy in Sung and Yuan Fu-chou." In *Kinship Organization in Late Imperial China, 1000–1940*, edited by Patricia Ebrey and James Watson, 95–136. Berkeley: University of California Press, 1986.

———. *Statesmen and Gentlemen: The Elite of Fu-chou, Chiang-hsi, in Northern and Southern Sung*. Cambridge: Cambridge University Press, 1986.

———. *Way and Byway: Taoism, Local Religion, and Models of Divinity in Sung and Modern China*. Berkeley: University of California Press, 2002.

Jay, Jennifer W. "Memoirs and Official Accounts: The Historiography of the Song Loyalists." *Harvard Journal of Asiatic Studies* 50, no. 2 (1990): 589–612.

Jiangnan tongzhi 江南通志. 1737. Shanghai Library.

Jin Dexuan 金德玹, comp. *Xin'an wencui* 新安文粹. In *SKCM*, 4.292.

Johnson, David. "The City-God Cults in Tang-Song China." *Harvard Journal of Asiatic Studies* 45 (1985): 363–457.

———. *The Medieval Chinese Oligarchy*. Boulder: Westview Press, 1977.

———. *Spectacle and Sacrifice: The Ritual Foundations of Village Life in North China.* Cambridge, Mass.: Harvard East Asian Monographs, 2010.

Ke, Dawei (David Faure) 科大衛 and Liu Zhiwei 劉志偉. "Zongzu yu difang shehui de guojia rentong: Ming-Qing Huanan diqu zongzu fazhan de yishi xingtai jichu" 宗族與地方社會的國家認同：明清華南地區發展的意識型態基礎. *Lishi yanjiu* 歷史研究 (2000.3): 3–14.

Ko, Dorothy. *Cinderella's Sisters: A Revisionist History of Footbinding.* Berkeley: University of California Press, 2007.

———. *Teachers of the Inner Chambers: Women and Culture in Seventeenth-Century China.* Stanford University Press, 1994.

Kuhn, Philip A. *Chinese Among Others: Emigration in Modern Times.* New York: Rowman and Littlefield, 2008.

———. *Rebellion and Its Enemies in Late Imperial China: Militarization and Social Structure, 1796–1864.* Cambridge, Mass.: Harvard University Press, 1970.

Lee, James, Wang Feng, and Danching Ruan. "Nuptiality among the Qing Nobility, 1640–1900." In *Asian Population History*, edited by Ts'ui-jung Liu, James Lee, David Sven Reher, Osamu Saito, and Wang Feng, 353–73. Oxford: Oxford University Press, 2001.

Lee, Sukhee. *Negotiated Power: The State, Elites, and Local Governance in Twelfth- to Fourteenth-Century China.* Cambridge, Mass.: Harvard University Press, 2014.

Lei Li 雷禮 (1505–81). *Guochao lieqing ji* 國朝列卿記. Taipei: Chengwen, 1970.

Li Linqi 李琳琦. "Ming-Qing Huizhou jinshi shuliang, fenbu tedian jiqi yuanyin fenxi 明清徽州進士數量，分佈特點及其原因分析." *Anhui shifan daxue xuebao* 安徽師範大學學報 (Feb. 2001): 32–41.

Ling Mengchu 凌濛初 (1580–1644). *Erke Pai'an jingqi* 二刻拍案驚奇. Jinan: Qilu shushe, 1995.

———. *Pai'an jingqi* 拍岸驚奇. Jinan: Qilu shushe, 1995.

Liu, Ts'ui-jung. "The Demography of Two Chinese Clans in Hsiao-shan, Chekiang, 1650–1850." In *Family and Population in East Asian History*, edited by Susan B. Hanley and Arthur P. Wolf, 13–61. Stanford: Stanford University Press, 1985.

Liu Ts'ui-jung 劉翠溶. "Ming-Qing renkou zhi zengzhi yu qianyi: Changjiang zhongxia you diqu zupu ziliao zhi fenxi 明清人口之增殖與遷移：長江中下游地區族譜資料之分析." In *Di'erjie zhongguo shehui jingjishi yantaohui lunwen ji* 第二屆中國社會經濟史研討會論文集, edited by Xu Zhuoyun 許倬雲, Mao Hanguang 毛漢光, and Liu Cuirong (Liu Ts'ui-jung), 283–316. Taipei: Hanxue yanjiu ziliao ji fuwu zhongxin, 1983.

Lu, Weijing. *True to Her Word: The Faithful Maiden Cult in Late Imperial China.* Stanford: Stanford University Press, 2008.

Lufrano, Richard John. *Honorable Merchants: Commerce and Self-Cultivation in Late Imperial China.* Honolulu: University of Hawai{okina}i Press, 1997.

Luo Yuan 羅願, comp. *Xin'an zhi* 新安志. 1175. Taipei: Shangwu yinshu guan, 1983.

Mann, Susan. "Suicide and Survival: Exemplary Widows in the Late Empire." In *Chūgoku no dentō shakai to kazoku: Yanagida Setsuko Sensei koki kinen ronshū* 中國の傳統社會と家族：柳田節子先生古稀紀念論集, edited by Yanagida Setsuko Sensei Koki Kinen Ronshū Henshū linkai, 23–39. Tokyo: Kyūko Shoin, 1993.

———. *The Talented Women in the Zhang Family.* Berkeley: University of California Press, 2007.

McDermott, Joseph. "How to Succeed Commercially as a Huizhou Book Publisher, 1500–1644." In *Yinshua yu shichang: Guoji huiyi lunwenji* 印刷與市場：國際會議論

文集, edited by Zhou Shengchun 周生春 and He Zhaohui 何朝暉, 383–99. Hangzhou: Zhejiang daxue chubanshe, 2012.

———. *The Making of a New Rural Order in South China*, vol. 1. *Village, Land, and Lineage in Huizhou, 900–1600*. Cambridge: Cambridge University Press, 2013.

———. *The Making of a New Rural Order in South China*, vol 2. *Merchants, Markets, and Lineages, 1500–1700*. Cambridge: Cambridge University Press, 2020.

———. "The Rise of Huizhou Merchants: Kinship and Commerce in Ming China." In *The Economy of Lower Yangzi Delta in Late Imperial China*, edited by Billy K. L. So, 233–65. New York: Routledge, 2013.

———. *A Social History of the Chinese Book*. Hong Kong: Hong Kong University Press, 2006.

Meyer-Fong, Tobie. *Building Culture in Early Qing Yangzhou*. Stanford: Stanford University Press, 2003.

———. "The Printed World: Books, Publishing Culture, and Society in Late Imperial China." *Journal of Asian Studies* 66 (2007): 787–817.

Nakajima Gakushō 中島樂章. *Mindai gōson no funsō to chitsujo: Kishū monjo o shiryō to shite* 明代鄉村の紛爭と秩序：徽州文書を資料として. Tokyo: Kyūko shoin, 2002.

Ong, Chang Woer. *Men of Letters within the Passes: Guanzhong Literati in Chinese History, 907–1911*. Cambridge, Mass.: Harvard University Asia Center, 2008.

Peng Hua 彭華. *Peng Wensi gong wenji* 彭文思公文集. 1503. In *Mingren wenji congkan* 明人文集叢刊1, compiled by Shen Yunlong 沈雲龍. Taipei: Wenhai, 1970.

Peng Ze 彭澤, comp. *Huizhou fuzhi* 徽州府志. 1502. Taipei: Xuesheng shuju, 1965.

Plaks, Andrew H. *The Four Masterworks of the Ming Novel*. Princeton: Princeton University Press, 1987.

Pomeranz, Kenneth. *The Great Divergence: China, Europe, and the Making of the Modern World Economy*. Princeton: Princeton University Press, 2000.

———. "Power, Gender, and Pluralism in the Cult of the Goddess of Taishan." In *Culture and State in Chinese History: Conventions, Accommodations, and Critiques*, edited by Theodore Huters, R. Bin Wong, and Pauline Yu, 182–204. Stanford: Stanford University Press, 1997.

Pu Xia 蒲霞. *Ming-Qing yilai Huizhou fangzhi bianzuan chengjiu*明清以來徽州方志編纂成就. Hefei: Anhui daxue chubanshe, 2013.

Queming闕名 (Anonymous). *Huitu sanjiao yuanliu soushen daquan* 繪圖三教源流搜神大全. Shanghai: Shanghai guji chubanshe, 1990. Reprint based on a late Ming edition.

Qian Hang 錢杭. *Zongzu de shixixue yanjiu* 宗族的世系學研究. Shanghai: Fudan daxue chubanshe, 2011.

Qing tan chang zou 請壇場奏. Early twentieth-century manuscript from Limu village, Huizhou.

Qinhuai Yuke 秦淮寓客, comp. *Lüchuang nüshi* 綠窗女史. 1621. Shanghai Library and National Library of China in Beijing.

Qishen zouge 祈神奏格. Ming and Qing versions. Shanghai Library.

Rowe, William. *Saving the World: Chen Hongmou and Elite Consciousness in Eighteenth-Century China*. Stanford: Stanford University Press, 2001.

Santangelo, Paolo. "Urban Society in Late Imperial Suzhou." In *Cities of Jiangnan in Late Imperial China*, edited by Linda Cooke Johnson, 81–116. Albany: State University of New York Press, 1993.

Shahar, Meir, and Robert P. Weller, eds. *Unruly Gods: Divinity and Society in China*. Honolulu: University of Hawai{okina}i Press, 1996.

Shanhe Chengshi zongpu 善和程氏宗譜. 1907. Anhui Provincial Library.

She Huarui 佘華瑞. *Yanzhen zhicao* 岩鎮志草. 1738. Reprint, Huangshan shi Huizhou qu difang zhi bianzuan weiyuanhui bangongshi 黃山市徽州區地方志編纂委員會辦公室, 2004.

Shen Defu 沈德符 (Ming). *Wanli yehuo bian* 萬曆野獲編. Reprint, Beijing: Wenhua yishu chubanshe, 1998.

Shexian zhi 歙縣志. 1937. Taipei: Chengwen chubanshe, 1975.

Sima Qian 司馬遷. *Shiji* 史記. Beijing: Zhonghua shuju, 1974.

Smith, Joanna Handlin. *The Art of Doing Good: Charity in Late Ming China.* Berkeley: University of California Press, 2009.

Smith, Paul Jakov, and Richard von Glahn, eds. *The Song-Yuan-Ming Transition in Chinese History.* Cambridge, Mass: Harvard University Asia Center, 2003.

So, Billy. *Prosperity, Region, and Institutions in Maritime China: The South Fukien Pattern, 946–1368.* Cambridge, Mass.: Harvard University Press, 2000.

Sommer, Matthew. *Sex, Law, and Society in Late Imperial China.* Stanford: Stanford University Press, 2000.

Song Lian 宋濂. *Yuanshi* 元史. Beijing: Zhonghua shuju, 1976.

Szonyi, Michael. *The Art of Being Governed: Everyday Politics in Late Imperial China.* Princeton: Princeton University Press, 2017.

———. "The Illusion of Standardizing the Gods: The Cult of the Five Emperors in Late Imperial China." *Journal of Asian Studies* 56, no. 1 (February 1997): 113–35.

———. *Practicing Kinship: Lineage and Descent in Late Imperial China.* Stanford: Stanford University Press, 2002.

Taga Akigōrō 多賀秋五郎. *Chūugoku sōfū no kenkyū* 中國宗譜の研究. Tokyo: Hihon gakujutsu shinkōkai, 1981–1982.

———. "*Shin-an meizoku-shi* ni tsuite 《新安名族志》について. *Chūō Daigaku Bungaku-bu kiyō* 中央大學文學部紀要, 6 (1956): 79–102.

Tang Lixing 唐力行. *Huizhou zongzu shehui* 徽州宗族社會. Hefei: Anhui renmin chubanshe, 2005.

———. "Ming Qing Huizhou de jiating yu zongzu jiegou" 明清徽州的家庭與宗族結構. *Lishi yanjiu* 歷史研究 1 (1991): 147–59.

———. *Shangren yu wenhua de shuangchong bianzou* 商人與文化的雙重變奏. Wuhan: Huazhong ligong daxue chubanshe, 1997.

———. *Shangren yu Zhongguo jinshi shehui* 商人與中國近世社會. Hong Kong: Zhonghua shuju, 1995.

Theiss, Janet. *Disgraceful Matters: The Politics of Chastity in Eighteenth-Century China.* Berkeley: University of California Press, 2004.

T'ien, Ju-k'ang. *Male Anxiety and Female Chastity: A Comparative Study of Chinese Ethical Values in Ming-Ch'ing Times.* Leiden: E. J. Brill, 1988.

Von Glahn, Richard. "The Enchantment of Wealth: The God Wutong in the Social History of Jiangnan." *Harvard Journal of Asiatic Studies* 51, no. 2 (1991): 651–714.

———. *The Sinister Way: The Divine and Demonic in Chinese Religious Culture.* Berkeley: University of California Press, 2004.

Wan Zhengzhong 萬正中. *Huizhou renwu zhi* 徽州人物志. Hefei: Huangshan shushe, 2008.

Wang Daojin 汪道謹, comp. *Wangshi zupu* 汪氏族譜. 1480. Shanghai Library.

Wang Daokun 汪道昆. *Lienü zhuan* 列女傳 16 *juan*. Illustrated by the famous late Ming Huizhou painter-cum-woodblock cutter, Qiu Ying 仇英. Hangzhou: Baoshi zhibuzhu zhai 鮑氏知不足齋, 1779. Facsimile reprint of the original Ming Wanli edition. Beijing National Library.

———, comp. *Lingshanyuan Wangshi shiliu zu pu* 靈山院汪氏十六族譜 (also listed as *Wangshi shiliu zu jinshu jiapu* 汪氏十六族近屬家譜). 1592. Recut by Wang Cun 汪存 in 1612. Beijing National Library.

———. "Qilie zhuan 七烈傳." In *Lüchuan nüshi* 綠牕女史 14 *juan*, compiled by Qinhuai Yuke 秦淮寓客, *juan* 9 titled Jiexia 節俠. 1621, Beijing National Library.

———. *Taihan ji* 太函集. 1591. Hefei: Huangshan shushe. Reprint, 2004.

Wang Heming 王鶴鳴, comp. *Shanghai tushuguan guancang jiapu tiyao* 上海圖書館館藏家譜提要. Shanghai: Guji, 2000.

Wang Ji 汪璣, comp. *Wangshi Tongzong shipu* 汪氏通宗世譜. 1787. Shanghai Library.

Wang Kui 汪奎, comp. *Chongxiu Wangshi jiacheng* 重修汪氏家乘. 1508. *MDJP*.

Wang Nanxuan 汪南軒. *Chongbian Xin'an Zhonglie miao shen jishi* 重編新安忠烈廟神紀實. Reprint, 1460 (or 1465?), National Library of China. First compiled by Zheng Hongzu 鄭弘祖 and printed in 1339; the new version containing an undated preface by Fang Mian 方勉 (*jinshi* 1415) and another penned in 1465 (?) by Jiang Bochen 江伯琛.

Wang Qiang 王強, comp. *Zhongguozhenxi jiapu congkan: Mingdai jiapu* 中國珍稀家譜叢刊：明代家譜, 32 volumes. Nanjing: Fenghuang chuban chuanmei, 2013.

Wang Rang 汪讓, comp. *Chengbei Wangshi zupu* 城北汪氏族譜. 1487. Anhui Provincial Library.

Wang Shanghe 汪尚和, comp. *Xiuning Ximen Wangshi zupu* 休寧西門汪氏族譜. 1527. Shanghai Library.

Wang Shixing 王士性. *Guangzhiyi* 廣志繹 (preface dated 1597). In *Yuan-Ming shiliao biji congkan* 元明史料筆記叢刊. Beijing: Zhonghua shuju, 1981, series 1, vol. 13.

Wang Songtao 汪松濤, comp. *Wangshi yuanyuan lu* 汪氏淵源錄. Reprint 1518, original edition Yuan dynasty. Beijing National Library.

Wang Tingfeng 汪廷俸. *Wangshi tongzong pu* 汪氏統宗譜. Compiled during the Jiajing era (1522–66). Shanghai Library.

Wang Tingyuan 王廷元 and Wang Shihua 王世華. *Huishang* 徽商. Hefei: Anhui renmin chubanshe, 2005.

Wang Xun 汪循. *Renfeng wenji* 仁峰文集. In *Siku quanshu cunmu congshu* 四庫全書存目叢書, compiled by Siku quanshu cunmu congshu bianzuan weiyuanhui. Jinan: Qilu shushe, 1997, series 4.

Wang Zhenzhong 王振忠. *Huizhou shehui wenhua shi tanwei* 徽州社會文化史探微. Shanghai: Shanghai shehui kexue chubanshe, 2002.

———. "Ming-Qing wenxian zhong 'Huishang' yici de chubu kaocha" 明清文獻中'徽商'一詞的初步考察. *Lishi yanjiu* 歷史研究 (2006.1): 170–73.

Wang Zhongjin 汪仲溍, comp. (*Shexian*) *Xixi Wangshi xianying bianlan* 西溪汪氏先塋便覽. 1539. Shanghai Library.

Wang Zhonglu 汪仲魯 et al., comps. *Wangshi tongzong zhengmai* 汪氏統宗正脉. 1571. *MDJP*, vols. 18–22.

Wangshi jiacheng 汪氏家乘. 1488. Shanghai Library.

Watson, Burton, trans. *Records of the Grand Historian of China*. New York: Columbia University Press, 1961.

Watson, James. "Standardizing the Gods: The Promotion of T'ien-Hou ('Empress of Heaven') along the South China Coast, 960–1960." In *Popular Culture in Late Imperial China*, edited by David Johnson, Andrew Nathan, and Evelyn Rawski, 292–324 (Berkeley: University of California Press, 1985).

Weller, Robert. *Unities and Diversities in Chinese Religion*. Seattle: University of Washington Press, 1987.

Wentang Xiangyue jiafa 文堂鄉約家法. 1572, Anhui Provincial Library.

Wilson, Thomas. "Genealogy and History in Neo-Confucian Sectarian Uses of the Confucian Past." *Modern China* 20, no. 1 (January 1994): 3–33.

———. *Genealogy of the Way: The Construction and Uses of the Confucian Tradition in Late Imperial China*. Stanford: Stanford University Press, 1995.

Wong, R. Bin. *China Transformed: Historical Change and the Limits of European Experience*. Ithaca: Cornell University Press, 1997.

Wu, Yi-li. *Reproducing Women: Medicine, Metaphor, and Childbirth in Late Imperial China*. Berkeley: University of California Press, 2010.

Wu Bosen 吳柏森, comp. *Ming shilu leizuan—Wenjiao keji juan* 明實錄類纂—文教科技卷. Wuhan: Wuhan chubanshe, 1992.

Wu Changgen 吳長庚, comp. *Zhu Lu xueshu kaobian wuzhong* 朱陸學術考辨五種. Nanchang: Jiangxi gaoxiao chubanshe, 2000.

Wu Xuande 吳宣德 and Zong Yun 宗韻, comps. *Mingren pudie xuba jilue* 明人譜牒序跋輯略. Shanghai guji chubanshe, 2013.

Wu Zhaolong 吳兆龍. "Wang Daokun de jiapu bianxiu huodong jiqi lilun chengjiu" 汪道昆的家譜活動及其理論成就. Master's thesis, Anhui Normal University, 2012.

Wu Ziyu 吳子玉. *Dazhang shanren ji* 大障山人集. In *Siku quanshu cunmu congshu* 四庫全書存目叢書, compiled by Siku quanshu cunmu congshu bianzuan weiyuanhui. Jinan: Qilu shushe, 1997, series 4.

Xia Xie 夏燮 (1799–1875). *Ming tongjian* 明通鑑. Reprint, Changsha: Yuelu shushe, 1999.

Xie Bi 謝陛, comp. *Shezhi* 歙志. 1609. Reprint, Hefei: Huangshan shushe, 2014.

Xie Kaichong 謝開寵, ed. *Lianghuai yanfa zhi* 兩淮鹽法志. 1693. Reprint, Taipei: Taiwan xueshen shuju, 1966.

Xin'an Censhandu Chengshi zhipu 新安岑山渡程氏支譜. 1741. Anhui Provincial Library.

Xin'an Chenshi zongpu 新安陳氏宗譜. 1507. Anhui Provincial Library.

Xin'an Wangshi chongxiu bagong pu 新安汪氏重修八公譜. 1535. Shanghai Library.

Xiuning Gucheng Chengshi zongpu 休寧古城程氏宗譜. 1570. Shanghai Library.

Xiuning Shuaikou Chengshi xubian benzong pu 休寧率口程氏續編本宗譜, 1570. Shanghai Library.

Xiuning xianzhi 休寧縣志. 1548. Shanghai Library.

Xiuning xianzhi 休寧縣志. 1693. Reprint, Taipei: Chengwen, 1970. Cited as *XXZ*.

Xixi Wangshi xianying bianlan 溪西汪氏先塋便覽. 1539. Anhui Provincial Library.

Xu Chengyao 許承堯. *Sheshi xiantan* 歙事閑譚. Reprint, Hefei: Huangshan shushe, 2001.

Xu Jianhua 徐建華. *Zhongguo de jiapu* 中國的家譜. Tianjin: Beihua wenyi chubanshe, 2002.

Xu Shuofang 徐朔方. "Tang Xianzu nianpu" 湯顯祖年譜. In *Wan Ming qujia nianpu* 晚明曲家年譜, Xu Shuofang, 3:201–495. Hangzhou: Zhejiang guji chubanshe, 1993.

————. "Wang Daokun nianpu" 汪道昆年譜. In *Wan Ming qujia nianpu* 晚明曲家年譜, Xu Shuofang, 3:1–104. Hangzhou: Zhejiang guji chubanshe, 1993.

Xu Zhuo 徐卓. *Xiuning suishi* 休寧碎事. 1811. Anhui Provincial Library.

Yang Jin 楊瑾. "Wang Daokun liulun" 汪道昆六論. Master's thesis, Anhui Normal University, 2004.

Yang Shen 楊慎. *Sheng'an ji* 昇庵集. *Siku* edition.

Ye Weiming 葉為銘, comp. *Shexian jinshi zhi* 歙縣金石志. Hangzhou: Zicheng Yeshi jiamiao, 1936.

Ye Xian'en 葉顯恩. *Ming-Qing Huizhou nongcun shehui yu dianpu zhi* 明清徽州農村社會與佃僕制. Hefei: Anhui renmin, 1983.

Yixian zhi 黟縣志 (1812). In *Yixian sanzhi* 黟縣三志. Reprint, Taipei: Chengwen chubanshe, 1970.

Yong Rong 永瑢, comp. *Siku quanshu zongmu* 四庫全書總目. Reprint, Beijing: Zhonghua shuju, 2003.

Yu, Ying-shih. *Rujia lunli yu shangren jingshen* 儒家倫理與商人精神. In *Yu Yingshi wenji* 余英時文集, compiled by Shen Zhijia 沈志佳, vol. 3. Guilin: Guangxi shifan daxue chubanshe, 2004.

————. *Song Ming lixue yu zhengzhi wenhua* 宋明理學與政治文化. Taipei: Yunchen, 2004.

Yu Chenghua 禹成華, comp. *Huizhou mingzu zhi* 徽州名族志, 2 vols. Beijing: Quanguo tushuguan wenxian suowei fuzhi zhongxin, 2003.

Yu Zhihuai 余志淮. *Yixian: Taohuayuan li renjia* 黟縣 : 桃花源里人家. Hefei: Huangshan shushe, 1993.

Yueguo Wanggong cimu zhi 越國汪公祠墓志. 1852. Shanghai Library.

Yuko Shibuya. "Min Shin jidai, kishū kōnan nōson shakai ni okeru saishi soshiki ni tsuite—Shukuseikaibo'no shōkai" 明清時代, 徽州江南農村社會における祭祀組織 について—'祝聖會簿' の紹介. Shigaku 史學 59, no. 1 (1990): 103–34; 59, nos. 2–3 (1990): 93–129.

Zhang Chao 張潮 (1650–?). "*Shewen* xiaoyin" 歙問小引. In *Zhaodai congshu* 昭代叢書, compiled by Zhang Chao, series 3, vol. 24. Cambridge, Mass.: Harvard University, Yenching Library, rare-book section, n.d.

Zhang Haipeng 張海鵬 et al., comp. *Ming-Qing Huishang ziliao xuanbian* 明清徽商資料選編. Hefei: Huangshan shushe, 1985.

Zhang Haipeng 張海鵬 and Wang Tingyuan 王廷元, eds. *Huishang yanjiu* 徽商研究. Hefei: Anhui renmin chubanshe, 1995.

Zhang Jian 張健. "Lun Mingdai Huizhou wenxianxuejia Cheng Minzheng" 論明代徽州文獻學家程敏政. *Anhui shifan daxue xuebao* 31, no. 5 (2003): 514–18.

Zhang Tingyu 張廷玉. *Mingshi* 明史. Beijing: Zhonghua shuju. 1974.

Zhang Yi 章毅. *Lixue, shishen he zongzu: Song-Ming shiqi Huizhou de wenhua yu shehui* 理學, 士紳和宗族 : 宋明時期徽州的文化與社會. Hong Kong: Hong Kong zhongwen daxue chubanshe, 2013.

Zhao Huafu 趙華富. *Liangyi ji* 兩驛集. Hefei: Huangshan shushe, 1999.

Zhao Pang 趙滂, comp. *Cheng-Zhu queli zhi* 程朱闕里志. 1612. Anhui Provincial Library. Cited as *CZQLZ*.

Zheng Limin 鄭力民. "*Xin'an dazu zhi* kaobian—jiantan *Shilu Xin'an shijia*" 《新安大族志》考辨—兼談《實錄新安世家》. *Anhui shixue* (1993.3): 24–29; (1994.3): 15–18.

Zheng Yu 鄭玉. *Shishan ji* 師山集 (*SIKU* ed.).

Zheng Zhizhen 鄭之珍. *Mulian jiumu quanshan xiwen* 目連救母勸善戲文. 3 vols. 1582. Reprinted in facsimile in *Guben xiqu congkan chuji*, series 1, vols. 80–82. Beijing: Guben xiqu congkan biankan weiyuanhui, 1955–1959.

———. *Qimen Qingxi Zhengshi jiacheng* 祁門清溪鄭氏家乘. 1583. Shanghai Library.

Zhongguo shehui kexueyuan lishi yanjiusuo 中國社會科學院歷史研究所, comp. *Huizhou qiannian qiyue wenshu* 徽州千年契約文書. Shijiazhuang: Huashan wenyi chubanshe, 1991.

———. *Qimen Qingxi Zhengshi jiacheng* 祁門清溪鄭氏家乘. 1583, Shanghai Library.

Zhou Xiaoguang 周曉光, *Xin'an lixue* 新安理學. Hefei: Anhui renmin chubanshe, 2005.

Zhu Baojiong 朱保炯 et al. *Ming-Qing jinshi timing beilu suoyin* 明清進士提名碑錄索引. Shanghai: guji chubanshe, 1984.

Zhu Wanshu 朱萬曙. *Huishang yu Ming-Qing wenxue* 徽商與明清文學. Beijing: Renmin wenxue chubanshe, 2014.

———. "Ming-Qing liangdai Huizhou de yanju huodong" 明清兩代徽州的演劇活動. *Huixue* 徽學 2 (2002): 208–226.

Zong Li 宗力 and Liu Qun 劉群. *Zhongguo minjian zhushen* 中國民間諸神. Shijiazhuang: Hebei renmin chubanshe, 1986.

Zuo Dongling 左東嶺. *Wangxue yu zhong wan Ming shiren xintai* 王學與中晚明士人心態. Beijing: Renmin wenxue chubanshe, 2000.

Zurndorfer, Harriet. *Change and Continuity in Chinese Local History: The Development of Hui-chou Prefecture 800 to 1800*. Leiden: E. J. Brill, 1989.

———. "Contracts, Property, and Litigation: Intermediation and Adjudication in the Huizhou Region (Anhui) in Sixteenth-Century China." In *Law and Long-Term Economic Change: A Eurasian Perspective*, edited by Debin Ma and Jan Luiten van Zanden. Stanford: Stanford University Press, 2011.

———. "Learning, Lineage, and Locality in Late Imperial China: A Comparative Study of Education in Huichow (Anhwei) and Foochow (Fukien) 1600–1800." *Journal of the Economic and Social History of the Orient* 35, no. 2 (May 1992): 109–44; 35, no. 3 (August 1992): 209–38.

Founded in 1893,
UNIVERSITY OF CALIFORNIA PRESS
publishes bold, progressive books and journals
on topics in the arts, humanities, social sciences,
and natural sciences—with a focus on social
justice issues—that inspire thought and action
among readers worldwide.

The UC PRESS FOUNDATION
raises funds to uphold the press's vital role
as an independent, nonprofit publisher, and
receives philanthropic support from a wide
range of individuals and institutions—and from
committed readers like you. To learn more, visit
ucpress.edu/supportus.